# www.wadsworth.com

wadsworth.com is the World Wide Web site for Wadsworth and is your direct source to dozens of online resources.

At wadsworth.com you can find out about supplements, demonstration software, and student resources. You can also send email to many of our authors and preview new publications and exciting new technologies.

**wadsworth.com**
Changing the way the world learns®

# FROM THE WADSWORTH SERIES IN SPEECH COMMUNICATION

**Adams/Clarke**   *The Internet: Effective Online Communication*

**Adler/Towne**   *Looking Out/Looking In Media Edition,* Tenth Edition

**Albrecht/Bach**   *Communication in Complex Organizations: A Relational Perspective*

**Babbie**   *The Basics of Social Research,* Second Edition

**Babbie**   *The Practice of Social Research,* Tenth Edition

**Benjamin**   *Principles, Elements, and Types of Persuasion*

**Berko/Samovar/Rosenfeld**   *Connecting: A Culture Sensitive Approach to Interpersonal Communication Competency,* Second Edition

**Bettinghaus/Cody**   *Persuasive Communication,* Fifth Edition

**Braithwaite/Wood**   *Case Studies in Interpersonal Communication: Processes and Problems*

**Brummett**   *Reading Rhetorical Theory*

**Campbell/Huxman**   *The Rhetorical Act,* Third Edition

**Campbell/Burkholder**   *Critiques of Contemporary Rhetoric,* Second Edition

**Conrad/Poole**   *Strategic Organizational Communication,* Fifth Edition

**Cragan/Wright/Kasch**   *Communication in Small Groups: Theory, Process, Skills,* Sixth Edition

**Crannell**   *Voice and Articulation,* Third Edition

**Dwyer**   *Conquer Your Speechfright: Learn How to Overcome the Nervousness of Public Speaking*

**Freeley/Steinberg**   *Argumentation and Debate: Critical Thinking for Reasoned Decision Making,* Tenth Edition

**Geist-Martin/Ray/Sharf**   *Communicating Health: Personal, Cultural and Political Complexities*

**Goodall/Goodall**   *Communicating in Professional Contexts: Skills, Ethics, and Technologies*

**Govier**   *A Practical Study of Argument,* Fifth Edition

**Griffin**   *Invitation to Public Speaking,* Preview Edition

**Hall**   *Among Cultures: Communication and Challenges*

**Hamilton**   *Essentials of Public Speaking,* Second Edition

**Hamilton/Parker**   *Communicating for Results: A Guide for Business and the Professions,* Sixth Edition

**Hoover**   *Effective Small Group and Team Communication*

**Jaffe**   *Public Speaking: Concepts and Skills for a Diverse Society,* Third Edition

**Kahane/Cavender**   *Logic and Contemporary Rhetoric: The Use of Reason in Everyday Life,* Eighth Edition

**Knapp/Hall**   *Nonverbal Communication in Human Interaction,* Fifth Edition

**Larson**   *Persuasion: Reception and Responsibility,* Ninth Edition

**Liska/Cronkhite**   *An Ecological Perspective on Human Communication Theory*

**Littlejohn**   *Theories of Human Communication,* Seventh Edition

**Lumsden/Lumsden**   *Communicating with Credibility and Confidence: Diverse Peoples, Diverse Settings,* Second Edition

**Lumsden/Lumsden**   *Communicating in Groups and Teams: Sharing Leadership,* Third Edition

**Metcalfe**   *Building a Speech,* Fourth Edition

**Miller**   *Organizational Communication: Approaches and Processes,* Third Edition

**Morreale/Bovee**   *Excellence in Public Speaking*

**Morreale/Spitzberg/Barge**   *Human Communication: Motivation, Knowledge, and Skills*

**Orbe/Harris**   *Interracial Communication: Theory Into Practice*

**Peterson/Stephan/White**   *The Complete Speaker: An Introduction to Public Speaking,* Third Edition

**Rothwell**   *In Mixed Company,* Fourth Edition

**Rubin/Rubin/Piele**   *Communication Research: Strategies and Sources,* Fifth Edition

**Samovar/Porter**   *Intercultural Communication: A Reader,* Tenth Edition

**Samovar/Porter**   *Communication Between Cultures,* Fourth Edition

**Sellnow**   *Public Speaking: A Process Approach, Media Edition*

**Sprague/Stuart**   *The Speaker's Handbook,* Sixth Edition

**Thomas**   *Public Speaking Anxiety: Conquering the Fear of Public Speaking*

**Ulloth/Alderfer**   *Public Speaking: An Experiential Approach*

**Verderber/Verderber**   *The Challenge of Effective Speaking,* Twelfth Edition

**Verderber/Verderber**   *Communicate!,* Tenth Edition

**Westra**   *Active Communication*

**Williams/Monge**   *Reasoning with Statistics: How to Read Quantitative Research*

**Wood**   *Communication Mosaics: An Introduction to the Field of Communication,* Second Edition

**Wood**   *Communication in Our Lives,* Third Edition

**Wood**   *Communication Theories in Action: An Introduction,* Second Edition

**Wood**   *Gendered Lives: Communication, Gender, and Culture,* Fifth Edition

**Wood**   *Interpersonal Communication: Everyday Encounters,* Third Edition

**Wood**   *Relational Communication: Continuity and Change in Personal Relationships,* Second Edition

# Communicating Health

PERSONAL, CULTURAL, AND POLITICAL COMPLEXITIES

# Communicating Health

## PERSONAL, CULTURAL, AND POLITICAL COMPLEXITIES

**Patricia Geist-Martin**
SAN DIEGO STATE UNIVERSITY

**Eileen Berlin Ray**
CLEVELAND STATE UNIVERSITY

**Barbara F. Sharf**
TEXAS A&M UNIVERSITY

**THOMSON**

™

**WADSWORTH**

Australia ■ Canada ■ Mexico ■ Singapore ■ Spain ■ United Kingdom ■ United States

# THOMSON

## WADSWORTH™

*Publisher:* Holly J. Allen
*Executive Editor:* Deirdre C. Anderson
*Assistant Editor:* Nicole George
*Editorial Assistant:* Mele Alusa
*Technology Project Manager:* Jeanette Wiseman
*Marketing Manager:* Kimberly Russell
*Marketing Assistant:* Neena Chandra
*Advertising Project Manager:* Shemika Britt
*Project Manager, Editorial Production:*
    Ritchie Durdin
*Print/Media Buyer:* Doreen Suruki
*Permissions Editor:* Bob Kauser

*Production Service:* Hockett Editorial Service
*Text Designer:* Seventeenth Street Studios
*Photo Researcher:* Kathleen Olson
*Copy Editor:* Wesley Morrison
*Illustrator:* Lotus Art
*Cover Designer:* Margarite Reynolds
*Cover Image:* "All of the Past Becomes the Future"
    by Andrea Gomez, by permission from the
    collection of Thomas Palmesano, Seattle, WA
*Cover Printer:* Transcon-Louiseville
*Compositor:* Thompson Type
*Printer:* Transcon-Louiseville

Printed in Canada

1  2  3  4  5  6  7  06  05  04  03  02

For more information about our products,
contact us at:

**Thomson Learning Academic Resource
Center**

**1-800-423-0563**

For permission to use material from this
text, contact us by: **Phone:** 1-800-730-2214

**Fax:** 1-800-730-2215

**Web:** http://www.thomsonrights.com

Library of Congress Control Number: 2002104125

ISBN: 0-534-53100-8

**Wadsworth/Thomson Learning**
**10 Davis Drive**
**Belmont, CA 94002-3098**
**USA**

**Asia**
Thomson Learning
5 Shenton Way #01-01
UIC Building
Singapore 068808

**Australia**
Nelson Thomson Learning
102 Dodds Street
South Melbourne, Victoria 3205
Australia

**Canada**
Nelson Thomson Learning
1120 Birchmount Road
Toronto, Ontario M1K 5G4
Canada

**Europe/Middle East/Africa**
Thomson Learning
High Holborn House
50/51 Bedford Row
London WC1R 4LR
United Kingdom

**Latin America**
Thomson Learning
Seneca, 53
Colonia Polanco
11560 Mexico D.F.
Mexico

**Spain**
Paraninfo Thomson Learning
Calle/Magallanes, 25
28015 Madrid, Spain

## Days of Awe

All that has come into existence and has been given
    becomes a path to the beyond,
    and to that which is in the process of becoming,
    to the world beyond and to the coming day.
All creation wants to be revelation,
    all of the past becomes the future.

*Leo Baeck*

# CONTENTS IN BRIEF

# CONTENTS

**PART II   COMMUNICATING HEALTH ACROSS THE LIFE SPAN   132**

**CHAPTER 5**

**Beginning Life Passages   132**

# PREFACE

"**I**t's always something!" That saying was the catchphrase of Rosanne Rosannadanna, one of the most popular characters portrayed by the versatile comedian Gilda Radner during the early days of *Saturday Night Live* (in the late 1970s, before many of you were probably born). Rosanne Rosannadanna's characteristic "shtick" was to go into a long, convoluted rant about some unpleasant event that had recently befallen her and then, with a philosophical shrug, inevitably comment, "Ya know, it just goes to show ya. It's always something."—shorthand for "No matter what, things like this happen; such is life." So, when Gilda Radner wrote about her actual experience of being diagnosed—after a long series of painful symptoms and misdiagnoses—and then treated for ovarian cancer, the disease that eventually ended her life at a young age, her book was aptly titled *It's Always Something,* an ironically comic take on a tragic situation.

While our circumstances writing this book were not comparable in scope or consequence to Gilda's, her phrase seems a fitting metaphor for our experience. Beginning in September 1996, we conceptualized a text that would incorporate aspects of health communication that had not been adequately explored in previous volumes. These topics included mental illness and health issues related to the developmental life cycle, the relation of theory to practice, and an awareness that cultural, political, and ethical concerns, as well as interpersonal and mass media formats and both clinical and public health emphases, are integral to—and integrated within—all health-related communication. Our book would take a storied approach, replete with interesting narratives from a variety of perspectives and reflected in popular culture. Our original, ambitious two-year plan for completion, however, eventually stretched into six years. The delay was not due to laziness but, rather, to a continuous succession of personal and professional, unplanned interruptions in all our lives, many of which were in some way health-related—serious personal and family chronic illnesses; reactions to medications and treatments; good and not-so-good experiences with health providers and institutions; stress related to work situations, competing deadlines, and a cross-country move; a miscarriage; and the death of a family member. These intervening events were, of course, problematic, but to be fair, we also experienced joyful interruptions—family celebrations, vacation trips, and travel to interesting conferences. Concurrently with this project, each of us also developed new courses and completed other research articles and book chapters. In effect, it was "always something" that either delayed or extended our writing. And to a much greater degree than we ever anticipated at the beginning of this work, our own evolving stories were incorporated in what we wrote.

For example, while working on her chapters, Barbara was involved in a project about the social construction of breast cancer in popular media (thanks to the U.S. Department of Defense [grant DAMD17-97-1-7240]), which resulted in her increased attention to patient involvement in health decision making and advocacy. She also experienced increasingly painful episodes of rheumatoid arthritis, leading to personal explorations with integrative healing practices. About the time we signed the contract for this book, Eileen's father was diagnosed with Alzheimer's disease. In addition to witnessing the impact of his decline on her mother's health, Eileen has gone several rounds with various members of the medical establishment as an aggressive advocate for her father's physical and mental health care. She has also seen her son and daughter make the transition from children to adolescents, and she has watched her uncle fight and, so far, beat malignant melanoma that was diagnosed over 12 years ago. These experiences remind her of the importance of being a well-educated and actively involved health citizen. Through the evolution of this text, Patricia experienced the joys of watching her daughter blossom from a three- to a nine-year-old as well as the devastations of miscarriage and the deaths of her father-in-law and her cousin's only child. Clearly, life passages from beginning to end offer insights regarding health and how we talk through these understandings. In the end, we now realize how extensively our own experiences of health citizenry and patienthood have influenced our scholarship, teaching, and theorizing about health communication.

Finally, we wish to comment briefly on the process of collaboration that resulted in this work. Our initial decision to be coauthors was based on mutual respect and admiration for the research that each of us had already published and on the common intellectual goals that we discussed for this text. We also were aware of unique qualities that each of us brought to the project—differences in theoretical perspectives, research methodologies, and subject-matter expertise. We had lived and worked in different regions of the country, and we had distinctly different professional responsibilities and student constituencies. Because we didn't know each other on a personal basis extremely well, we began by meeting in a common place to advance both our task (the initial outline of the chapters and their content) and our relationships. This foundational meeting was very important—we highly recommend it to others—but it did not ensure smooth sailing. In fact, further development of the book as a whole and of each chapter individually was accompanied by subsequent get-togethers (at professional meetings and visits to one another's homes), periodic conference calls, and innumerable e-mails. Each chapter had a primary author but was critiqued and modified by the other two. Deirdre Anderson, our project editor from Wadsworth, became an influential fourth voice, whose opinion contributed to decision making and significantly shaped the final product. Throughout this process, many of our differences came to the surface—and initially, not always in harmonious ways. Periodically, there were clear conflicts and even hurt feelings, the working through of which may well be necessary steps in such an undertaking. What we think is important to underscore, however, is the joint ownership and unbroken mutual respect with which we conclude our work.

We end this preface with our appreciation of several people and institutional resources that have supported us and contributed throughout to this project. We appreciate the students in our respective health communication classes at Cleveland State, San Diego State, and Texas A&M universities who provided feedback on earlier versions of this text. We appreciate the thorough work of Jen Anderson, author of the accompanying instructors' manual. And we are thankful for the patience and encouragement offered by Deirdre Anderson, our editor, for the practical wisdom and negotiating skills of Rachel Youngman of Hockett Editorial Service, who shepherded the book through production; and for the useful feedback, based on their pedagogical experiences and content expertise, that we received from the following reviewers:

Carolyn Anderson, University of Akron

Judy Berkowitz, Emerson College

Dale Brashers, University of Illinois, Urbana-Champaign

Donald Cegala, Ohio State University

Kelly Herold, Winona State University

Pamela Kalbfleisch, University of Wyoming

Gary Meyer, Marquette University

Lisa Murray-Johnson, Ohio State University

Stuart Schrader, Indiana University-Purdue University

Karen Leigh Spicer, Wright State University

Kevin Wright, University of Memphis

Gust Yep, San Francisco State University

Finally, each of us also would like to offer some personal thanks.

*Barbara:* I would like to thank my colleagues in Medical Humanities and Medical Education at the University of Illinois at Chicago, the Narrative and Medicine Study Group at Chicago, my research collaborators at the Houston Center for Quality Care and Utilization Studies, and my esteemed writing partner, Dr. John Kahler from Cook County Hospital, all of whom shaped my understanding of how communication works in clinical practice. In addition, I would like to thank my colleagues in Health Communication at Texas A&M University, who helped me to reimmerse myself in the literature and pedagogy of academic communication. Appreciation goes also to Marsha Vanderford, my friend and colleague who brought Canada's harm reduction program to my attention, and to April Caires, assigned as my research assistant in Spring 2001 and who acquired many of the permissions required for special materials used in this book. I am thrilled that the gorgeous and inspirational painting created by my loving sister, Andrea Gomez, graces our cover. Finally, I am very grateful to my caring, loving, and understanding husband, Marlynn May, who introduced me to a whole new aspect of intercultural health issues in the *colonias* of the South Texas borderlands and who endured many delayed dinners and late-night writing jags while this book was in progress.

*Eileen:* I want to thank the students in my Health Communication 362 class, Fall semester 2001, for their constructive feedback on drafts of the book chapters and for their openness to thinking about health communication in different ways. My colleagues at Cleveland State, Jill Rudd, Renee Botta, Jen Kopfman, and Loreen Olson, always offered encouraging words, relevant articles, and frequent lunches at our favorite Chinese restaurant, and they remain the "fun folks." My friends outside of academia have been listening to me talk about this book for a very long time. Among them, Lisa Deinhardt, friend and neighbor, and Laurie Zittrain Eisenberg, my cousin, deserve special recognition for accompanying me through the various stages of this project and for helping me to keep a balanced perspective. Finally, my most heartfelt thanks go to my husband, George Ray, for his calmness, humor, insights, support, and love. And to our children, Bryan and Lesley, for making me laugh so much and so hard.

*Patricia:* I offer sincere gratitude to my colleagues and friends at San Diego State and other universities who were always ready to reflect on good ideas and good questions. I especially want to thank all the diligent research assistants who read—and reread—each chapter, tracked down hard-to-find references, and remained passionate about what they read as the book evolved: Marion Cabuto, Juan Cephas, Amy Fryer, Elissa Fischer, Chuck Goehring, Carolyn Hartigan, Lindsay Flemming, Melissa Karaiscos-Cornwell, and Sarah Bourke. I would like to thank my good friends Linda Perry and Beth Martin for their contributions to my sanity by always being willing to go to a movie or for a run. Most importantly, I am so very thankful for my husband, J.C., and my daughter, Makenna, who distracted me whenever they could and who knew not to ask "Are you done with the book yet?" The very day the final version of the book was e-mailed to the publisher, Makenna taped a new sticky note to my computer stating "New job! Spend time with Makenna!"

Finally, we all extend a very special thank you to the people whose stories grace the pages of this book and reveal the complexities of health communication. We hope that you will find what follows to be meaningful and relevant in your own lives as practitioners, patients, and health citizens. And for all of us, both readers and authors alike, we begin the text with a universal wish and invocation: *salud, l'chaim,* "to our health."

*PGM,* San Diego
*EBR,* Cleveland
*BFS,* College Station

Eileen (left), Barbara, and Patricia. *Photo by Ruth Zittrain.*

# 1

# Communicating Health

*Photo reprinted with permission of Deena Metzger. To order the poster, please contact Donelly/Colt, 202 Station Rd., Hampton CT 06247, phone (860) 455-9621 or fax (800) 533-0006.*

**Tree**

I am no longer afraid of mirrors where I see the sign of the amazon
the one who shoots arrows.
There was a fingered line across my chest where a knife entered,
but now a branch winds above the scar and travels from arm  to heart.
Green leaves cover the branch,
grapes hang there and a bird appears.

What grows in me now is vital and does not cause me harm.
I think the bird is singing.
I have relinquished some of the scars.
I have designed my chest with the care given to an illuminated
    manuscript.
I am no longer ashamed to make love.
Love is a battle I can win.
I have the body of a warrior who does not kill or wound.
On the book of my body,
I have permanently inscribed a tree.

DEENA METZGER (1992, p. 91)

Consider the photo of the woman on the first page of this chapter. Her name is Deena Metzger, and she is a well-known writer who lives in California. This portrait, which is called "The Warrior," was commissioned for a book of her poetry called *Tree*. In it, she seems to be in a state of general well-being: Her face is radiant, her body up-lifted in a joyful way, but no observer can miss that she carries a long scar in place of a breast, the remnant of a mastectomy. Would you say this is a picture of health? What might we infer from the picture about this woman's story? What might she tell others about what she has lived through and discovered about herself? How do we make sense of symbols that convey mixed meanings related to health status?

Now consider Metzger's poem that accompanies the photograph. What kinds of verbal imagery are emphasized in this poem? Are these different than what you observed by looking at the picture alone? Do the words confirm, contradict, or extend the meaning that you first understood from the photo? How so? In what ways do the visual image (nonverbal communication) and the word-pictures (verbal communication) interact to help you better understand this woman's story?

Deena Metzger continues to write and conducts workshops on healing and creative writing. Her photo has been an inspiration to survivors of breast cancer for the past 25 years, and if you could look closely at her elaborate tattoo, you would see incorporated within the tree limb that spans the scar grapes on a vine, the Book of Life, and a bird—each a symbol of regeneration and vitality (Sharf, 1995). What is central in both the image and the poem is that how the meaning of **health** and well-being is communicated shapes our experiences of health-related situations. Such meanings are conveyed in this photo, the poem, and a broad array of other cultural stories and images, in a variety of media, that surround and influence us on a day-to-day basis (Morris, 1998).

Consider how health is communicated to and by you. What are the meanings of *healthy, unhealthy,* and *healing* when talking with friends, going to the gym, visiting the doctor, coping with depression, noting headlines in the paper and on the TV news, perusing magazine ads, considering items on restaurant menus, worrying about sick relatives, debating the morality of physician-assisted suicide, understanding new HMO (health maintenance organization) rules, or negotiating safe sex? We are surrounded by health-related themes in our daily lives, and these themes impact us in many ways. As patients, practitioners, public citizens, or private individuals, we respond to texts, are drawn into interactions, and create discourse; in short, we participate in a variety of communicative interactions.

This book defines **health communication** as the symbolic processes by which people, individually and collectively, understand, shape, and accommodate to health and illness.[1] The definition used in *Healthy People 2010* (2001), an influential report documenting the national plan for improving public health, emphasizes the investigative and applied nature of health communication as an academic discipline: "the study and use of communication strategies to inform and influence individual and community decisions that enhance health." Essentially, health communication involves a wide range of messages and media in the context of health maintenance, health promotion, disease prevention, treatment, and advocacy, including variations in:

- Situations
- Structures
- Roles
- Relationships
- Identities
- Goals
- Strategies of social influence

We have tried to write clearly, using many kinds of examples. At the same time, we hope to challenge and encourage you to stretch intellectually.

---

[1] We would like to acknowledge Professors Austin Babrow and Bruce Lambert for their ideas that helped in constructing this definition.

Rather than tailor our discussions of communicating health according to how many people are communicating (such as in a relationship, group, or public setting), we want you to think about the context of communicating health—the set of circumstances that surround an event or a situation concerning health or illness. We also want you to consider the stories not told, and how these omissions communicate health. What information, thoughts, or feelings are communicated or invalidated by their exclusion? Think about mental illness, for example. Famous people such as Tipper Gore, William Styron, Mike Wallace, and Art Buchwald have written and spoken publicly about their bouts with clinical depression, but many Americans still feel shame and stigma if they or family members are diagnosed with a mental illness. It is either not discussed, alluded to in euphemisms, or denied when communicating health. By its exclusion, people with mental illness are isolated, marginalized, and disenfranchised from others (Ray, 1996b). As we begin to tell our stories, however, in our interpersonal relationships or through the media, we move from the margins toward the center and gain personal and political power through our individual and collective voices. Adult incest survivors, for example, have reported that just telling their stories to a researcher helped them to make sense of their experience by increasing their self-knowledge, validating their feelings, and expanding the opportunities for their stories to help others (Varallo, Ray, & Ellis, 1998). Thus, the personal, political, and cultural complexities of communicating health tell us much more about health beyond medicine—our own theories, stories, citizenry, representations, and boundaries.

The thread drawn through this text is the notion that we are constantly **theorizing** from the stories we tell and hear about everyday health practices. That is, we form theories—rationales, guesses, or explanations—from these stories. So, throughout this book, we offer opportunities for theorizing practice in boxes set off from the text. In this chapter, we continue by discussing the **narrative perspective,** which emphasizes stories as a way of learning, both in how we have designed this text as well as in the storied lives we all live. Hopefully, through reading and discussing this book, you will reflect and act on your own **health citizenry** and the interpretive task of constructing what such terms as *healthy* and *unhealthy, wellness* and *illness,* and *medicine* and *healing* mean to you. In other words, you will contemplate how health is represented in your everyday life and the ambiguous boundaries drawn among biological, psychological, social, and spiritual health. Blurring these boundaries is important in order to explore and understand what communicating health means, especially in light of dramatically changing contexts of health care. We want you to consider health beyond medicine and how we communicate to negotiate, maintain, and rationalize healthy and unhealthy behaviors. We close this chapter with a section entitled "Moving Forward" to highlight the three primary sections of this text.

# THEORIZING FROM OUR EVERYDAY HEALTH PRACTICES

We invite you to theorize about your own processes of communicating health. Theorizing provides a framework within which we can think about, understand, and explain our experiences. We believe that we gain a great deal from theorizing about our daily communicative practices of representing and narrating health, but how is theory integrally related to practice? bell hooks (1991), an educator, author, feminist activist, and social critic, believes in theory as a liberatory practice in which we participate as a way of resisting how others have theorized:

> The privileged act of naming often affords those in power access to modes of communication that enable them to project an interpretation, a definition, a description of their work, actions, etc. that may not be accurate, that may obscure what is really taking place. (p. 3)

Theorizing is a lived experience of critical thinking, of narrating and explaining the things that hurt or bother us, that makes them go away or, at least, seem less threatening. Theory is a location for healing—a place where we can imagine possible futures, a place where life could be lived differently (hooks, pp. 1–2). But as hooks points out, theory is not inherently healing, liberating, or revolutionary. It fulfills this function only when we ask that it do so and direct our theorizing toward this end (p. 2). Throughout this text, we invite you to examine significant stories in your own and others' lives and to theorize about the everyday health care practices we all engage in, sometimes unconsciously and sometimes habitually.

The next section, "Narrating Life and Communicating Health," provides the framework that underlies the perspective in this book. We ask you to embrace this framework as a way of thinking about, analyzing, and reconsidering your own and others' health care beliefs, behaviors, and communication. Listening to others' stories—and writing and telling your own—is vital to your development as a health communicator.

# NARRATING LIFE AND COMMUNICATING HEALTH

If it is true that when people talk with others about their own health and illness they are searching for ways to think and talk differently about their lives, then healing necessarily must be tied to the stories that we tell. In describing his belief

---

in authentic health communication that balances biological, personal, and societal well-being, health care communication consultant Eric Zook (1994) suggests that when patients come to medical encounters saying "Doctor, I am sick," they actually want to ask "Can you heal my story?" (p. 355), because the ways of talking about our health can be much more open to variation and revision than the biological processes that underlie our health problems. Pushing the point further, writer David Morris (1998) argues that this is an age in which many people, when challenged by health problems, strive to incorporate, supercede, and even resist the "authorized medico-scientific" narratives typically offered by clinicians and to "reclaim power as creators and narrators of their own distinctive stories" (p. 25). Thus, patients may be "wounded storytellers" (Frank, 1995), but they are no longer victims of their diseases. Rather, we now say that someone is a "person with cerebral palsy" or a heart attack survivor, and the increasingly public telling of their stories is a way of regaining voices previously lost to illness (Frank; Morris).

Rhetorical theorist Walter Fisher (1984, 1985, 1987) posited a decade ago that humans can be distinguished by their innate storytelling tendency, what he called **Homo narrans.** In other words, people are, by nature, storytellers, so our communication takes the form of narratives, stories that we use to explain and exemplify our ideas, and to recount and account for our decisions. This is a perspective with which we resonate. This text proceeds on the assumption that much of human communication is narrative in nature, and that storytelling is the form of communication that best commands attention and involvement.

Not coincidentally, medical, communication, and other humanities and social science scholars (Polkinghorne, 1988; Rabinow & Sullivan, 1987) have applied a narrative perspective to understand interactions in the contexts of medicine, family, and relationships. They refer specifically to "stories of sickness" (Brody, 1987, 1992; Coles, 1989), "illness narratives" (Kleinman, 1988), "illness experiences" (Frank, 1991), "doctors' stories" (Hunter, 1991), "emotional experience" (Ellis, 1991), "personal narratives" (Riessman, 1993), "relationships as stories" (Bochner, Ellis, & Tillmann-Healy, 1996), and case studies (Ray, 1993a, 1996a). At their best, narratives can be open-ended resources—sources of healing and comfort, spiritual maturation, privileged moments of self-change, epiphanies, turning points, and lessons to live by.

The influence of the narrative perspective in understanding medical encounters has the potential to be revolutionary. For instance, doctors traditionally have been trained to "take" a medical history from patients to complete the task of "data-gathering." Think how different it is to conceptualize this same process as physicians and patients each having their own stories to tell the other (Geist & Gates, 1996; Geist-Martin & Dreyer, 2001). In this way of seeing the world, collaborative problem-solving related to the patient's illness depends, in great part, on how well the two participants can enmesh significant portions of their respective accounts (Geist & Hardesty, 1990; Sharf, 1990).

While you may be unfamiliar with the literature on narrative theory, all of us are familiar with the elements of story. The *scene* is the physical or geographic setting in which the story takes place. Because narratives are events that are somehow sequenced through time, stories tend to be oriented in the past, present, or future, though more complex time structures, like a flashback to the past from the present, may also be employed. The *characters* are, of course, the people featured in the story and are cast as heroes, villains, victims, innocent bystanders, and the like. The characters' *motives* are the underlying reasons why these individuals take certain actions, whereas the *plot* is the development of the story, or what results from the interactions and conflicts among motives and characters' choices. Every story, by necessity, is told in the *voice*, or from the point of view, of the narrator. Therefore, depending on who tells the story, the same set of events is depicted differently from one version to another. In addition to the content of the story, the *telling*, or the manner of how the story is actually told, will color the meaning that is conveyed.

This book makes use of the narrative perspective in several ways. First, we intentionally use storied illustrations throughout. These come from a variety of sources, including actual personal accounts, written and media fiction, news reports, songs, poetry, and art. We do so to clarify our accounts of what health communication is and our explanations of how it plays out—and because we think it is the most interesting way to go. Second, from time to time, we use narrative analysis as a conceptual framework or methodology for examining specific pieces of discourse from a critical stance. Third, we continuously encourage you, as readers, to use your own stories to respond to our questions, test our assertions, and expand the viewpoints conveyed here by theorizing from your everyday (healthy and unhealthy) practices. We ask you to engage in these practices so that you may begin enacting health citizenry in the ways described in the next section.

## ENACTING HEALTH CITIZENRY

When it comes to the identities that individuals assume as health communicators, the descriptive vocabulary has been quite limiting. We can be experts or professionals (categories that typically include clinicians, health care managers, policy makers, and researchers)—in short, those who provide medical care, formulate standards of practice and rules for the receipt of care, or study medical science. Alternatively, we can be patients or health consumers—that is, the recipients of health care, as well as those who pay for it. These words are rooted in the world of medicine and do not speak to the much broader contexts of health communication that we have been describing. Thus, we make extensive use of the term *health citizen* (Arntson, 1989; Rimal, Ratzen, Arntson, & Freimuth, 1997). By this, we refer to the full range of health-related activities in which people (who at certain times also may assume the specific roles of patient or practitioner) participate and interact with one another. We intend the term *citizen* to convey the sense of universality among all members of a society as well as the notion of responsibilities and privileges that accompanies such participation. A primary goal of this text is to help you maximize your effectiveness as communicators in those multiple situations in which you assume the identity of health citizens. In the process of "Representing Health in Everyday Life," you will discover avenues for narrating health and illness and for enacting your health citizenry.

## REPRESENTING HEALTH IN EVERYDAY LIFE

Analyzing how health is represented in everyday life means considering the language, images, and other symbol systems used to create shared meaning among people. Thus, we begin our discussion of communicating health by focusing on how matters of health are represented symbolically. Consider the official slogan of the WHO (World Health Organization). For more than three decades, the slogan had been "health for all by the year 2000" (WHO Executive Board, 1979), though the date has now been extended to 2020. The WHO has had specific objectives within its own agenda, but how are we, as the public, to understand this phrase? Obviously, it was impossible that all diseases could or would be eliminated by the end of the twentieth century (or ever); however, working toward the progressive eradication of some diseases or a significant decrease of overall sickness on the planet is a credible goal. As ambitious as that objective still is, the focus is limited.

Another way to interpret "health" is by considering the ideals of providing adequate nutrition, shelter, and medical care for every citizen. Since September 11, 2001, many people in the United States would add safety from terrorism and biochemical warfare to the list. In addition, does "health for all" also imply meaningful employment, sufficient rest, and protection from human violence, natural disaster, and environmental hazards? Is health linked to emotional stability and enrichment of spirit? In fact, since 1948, the WHO has defined health as "a state of complete physical, mental, and social well being and not merely the absence of disease or infirmity" (WHO, 2001).

Conversely, what does it mean to undergo illness, to experience disease or what others have described as **dis-ease,** a feeling of deep discomfort with the way things are (Eisenberg & Goodall, 2001, pp. 12–13)? The act of diagnosis, of naming the problem, is essential to proper treatment but also has symbolic importance to the individual whose equilibrium has been disrupted. An example is the addition of the concept of date rape to our public vocabulary over the past two decades and the recognition of sexual victimization as a significant health problem in the United States (Spitzberg, 1999a). Many women have experienced nonconsensual sex but believed it was their fault. Many felt self-blame, guilt, and that "boys will be boys." Often they kept their experiences to themselves, feeling too isolated and humiliated to disclose their experience. However, once date rape was redefined publicly, women started sharing their stories with each other informally, in support groups, with rape crisis counselors, and in the media. As a result, women's self-definitions changed from victims to survivors, our definition and understanding of rape expanded, education programs began, laws were passed, and the definitions of sex and rape were dramatically altered.

With physical illnesses, one curious set of complications arises when people are diagnosed with a serious disease but have no immediate overt symptoms; the map does not appear to match the territory. For instance, many who have been pronounced hypertensive (having high blood pressure) typically do not experience symptoms. Thus, they unwisely skip daily medications that would enable them to maintain a lower blood pressure, because the label does not seem to fit how they feel.

To be told one has cancer is a fearsome diagnosis that nearly always alters one's perception of self and the world, but it can be ironically disconcerting while no bodily pain or changes are felt. Indeed, in such cases, the treatment may feel much crueler than the disease. The picture changes when an individual has been experiencing symptoms with no explanation. In these circumstances, having an official name for a perceived problem, however serious or frightening, is also validating. As sociologist Arthur Frank (1991) says about his diagnosis of prostate cancer, "[I]t was reassuring to have other physicians acknowledge that the problems were as real as I felt they were" (p. 44). It is not surprising, then, that groups of sufferers, whose symptoms are perceived by medical experts as being vague or diffuse, fight to confirm the legitimacy of such diagnostic categories as Gulf War syndrome, chronic fatigue syndrome, or posttraumatic stress disorder to validate their pain and justify reimbursement for treatment. In Theorizing Practice 1.1, we ask you to consider the origins and power of words by engaging in Webster Work.

Interrelated with our emphasis on considering health in other sites and relationships beyond the medical milieu is the need to blur the boundaries between wellness and illness. Beyond the emphasis on biological vocabularies of disease, we need to elicit and learn from individuals' vocabularies of experience when they speak of wellness, illness, and healing. That is, now more than ever, we are recognizing that the stories we tell about our healthy and unhealthy behaviors and the

## Webster Work

Theologian and philosopher Mary Daly (1973) discusses the importance of what she calls "**Webster Work.**" For her, a Webster is a weaver who considers carefully the meaning of words, both in their original definitions and in the diverse connotations that people assign to them. She suggests that too often we engage in *verbicide,* which is killing of the living, transformative energy of words and muting of the metamorphic, shapeshifting powers inherent in them (pp. xvii-xviii). She suggests we engage in Webster Work by strategically hyphenating words to re-consider their meanings.

- How might you re-consider the transformative power of the following newly hyphenated words: re-writing, be-friending, re-member, be-longing, e-motional, dis-ease, re-turn, dis-cover, full-filled, and dis-illusionment?

- Now re-consider words related to communicating health, such as re-covering, dis-abled, dis-order, life-time, and pro-motion. Brainstorm a list of possible meanings for these words, and generate a list of additional health-related words that could be trans-formed through Webster Work.

- Become a weaver in your own thinking, speaking, and writing. Weave words into their active form, creating movement that re-considers reality and trans-forms the energy of our communication with one another.

"medicine" we take represents more about our biographies than our biology (Zook, 1994)—and even less about the categories of disease that label our identity as well or ill.

# BLURRING THE BOUNDARIES BETWEEN WELLNESS AND ILLNESS

In contemporary American culture, concerns about health are most often framed within a disease-oriented medical model. The results of this association, the blurring of the boundaries between medical pathology and problems of everyday living, are often confusing and play out in a variety of ways. The medical perspective is so ingrained within our society that its metaphors often spill into other non-health-related areas. Writer and cultural critic Susan Sontag (1978) has eloquently explained how the popular application of medical figures of speech abound, often stigmatizing people with certain diseases. Thus, computers become *infected* with *contagious viruses,* which can be deadly to the information stored within. Similarly, the Watergate scandal during the Nixon administration revealed a so-called *cancer* within the American presidency (a metaphor more recently revived during the Congressional impeachment of President Clinton). Imagine the impact of such negative figurative language on people suffering with AIDS (acquired immunodeficiency syndrome) or with malignancies and who struggle to define themselves as people apart from the stigmatizing communication surrounding the disease.

With the advent of advanced biotechnology and specialization, many ordinary and crucial aspects of human development have become "medicalized," subject to the expertise of physicians and other health professionals. Examples include fertilization, pregnancy and birth, and lifestyle issues. While medical management can be helpful, sometimes improving quality of life and/or longevity, a pervasive feeling now exists that control has shifted away from the individuals whose lives are at stake.

In some cases, **medicalization** of routine living is open to question. At the center of a recent controversy, Susan Love (Love & Lindsey, 1997), a breast surgeon and women's health activist, describes her opposition to the movement to name menopause as an estrogen-deficiency disease. She views efforts by pharmaceutical companies to develop "educational" (advertising) campaigns directed at doctors and women to recommend "replacement" hormone therapy for the rest of their lives as problematic. The "replacement" hormones may be unnecessary, may increase a woman's risk of developing breast cancer, may increase the development of blood clots and gallbladder disease, and may increase the risk of uterine cancer. Love supports the view that estrogen therapy may be beneficial for some, but not all, women. By naming a normal part of life, such as menopause, a disease, we too often find aggressive measures being taken when such "prolonged" use of therapy is unnecessary and, in some cases, causes more harm than good.[2]

In another instance, the American Academy of Pediatrics (1995) has recommended that pediatricians include children's TV viewing habits as part of a routine check-up. While children's exposure to media violence is a major societal concern, whether physicians are the most appropriate monitors and advisers in this area is a matter for debate. In other situations, however, clear harm has been done by pathologizing natural processes. Until 1973, homosexuality was listed as a diagnostic category in the American Psychiatric Association's *Diagnostic and Statistical Manual* (Kaplan & Sadock, 1985). Intense, organized advocacy was required to force the removal of this stigmatizing and arbitrary label.

Blurring the boundaries also means considering the overlapping and multiple forms of knowledge and experience that contribute to wellness and illness. For

---

[2]Remember, however, that Love's opinion is just that—a subjective statement, not an absolute truth. For a contrasting viewpoint, see Gladwell (1997).

some individuals, cultural or religious belief systems take priority where decisions about health and illness are concerned (Galanti, 1997; Geist, 1999; Giger & David-hiza, 1991; Kleinman, 1980; Leininger, 1991). For others, spiritual health guides a philosophy that transcends the entrapment of dualities such as life and death, illness and health, healthy and destructive behaviors (Gonzalez, 1994; Remen, 1988, 1994). Rather than experience the dualities as opposition, we gain understanding by considering one through the other and then using this knowledge to make choices about how we communicate (Lorde, 1980). For example, on an episode of the popular TV series *ER,* a patient waiting for a heart transplant expressed his concern about the "goodness" of the person whose heart he would receive. Respecting the patient's value system, the doctor communicated in a way that honored the patient's spiritual belief in life as integrating the biological, social, and spiritual aspects. The doctor investigated the donor and provided information about the person, not just the quality of the biological part. For many, the increasing emphasis and development of preventive and integrative medicine offers support for these varied belief systems by its main focus on caring as well as curing, and on the person rather than the disease (Lowenberg, 1989; Wallis, 1991). Hopefully, this emphasis avoids dichotomizing biomedical and alternative medicines (Coward, 1989).

Cultural forms of knowledge can both facilitate and constrain health behaviors. For example, Lynn Payer (1988), in her research on the varieties of medical treatment in the United States, England, West Germany, and France, discovered profound differences among the four systems, with grave implications:

> *Many of the medical mistakes made in each country can be best understood by cultural biases that blind both the medical profession and patients, causing them to accept some treatments too quickly and other treatments reluctantly or not at all. (p. 34)*

Without these more global and political insights, we possess only limited understanding of similarities and differences among cultures with respect to human care, health, and illness.

In short, the language and other symbols representing vitality and illness, disease and treatment, and well-being and disability are laden with ambiguity and connotations that function—sometimes obviously, sometimes subtly—to add layers of meaning and often difficulties in mutual understanding during attempts to communicate health. Without doubt, the changing landscape of health care also significantly increases the ambiguity, complexity, and sheer diversity of health care services. By recognizing these changes, we may feel less confused and more empowered to enact our health citizenry.

# RECOGNIZING THE CHANGING LANDSCAPE OF HEALTH CARE

One of the most prominent features in health communication is what happens when we receive care from health professionals. We are living in a time when many of the established ways in which professional practice occurs are undergoing significant changes. To further complicate matters, several forces intrinsic to the quality of care are directly intersecting.

Many of us have a vision of the ideal doctor-patient relationship modeled on the kindly family practitioner (or pediatrician, internist, or even heroic surgeon) who knows his or her patients well, takes a personal interest in the problems of each patient, establishes a relationship of trust and good will, and without question, acts in the patient's best interest. This image was epitomized by the fictional Marcus Welby, M.D., of the 1970s TV series. Interestingly, the same altruistic characteristics were portrayed by the funnier, more cynical Hawkeye Pierce, an army surgeon in the TV show *M\*A\*S\*H* (1972–1983). More contemporary doctors in TV shows like *ER* do the same when they are at their best, but now they are often depicted as conflicted and compromised in coping with new technologies; balancing home, work, and family stressors; and financial challenges to professional ethics.

The reality of service that many of us have experienced had its roots in the medical science research boom that took hold following World War II and that continues to this day. As knowledge and technology evolved, medical care grew more specialized and fragmented. One of the significant social revolutions of the 1960s was the governmental assurance of medical care for the elderly and the indigent with the passage of legislation establishing Medicare and Medicaid (Geist & Hardesty, 1992). Specialty care formerly took place mainly in hospitals, many of which sponsored programs for training health professionals. Over time, the United States came to have the most advanced system of health care in the world. Though Americans in urban and suburban areas eventually lost the sense of familiarity and personalized services, such as home visits, that once characterized relationships with general practitioners, they gained confidence in medical miracles and expectations that science could deal effectively with most medical problems. Rural areas continued to experience age-old problems of sufficient access to care, particularly specialty care, though technologies of telemedicine and computer-mediated communication have started to remedy this situation (Bauer, Deering, & Hsu, 2001; Rice & Katz, 2001).

At present, we are reaping the results of that history. As technology escalated, so did health care costs, eventually skyrocketing out of control. A two-tiered system of health care, which had always existed to some degree, became more institutionalized, so that the poor—and, perhaps most of all, the uninsured working poor—have access to fewer services than middle-class and wealthy citizens do. The erosion of trusting relationships between providers and patients was evidenced during the 1980s by a steep rise in malpractice litigation and a public yearning for patients to be regarded as "whole persons" (as opposed to fragmented body parts or ailments) who need to be listened to attentively and to have their health care preferences honored whenever possible.

In response to the crisis in health care costs, gradual but steady changeovers have occurred in the way health care is delivered, managed, and paid for, a trend that sociologist Paul Starr (1982, p. 421) identified in the early 1980s as "the rise of corporate enterprise in health services" in America and that has evolved to what is now known as managed care. **Managed care** is an arrangement in which an insuring organization accepts the risk for providing a defined set of health services, using an identified set of providers, for a specified population in return for a fixed payment rather than a fee for service (Lammers & Geist, 1997; Sofaer, 1996). Managed care arrangements have taken a variety of forms, including prepaid health services, commonly known as HMOs and PPOs (preferred provider organizations), and other reimbursement networks. The site of much health care provision has shifted from in-patient hospital sites to ambulatory centers. Primary care physicians have become the organizationally designated gatekeepers to more specialized services. Days of hospitalization have decreased significantly. With regional variations in place, physicians increasingly continue to shift from self-managed, fee-for-service practice to employment with local and national health management corporations. Both patients and physicians find themselves operating according to guidelines and constraints imposed by higher administration. Mental health care, for example, has changed dramatically. Mental health practitioners are now only reimbursed for brief therapy (typically limited to 20 visits/year), and psychiatrists find that their role has shifted from therapist to medication manager.

These complex, pervasive changes at the organizational level give rise to an array of new communication issues to be examined. Is it possible for bureaucracies to be hospitable environments for the nurture of caring relationships? How best can trusting physician-patient relationships be fostered when cost containment is an overarching organizational goal? Despite the negative image that HMOs and other managed care systems have received in the popular press, what are the possibilities for improved health care outcomes through newer organizational structures? Would it mean, for example, that we place more emphasis on preventive as well as curative medicine, or better surveillance of individual physician practices (a process called quality assurance) as well as attention to more systematic patient feedback? How can patient members of managed care organizations best be prepared to communicate effectively through the various structural configurations that now mediate health care decision making? Take a look at Theorizing Practice 1.2, and consider what you can do to become a more informed consumer of health care. Finally, how can workers advocate for better benefits when the trend is toward first-class benefits for executives and cut-rate benefits for workers (Myerson, 1996)? These questions must be raised if we are to consider health beyond medicine.

## CONSIDERING HEALTH BEYOND MEDICINE

Health communication scholars have a tradition of conceptualizing their interests to include, but not be limited to, the medical milieu. Thus, our talk of health-related issues crosses a myriad of contexts within which we live, work, and play.

*Home* is the site in which routine health practices are frequently negotiated and maintained. It is where patterns of nutrition, exercise, rest, and relaxation are created and reinforced; relationships with family and significant others are carried out; and the effects of cultural and community contexts are most strongly felt. Exploring family conversations about one member's eating disorder of bulimia, communication researcher Wayne Beach (1996) captures how even the family's delicate and well-intended discussion of concerns about the disorder guarantee neither agreement on the nature of the "problems" nor commitment to seek professional

---

**THEORIZING PRACTICE 1.2**

### Managed Care and Health Citizenry

Discuss with friends, family, and your health care providers how you can become a more informed consumer of health care, adding to the following list of strategies:

- Investigate costs and benefits provided by health care plans.
- Speak frankly with your providers about choices and costs.
- Ask your providers' views of the system and ways you can work together.
- Voice your requests and concerns to administrators of your health care plans.
- Engage in preventative health care on a daily basis.
- Construct activities with friends to sustain healthy behaviors.
- Use your citizenship to advocate for underserved people in your community.

help. This study represents a movement to consider health beyond medicine, the complicated interactions that cross and intermix both the roles of family and health professional and the boundaries of institutions and homes. Considering health beyond medicine also means conducting your own health communication assessment, as described in Theorizing Practice 1.3. In this way, you become an active participant in evaluating and responding to your own healthy or unhealthy behaviors.

Despite the primary influence of home, family, and friends, the *workplace* is where many people spend much, if not most, of their waking hours. Interactions with colleagues may have an important influence on attitudes and opinions. The workplace is the site of occupational hazards as well as institutional resources. It is also, typically, the necessary link to health care insurance. Broad health concerns like stress, social support, preventive practices and management of chronic problems, sexual contacts, balancing work and family, exposure to violence, lay remedies, and nontechnical health beliefs cut across both work and home environments (Miller & Ray, 1994; Ray, 1993a). Considering health beyond medicine raises questions about the relationship between organizational structures and individuals' health and prompts us to explore new priorities and values in the pursuit of health (Bellah, Madsen, Sullivan, Swidler, & Tipton, 1985; Eisenberg & Goodall, 2001; Miller, Ellis, Zook, & Lyles, 1990).

The *public arena* tends to be more a socially formulated environment than an actual physical site. Though it may include any situation that places citizens in contact so that the interchange of ideas may occur, media forums (newspapers and magazines, films, TV, radio, the Internet) increasingly are stimulating and facilitating dialogue among various sectors of the society. In these contexts, public arguments regarding health-related controversies like the rights of people with AIDS versus protection of public health, the promise and problems with stem cell research, and the rationing of health care are articulated, attacked, and defended. The saliency and persuasiveness of these arguments in turn provide the basis for policy making.

The public arena is also the major informational channel for conducting health promotion and education campaigns, such as those focused on curbing smoking and drug abuse. Moving health beyond medicine means engaging in what has been called "public moral argument" (Fisher, 1984, 1987). In rhetorician Michael Hyde's view (1990), too often the public is cut off from open discussion and debate with the experts concerning their own health. Using technologies such as CAT scans, ventilators, and organ transplants, experts often make decisions based on technical knowledge without considering the social knowledge that could be gained through dialogue with the general public. By bringing topics into public discourse, we avoid "legitimation masquerading," circumstances wherein what we accept as legitimate in our society often has never endured any public scrutiny

## Health Communication Assessment

To gain firsthand knowledge of health communication, write a daily journal about your own health care beliefs and behaviors. In a notebook, write an entry each day that describes the following:

- Describe one behavior you engaged in today that you believe contributes to or detracts from your health, such as engaging or not engaging in taking vitamins, exercising, smoking, going to yoga, or positive mental thinking.

- Explain why you do this behavior and how you believe it contributes or detracts from your health.

- Describe how communication was part of engaging in this behavior today; for example, you told a friend or a health care provider, talked with someone while engaging in this behavior, conversed with a friend who also engaged in this behavior, and so on.

- Describe how you might ensure continuing this healthy behavior or reducing/eliminating this unhealthy behavior.

Once you have faithfully written in this journal for a month, take the time to analyze the frequency/nature of your healthy and unhealthy behaviors. Write a report describing the patterns in your behaviors. Try to provide an understanding of the multiple influences, such as culture, family, work, and politics, on your behaviors.

(Hyde, p. 116); instead, we create the opportunities for individuals to learn the "expert" knowledge concerning decisions about their treatment and their lives.

The final section of this chapter, "Moving Forward," previews the content and format of this text. We want you to move forward, connecting your own stories with those that we offer, creating your own expertise, and learning how to learn from your own and others' experiences.

# Moving Forward

The contents of this text have been divided into three major parts.

- Part I: Communicating Health Complexities

- Part II: Communicating Health Across the Life Span

- Part III: Communicating Health Competencies

We close this chapter with a brief description of the ten other chapters included in this book.

Along with this chapter, the purpose of the additional three chapters in Part I, "Communicating Health Complexities," is to reveal the variety of identities operating at several communicative levels that shape our health beliefs and practices. In other words, identities are subtly embedded in and imposed on our ideas of how the world is and the way we live our lives, including our conceptions of health status and medical care. For instance, mainstream American society privileges the rights of the individual above all else. This core belief is reflected in our country's history, laws, and social customs, though it is occasionally contested by an opposing ideology of the primacy of communal interests (Bellah et al., 1985). The celebration of this individual identity is evidenced in health care by the official sanctioning of patient autonomy; both legal and ethical authorities have repeatedly upheld the right of patients to make their own health care decisions, even when those decisions conflict with medical advice. In a society as diverse as the United States, especially in light of the multiple forces of change impacting health care, it is not surprising that personal, political, and cultural identities generally accepted in previous decades are now open to question and competition.

Part I begins with this chapter and continues with Chapter 2, "Personal Complexities of Communicating Health and Illness." The chapter begins with Christopher Reeve's story of his horse-riding accident and adjustment to life with a spinal cord injury. Providing an introduction to the personal complexities of communicating health, the chapter explores how people tell the stories of their lives to frame, understand, confront, manage, and change their identities. Narrating health and illness represents healing as epiphany through stories of suffering and comfort, disability and capability, loss and recovery. The chapter discusses how stories speak about the pain of being silenced, discredited, excluded, and stigmatized by a dominant culture that defines ill persons as the "other." Stories address the importance of communicating about the constraints on voice and bringing into the open the stigma, stereotypes, and suppression that people experience daily in health and illness.

Chapter 3, "Understanding Health in Cultural Communities," draws on Anne Fadiman's book *The Spirit Catches You and You Fall Down*, beginning with a description of the two cultural communities of medicine and the Hmong as an exemplar for the cultural complexities of communicating health. The chapter discusses the vital role of understanding health in cultural communities. A culturally sensitive model of communication is offered for educating health care providers, for clinical practice, and for patient empowerment. The utility of this model for understanding culturally sensitive communication is elaborated through discussion of the cultural complexities surrounding AIDS. We then discuss three dialectics that can become both barriers to and avenues for understanding the borderlands of cultural communities.

Beginning with the case of medical marijuana, Chapter 4, "Political Complexities of Medicine and Healing," explores the politics of medicine and healing. The chapter provides a historical perspective of health care in the United States, tracing the development of roles and perceptions of health care providers and institutions. It also discusses traditional and biomedical models and their impact against the backdrop of major changes in the U.S. health care landscape and how the politics of health care directly affect who has access to what care. The politics surrounding three specific, controversial health issues are discussed: venereal disease, breast implants, and prostate cancer.

The four chapters in Part II, "Communicating Health Across the Life Span," focus on the discoveries, changes, and dilemmas that we live with and learn from across our own and others' lives. Each and every one of us undergoes life-changing experiences of births and deaths—of beginning, sustaining, enduring, and ending life passages. In the process, our personal, cultural, and political identities are affected, challenged, confirmed, and even transformed. So, too, are the ways we communicate health and illness impacted. We may settle into negative patterns, discover valuable changes, or develop new competencies.

Chapter 5, "Beginning Life Passages," explores the communication surrounding life passages such as prenatal care, miscarriage, infertility, birth, postnatal care, and family health. Focus is placed on the inevitable changes in communication and relationships as families and their health care providers commence and move through these beginning life passages. Attention also is paid to the personal, political, and cultural complexities of communication surrounding three specific health issues: birthing, miscarriage and infertility, and the birth of a child with a disability.

Chapter 6, "Formative Life Passages," explores the communication surrounding the formative life passages of adolescence—the changing identities concerning their bodies and the emotions of such changes. We begin generally, with communicating a sense of self, but then move specifically to particular changes, events, or behaviors that are part of young people's formative life passages, focusing especially on communicating about sexuality and risk-taking behaviors. Life passages such as puberty, menstruation, sex education, and teenage pregnancy are discussed. The chapter also turns to the communication surrounding adolescent risky behavior, including unhealthy eating habits, drinking, and smoking.

Chapter 7, "Sustaining and Enduring Life Passages," focuses on the impact of chronic health challenges throughout the life span. The chapter examines mental, physical, and social health turning points through the examples of depression, blindness, and aging. Those faced with these challenges are often stigmatized and communicatively marginalized by society. Formal and informal interpersonal relationships provide important social support that can buffer this marginalization.

Chapter 8, "Ending Life Passages," discusses communication issues related to death and dying. Interwoven throughout this chapter are the stories of two women. One is terminally ill; the other describes the terminal illness of her mother. Through their stories, we see how our language reflects our values and beliefs about death and dying, from how health care professionals deliver bad news to how we deal with the process of dying during illness and after the death.

The three chapters of Part 3, "Communicating Health Competencies," delve into the communication dilemmas we face and the competencies we may develop as we attempt to comprehend health care information, systems, and empowerment.

Chapter 9, "Using and Evaluating Health Information," examines issues that arise while seeking and assessing information related to our health needs and practices. First, questions of quantity and quality are explored: How much information is enough? What kind of information is appropriate to educate ourselves? How do we attribute health expertise? Second, questions of value are addressed: How is public health information framed? What—and whose—values underlie and color that information? Third, questions of accessibility are investigated: What forces control and limit information? What dynamics increase the public's ability to access specialized health information? Finally, the relationship between information and decision making is considered.

Chapter 10, "Navigating Health Care Organizations," introduces the varied health care systems that citizens use to maintain health, both through preventive care and through treatment of illnesses. These changes have had a dramatic impact on patient care as well as on relationships within health care organizations. We consider changes in organizational communication, increases in care providers' job stress and burnout, and how supportive communication can mediate job stress in functional as well as dysfunctional ways.

Finally, Chapter 11, "Empowering Citizens and Advocating Issues," reflects on the ways in which people can feel more willing and competent to participate fully and proactively in patterns of communicating that facilitate wellness, prevent disease, cope with medical crises and chronic illnesses, and promote physical and spiritual healing. These patterns may span a wide range of activities, including improved partnerships between patients and providers, expanded social support, better use of media and other public awareness resources, and increased participation in the political process. The incorporation of health awareness and activism is reviewed from the perspectives of everyday social interactions and national policy making.

We chose this three-part structure in order to integrate into our text a variety of essential considerations of communicating health, just as they occur in our real lives: (a) interpersonal, organizational, and public identities; (b) cultural, political, and ethical influences; (c) physical, psychological, and spiritual concerns; and (d) health promotion, care, education, and advocacy goals. Our hope is that this book will be useful to you and gain in significance as you continue to develop your identities as health citizens.

## SUMMARY

This chapter introduces you to our book and our perspective on health communication. We offer our definitions of *healthy, unhealthy,* and *health communication* to set the stage for what follows in the next 10 chapters. Specifically, we ask you to consider what it means to theorize from your everyday health practices, to narrate life and communicate health, to enact health citizenry, to take into account how representations of health abound in everyday life, to blur the boundaries between wellness and illness, to recognize the changing landscape of health care, and to think of health beyond medicine. The thread we draw through this book is the notion that we are constantly theorizing from the stories we tell and hear about everyday health practices. So, we ask you to consider your own stories as valuable knowledge for making sense out of what you read and learn.

## KEY TERMS

| | | |
|---|---|---|
| health | health citizen | medicalization |
| health communication | *Homo narrans* | managed care |
| theorizing | dis-ease | |
| narrative perspective | Webster Work | |

## DISCUSSION QUESTIONS

1. How might our personal definitions of terms like *healing, disease,* or *disability* influence our decisions to talk about our health or illness in social settings? How might they influence our willingness to actively seek out information or to see a health care provider?

2. Provide an example of how you have theorized about an everyday communicative practice. Based on this example from your own life, what do you think prompts moving from experience to theory, and what functions do you think theorizing serves?

3. Is there a certain person you tend to seek out or trust when it comes to discussing your own experiences with sickness or disease? If so, why do you believe you feel comfortable or trust this particular individual?

4. How do discussions of the same health issue vary when the context changes, such as in your home with family or with roommates? In the classroom or workplace with other students or coworkers? In the health care environment with professional caretakers? In the mass media or other public forums?

5. Consider how various aspects of your life have become "medicalized" through the ways in which we conceptualize them or use particular language to refer to them.

6. What specific concept or idea from this chapter do you believe will be most useful in considering your own health or illness?

## INFOTRAC COLLEGE EDITION

1. Under the subject heading "health" on the InfoTrac database are 35 newspaper citations and 924 periodical citations. Briefly review at least 50 of these citations, and note how many different ideas (for example, exercise) are associated with the concept of health.

2. Read Fazlur Rahman's 1998 essay, "Angels and Spirits in the World of Illness." First, identify the elements within this essay that contribute to its functioning as a health narrative. Next, determine the personal, cultural, and political complexities that are integrated within this story of health beliefs and practices. Finally, consider the implications of this story for our experiences of health and illness in American society. For instance, in what ways do angels and spirits figure into our own health beliefs and practices, including how we communicate about health issues?

3. Dr. Dean Ornish, one of the leading authorities on heart disease and preventive treatment, made the argument reported in an April 3, 1998, newspaper article that spiritual and physical health are connected. He suggests redefining medical practice to deal with patients' emotional and interpersonal needs. After reviewing this article, prepare your own response to Dr. Ornish's suggestion that heart disease is emotional and spiritual as well as physical. How do you think communication between doctors and patients would change if Ornish's argument were generally accepted by medical schools, health care organizations, and health insurers?

# 2

## Personal Complexities of Communicating Health and Illness

**Actor Thrown from Horse Is Dependent on Respirator**

The actor, Christopher Reeve, remains paralyzed, breathing only with aid of a mechanical respirator at the University of Virginia Medical Center in Charlottesville, his doctor said yesterday.

Mr. Reeve, 42, who starred as Superman in several movies and recently played a wheelchair-bound detective in a cable television movie is alert and can communicate "by mouthing words," but cannot make sounds because a breathing tube has been inserted into his windpipe, said Dr. John A. Jane, who heads the hospital's neurosurgery department.

Mr. Reeve is paralyzed from the neck down, Dr. Jane said at a news conference on Thursday afternoon. He was thrown from a horse at a horse trial last Saturday and was reported in "serious but stable" condition last night.

Mr. Reeve, who wore a helmet, suffered fractures of the first and second cervical vertebrae in the fall, damaging the spinal cord at the base of the brain where it joins the spinal cord. Such damage is known as a high cervical injury. It is generally irreversible, experts in spinal cord injuries said in interviews.

"This is a devastatingly dreadful injury," said Dr. Paul Cooper, a brain surgeon at New York University Medical Center who is not involved in Mr. Reeve's case. "If you are demented, you don't know it, but here you know it and you can't do anything about it."

Common causes of high cervical injury are car and diving accidents, which usually result in death before the person can be rescued.

Mr. Reeve may have survived because paramedics were on the scene and gave him mouth-to-mouth resuscitation when they found he was not breathing after the fall.

The accident occurred when Mr. Reeve's horse, Eastern Express, bolted as it approached a hurdle during the first day of a three-day Spring Horse Trials of the Commonwealth Dressage and Combined Training Association in Culpeper.

(ALTMAN, 1995, p. A12)

May 27, 1995, is when Christopher Reeve's life and the lives of his family changed dramatically. While the newspaper account provides a brief synopsis of what occurred that fateful day, Christopher Reeve's 1998 autobiography, *Still Me*, published three years later, sheds light on the personal, cultural, and political complexities of his "new" life and his changed perspective. Here is how Reeve describes his recollection of the accident and the compelling words spoken by Dana, his wife, at his bedside when he regained consciousness:

*When I arrived back at the stables, I ran into John Williams, an Advanced Level rider and trainer and a good friend. . . . I told him that I liked the course and was glad I'd come to Virginia, that I had a great new horse and was looking forward to a good ride. He wished me luck. From that moment until I regained consciousness several days later in the intensive care unit at the University of Virginia, I have no memory of what occurred. . . . Witnesses said that Buck [the horse] was absolutely willing and ready. First jump, no problem. The second jump was a medium size log pile. No problem. Then we came to the zig zag . . . Apparently Buck started to jump the fence, but all of a sudden he just put on the breaks. No warning, no hesitation, no sense of anything wrong. The judge reported that there was nothing to suggest Buck was worried about the fence. He just stopped. It was what riders call a dirty stop; it occurs without warning. Someone said that a rabbit ran out and spooked Buck. Someone said it could have been shadows. . . . My hands probably got caught in the bridle because I was making every effort to stay on. If you fall off during your cross-country ride, you lose sixty points and have no chance of placing in the competition. If my hands had been free, my guess is that I would have broken a wrist. Or I would have just rolled over, gotten up, cursed quietly to myself, and hopped back on. Instead I came straight down on the top rail of the jump, hy-*

*perextended my neck, and slumped down in a heap, head first, six feet, four inches and 215 pounds of me straight down on the rail. Within seconds I was paralyzed and not breathing.*

*After five days, I became fully conscious and able to make sense. Henson and Jane came in to explain my situation. [Dr. John Jane is the chief of neurosurgery, and Dr. Scott Henson is his second in command.] They told me in detail about the extent of my injury, and that after the pneumonia cleared from my lungs they would have to operate to reconnect my skull to the top of my spine . . . and now I understood how serious it was. This was not a C5-C6, which means you are in a wheelchair but you can use your arms and breathe on your own. C1-C2 is about as bad as it gets. Why not die and save everyone a lot of trouble.*

*Dana came into the room. She stood beside me and we made eye contact. I mouthed the words to her: "Maybe we should let me go." Dana started crying. She said, "I'm only going to say this once: I will support whatever you want to do, because this is your life, and your decision. But I want you to know that I'll be with you for the long haul, no matter what." Then she added the words that saved my life: "You're still you. And I love you."*

*If she had looked away or paused or hesitated even slightly, or if I had felt there was a sense of her being—being what?—noble, or fulfilling some obligation to me, I don't know if I could have pulled through. Because it had dawned on me that I was going to be a huge burden to everybody, that I had ruined my life and everybody else's. Not fair to anybody. The best thing to do would be to slip away.*

*But what Dana said made living seem possible, because I felt the depth of her love and commitment. I was even able to make a little joke. I mouthed, "This is way beyond the marriage vows—in sickness and in health." And she said, "I know." I knew then and there that she was going to be with me forever. My job would be to learn how to cope with this and not be a burden. I would have to find new ways to be productive again. (Reeve, 1998, pp. 15-16, 28)*

Not only has Reeve's life changed, so have the stories he tells. Although he would still describe his life as a roller-coaster ride, now it is not a very dangerous one, "more something you might find at a country fair than at Coney Island or Great Adventure" (Reeve, 1998, p. 293). He misses the "freedom, spontaneity, action, and adventure" of the physical, active life he led before the accident. The transition from participant to observer often leaves him feeling like everything he sees from his wheelchair on the deck of his home looking across his pastures is just scenery: "[S]till beautiful, but almost as if cordoned off behind velvet ropes. I feel like a visitor at a spectacular outdoor museum" (p. 266). He titled his autobiography *Still*

Christopher Reeve, *Still Me*. Photo reprinted with permission from the Christopher Reeve Paralysis Foundation; photo by Don Flood.

*Me* to capture the double meaning to the word *still*, "that I am still me, I continue to be me. And also the fact that I don't move. So it's both" (Larry King Live, 1998).

This chapter uses excerpts from Reeve's story, and from those of others, to understand how our narratives, our stories, about health both impact and are impacted by the personal, cultural, and political complexities of our lives. From our perspective, vital to understanding and theorizing about communicating in health and illness is understanding these complexities of health as revealed in narratives. Narratives of health and illness surround us, and more often than not, they are complicated by the politics of interaction between family members, between providers and patients in medical settings, between friends and coworkers, and by our own identity struggles.

We begin by defining **narratives** or **stories** and discussing their complexities. In this chapter, we turn to narratives as a foundation for understanding health communication. We do not offer this perspective as a prescription or a method for studying health communication. Instead, we use narratives as a framework for understanding the personal complexities of communication in health and illness in diverse contexts—families, health care settings, policy and legislation, and mass media campaigns. (Chapters 3 and 4 elaborate our perspective on the cultural and political complexities of communicating health and illness.) We continue by discussing what narratives reveal about embodiment and identity in the contexts of health and illness. Finally, we consider what we can learn from theorizing about narratives.

## NARRATING PERSONAL, CULTURAL, AND POLITICAL COMPLEXITIES

*The story of a life is less than the actual life, because the story told is selective, partial, contextually constructed and because the life is not yet over. But the story of a life is also more than the life, the contours and meanings allegorically extending to others, others seeing themselves, knowing themselves through another's life story, re-visioning their own, arriving where they started and knowing "the place for the first time."*

(Richardson, 1997, p. 6)

Narratives become the primary means for negotiating our way through the demanding moments of our personal lives and our changing identities (Hanne, 1994). Through stories, we explain, exemplify, recount, and account for our decisions (Fisher, 1987). We can think of narratives as something we construct for ourselves and with others to make sense of our lives (Bruner, 1987; White, 1981).

### Defining Narrative

So what is a story or a narrative? The word **narrative** can refer to both the process of making a story and to the result of that process—the story, tale, or history (Polkinghorn, 1988, p. 13). According to Laurel Richardson (1997), a sociologist, **narrative** is a mode of reasoning used to make sense of or apprehend the world, and it is a mode of representation used to tell about the world. Each day, we use the two primary and complementary forms of reasoning—narrative and logico-scientific—each of which relies on different communication codes to get messages across. **Narrative reasoning** is designed to understand the whole by integrating parts of our experience, often in ways we cannot "prove" but know intuitively; **logical reasoning,** however, is based on structured observations that "prove" what we experience.

Similarly, psychologist Jerome Bruner (1986) contrasts the paradigmatic and the narrative as two modes of thought. Whereas the paradigmatic utilizes logical reasoning and hypothesis testing, the narrative "allows for examination of felt personal experience and the individual's struggle with meaning-making in a social context" (Fiese & Grotevant, 2001, p. 579). Barbara Czarniawska (1997), an organizational scholar, suggests that the boundaries between narrative and scientific knowledge are permeable, and that loans from both forms of reasoning arrive in packages that are inseparable aspects of the same thing—both frame and picture.

A vivid example of how both forms of reasoning are often inseparable is revealed in my (Patricia's) experience with losing a family member. My cousin, Jeanne, and her husband, Bill, lost their only child, Billy. On Saturday, October 2, 1999, at the age of 28, Billy died of a drug overdose. During the week I spent with Jeanne and Bill, everyone talked about what happened, how it happened, and who was responsible. Raising these questions led friends and family to use logical reasoning, focusing on what could be proven from the observations of people who were with Billy before he died, what the paramedics observed and reported, what the autopsy report contained, and even what family and friends knew to be true about Billy. At the same time, and often in the same sentence, family and friends told stories, reasoning narratively to answer these difficult questions. People talked about the could have's, should have's, would have's, might have's, and why didn't I's. The logical and narrative reasonings were spoken softly, angrily, in between sobs and all around the memories tied to "What if?" Like a hologram, our communication about health and illness interconnects both forms of reasoning, and each story we tell reflects the whole of who we are and how we reason about our life experiences with health, illness, and death.

Along with the notion of narrative as a process of reasoning and communicating or representing what we apprehend, these narrative representations become products that others listen to, learn from, disagree with, and generally use as a resource, either personally or politically. In addition to representing moral dilemmas or opportunities for others to be moved by or resonate with a story, narratives often become significant vehicles for social change. Usually, members of particular cultural communities who know firsthand the issues at stake make the personal political. "To tell a previously 'untold story' is an act which can be extraordinarily disruptive to the way things are or the way people think things are" (Hanne, 1994,

p. 12). For many, Christopher Reeve's account was an "untold story" that raised awareness and prompted them to become politically active concerning issues facing the cultural community of persons with spinal cord injuries. In this way, personal stories are not just representations of some event, belief, or campaign; they become sites of political action and negotiation (Denzin, 1997).

We can think of Christopher Reeve's narratives as both a process and a product. He says that the process of writing *Still Me* was a powerful source of motivation and satisfaction, so much so that he experienced separation anxiety when it was completed (Reeve, 1998). Reeve suggests that "writing the book was one of the highlights of my life, before and after the accident" (Christopher Reeve Homepage), that "it was therapeutic and also emotionally difficult . . . [it was] cathartic . . . and I remembered some wonderful stories" (Larry King Live, 1998).

Reeve's narratives become a product in that he and others may use his stories to inspire, persuade, comfort, or motivate. The stories, tales, and historical details of his life before and after the accident depict a range of devastations and elations. As a result, they have inspired thousands to write him with their own stories, helped to raise funds for spinal cord injury research, and facilitated the development of legislation for an insurance company tax to increase monies for medical research, and generally engaged others to think differently about disability and medical research.

Reeve's optimism about the future remains intact. He is committed to his creative work of directing, writing, and acting and to his responsibility to help other disabled individuals by changing legislation to increase insurance coverage and by promoting research on spinal cord injuries. He delivers more than 40 speeches a year, frequently meets with legislators and scientists, and regularly attends social events and political fundraisers (Christopher Reeve Homepage). Rather than seeing his life as two parts, divided by what happened on that fateful day, he now sees his life as a journey, with more possibilities than limitations (Reeve, 1998, p. 295). It is not surprising, then, that his definition of a hero has changed:

> *When the first Superman movie came out, I gave dozens of interviews to promote it. The most frequently asked question was: "What is a hero?" I remember how easily I'd talk about it, the glib response I repeated too many times. My answer was that a hero is someone who commits a courageous action without considering the consequences. A soldier who crawls out of a foxhole to drag an injured buddy back to safety, the prisoners of war who never stop trying to escape even though they know they may be executed if they're caught. And I also meant individuals who are slightly larger than life: Houdini and Lindbergh of course, John Wayne and JFK, and even sports figures who have taken on mythical proportions, such as Babe Ruth or Joe Di Maggio.*

> *Now my definition is completely different. I think a hero is an ordinary individual who finds the strength to persevere and endure in spite of overwhelming obstacles.*

*The fifteen-year old boy down the hall at Kessler who had landed on his head while wrestling with his brother, leaving him paralyzed and barely able to swallow or speak. Travis Roy, paralyzed in the first eleven seconds of a hockey game in his freshman year at college. . . . These are real heroes, and so are the families and friends who have stood by them. (Reeve, p. 267)*

Christopher Reeve's stories capture his soul-searching and the discoveries he makes about himself and about the family, friends, and providers who support him. He chronicles his movement into the cultural community of the disabled, specifically the community of persons with spinal cord injuries. We see boundaries collapsing and new forms of communication among diverse communities—his family; peers in his professional world of acting; health care providers, particularly those specializing in spinal cord injuries; neurological researchers; the National Spinal Cord Injury Association; the community of others who are living with a spinal cord injury; and people who reach out to Reeve through mail, e-mail, telephone, and daily contact during his health care visits, political activism, and social life.

## ▇ Complex Meanings in Health Narratives

The storied nature of health **identity** is personal, cultural, and political. That is, our sense of self, our identity, is decidedly a process and product of our personal experience of life and of the cultural and political systems we inhabit (Bordo, 1989; Shilling, 1993). Through Christopher Reeve's stories, we see the layers of political complexities surrounding the need for better health insurance coverage, the need for increased funding for medical research, and the significant role that a public and charismatic figure can play in advocating change. Through Christopher Reeve, we learn about the magnitude and politics of spinal cord injuries. Links from an extensive Christopher Reeve Web page, created by one of his fans, take us to the Web site of the National Spinal Cord Injury Association, where we learn that more than 400,000 persons are living with spinal cord injuries and more than 7,800 individuals sustain a spinal cord injury every year (National Spinal Cord Injury Association, 1999).

Dramatically, the cultural boundaries collapse between the public personae of Christopher Reeve the actor, the activist, and the mythical hero, Superman, and his private struggle with "ordinary" life events as a disabled person. In his autobiography (Reeve, 1998), he describes his struggle with something most of us take for granted every day, a shower:

*Every couple of nights you need to take a shower. The prospect absolutely terrified me: What if something happened to the vent [ventilator—the apparatus that assists with his breathing] in the shower? What if water got into the trach or the tube from the ventilator to the opening in my throat? . . . The idea of immersing myself in water petrified me. I kept putting it off, saying, "Just give me a sponge bath. I can't face a shower." (p. 95)*

In this passage, we learn about Reeve's personal fears and the necessity of communicating those fears to others. We learn how critical each and every technological device is to his life and about the safety precautions he and his caregivers must take and talk about when caring for him, sometimes in ways that publicly display bodily functions that normally are private (such as bowel movements). From this story, and from other stories of "ordinary" routines in his life, we learn how vital the communication is between Reeve and his providers. We learn how essential each and every caregiver is to ensuring that Reeve moves through each of these routines safely. The personal reflects the political when we realize what he and others have learned by living life with a disability: Insurance caps on health care often do not allow for the 24-hour professional care that is vital to life. Reeve's story, in relating very personal and specific examples of his needs for medical equipment and professional care, bring to the public's attention the need to re-examine our health care insurance policies. The personal becomes public, and the public becomes political.

Narratives, therefore, are not neutral representations of some "truth." The story told is different from the story lived, and the story told varies from one situation to the next and from one person to the next. Narratives represent different versions of different stories, not one "truthful" story (Denzin, 1992). As Arthur Frank (1995), sociologist and cancer survivor, points out:

> *The truth of stories is not only what was experienced, but equally what becomes experience in the telling and its reception. . . . Life moves on and stories change with that movement, and experience changes. Stories are true to the flux of experience, and the story affects the direction of that flux. If calling stories true requires some category of stories called false, I confess to being unsure what a "false" personal account would be. I have read personal accounts I considered evasive, but that evasion was their truth. The more reconstructed the story, the more powerful the truth of the desire for what is being told, as the corrected version of what was lived. Hearing the desire in the story takes me back to the need for a different level of attention to stories. (p. 22)*

To understand personal narratives, we must assume that they are "true" and try to imagine the context of their creation.

## ▓ The Context of Health Narratives

Understanding narratives necessitates considering the discourse of the story and the context of the people who are communicating based on their cultures and political beliefs. Consider the origins of the word **context**: Its Latin roots: *com-*, which means "together," plus *textere,* which means to join, to weave, or to plait, indicate that individuals create coherence or meaning based on what is "true" from their positioning in particular cultural communities or political contexts (Chenail, 1991). Language in medical settings acts to perpetuate the interests of some groups and not those of others. Culture and politics speak through stories in ways that may seem natural and neutral. However, communicating about our health and illness means that our economic status, language proficiency, education, professional training, and assertiveness may all play a part in whose views are considered and influence decision making (Lupton, 1994). For example, indigent patients who are not well educated or who speak English poorly are not likely to get as good an explanation of a diagnosis or an illness management plan as a more middle-class or well-educated person. The professional training of nurses, physicians, hospital administrators, and physical therapists also often leads them to communicate differently about what to focus on when caring for patients.

We can learn a great deal from juxtaposing narratives and the process of interaction surrounding the construction of narratives in diverse contexts. Theorizing Practice 2.1 looks at three separate contexts in which different meanings may be composed and considered. In this comparison, we often see how "stories are incomplete, tentative, and revisable according to contingencies of our present life circumstances. . . . Stories rearrange, redescribe, invent, omit, and revise" (Ellis & Bochner, 2000, p. 745). Clearly, considering narratives and the process of narrating is valuable in almost any context, but our attention now turns to that of narrating identities of health and illness.

Who participates in the construction of narratives of health and illness? What forms do these narratives take? What can we learn by juxtaposing narratives? The next sections attempt to address these questions.

# N ARRATIVES OF HEALTH AND ILLNESS

*A story houses us. Often more utterly than does our flesh.*

*I do not mean just the collected wake of events accruing and intersecting into a kind of minor history; rather the revelation of these events in the realm of conscious meaning. This is our story. Each of us may follow this or flee from it. In either case we make a pattern in space, one beginning in a given time and one that is in its relentless design beautiful.*

*We all live in this way: in a story, in and out of place; living and dying in this way, speaking in search and prevention of ourselves, in places and alien to them, given*

## Personal, Cultural, and Political Contexts of Narratives

Imagine construction of a narrative about abortion in the context of the family living room during a conversation between a 1-month pregnant, 15-year-old young woman and her parents, who do not believe that abortion is an option. The parents are loving, caring, and concerned about the welfare of their daughter.

Imagine another situation in which a narrative about abortion is constructed in the context of a small, private office at Planned Parenthood during a conversation between the same teenaged girl and a counselor. In this case, abortion is discussed as her "choice" among other options such as giving the child up for adoption.

Imagine a third situation in which a narrative about abortion is constructed during a conversation between the 15-year-old young woman and the 15-year-young man who impregnated her. He believes that abortion is the best option and wants nothing to do with the situation.

Consider what cultural or political contingencies might lead the abortion narratives to be constructed differently in each situation—with the parents, with the boyfriend, or with the Planned Parenthood counselor. These contingencies might include religion, Planned Parenthood's mission statement, the relationship between the young woman and her parents or her boyfriend, and so on.

What might we learn by juxtaposing these three narratives?

*to and taken from a family, suspecting, betraying and worshipping that great space that dwells within the story and the storyteller.*

(Ronan, 1982, p. 7)

In sickness and in health, we tell, listen to, and construct stories about our bodies—its functioning, its malfunctioning, and even goals that we have for changing its shape, strength, and capacity. Such stories confirm, disconfirm, and challenge our identities. They offer advice, remedies, and motivation, and they build and question the guiding philosophies for living life and for surviving illness and loss. We construct and listen to such stories with our friends, family, health care providers, athletic coaches, instructors, and even strangers who initiate narratives or are willing to participate in a story we want to tell.

### Patients' Stories

A great deal of emphasis has been placed by theorists on patients' narratives and the forms their stories take. Frank (1995) says that "people tell stories not just to

## Anesthesia as Overkill: One Patient's Story

The patient, now in the hospital gown, paper cap, and paper shoes and under the warm covers of the hospital bed, situated in the curtained-wall cubical of pre-op and awaiting surgery, is discussing her choice of a local rather than a general anesthetic and minimal amounts of sedation. The anesthesiologist, relaxing in a chair beside her bed and wearing a Hawaiian-print head cap, states, "You are what we call a minimalist."

"What does that mean?"

"That means you prefer to use anesthesia minimally."

"Is that a negative term, minimalist?"

"No, no, not at all. It has more to do with your tolerance for pain and the kind of control you want to have. But some people have trouble with the consciousness that minimal anesthesia allows. They may feel more in control because they are more conscious, but they are not truly in control in the sense that they cannot get up and leave in the middle of the operation. So rather than experience the contradiction, they prefer to have a stronger sedation or a general rather than a local."

"But isn't a general really an overkill for this type of operation?"

"Well, yeah, it is like using an elephant gun to kill a mouse."

"Oh, I guess overkill isn't the best choice of words here, but . . ."

"Yeah, I wouldn't use the word overkill, but yes, it's much more than you need. So there you have my philosophy of anesthesia in *Reader's Digest* form. Okay then, we will administer a local with minimal amounts of sedation."

"So, do I even need sedation?"

"Well, it is up to you, but most patients prefer to have at least some sedation to calm their nerves going into surgery."

"But I have been through this surgery so many times before, I really don't think I need any sedation."

"Maybe not, but most people don't realize they're nervous or anxious until they actually are wheeled into the surgical unit, so a little sedation just takes the edge off."

"Well, I'm just not sure. I guess just a little. Minimal sedation would be okay."

No one really explains to the patient the possible variance in amounts of sedation, or even what the "minimal" amounts are that they begin to

work out their own changing identities, but also to guide others who will follow them" (p. 17). We offer one person's story in Theorizing Practice 2.2 as a vehicle for exploring communication and the multiple identities of patients and providers. The story raises issues concerning context, complexities, and how what might be true for the patient might not be true for the provider. Try to put your-

*(continued from previous page)*

administer through her intravenous line. But one thing she is certain of—she is glad to be aware enough to ask for the Windham Hill sampler CD. As the music begins to play, she realizes that the anesthetist (at least, she assumes the woman monitoring her intravenous line is the anesthetist) may or may not know her preferences for minimal sedation. Just as she is about to communicate these preferences once again, the woman takes her hand and says, "I think a bit more sedation would be good. . . . Now doesn't that feel better?"

"It feels like a truck has run over and crushed my hand," she states before the fuzzy feeling takes over.

The next day, the patient vividly recalls, with a surprising degree of anger, her feelings of loss of control, being misunderstood, and not listened to. But it's over now. She can't help but feel like she should call the doctor who performed the surgery and ask about the dark-haired anesthetist. She desperately wants to exert her control by reporting this incident to the doctor, and she is curious how the doctor will respond.

(Geist & Gates, 1996, pp. 222)

**Questions to Consider**

- How might we better interpret this story if we knew something about the hospital's health care policies?

- What other factors may need to be considered in this situation beyond the patient's request for minimal sedation?

- What other stories could be told about this situation, and from whose perspective?

- Do you think the patient was justified in her feelings of betrayal and anger? Why?

- Would you contact the anesthetist?

- If you would not contact the anesthetist, why not?

- If you would contact the anesthetist, how would you do so—by a phone call, personal appointment, or some other way (such as a letter or through the Internet)?

self in the places of this patient and the providers with whom she interacts, then try to answer the questions that follow the story.

Much of this chapter concerns the patient as the central construct, but we recognize the problematics of using this word because of its connection to illness rather than to health and recovery. We recognize the therapeutic and recuperative value of patients' narratives and what they convey about their biographical emotions, turning points, and identity struggles, but we also want to emphasize others who participate in constructing health narratives, including family members, friends, and providers.

## ▪ Providers' Stories

In addition to considering what patients' accounts reflect about their illness or wellness experience, we should also consider the narratives of health care providers and what these stories reflect about their experiences of providing care. As health communication scholar Athena du Pré (2000) points out, becoming a health professional is both a matter of acquiring technical expertise and a process of socialization in which providers learn the responsibilities, demands, expectations, and privileges of a particular profession.

Providers may be limited in their ability to listen to patients' stories based on their professional training; their negative characterizations of the patient; the politics of the medical setting, which may privilege organizational routines over quality of care; or managed care mandates, such as limiting the time that providers can see each patient (Geist & Dreyer, 1993a, 1993b). The danger is that disproportionate privilege may be granted to providers' narratives, allowing talk of scientific knowledge gained through diagnostic tests to dominate so that the "voice of medicine" interrupts—or even silences—the "voice of the patient" (Mishler, 1984).

This isn't the whole story, however. Providers' communication also can be constrained in several ways: (a) by the voice of medicine, which gives little opportunity to share their emotions or to solicit emotions from patients; (b) by their socialization to be confident and in control, especially with the threat of lawsuits, which limit what providers can talk about (such as their self-doubt, medical mistakes, or stress and burnout); and (c) by the contradictory demands on providers to be quick but thorough, strong but emotionally accessible, always available but never tired, and honest but infallible (du Pré, 2000).

Many sensitive providers offer insight into their experiences with medical school, caring for patients, communicating with colleagues, and managing the work of the hospital or clinic. For example, Rafael Campo, a general internist at Harvard and an accomplished poet, uses the clinical/technical style of writing in some of his poems but then offers a very humane twist at the end. Theorizing Practice 2.3 reveals how some of his poetry provides both a commentary on medical practice and an empathic insight regarding patients.

Along with highlighting personal complexities, providers' narratives capture the political complexities of medical work (Atkinson, 1995; Hunter, 1991). Featured prominently in providers' stories is a hierarchy of authority, where certain

## Humanizing Medicine

Read the following two selections from Rafael Campo's (1996) "Ten Patients and Another," and consider what you learn about medicine, patients, providers, and the personal, cultural, and political complexities of communication in the medical setting.

II. Jamal
The patient is a three-year-old black male,
The full-term product of a pregnancy
That was, according to his grandmother,
Unplanned and maybe complicated by
Prenatal alcohol exposure. Did
OK, developmentally delayed
But normal weights and heights, until last week
When he ingested what's turned out to be
Cocaine, according to the lab results;
His grandmother had said she'd seen him with
Some baby powder on his face and hands
Before he started seizing and they brought
Him in. The vital signs have stabilized.
The nurse is getting D.S.S. [Department of Social Services] involved.
The mom? She left it on the kitchen table.
That's her—the one who sings to him all night.

IV. Kelly
The patient is a twelve-year-old female.
She's gravida zero, no STD's. [no previous pregnancies, no sexually transmitted diseases]
She'd never even had a pelvic. One
Month nausea and vomiting. No change
In bowel habits. No fever, chills, malaise
Her school performance has been worsening.
One states that things at home are fine.
On physical exam, she cried but was
Cooperative. Her abdomen was soft,
With normal bowel sounds and question of
A suprapubic mass, which was non-tender.
Her pelvic was remarkable for scars
At six o'clock, no hymen visible,
Some uterine enlargement. Pregnancy
Tests positive times two. She says it was
Her dad. He's sitting in the waiting room.

physicians have rights to claim the floor and tell particular types of stories to an audience. Through these stories, we learn about the politics of working in the health professions as providers engage in daily "rounds" of orations, narratives, and disputes:

> *The late modern clinic with its ultracomplex division of labor draws on and engages a large number of techniques and technologies. The patient and her or his illness are translated into a multiplicity of measurements and representations. The sites of such representations are numerous, in laboratories and diagnostic specialisms. Yet these technologized representations are by no means the whole story. Indeed, the whole story is precisely what counts. Dispersed in time and space in the clinic are the numerous tellings of the patient. "Telling the case" is a powerful mechanism for the enactment of professional work. . . . At daily working rounds, and in the multiplicity of daily collegial contacts, cases are narrated. There is a generalized exchange of narratives. One can think, indeed, in terms of a kind of economy in which the stories of medical work are the tokens. (Atkinson, 1997, pp. 328–329)*

The political complexities of communication are evident in providers' stories in other situations as well. For example, in a series of studies that I (Patricia) conducted with my colleague, sociologist Monica Hardesty, we found through interviews that as health providers communicate with one another, they may disagree with or misunderstand one another because of their "competing" definitions of quality of care (Geist & Hardesty, 1990). Nurses often suggested that quality is caring, administrators that quality is efficiency, and physicians that quality is effective decision making. Political complexities are also revealed as physicians experience uncertainty in communicating with patients. Physicians' stories of difficult and nonroutine decisions often weave in references to themselves in ways that establish their own authority or credibility as a strategy for managing uncertainty (Hardesty & Geist, 1990). Hospital administrators recognize their ability to gain cooperation from physicians through construction of narratives that combine both anecdotal evidence of cases and statistical evidence of general patterns (Geist & Hardesty, 1992).

## ▩ Voices of Significant Others

Finally, the narratives of family members, friends, and others are constructed in the process of providing support, care, and struggling with their own identities in relation to those who are ill or diseased. One rich example is the evocative, autobiographical narrative composed by Carolyn Ellis (1995a, 2000), sociologist and communication researcher. She writes about her experiences as a long-term caregiver for her critically ill partner, Gene, who eventually died of emphysema, a severe lung disease that interferes with normal breathing. By juxtaposing her private and intimate conversations with Gene and her conversations with four different doctors over the course of eight years, she creates a powerful story that captures the dynamic, long-term process of negotiating the illness experience.

Another vivid example of interweaving the diverse voices of patients, providers, and families is the work of communication scholars Mara Adelmen and Lawrence Frey (1997). For two years, they explored the narratives constructed by individuals living in Bonaventure House, a residential facility for people with AIDS. Through the stories of the facility's residents and administrators, we discover how residents communicate with one another to provide social support and resolve tensions in their fragile community.

Research that juxtaposes the narratives of patients with those of providers or family members helps us better understand the personal, cultural, and political complexities involved. The next section looks at what we learn from considering individuals' personal narratives of embodiment, disembodiment, and identity. Through this discussion, we begin to see the forms that narratives take and what we can learn by juxtaposing narratives of health and illness.

# NARRATING EMBODIMENT AND IDENTITY

*Our bodies are with us, though we have always had trouble saying exactly how. We are, in various conceptions or metaphors, in our body, or having a body, or at one with our body, or alienated from it. The body is both ourselves and other, and as such the object of emotions from love to disgust. . . . Most of the time, the body maintains an unstable position between such extremes, at once the subject and object of pleasure, the uncontrollable agent of pain and the revolt against reason— and the vehicle of mortality. As such, it is always the subject of curiosity, of an ever-renewed project of knowing.*

(Brooks, 1993, p. 1)

We are surrounded by discourse in stories about height, weight, physique, breast size, penis size, skin color, hair color, baldness, performance, strength, and even mood from childhood through our elder years. I (Patricia) remember how preoccupied my then-five-year-old daughter was with saying, "Look how strong I am!," "Look how tall I am!," or "Look how fat I am!" (though most would describe her as tiny). We describe ourselves and tell stories about conforming—or not conforming—to what we have heard, read, or talked about concerning our health in the context of political and cultural communities.

Bodies have occupied a central place in theories from a variety of disciplines, including sociology, political science, psychology, literature, theology, and communication. Yet as Brooks (1993) points out, "[W]e still don't know the body. Its otherness from ourselves, as well as its intimacy, make it the inevitable object of an ever-renewed writing project" (p. 286). Through our bodies, we are enabled, constrained, managed, disciplined, accepted, and rejected by others and ourselves.

In our everyday lives, we move between dualities of wellness and illness, ability and disability, presence and absence, and **embodiment** and **disembodiment**. At times, we even experience both simultaneously. As embodied selves, we may be conscious of the body, looking at it, sensing it, but at the same time feeling disembodied by the alien nature of novel sensations in illness, cyclical body changes, and dysfunction (Leder, 1990). A skier, skater, runner, or walker may feel a sense of embodiment after a good workout, but at the same time, they may feel disembodied by the sensations of chronic pain from a previous injury. Drew Leder (1990), a philosopher, captures these dualities in his book, *The Absent Body*, when he states:

> *Insofar as the body tends to disappear when functioning unproblematically, it often seizes our attention most strongly at times of dysfunction; we then experience the body as the very absence of a desired or ordinary state, and as a force that stands opposed to the self.* (p. 4)

Leder suggests that at moments of breakdown, we experience **dys-appearance**. That is, in contrast to the disappearances that characterize ordinary functioning, in dys-appearance we experience a limit on vital functioning but also a personal disturbance that tends to make us feel self-consciousness. Leder explains dys-appearance in this way:

> Dys *is from the Greek prefix signifying "bad," "hard," or "ill" and is found in English words such as "dysfunctional."* . . . *However, dys is also a variant spelling, now somewhat archaic, of the Latin root dis. This originally had the meaning of "away," "apart," or "asunder."* . . . *The body in dys-appearance is marked by being away, apart, or asunder.* (p. 87)

Essentially, our bodies in dys-appearance or disembodiment can be experienced in two ways: as a reversal of a normal or desired state; and as away, apart from self, an alien thing or painful prison or tomb that one is trapped in (Leder).

The root of disembodiment lies in defining our own or others' self-identities solely based on the physical body (Scheman, 1993). In this way, those persons who do not possess what the culture has defined as the "ideal body" are the ones who are subordinated, othered, and considered less than or inferior to the ideal. When we are sick, diagnosed with a particular disease, or in some way disabled, the unobtainable body image becomes even more impossible, because we or others (or both) define our bodies as damaged and changed, which implies we are less than whole, complete, able, or "perfect." Any visible "flaws" become scars for the world to see, and we may fear our "invisible flaws" will be discovered. We also may expend great energy denying the "flaw" in our body—our flaws become the basis on which we (and others) reject our own bodies as being different or other. Undoubtedly, these changes, these "flaws," may alter our communication in ways that intensify dys-appearance and disembodiment.

Embodiment and disembodiment are natural processes that operate every day, habitually, and often unconsciously. Most people experience a tolerable, even comfortable ebb and flow of their "healthy" and "sick" identities. Yet when the sick or diseased identity becomes all-encompassing, so that everything we do or say becomes centered on our illness (be it an injury, chronic illness, or disease), we may find that our communication with others can intensify self-consciousness to the point that our dys-appearance is uncomfortable (Do & Geist, 2000). Leder (1990) suggests that this uncomfortable intensification of self-consciousness often relates to a discrepancy in power. When we are sick, ill, or diseased, others have the power to heal, to provide care, and to help us feel whole again.

Erving Goffman (1963), a sociologist, has written about **stigma.** He suggests that loss of control over our bodies creates a **spoiled identity** that for most people is embarrassing and stigmatizing. Goffman coined the term **passing** to describe what people do when they keep invisible from the public's gaze what is spoiled about their identities. Spoiled identities create crises of communication that lead people to engage in strategies to feel more in control and to become embodied in ways that manage their "sick" identity.

Times are changing, however. Many of us talk more openly now about our health and illness. Frank (1991) says that "when I wear the lapel pin of my own cancer support group I am doing a kind of reverse passing, proclaiming my identity to be spoiled even though I could easily pass" (p. 32). Though people cannot always do something to change their illnesses, this "coming out" tells others that they are doing something about their spoiled identity. Thus, it becomes a form of control. Coming out in this way—through lapel pins, bumper stickers, t-shirts, support groups, Internet chat rooms, and health-oriented classes—provides opportunities to share stories and to learn about others' spoiled identities and strategies for communicating.

Turning illness into story is a form of control as well as an opportunity for others to communicate caring and understanding. It is compassion, in the sense of experiencing and sharing another's perspective, that allows us to become transformed into real, dimensional, embodied selves and not to be defined solely by a physical characteristic, an illness, or a disease (Leder, 1990). Communication can be a vehicle for **transformation,** for experiencing compassion, and for crossing the boundaries between embodied and disembodied selves. Resisting disembodiment through communication can transform interaction in ways that build understanding and compassion. Transformation from disembodiment to embodiment may ease tensions of difference/indifference, stimulate interest in understanding those afflicted in ways we have not personally experienced, and thus, transcend the "othering" (distancing) that routinely occurs for persons who are ill, disabled, or feel disembodied (Do & Geist, 2000).

One step toward transformation is listening to the voices of people in sickness and in health. We can learn a great deal about the everyday processes of embodiment and disembodiment through narratives. And we can begin to understand the significant role of communication in intensifying or transforming the debilitating self-consciousness and stigma of a spoiled identity that restricts understanding, compassion, and acceptance of both ourselves and others.

## ∫ TORIES OF EMBODIMENT AND DISEMBODIMENT: COMMUNICATING TRANSFORMATION

*Illness is the night-side of life, a more onerous citizenship. Everyone who is born holds dual citizenship, in the kingdom of the well and in the kingdom of the sick. Although we all prefer to use only the good passport, sooner or later each of us is obliged, at least for a spell, to identify ourselves as citizens of that other place.*

(Sontag, 1989, p. 3)

Never underestimate the power of story to reflect—and to affect—people's dual citizenship. Such narratives give voice to the concerns of persons who are usually not heard because of the stigma of their spoiled identities. More often than not, our society privileges those with undamaged bodies and minds to speak with a stronger voice than the voice of "others."

Narratives reflect people's lives and the changes in identity experienced when they become ill or grapple with their spoiled identity, allowing others to glimpse the experiences and emotions of persons who feel embodied or disembodied in some way. Stories as "identity work" represent an overarching narrative that might also be described as a journey (Jackson, 1989), a performance (Denzin, 1997), or a ritual of community (Richardson, 1997). Identity work for persons who are ill involves articulating what it means to live a life circumscribed by illness (Mathieson & Barrie, 1998). From the moment they are diagnosed with an illness or begin some physical or psychological therapy, individuals face a process of composing

## "Sharing the Secret"

Rita: I never told anyone about what my father did to me until just before Steve and I got married. I can't even tell you why I told him. We were in the living room watching TV and I just turned around and said, "I have something to tell you." He didn't say much of anything, and we never talked about it after that. But then when my daughter turned three, it was bothering me, just seeing Steve and Emmy together. I used to want to spy on them to see if he was doing something to her. When I told him, he got really upset. He couldn't believe I would think that of him. And I had to try to tell him that it wasn't him; it would be anybody. Now Emmy's eight and I've been in therapy for about four years. But as time goes on, I keep having trouble with sex. I expected that it would get better. But it's gotten worse. Sometimes I have flashbacks and sometimes I just can't feel anything. That puts a strain on us. I don't like to talk about the abuse, not with him. It's so personal, and it may get into something that I don't want to deal with, or *I think I don't want to open this up again.*

(Ray, Ellis, & Ford, 2000, p. 221)

**Questions to Consider**

- How would you describe Rita's illness narrative?
- What changes is Rita trying to compose about her identity?
- What tensions does Rita experience?
- What tensions does Steve experience?
- How you think our societal norms or pressures may contribute to Rita's spoiled identity?

and renegotiating their identities with family, friends, coworkers, and health care providers (Mathieson & Stam, 1995).

Survivors of abuse experience intense anguish in their efforts to live a "normal" life unspoiled by memories, flashbacks, and self-destructive behaviors. Disembodiment is experienced daily in communicating with others and attempting to compose an identity unspoiled by past abuse. Theorizing Practice 2.4 offers Rita's story of sexual abuse and the stigma and pain that continually haunt her present relationships.

## Illness Narratives and Changing Identities

Composing identities in the face of uncertainty, pain, stress, stigma, and in some cases, the prospect of death occurs during the course of illness. A broad range of research focuses on the identity work by members of varied cultural communities as they face injury, illness, and disease, including athletes (Sparkes, 1996, 1997, 1998), individuals who are chronically ill (Charmaz, 1983, 1987, 1991, 1994, 1995), and individuals with cancer (Frank, 1991; Lorde, 1980; Ott, 1999). Other research has focused on the healing powers of the stories we tell over the course of illness (Pennebaker, 1993; Pennebaker & Beall, 1986; Pennebaker, Kiecolt-Glaser, & Glaser, 1988). Narratives function as medicine for those who are ill, allowing them to use story as a process of understanding both themselves and their relationships (Brody, 1987).

Arthur Frank (1993) suggests that viewing an illness experience as a narrative allows us to experience illness as something more than a deviation from health. He suggests that illness narratives are not illnesses, but that they invoke change "based on understanding illness as a moment at which change is especially possible" (p. 41). People change their lives through narratives, and these narratives may convey at least three different types of changes.

One type of change is that a person may discover themselves anew as "what I have always been" (Frank, 1993, p. 42). For example, Audre Lorde (1980) tells the story of her breast cancer and postmastectomy identity in a way that embodies her unique identity as a black, lesbian poet. Pressure from the medical community or volunteer groups such as Reach for Recovery for her to accept a breast prosthesis represents what Lorde has always known and experienced—a normalizing demand to make difference invisible.

A second type of change is that a person discovers "who I might become" (Frank, 1993, p. 42). For example, Lisa Tillmann-Healy (1996), a communication scholar, tells the story of her life-long battle with bulimia. She describes her movement toward "a new and better place, a place of self-acceptance and empowerment" (p. 104), but she reminds us this is not a story with a neat and tidy resolution of living happily, healthily ever after:

> Before I began this project, I couldn't understand why someone like me—bright, educated, feminist—would binge and purge. I have since looked long and hard at the family and cultural stories that surround(ed) me. In the context of those stories—stories that teach all of us to relate pathologically to food and to our bodies, stories told and repeated at home, at school, and in the media—bulimia no longer seems an illogical "choice." (p. 104)

The new relation to self and others is not one of "cured" but of acceptance, of comfort and companionship for those who read her story and see themselves in it.

A third change is **cumulative epiphanies** (Frank, 1993). That is, the narrative does not describe one moment of discovery that is life changing. Instead, it represents a discovery of what one has always been but has never understood—the cumulative epiphany is "I am what I have always been" (Frank, p. 42). For example, Irving

Zola (1982), a sociologist who has been disabled since childhood, writes about visiting a community for the disabled in The Netherlands and recognizing that who he is, in fact, is who he has always been, even though he had invested his life energies in passing as a "normal," unimpaired person. This is a different change than what Lorde experienced. She discovers that her preillness identity can be extended to express the contingencies of her "ill" life, and she expresses a deeper truth of what she has always been. In contrast, Zola develops "the truth of his *difference* from what he has tried to make himself. He discovers his 'old self' never was what he tried to believe it was and force it to be" (Frank, p. 46) and, thus, does not claim to be anyone radically new.

Finally, the narrative also might reveal a person's claim of little, if any, self-change following the illness (Frank, 1993). There is no epiphany. There is no reappraisal. There is only ambivalence. Physician Fitzhugh Mullan (1975) expresses this:

> *Even as I write about it I feel a kind of terminal ambivalence about the entire experience. Though I would never have chosen to have cancer, it is part of me and therefore something that I can't hate, deny, or discard. Like a lame leg or a blind eye, it is with me for the rest of my life. For better and worse, I will live with it and quietly work and rework my personal history in an effort to accommodate it as much as possible. (p. 195)*

As Frank points out, however, even in narrating his story there is an opportunity to witness his own suffering, and perhaps in the process of writing and reading his own story as well as in listening to the responses to it, he may discover some changes.

In addition to reflecting people's lives, narratives of health and illness also allow readers to reflect on themselves and their own experiences. For instance, Carolyn Ellis (1996) reflects on Tolstoy's fictional account, the "Death of Ivan Ilych," by writing:

> *The story made me think about how I was living my life and working my work. I thought further about the role of family relationships, career, and social support in one's life, and even more abstractly about mortality, meaning, and life after death. This cognitive awareness was accompanied by emotional, bodily, and spiritual reactions. For a while, I became a part of Ivan Ilych's life and experienced his story in the role of each character in the narrative. (p. 3)*

Through Tolstoy's personal narrative, Ellis gained unique insight in understanding Tolstoy's experience and reflected on her own relationships and experiences.

The narratives we tell also provide a means to heal wounds, to create meaning, and to move ahead. According to Ellis (1996):

> *An experience of loss can scatter the pieces of the meaningful world we have assembled for ourselves. Coping, understanding, and recovering are hard work. Part of this work entails creating an account . . . recovery from loss is contingent on both*

*the private experience of formulating that account and the public experience of disclosing it to others. (p. 157)*

Clearly, narrative is a way to understand and make sense of our own and others' lives (Bochner, Ellis, & Tillmann-Healy, 1996; Ellis, 1993, 1996, 1997; Ellis & Bochner, 2000).

### ▨ Narratives and Understanding

Narratives speak words that humanize persons who may have experienced something we know nothing about. This was the case for many people when they heard Christopher Reeve's story of his life before and after his spinal cord injury. Stories such as his, told by members of a cultural community who feel embodied or disembodied in some way, transform our stereotypes and allow people to become "selves," making them *persons* and not *others* (Fine, 1994).

Humanizing women who have been victims of violence is precisely the goal of the Clothesline Project, which was initiated by a group of Massachusetts women who were inspired by the AIDS quilt. T-shirts are created by survivors of violence, or by someone who cares about them, and are presented in a display of multicolored t-shirts (each color representing a specific form of violence). The project "focuses on providing healing for survivors of violence, educating the public about violence, and providing solutions through individual action to prevent violence" (Fraser-Vaselakros, 2002). FYI 2.1 offers a powerful story told by one man who viewed the Clothesline Project in his hometown.

### ▨ Disabling Narratives

In addition, we sometimes may feel **othered** by the stories people tell us. On occasion, stories are offered with the best intentions, but instead, we experience them as not supportive or understanding. I (Patricia) remember all too well the horror stories friends told to me about giving birth when I informed them I was pregnant. Even strangers told me, from the moment they assessed my condition as pregnancy and not just being overweight. In fact, because all I was told were horror stories of lengthy and intensely painful labor, "barbaric" hospital practices and procedures, and unsupportive family or medical professionals, I was determined to have a birth experience that would be a "happy" pregnancy story.

In a similar vein, I discovered also that when I shared the story of my painfully devastating experiences with multiple miscarriages, people told me, in caring ways and with good intentions, stories of someone they knew who had experienced even more miscarriages than I, but who now had the child or children they always wanted. I found little comfort in thinking or believing that I only needed to experience a few

If you take a couple of minutes to read this, maybe while you enjoy a Sunday morning cup of coffee, you should know that while you're reading and sipping, thirteen women will be physically abused in America. Two of those women will be raped, one or both of them by a man she knows. Eight or more of those women will resist the attacks, verbally and/or physically.

Half the women in America will be in abusive relationships during their lives. Women are nine times more likely to be attacked at home than on the street, and they're more likely to be raped by someone they know than by a stranger. When they know their attackers they're more than twice as likely to suffer injuries as they are when they don't know them. Many of those injuries will be so severe the victims won't be able to drink coffee for a long time, if ever again. Put your cup aside and I'll tell you how I know these statistics: I have had the pain and the awakening of seeing the Clothesline Project on display.

The National Clothesline Project was started in 1990. It consists of t-shirts created by women who have been the victims of violence, or by their surviving family or friends. There's a color scheme to the shirts, though it's not rigidly followed: yellow or beige is for women who have been battered or assaulted; red, pink or orange is for women who have been raped or sexually assaulted; blue or green is for women survivors of incest or child sexual abuse; purple or lavender is for women attacked because of their perceived sexual orientation; black is for women who have been gang-raped; and white is for women who have died as a result of violence.

The Ventura County Clothesline Project currently has fifty-five shirts, all made by local victims, or by their families. I assure you that every color and category listed above is included in the display. I have never in my life experienced a more moving, more haunting, more shaming feeling than what I felt while I stood before the silent cloth witnesses to what is happening to women and girls in this nation. In fact the point, the purpose of the Clothesline Project, nationally and locally, is to "Break the Silence" and put an end to this cycle of cruelty.

More than 58,000 Americans died in the Vietnam War. During that war 51,000 American women were killed in the U.S. by men who supposedly loved them. We built a wall to honor those who died in Vietnam, a long, black slash across the national conscience, so that we would not forget those who gave their all. But we have built no such wall, no monument, to the women who died and continue to die in such awful numbers, or to so many more women who suffer emotional and physical injuries yet somehow survive. We hope that as a nation we learned something from Vietnam, but there is no indication that we have learned what a price we all pay when we continue to allow this epidemic of violence.

Stand before the clothesline, read the stories the t-shirts tell. They're all graphic and compelling, regardless of the words used to describe what their creators went through. Those women, and all the women who have created shirts, all the women who have been victims of violence, are as courageous as any decorated combat veteran, any soldier who stood

*(continued)*

*(continued from previous page)*

before an enemy, any Medal of Honor winner—they were all those things and more, because they too often had to stand alone.

One definition of society is "The institutions and culture of a distinct self-perpetuating group." We are certainly a society, markedly so when we realize that the institutions and culture with which we surround ourselves seem so intent on perpetuating violence against women. But no society can rightfully call itself a civilization, civil being the operative part of the equation, so long as it allows such violence to continue, or depends on the victims of that violence to stop it.

It's time to "Break the Silence" and become a civilization. You can help do so by seeing the Clothesline Project, and by supporting it. For information on how you can do both, contact your local NOW chapter (National Organization for Women) or Victims of Abuse Hotline.

Make a difference, and your coffee won't taste as bitter as it does right now.

(Hunt, 1996)

more miscarriages to give birth to the child I wanted. And I am not alone. Many women who have experienced miscarriage find that even though they really want to talk about the baby they lost, people comfort them in ways that do not allow them to tell their story. In reality, most women desperately want to talk about what they planned to name the baby, what month the baby was to be born, and what hopes and dreams they had for their new life (Ross & Geist, 1997).

## SUMMARY

We can begin to theorize about communicating health in our lives and those of others by considering the personal complexities revealed in stories. Frank (1995) suggests that theory meets story when we think *with* a story rather than *about* it:

> To think about a story is to reduce it to content and then analyze the content. . . .
> To think with a story is to experience its affecting one's own life and to find in that
> effect a certain truth of one's own life. (p. 23)

Arthur Bochner (1997), a communication scholar, echoes Frank's recommendation:

> We do not turn stories into data to test theoretical propositions. Rather, we link theory to story when we think with a story, trying to stay with the story, letting ourselves resonate with the moral dilemmas it may pose, understanding its ambiguities, examining its contradictions, feeling its nuances, letting ourselves become part of

*the story (Ellis, 1995a). We think with a story from the framework of our own lives. We ask what kind of person we are becoming when we take the story in and consider how we can use it for our own purposes, what ethical directions it points us toward, and what moral commitments it calls out in us (Coles, 1989). (p. 436)*

Theorizing Practice 2.5 asks you to consider what it means to think with the story "Tigger," written by a medical student.

Focusing on narratives in the contexts of health, illness, and providing care creates opportunities for understanding and participating in our own health care with greater vigor and freedom. Each of us should consider how useful it is to compare our interpretations with those of others and be aware of the personal, cultural, and political complexities of health care decisions. This is especially vital in health communication encounters that are tied to **fateful moments** (Giddens, 1991). For example, waiting for the results of a diagnostic test may be routine procedure for many health care providers, but that singular test may be what informs a person whether they have a life-changing disease or illness. Fateful health care moments, such as pregnancy, miscarriage, surgery, and a life-threatening diagnosis, are filled with uncertainty and may also have spiritual implications for the patient (Gonzalez, 1994). When such moments are treated as opportunities for constructing narratives that interweave the voices of care providers, individuals, and families, the potential exists for people to feel they have some control. And that sense of control may be vital to a person's healing, comfort, and feeling understood through the difficult and enlightening moments of the illness journey (Anderson & Geist-Martin, in press). The vital insight and information that individuals bring to the medical encounter—knowledge about self, motivations, and experience connected to a wider social context—become essential to the diagnosis, negotiation, and treatment of illness (Sharf, 1990). Christopher Reeve, who can now move his diaphragm and breathe on his own for short periods, suggests that by limiting the amount of time he is allowed to feel sorry for himself, he has made tremendous improvement. Because he has received awards for his performances after the accident in *Rear Window* and *In the Gloaming*, Reeve even jokes that "some people have said to me that breaking my neck was a good career move" (Ciabattari, 1999, p. 10).

We learn from stories of health and illness—the stories others tell, the stories we tell, and the stories we construct in conversation. Critical to learning from these stories is encouraging people to tell their own stories of being silenced, discredited, excluded, and stigmatized as well as those of being heard, encouraged, comforted, and included. A sincere desire on our part to learn about, theorize from, and understand the personal complexities of our own and another's experience is vital to communicating health.

## Thinking with a Story

Consider what it means to think with this story, "Tigger," written by Juanita Redfield (1997) during her last year as a medical student at the University of Illinois at Chicago.

### "Tigger"

I had a cold that day, I remember. I'd taken one of those "non-drowsy" cold-relief formulas, which had lived up to its claim so well that I was feeling hyper-alert. All of the details of the encounter are imprinted in my memory—the colors, the sounds, the smells.

I was warned about her by the nurses.

"She's totally wild," they said.

"ADHD—bouncing off the walls."

I took her chart from the door. Numerous visits, all with different doctors. Various colds, aches and pains; a sprained wrist. I summoned up my courage, knocked on the sliding wood door to the tiny exam room (I remember the coarse, unyielding surface against my knuckles), and entered.

She was sitting a few feet from her mother when I walked in. Naturally that didn't last long. As soon as she saw me, she sprang to meet me, singing, "my stomach hurts HERE," throwing up her patterned exam gown and pointing dramatically to her midriff. I introduced myself and took her small, nine-year-old hand with the (I learned later) still bruised wrist in my own. I sat her down in a chair, and, sitting opposite, I concentrated every ounce of my attention on her.

"What I need you to do, sweetheart," I told her, "is to sit right here and tell me everything you can about your stomach-ache." I will never forget her long, tousled black hair, her brown doe eyes as she stared at me and tried, in a rush of words, to describe it. Her eyes told a different story. I knew the diagnosis, saw it in the hunger those eyes express.

I turned to her mother, inhaling the stale smell of old cigarette smoke, which hung in a veil around her, dulling her skin and deadening her eyes. "How long has this been going on?" I asked. She answered me, hardly changing the sullen, resentful set of her mouth. "About a week, I guess. I just figured she was playing one of her tricks to get at me. She's always doing that. I decreased her meds on my own because she was falling asleep in school." I asked her about family counseling. "Yeah, we go, but it's real boring."

The little girl had started to bounce. I turned from her mother's apathetic figure and put my hand on her thigh. "I need you to sit quietly now so I can examine you," I said, cutting off her mother's impatient "will-you-shut-up" remarks. "But I'm Tigger," she told me.

"I know, and that makes you a Very Bouncy Animal, right?" I grinned. This threw her, and she sat still for a moment.

*(continued from previous page)*

"How do you know about Tigger?" she asked.

"Well," I replied, "You're not the only one who reads *Winnie the Pooh*."

I remember completing the exam, asking more questions, always with my hand on her arm, her thigh, as if, through the laying on of hands, I could make her whole. I remember she seemed almost to burrow into me, starved for touch.

I left the room and went to present her to the attending. "This is a nine-year-old female with ADHD who presents with a one-week history of abdominal pain, located in the periumbilical area . . ."

Attention Deficit Hyperactivity Disorder.

What inadequate words to describe her illness.

She was suffering from an attention deficit, all right. But how do you tell a mother that her child is dying inside for something she may simply be unable to give?

I tried, of course. I spoke of the importance of continuing family therapy, of spending time together, of choosing one doctor for her daughter so she could begin to build a relationship ("I want YOU to be my doctor," the little girl piped up at this point, giving the knife another twist). But in the end, as I looked into those dead eyes, I felt I was speaking a foreign language.

That night, as I lay in bed once again in the throes of my own illness (the cold-relief formula having worn off hours ago), I remembered something else about Tiggers.

They're one of a kind.

Juanita Redfield (Class of 1997)

## What Does It Mean to Think with This Story?

- What resonates with you?
- What moral dilemmas does the story make you think about?
- What curiosities remain?
- What other types of tensions can you identify in the story?
- What nuances made you think?
- In what part of the story did you discover your own presence?
- Now what?

## In Thinking with This Story:

- Where do you end up?
- What commitments do you find yourself wanting to make?
- How is your theory a healing place?

---

## KEY TERMS

narrative

narrative reasoning

logical reasoning

identity

context

embodiment

disembodiment

dys-appearance

stigma

spoiled identity

passing

transformation

cumulative ephiphanies

othered

fateful moments

## DISCUSSION QUESTIONS

1. How would you describe what Christopher Reeve has been learning as a new member of the disabled cultural community?

2. If you were to select a story about your health or illness to tell others again and again, what would it be? How do you see that story as both a product and a process of your identity?

3. Most people are unaware of the many persons living with a spinal cord injury unless they know someone who is or they are members of this community themselves. What other types of illnesses tend to be overlooked in our society? Why?

4. Most of us have a part of our body that we are not satisfied with or are uncomfortable or self-conscious about. It is the part of ourselves that "spoils" our identity. What part of your own body has been a site of struggle? How do you compensate for this "othered" part? What communicative strategies do you use to feel more in control?

5. Consider a recent illness you experienced or are currently living with. How has it changed the way you understand or talk about yourself or your life? Have you witnessed such changes in others whose lives may have been affected because of their illness experience?

6. What illness narrative have you heard that has had an impact on you? It could be a story told by a health care provider, family member, or friend. Why has this particular story stuck with you?

## INFOTRAC COLLEGE EDITION

1. Read James W. Lynch's 2002 article, "A Lesson in Empathy: Among All the Things We Do, What Our Patients Are Most Likely to Remember Is Our

Compassion." What personal, cultural, and political complexities are part of this story? How does this story lead you to think differently about physicians or about patients? In addition to compassion, what other characteristics are essential in providing care? What do you see as the most important lesson that this story provides?

2. How does Stephen Lurie define physicians' *narrative competence* in his 2002 essay, "Patients' Stories as Narrative"? Also, read the 2001 article by Rita Charon, "The Patient-Physician Relationship: Narrative Medicine: A Model for Empathy, Reflection, Profession, and Trust." What is narrative medicine as described by Charon? What problems does she see narrative medicine addressing?

3. Using the key words *patients' stories*, summarize what you find: the type of citations (for example, newspapers, medical journals, other types of journals, or editorials), the topics, and the authors (for example, journalists, physicians, or patients). Pick five sources that you find especially interesting, and write a brief summary for each.

# 3

## Understanding Health in Cultural Communities

Under my desk I keep a large carton of cassette tapes. Even though they all have been transcribed, I still like to listen to them from time to time.

Some of them are quiet and easily understood. They are filled with the voices of American doctors, interrupted only occasionally by the clink of a coffee cup or the beep of a pager. The rest of the tapes—more than half of them—are very noisy. They are filled with the voices of the Lees, a family of Hmong refugees from Laos who came to the United States in 1980. Against a background of babies crying, children playing, doors slamming, dishes clattering, a television yammering, and an air conditioner wheezing, I can hear the mother's voice, by turns breathy, nasal, gargly, or humlike as it slides up and down the Hmong language's eight tones; the father's voice, louder and slower and more vehement; and my interpreter's voice, mediating in Hmong and English, low and deferential in each language. . . .

I sat on the Lees' red folding chair for the first time on May 19, 1988. Earlier that spring I had come to Merced, California, where they lived, because I had heard that there were some strange misunderstandings going on at the county hospital between its Hmong patients and its medical staff. One doctor called them "collisions," which made it sound as if two different kinds of people had rammed into each other, head on, to the accompaniment of squealing brakes and breaking glass. As it turned out, the encounters were messy but rarely frontal. Both sides were wounded, but neither side seemed to know what had hit it or how to avoid another crash.

I have always felt that the action most worth watching is not at the center of things but where the edges meet. I like shorelines, weather fronts, and international borders. There are interesting frictions and incongruities in these places, and often, if you stand at the point of tangency, you can see both sides better than if you were in the middle of either one. This is especially true, I think, when the apposition is cultural. When I first came to Merced, I hoped that the culture of American medicine, about which I knew a little, and the culture of the Hmong, about which I knew nothing, would in some way illuminate each other if I could position myself between the two and manage not to get caught in the cross fire.

(FADIMAN, 1997, pp. ix–x)

hrough these words, Anne Fadiman (1997), journalist and author, introduces us to the Lee family and to the cultural miscommunication that occurs when American doctors attempt to care for their daughter, Lia Lee, from the age of three months old, when she is first misdiagnosed with pneumonia and eventually correctly diagnosed as epileptic, to the age of four, when she entered a "persistent vegetative state . . . quadriplegic, spastic, incontinent, and incapable of purposeful movement" (p. 210). Her brain was destroyed by septic shock, which was caused by *Pseudomonas aeruginosa* bacillus (bacteria) in her blood (p. 254). *The Spirit Catches You and You Fall Down: A Hmong Child, Her American Doctors, and the Collision of Two Cultures* (Fadiman) chronicles the dilemmas that inevitably arise when health care providers and patients do not understand each others' perspectives and experience a multitude of cultural misunderstandings.

The story captures the complexity of what creates and contributes to the seemingly unbridgeable chasm between the culture of American medicine and the culture of the Hmong. The Hmong, who immigrated to the United States, came from a tribe of peasant farmers from "small mountaintop villages in the forbidding terrain of Northern Laos where they tended their animals and grew dry rice and corn in fields cleared from forest" (Conquergood, 1988, p. 188). The narrative captures the traumatic life passage of the Lee family before their exodus to the United States—leaving their war-torn Laos, being captured and abused by Vietnamese soldiers, and trekking on foot across the Mekong River to the Ban Vinai refugee camp on the Lao-Thailand border with more than 42,000 inhabitants (Fadiman, 1997).

Through this historical account, we can better understand the stark contrasts in the two cultures' belief systems about illness and treatment. We learn how often refugees and other displaced people find themselves "suspended between infinite layers of identities, between a shattered past and insecure future, between discontinuity and stability . . . living on the edge of a borderlands life" (Conquergood, 1991, pp. 184–185). In this story, we recognize how many patients, families, and providers find themselves in the borderlands between diverse beliefs, values, and behaviors: the Lees' reasoning for not following Lia's anticonvulsant regimen, the court's order to place Lia in a foster home, the inability and/or unwillingness of people to communicate in the face of a language barrier, and the other frequent misinterpretations by both the Lees and the American doctors. As one provider told Anne, "It felt as if there was this layer of Saran Wrap or something between us, and they were on one side of it and we were on the other side of it. And we were reaching and reaching and we could kind of get into their area, but we couldn't touch them" (Fadiman, 1997, pp. 47–48).

Early in the book, Fadiman offers the Lees' perspective on the cause of their daughter's illness:

> *When Lia was about three months old, her older sister Yer slammed the front door of the Lees' apartment. A few moments later, Lia's eyes rolled up, her arms jerked over her head, and she fainted. The Lees had little doubt what had happened. Despite the careful installation of Lia's soul during the* hu plig *ceremony, the noise of the door had been so profoundly frightening that her soul had fled her body and become lost. They recognized the resulting symptoms as* qaug dab peg, *which means "the spirit catches you and you fall down." The spirit referred to in this phrase is a soul stealing* dab; peg *means to catch or hit; and* qaug *means to fall over with one's roots still in the ground, as grain might be beaten down by wind or rain. (p. 20)*

When Foua and Nao Kao Lee brought their daughter to the emergency room for the third time, three things were different that assisted in diagnosing Lia as epileptic. First, Lia was in the middle of a seizure. Second, their cousin, who spoke some English, was with them. Third, the on-duty physician, Dan Murphy, was considered the most interested and knowledgeable physician about the Hmong. However, these circumstances do not go far in bridging the cultural chasm that pervades diagnosis and treatment. In this particular hospital visit, neither the provider nor the patient's parents had—or took—the time to explain their perspectives. They may not have taken—or been given—the opportunity to communicate.

> *Dan had no way of knowing that Foua and Nao Kao had already diagnosed their daughter's problem as the illness where the spirit catches you and you fall down. Foua and Nao Kao had no way of knowing that Dan had diagnosed it as epilepsy, the most common of all neurological disorders. Each had accurately noted the same symptoms, but Dan would have been surprised to hear that they were caused by*

*soul loss, and Lia's parents would have been surprised to hear that they were caused by an electrochemical storm inside their daughter's head that had been stirred up by the misfiring of aberrant brain cells. (p. 28)*

Dan's view of medicine was not unlike that of his colleagues, who as medical students spent hundreds of hours dissecting cadavers, identifying anatomical parts, and reviewing bodily functions.

*To most of them, the Hmong taboos against blood tests, spinal taps, surgery, anesthesia, and autopsies—the basic tools of modern medicine—seemed like self-defeating ignorance. They had no way of knowing that a Hmong might regard these taboos as the sacred guardians of his identity, indeed, quite literally, of his very soul. (p. 61)*

While medical doctors eventually diagnosed and treated Lia's epilepsy, throughout Lia's treatment—with more than 30 hospital admissions and the construction of her 400,000-word medical chart—frequent frictions and incongruities in communication occurred between family and providers that proved insurmountable and may have contributed to her "neurological crisis."

In addition to these stark differences in their perceptions of diagnosis and treatment were several communication barriers to complying with the specified treatment regime, eventually leading to Lia being taken from her family and put into a foster home. First, Lia did not like or want to take her medications. Her parents constantly struggled with convincing her to take them. Second, Lia's parents experienced difficulty in keeping track of and understanding the information provided about her treatment regime, especially because her prescriptions changed 23 times in less than four years, they could not read the medication directions written in English, and they could not interpret the measurement lines on the droppers used for dispensing the medications. Third, the problems already described were intensified by the absence of good interpreters and providers' interpretations of the Lees' responses to questions. Under the circumstances, it was difficult for medical providers to know if the Lees were "confused," "lying," "stupid," or if they were even getting through to Lia's parents because of the cultural barriers.

The Lees wanted their story told and willingly agreed to be interviewed by Anne Fadiman (1997). They wanted others to understand Hmong culture. As Lia's father, Nao Kao, stated,

*"Sometimes the soul goes away but the doctors don't believe it. I would like you to tell the doctors to believe in our* neeb." *(The word* neeb, *or healing spirit, is often used as shorthand for* ua neeb kho, *the shamanic ritual, performed by a* txiv neeb, *in which an animal is sacrificed and its soul bartered for the vagrant soul of a sick person.) . . . "With Lia it was good to do a little medicine and a little* neeb, *but not*

---

*too much medicine because the medicine cuts the* neeb's *effect. If we did a little of each she didn't get sick as much, but the doctors wouldn't give us just a little medicine because they didn't understand about the soul." (p. 100)*

Undoubtedly, the providers wanted to help Lia, but too often they found themselves positioned in the **borderlands** between their views of what constituted efficient and effective care and of what constituted noncompliance by the Lee family.

In the end, there is no one truth. There are no pat answers for how best to communicate in the borderlands between these two cultures. There are only similar and contradictory explanatory models—that is, descriptions of illness episodes, representations of the cultural flow of life experience, and justifications for practical action (Fadiman, 1997; Kleinman, 1988; Kleinman, Eisenberg, & Good, 1998). Lia's parents think that the neurological crises that left her brain dead were caused by too much medicine. One of the pediatric neurologists, who treated her early on, agrees, suggesting that the focus on prescribing medicine for her epileptic seizures may have compromised her immune system and made her more susceptible to the *Pseudomonas,* setting her up for septic shock (Fadiman, pp. 254–255). Lia's parents believe she would not be sick today if the family had stayed in Laos and not given their child American medicine. At the same time, Fadiman points out, if the Lees were still in Laos, "Lia would probably have died before she was out of her infancy, from a prolonged bout of untreated status epilepticus. American medicine had both preserved her life and compromised it. I was unsure which had hurt her family more" (p. 258).

Understanding health in communities means recognizing the equally powerful roles played by the culture of communities (in this case, the cultural community of the Hmong people and the cultural community of biomedicine). Interpretation and communication about illness and disease, diagnosis and treatment, and caring and curing often is complicated by the "collision" of cultural communities, whose versions of what is at stake may be very different. It also means recognizing that in today's interconnected world, with the "drastic expansion of mobility, including tourism, migrant labor, immigration, urban sprawl . . . [we are] always, to varying degrees, 'inauthentic': caught between cultures, implicated in others" (Clifford, 1988, pp. 11, 13).

Communicating health and understanding in the borderlands of cultures is not a matter of learning everything there is to know about every cultural community before providing or seeking care. It is more a matter of realizing that all of us, to some degree, live in the borderlands between cultures that make up our identities—including our gender, race, ethnicity, religion, health histories, and even the geographic region we grew up in or live in today. In this way, we have much to learn about communicating with each other in our communities. We need to recognize and appreciate the emergent, revived, or invented cultural fragments in our own and others' talk about health and illness. As Arthur Kleinman (1988), a physician and anthropologist, points out, eliciting patient and family explanatory models

> *helps practitioners to take the patient's perspective seriously in organizing strategies for clinical care. Practitioners' effective communication of their models in turn assists patients and families to make more useful judgments of when to enter treatment, with which practitioner, for what treatments, and at what ratio of cost and benefit. (p. 122)*

It means developing sensitivity to communication in ways that allow us to learn from one another. In that process of communicating, we negotiate with providers for the care, support, and empathic treatment we need and desire, deciding what is critical and compromising as we go.

This is the focus of this chapter. We begin by considering the diversity of our multicultural health and illness communities, defining *culture* and *community*. We then continue by discussing how the vital role of communication is enhanced when we incorporate cultural knowledge in health care interactions through the Culturally Sensitive Model of Communication (Sharf & Kahler, 1996). Communicating in culturally sensitive ways is often constrained by the complex layers of meanings described in the model, and communicating becomes further complicated by our lack of awareness or inattention as to how these layers interact among all the communicators involved in the health situation. We then turn to an examination of AIDS as a case study, demonstrating the utility of this model to enhance our understanding of health and illness in the cultural communities surrounding AIDS. Finally, we discuss avenues for practicing cultural sensitivity through consideration of three intercultural dialectics in health care, which can become both barriers to and avenues for communicating in the borderlands.

# Multicultural Health/Illness Communities

*Cultures are now less bounded and homogeneous and more porous and self-conscious than ever before, and cultural differences—of religion, gender, language, class, ethnicity, sexual orientation, and so on—are no longer contained within old geopolitical boundaries. Subcultures, cultures, and supercultures merge and emerge anew, ceaselessly. In the rough-and-tumble of transnational migration and capitalism, what was exotic yesterday may be domestic today. And what is domestic today may be exotic tomorrow.*

(Barbash & Taylor, 1997, p. 5)

By the year 2000, the U.S. population reached more than 281.4 million (U.S. Census Bureau, 2001), with more than 660,000 immigrants admitted in 1998 (Table 3.1). California is expected to be the first mainland state with a nonwhite majority in the coming decades, with 39 percent of the national Asian population, 34 percent of the Hispanic population, and 12 percent of the Native-American population (Purnell & Paulanka, 1998b; Howe-Murphy, Ross, Tseng, & Hartwig, 1989). Other states are expected to mirror this trend, but at a slower pace (Norbeck, 1995; Purnell & Paulanka). With the diversity both of individuals entering the United States and of our present population, differences in health care beliefs and practices are increasing.

Let's begin by considering what we mean by *culture*. At the most general level, we can define **culture** as a group or community of people who share a set of beliefs, values, and attitudes that guide their behavior (Geertz, 1973; Gudykunst, Ting-Toomey, & Chua, 1988; Kreps & Kunimoto, 1994). Table 3.1 reveals that the largest numbers of people immigrating to the United States in 1998 were from Mexico, China, and India. The people immigrating to the United States are members of diverse national cultures, however, and of unique regions within these countries, which have a great influence on their health beliefs, values, attitudes, and behaviors (Purnell & Paulanka, 1998b).

Members of cultural groups often conceive of health, disease, pain, and health care practices differently. For example, some cultural groups, such as African Americans, Irish Americans, Mexican Americans, and many others, often turn to the ethnocultural practice of self-care using folk or traditional medicines, such as prayers, herbal medicines, acupuncture, or teas, before seeking professional care (Purnell & Paulanka, 1998c). The increasing practice of blending traditional and biomedical heath care practices has led to establishment of an Office of Alternative Medicine at the National Institutes of Health, where millions of dollars in grants are awarded "to bridge the gap between traditional and nontraditional therapies" (Purnell & Paulanka, p. 43). Purnell's model of cultural competence suggests a number of guidelines for assessing the cultural domain in health care practices, including beliefs and behaviors, concerning health-seeking, responsibility for health care, folklore practices, barriers to health, cultural responses to health and illness, and blood transfusion and organ donation (Purnell & Paulanka, p. 46). Although we may be born into and influenced by our country of origin, ethnicity, and membership in a particular cultural group, our health communication also is influenced significantly by our present memberships in several other cultural communities.

## TABLE 3.1

### Immigrants Admitted to the United States

| COUNTRY OR REGION | NUMBER OF IMMIGRANTS | PERCENTAGE OF IMMIGRANTS |
|---|---|---|
| 1. Mexico | 131,575 | 19.92 |
| 2. China | 36,884 | 5.58 |
| 3. India | 36,482 | 5.52 |
| 4. Philippines | 34,466 | 5.22 |
| 5. Dominican Republic | 20,387 | 3.09 |
| 6. Vietnam | 17,649 | 2.67 |
| 7. Cuba | 17,375 | 2.63 |
| 8. Jamaica | 15,146 | 2.29 |
| 9. El Salvador | 14,590 | 2.21 |
| 10. Korea | 14,268 | 2.16 |
| 11. Haiti | 13,449 | 2.04 |
| 12. Pakistan | 13,094 | 1.98 |
| 13. Columbia | 11,836 | 1.79 |
| 14. Russia | 11,529 | 1.75 |
| 15. Canada | 10,190 | 1.54 |
| 16. Peru | 10,154 | 1.54 |
| 17. United Kingdom | 9,018 | 1.37 |
| 18. Bangladesh | 8,621 | 1.31 |
| 19. Poland | 8,469 | 1.28 |
| 20. Iran | 7,883 | 1.19 |
| 21. Guatemala | 7,759 | 1.17 |
| 22. Nigeria | 7,746 | 1.17 |
| 23. Ukraine | 7,448 | 1.13 |
| 24. Taiwan | 7,097 | 1.07 |
| 25. Ecuador | 6,852 | 1.04 |
| 26. Honduras | 6,463 | 0.98 |
| 27. Germany | 5,472 | 0.83 |
| Others | 168,575 | 25.53 |
| All Countries | 660,477 | 100.00 |

Note: From United States Immigration Service (1998)

Each of us thinks, speaks, and behaves in ways that are influenced by our membership in multiple cultures, multiple **communities.** A community emerges through communication. It is where culture gets made and remade through emotional connection, a sense of belonging, and a common set of customs, rules, rituals, and language (Adelman & Frey, 1997; Conquergood, 1994; Tinder, 1995). Yet any community is more than a set of customs, behaviors, or attitudes about other people. A community is also a collective identity; it is a way of saying who "we" are (Sennett, 1976). We each, therefore, develop our own idiosyncratic multicultural identities through the combination of different cultural orientations and influences of the many cultural communities to which we belong (Kreps & Kunimoto, 1994, p. 3). Consider your own membership in multicultural communities based on your age, language, friendships, year in school, birthplace, region of upbringing, choice of exercise (or not), hobbies, intellectual interests, religion, gender, political affiliation, and the many other factors that lead you to talk and to act in certain ways, to make and to remake a cultural community.

One avenue for understanding and addressing health in cultural communities is to consider how people's multicultural memberships in different communities are based on their past, present, or anticipated health or illness status:

*People of different ages, educational levels, socioeconomic standing, occupations, sexual orientations, and even of different health conditions belong to their own cultural groups. Even persons who share certain health conditions, such as people who are blind, deaf, or paralyzed, have their own cultural orientations, as do people who are dying, or who have diabetes, cancer, or AIDS.*

(Kreps & Kunimoto, 1994, pp. 2–3)

By defining ourselves—or being defined by others—as healthy or unhealthy, we may affiliate with particular **cultural communities.** We may join a gym, Alcoholics Anonymous, a cancer-survivor support group, Gamblers Anonymous, or other wellness or disease-related groups. For example, I (Patricia) belong to a number of cultural communities based on my age and gender: I find myself influenced by friends and family members of my same age and gender who have experienced what I am experiencing or anticipate experiencing, including menopause, infertility, and arthritis. I am also influenced by my membership in a culture of women who have experienced the trauma of multiple miscarriages (Ross & Geist, 1997), eventually joining Empty Cradle (a support group for people who have suffered from miscarriage or loss of a child during infancy). I find myself reading and talking a great deal about cancer, because my mother succumbed to it at the age of 48 and I have lost other family members and friends to this disease. As a runner my whole life, I am greatly influenced by a culture of runners who talk about races, injuries, and the physical, emotional, and spiritual benefits of running. Finally, as a professor, I find myself privileged to have access to health care benefits that someone else may not have.

We need to think of cultural communities in another way as well. Most of our discussion so far has focused on individuals as citizens who belong to and are influenced by the diverse cultural communities to which they belong. In addition, we need to consider the cultural communities that influence providers and how they communicate in delivering care. They too develop their own idiosyncratic, multicultural identities through different cultural orientations and the influences of the many cultural communities to which they belong—country of origin, gender, ethnicity, profession, training, institutional affiliation (ranging from a small clinic in a lower socioeconomic neighborhood to a large, managed care hospital). The American Medical Association estimates that 21.4 percent of U.S. doctors licensed in 1990 were international medical graduates (Roback, Randolf, & Seidman, 1992; Rubin, Healy, Gardiner, Zath, & Moore, 1997), and between 1970 and 1992, the number of international medical graduates practicing in the United States increased by 132 percent (U.S. Department of Commerce, 1994).

Complex layers of meaning accompany all our conversations about health, wellness, illness, and medicine in any of these cultural communities. For most of us, our definitions of what is healthy or unhealthy often vary. At home, at work, at the gym, at the hospital, in support groups, and in emergency rooms, we talk about our health, illnesses, and healthy and unhealthy behaviors. Our conversations may center on smoking, not smoking, exercising, not exercising, feeling depressed, or feeling energized, or they may center on prescriptions, home remedies, what works, what doesn't work, and what we generally consider to be our state of health and what impacts our health the most.

Providers too may develop similar or different interpretations, including definitions of what is healthy or unhealthy, what is focused on as the cause of illness, what is the most effective treatment, and even what is important to know or talk about in providing care. Read over the assignment described in Theorizing Practice 3.1, and think about how writing up this assignment may provide a more complete understanding about the complex layers of meaning that are part of talking about health and illness.

The many layers of meaning are complicated further by a wide variety of cultural differences as we communicate across, between, and within cultural communities. Our contemporary society is composed of multicultural communities with many different national, regional, ethnic, racial, socioeconomic, and occupational orientations that influence interactions in health care settings (Kreps & Thornton, 1992).

Because we live, work, play, and seek health care in the borderlands of multiple communities that are diverse in gender, ethnicity, religion, sexual orientation, and

## Assessing Your Own Cultural Communities

Examine your own health beliefs and practices by answering the questions below from your personal and cultural perspectives. Summarize your response in written form (two or three typed pages), including a final paragraph describing your reaction to this exercise.

1. With what ethnic or cultural communities do you most identify? (Think about your family's country or countries of origin, how many generations your family has been in the United States, your religious background, and where you were born and raised.)

2. How do you define health (ability to work, feel good, lack of symptoms, spiritual grace, being well fed, mental outlook, and so on)? Does your view differ from those of your friends, partner, spouse, parents, or grandparents; if so, how? How concerned about health was your family as you were growing up?

3. What factors does your cultural group believe cause illness (neglect, punishment from God, natural causes, exposure to drafts and wet, germs, evil spirits, body imbalances, eating poorly, and so on)?

4. How are/were common illnesses like colds, stomachaches, and headaches treated within your cultural group? What home remedies are/were used most often?

5. What are some practices to prevent illness that are used within your cultural group (laxatives, herbs, spiritualist consultations, regular visits to a doctor, prayers, vitamins, exercise, special nutrition, self-medications, and so on)?

6. Who do people in your cultural group consult when someone is ill? What other sources of health care are used outside the mainstream U.S. medical system (ministers, folk healers, herbalists, and so on)? Who makes the major health care decisions?

Questions adapted from Orque, Block, & Monroy (1983) and from Spector (1996).

language, our conversations about health and our efforts to sustain or improve health are complicated by varied health beliefs, practices, and concerns. The reality of this diversity is that differences in health care needs often go unrecognized or unserved. For example, one community in particular, individuals living in poverty, generally have poorer health and remain unreached, often because of how society labels them as "unreachable, disenfranchised, indigent, hard-to-reach, and chronically uninformed" (Marshall & McKeon, 1996, p. 137).

The reality of this diversity is also that often we communicate in ways that devalue others based on their membership in a particular cultural community. Imagine what persons born with a physical disability experience in communication during their lifetime when they are stereotyped as "mentally handicapped" (Do, 1997; Kleinfield, 1977; Morris, 1991; Shapiro, 1993); when they are referred to as "victims," "sufferers," and "handicapped" (Braithwaite, 1996); when they are verbally accepted but nonverbally rejected (Braithwaite, 1990; Braithwaite & Braithwaite, 1997; Emry & Wiseman, 1987; Thompson, 1982); when they are routinely asked by strangers to reveal private information about their health, bodies, sexuality, or personal habits (Braithwaite, 1986, 1991); and when they realize it is simply better to avoid communication than to be disrespected or degraded (Braithwaite & Labrecque, 1994). It is our hope that by comparing our responses to Theorizing Practice 3.1, we may begin to identify and to learn from our own diversities and dilemmas.

Increasingly, we are taking seriously the need to develop effective multicultural relations in health care systems. *Healthy People 2010*, a document published by the U.S. Department of Health and Human Services (Healthy People 2010, 2001), provides national health promotion and disease prevention objectives targeting our diverse populations. The document suggests that special population groups need targeted preventative efforts, and that such efforts require understanding the needs and particular disparities experienced by these groups. In addition, the significant influence of culture on health perceptions, treatments, and interactions is being recognized in a wide array of disciplines, including communication, social work, nursing, medical anthropology, sociology, literature, allied health, public health, and medicine.

Recommendations for building successful health promotion campaigns emphasize the significance of investigating cultural factors and of using this information to create culturally sensitive messages:

> *In planning health promotion programs, the following background factors of the target population must be considered: endogenous characteristics (e.g., knowledge, attitudes, beliefs, cultural values), sociostructural factors (e.g., environmental support, peer influences, role of the family), and structural inequities (e.g., racism, poverty). (Bird, Otero-Sabogal, Ha, & McPhee, 1996, p. 105)*

Bird et al. recommend that programs not only demonstrate cultural sensitivity but use culturally relevant symbols to communicate a message. Program personnel must become culturally competent and draw on the support of community members who work with and are knowledgeable about particular cultural groups (see Theorizing Practice 3.2).

## Cultural Factors and Health Care Promotion

Read the following descriptions of findings about women, ethnicity, and cancer. Consider what implications each finding would have on gathering information and constructing a health promotion campaign targeted to each of these cultural groups. Keep in mind the factors of the target population suggested by Bird et al. (1996).

1. African-American women have a higher death rate from breast cancer than whites in part because of cultural differences that delay treatment, according to a study of a rural area in the southeastern United States (Lannin et al., 1998). The study concluded that economic factors, such as low income, lack of transportation, and inadequate health insurance, all affect why some black women are not diagnosed until the disease is advanced ("Study links," 1998).

2. In California, rates of cervical cancer among Vietnamese women are four times higher than in the general population and twice the national rate for either Anglo-American or African-American women. Research indicated that many of these Vietnamese women did not speak English, were recent immigrants, and lived in crowded housing with a lack of child care assistance (Bird et al., 1996).

An exemplar of this approach is the Native American Community Board that opened the Native American Women's Health Education Resource Center in South Dakota in 1988, the first of its kind on a reservation in the United States (Morrison, 1996). In addition to facts about health issues, the center offers programs that help Native-American women become involved in their tribal communities both to improve policy and to become leaders in promoting change. The first health promotion project constructed by the center focused on preventing fetal alcohol syndrome. Part of this project was creating a poster that states "Everyone in the Sacred Circle of Life is Responsible for the Creation of a Healthy Generation" (see FYI 3.1). The poster is an excellent example of the incorporation of cultural symbols, including the Medicine Shield or Wheel, representing the sacred hoop of the nation; the braided and unbraided hair, representing the dichotomy between traditional and modern values and between different generations; and others, such as the sacred pipe, the seeding of life, and the four winds, representing strength and pride. We see this poster as a powerful vehicle for drawing on cultural symbols to address the problem of alcoholism and the trauma and stigmatization of a cultural community.

Clearly, we need to deepen our understanding of the health beliefs and practices of individuals in cultural communities to meet their diverse—and often

Everyone in The Sacred Circle of Life
is Responsible for the Creation of a Healthy Generation.

# PREVENT FETAL ALCOHOL SYNDROME

The art work for this poster was provided by "PIPES" (People In Prison Entering Sobriety) of the
South Dakota State Penitentiary in Sioux Falls, South Dakota and presented to the Native American Women's
Health Education Resource Center as a joint project to promote awareness of Fetal Alcohol Syndrome.

**Native American Women's Health Education Resource Center**
P.O. Box 572 • Lake Andes, SD 57356-0572 • 605-487-7072 • FAX # 605-487-7964

Prevent Fetal Alcohol Syndrome. *Native American Women's Health Education Resource Center.*

unserved—health care needs and expectations. What is clear from nearly all examinations of health and culture is that "miscommunication, noncompliance, different concepts of the nature of illness and what to do about it, and above all different values and preferences of patients and their physicians limit the potential benefits of both technology and caring" (Payer, 1988, p. 10). Cross-cultural caring considers health care to be a social process in which professionals and patients each bring a set of beliefs, expectations, and practices to the medical encounter (Waxler-Morrison, Anderson, & Richardson, 1991).

We must recognize that our multicultural health communities are not static—people get sick; get well; exercise at certain times but not at others; gain weight; lose weight; come close to dying and survive; care for a dying parent or friend; are diagnosed with cancer; go into remission; lose their hearing, sight, or use of particular limbs; choose to remove life support; and are denied access to—or cannot afford—health care because of socioeconomic factors, such as age, race, gender, sexual orientation, and economic status. Each of these changes can occur sequentially, simultaneously, to others, or to us, and these changes can be feared, embraced, not of our choosing, or even celebrated. Whatever the case, with changes in a person's multicultural health memberships come changes in identities that often place that person in the borderlands between well and ill, living and dying, and hope and despair.

At the same time that illness and wellness identities are shaped by membership in multiple cultural communities, all of us (providers, patients, and families) communicate within contexts of cultural systems that influence the flow of knowledge and power. Consider, for example, what you might learn from examining your own multicultural health identity and from interviewing someone who does not share your identity (see Theorizing Practice 3.3). We must recognize "that maladies, while always biological, are also in part cultural artifacts, in the same way that medicine is a cultural artifact as it operates through discourses that distribute social power across institutions and individual lives . . . so that selfhood, like illness, is a biocultural construction" (Hsu, 1985; Morris, 1998, pp. 74–75; see also Kuipers, 1989). Morris exemplifies this point well in his discussion of AIDS:

> AIDS is never simply about the science of a microbe. People infected with the HIV live within cultures that directly affect their health: Cultures marked in the developed world, for example, by homophobia, government funding, gay rights activists, research grants, racism, pharmaceutical companies, addicts, and blood transfusions. Outside the lab, microbes follow the terrain of cultural geopolitics. Life-extending multiple drug therapies available to a U.S. citizen in San Diego are unavailable—because they cost too much—to a patient in Port-au-Prince or Kinshasa. HIV was not simply discovered like a comet, but slowly put together as a legitimate diagnosis through a process of social consensus that included de-

## Understanding Another's Multicultural Health Identity

First, make a list of all the cultures that compose your own multicultural health identity. Then write a one-page narrative that describes your multicultural health identity in a way that provides an understanding of the changes that you have experienced in your health or that you anticipate occurring.

Second, interview someone you consider to be part of a health/illness culture that is outside of your own multicultural health identity. Write a one-page description of what you have learned about their multicultural health identity.

Third, summarize your reactions to what you have written in the first two steps in a way that identifies the similarities and differences of the two multicultural health identities.

*bate among international laboratories, sometimes stormy annual conferences, peer-reviewed journals, grant proposals, and the exclusion of contrary views deemed extreme, incorrect, or merely annoying . . . What underlies these changed assumptions, assumptions that destabilize a traditional biomedical reading of disease and illness, is a new understanding of culture. (pp. 40–41)*

Negotiating understanding both within and among these multicultural health and illness communities, amidst the cultural and political systems, is complicated and challenging.

Enhancing understanding of health in cultural communities necessitates a willingness by providers and patients to communicate honestly and to build a supportive, trusting relationship—"a relationship based not on unrealistic certainty, but on honesty in facing the uncertainty in clinical practice" (Inlander, Levin, & Weiner, 1988, p. 206). We need to understand illness and care as embedded in the social and cultural world (Kleinman, 1980).

The call to expand our understanding and appreciation of cultural communities implies that we need to acknowledge our own **ethnocentrism** (our view that our culture's way of doing things is right and appropriate) in dictating the proper way to provide care (Leininger, 1991), to internationalize our professional education system (Linquist, 1990), to consider the sociocultural background of patients and practitioners (Boyle, 1991; Giger & Davidhizar, 1991), to understand traditional (folk-healing) health care beliefs and incorporate them into care (Krajewski-Jaime, 1991), to develop our cultural sensitivity (Waxler-Morrison et al., 1991), and in general, to communicate interculturally, recognizing the problems, competencies, prejudices, and opportunities for adaptation (Barna, 1993; Brislin, 1991; Kim, 1991; Purnell & Paulanka, 1998a, 1998b; Spitzberg, 1999b). A significant contribution to our understanding of health in cultural communities is the Culturally Sensitive Model of Communicating.

# A CULTURALLY SENSITIVE MODEL OF COMMUNICATING HEALTH

Differences in race, ethnicity, socioeconomic status, and/or education can create distance, lack of understanding and of shared meaning, and problematic communication between providers and patients (Sharf & Kahler, 1996). Co-author and communication researcher Barbara Sharf and pediatrician John Kahler have devised a **culturally sensitive** model of patient-physician communication that can be used as a teaching model, as a clinical practice model, and as a model of patient empowerment. Although specifically designed to increase understanding between patients and physicians, this model is clearly relevant to what we may experience when attempting to make sense of our conversations about health with anyone—family, friends, providers, even acquaintances and strangers.

The Culturally Sensitive Model provides insight regarding the complex and multiple **layers of meaning** that each participant brings to their relationships and conversations about health and illness (Figure 3.1). The five layers include:

- **Ideological Layer of Meaning:** The philosophical "truths" or the ethical underpinnings of society; for example, the American emphasis on values of independence and individualism versus other societies' emphasis on values of community.

- **Sociopolitical Layer of Meaning:** The politics surrounding the primary social bases of power; for example, race, class, and gender.

- **Institutional/Professional Layer of Meaning:** The organization of health care and related services by professional and corporate categories; for example, federal and state governments, HMOs (health maintenance organizations), and professions such as medicine, nursing, and social services. This layer also includes professional versus lay understanding of health problems and issues.

- **Ethnocultural/Familial Layer of Meaning:** The cultural traditions, styles, customs, rituals, and values that form patterns of everyday living, expression, and social interaction, which are often inculcated or learned through the family.

- **Interpersonal Layer of Meaning:** The dynamics of style, intimacy, and roles played out in human interactions.

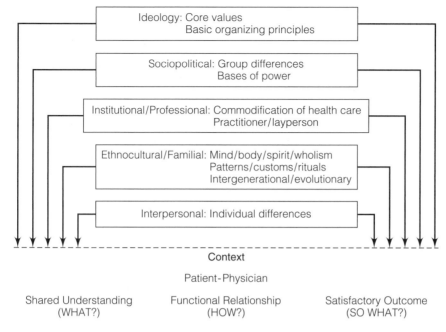

Ideology: Core values
Basic organizing principles

Sociopolitical: Group differences
Bases of power

Institutional/Professional: Commodification of health care
Practitioner/layperson

Ethnocultural/Familial: Mind/body/spirit/wholism
Patterns/customs/rituals
Intergenerational/evolutionary

Interpersonal: Individual differences

Context

Patient-Physician

| Shared Understanding (WHAT?) | Functional Relationship (HOW?) | Satisfactory Outcome (SO WHAT?) |

**FIGURE 3.1**  The culturally sensitive model of patient–physician communication.

The model focuses on these five layers to assist us in considering what meanings we must be aware of to be culturally sensitive when conversing about health and illness. The five layers indicate sources of meaning that underlie people's communication and sources of understanding for clinical practice and health promotion, for teaching health professionals, and for patient, family, and community empowerment. In essence, the model has utility for anyone as they communicate about health and illness—patients, families, health care policy makers, professionals, and administrators.

Each layer reciprocally influences the others in the process of communicating. For example, let's examine the dilemma of using technology, such as respirators, to extend the lives of people who are critically ill or have a poor prognosis for remaining alive. Ideologies of quality of life versus quantity of life clearly impact the sociopolitical and ethical debates that family, friends, and health professionals engage in when deciding whether to use life-support systems in hospitals. Professional personnel in these discussions attempt to follow institutional guidelines that clearly affect decisions regarding whether—and when—to withdraw life support. Simultaneously, family members discuss the dilemma with each other, considering their own spiritual, cultural, and personal beliefs. In the best of circumstances, individual patients have discussed their own values and preferences regarding life-sustaining measures with family members and personal physicians before getting sick or entering the hospital. Through such discussions, family members and providers have a sense of what patients will prefer if they become unable to speak during a critical illness. Unfortunately, this kind of interpersonal exchange often is neglected, as we discuss in Chapter 8, "Ending Life Passages." Creating a living will and establishing a durable power of attorney are two steps that you can take in the area, as also discussed in Chapter 8.

Importantly, the model helps us to see the powerful influence of ideologies on our communication and how ideological layers of meaning permeate the other four layers. Also significant is that while institutional policies and resources may be the main concern for professionals, families may be focusing on spiritual and cultural values. Thus, two different layers of meaning may be operating and, perhaps, conflicting among communicators. This was the case for the Lee family and the providers who cared for their daughter. Which layers do you believe have the greatest influence on the miscommunication that occurred in this case?

In applying the model, using the metaphor of a computer "Windows" program, in which all five layers operate simultaneously but are not all visible on the "screen," is useful. One or more layers may predominate in conversation, and the layer that is salient at one point for one person may not be for another. The subtleties and complexities of what is on your screen become the focus of your attention and talk.

Now we turn our attention to AIDS to demonstrate the utility of this model for enhancing our understanding of health in making and reconsidering the cultural communities surrounding this serious disease.

# AIDS AS A CASE STUDY

*AIDS is never simply about the science of a microbe. People infected with [HIV] live within cultures that directly affect their health.*

(Morris, 1998, p. 40)

We may begin to understand how people who are infected with HIV live within layers of cultural communities that directly affect their health by discussing some of the research about communication and HIV as it relates to the five layers of the Culturally Sensitive Model. Each layer provides insight regarding the complex and multiple meanings that people bring to their relationships and to their conversations about AIDS. It is critical to consider the meanings formed by patients, providers, families, caregivers, lawmakers, activists, and others in the communities that are made and remade surrounding AIDS. From this research, we learn that culture influences who is infected with HIV, how HIV is transmitted, who is diagnosed, what means of prevention are discussed and used, and even who benefits from new drug therapies (Morris, 1998).

## Ideological Layer of Meaning

The ideological layer of meaning reveals the philosophical "truths" about HIV. From its first description as the "Gay Plague," infection with HIV carried the stigma of being attached to high-risk groups such as homosexuals and, later, intravenous drug users and prostitutes (Morris, 1998). The disease is stigmatized by a history of medical, political, ethical, and scientific debate (Shilts, 1987). Early media coverage perpetuated an image of AIDS as the hazard of a gay lifestyle and its assumed deviant behaviors; as a result, the media encouraged an ideology of AIDS as deviant, distant, and not affecting "us" ("Gays are not like us.") (McAllister, 1992, p. 213).

The truths that people hold about AIDS manifested in at least four characteristics this disease shares with any other disease likely to evoke **stigma:** (a) it is perceived to be the bearer's responsibility—contracted through voluntary and avoidable behaviors; (b) it is associated with illness and conditions that are unalterable, degenerative, and fatal; (c) it is associated with conditions that are perceived to be contagious; and (d) it is readily apparent to others and is perceived as repellent, ugly, or upsetting—in advanced stages, AIDS affects an individual's physical appearance and stamina, evoking distress and stigma from observers (Herek, 1999, pp. 1109–1110).

This ideological layer makes it easy for some to forget that patients with AIDS are *people* who are ill:

> Patients are too often viewed as helpless victims. The science-based public television series Nova employed the horror film scenario of victims in the grasp of a hideous creature to provide the structure for a widely shown documentary on AIDS, with doctors and scientists cast as heroic dragon slayers. The person who falls ill with AIDS today falls unavoidably into this net of tacit meanings and subliminal narratives. (Morris, 1998, pp. 191–192)

Manifestations of the stigma remain today in AIDS-related prejudice and discrimination. Persons with AIDS have been evicted from their homes, fired from their jobs, shunned by family and friends, and as recently as 1998, an eight-year-old New York girl "was unable to find a Girl Scout troop that would admit her once her HIV infection was disclosed" (Herek, 1999, p. 1106; see also "HIV-positive girl," 1998). Although this ideological level of meaning is solidified and seemingly unchangeable, it is essential that we view AIDS as a "regular" disease that can be contracted by anyone and that kills its victims just as heart disease, cancer, and stroke do (Duh, 1991).

The stigma—and stigmatizing—language of AIDS frames the experience of affected persons at all other levels of the model, especially the sociopolitical layer.

## ■ Sociopolitical Layer of Meaning

In the sociopolitical layer of meaning, we explore the politics surrounding AIDS. The inseparable connection between AIDS and power in society is evident in "how AIDS is discussed, how resources are allocated, who are defined as in the 'risk groups,' and who makes the decision about AIDS" (McAllister, 1992, p. 196). In his edited book *Power in the Blood: A Handbook on AIDS, Politics, and Communication,* communication researcher William Elwood (1999a) offers unique insights regarding the politics and communication surrounding AIDS and the intersection of government, policy, media, public opinion, and people both affected by and infected with HIV and AIDS. In the closing chapter of the book, Elwood (1999b) tells us:

> *HIV/AIDS has taught us that there is more than one kind of power in the blood; moreover, the epidemic has revealed how reluctant many of us are to discuss the behaviors that facilitate or prevent the transmission of a lethal virus. It also has revealed anew our prejudices and the inequities of resources, access, and control over one's own body. (p. 419)*

This reluctance to discuss AIDS occurs everywhere. In China, where more than 600,000 people have been diagnosed with the disease, reluctance and prejudice are vividly revealed in a recent survey by China's State Family Planning Commission that reports one in five Chinese said they have never heard of AIDS and that half did not know it was spread by sex (Rosenthal, 2001). The politics of communication about AIDS is explained by Pan Cuiming, a professor of Sociology at People's University in Beijing, who indicates that programs seek to educate sex workers but not the men who bring the virus back to their spouses: "The government always wants to say AIDS and sexually transmitted diseases are from prostitutes, but most of these girls are just poor children—they are victims—they didn't have diseases when they started" (Rosenthal, 2001, p. A8). In addition, some of the girls are paid as little as $1.20 for sex and lack the power to insist on condoms (Rosenthal).

From its first detection (or naming) in the early 1980s to the present (and certainly into the future), AIDS has been politicized by constructing the meaning of this disease based on race, class, gender, and sexual orientation. Lack of information and early media coverage reveals the power to ignore exceptions:

*For example, one 1982 study was entitled "Gay-related Immunodeficiency (GRID) Syndrome: Clinical and Autopsy Observations." The GRID label was used in this title even though 2 of the 10 subjects in the study were exclusively heterosexual (Oppenheimer, 1988). Likewise despite the fact that the first women with immune suppression were noted by the CDC [Centers for Disease Control and Prevention] in August 1981 (Oppenheimer, 1988), women with AIDS were usually placed in the more general epidemiological category of "Other," marginalizing the impact on their lives (Treichler, 1988). (McAllister, 1992, p. 213)*

The politics and controversy surrounding the first discovery of HIV infection in the already stigmatized group of gay men divided the world of AIDS into "us" and "them," rendering woman, heterosexuals, and others invisible and, supposedly, not at risk of infection (Cline & McKenzie, 1996a).

Today, 70 to 75 percent of all HIV transmissions occur through heterosexual contact, with women and minorities comprising the two fastest-growing segments of the infected population (Morris, 1998, p. 102). The greatest increase of new cases and the poorest survival rates are among African-American and Hispanic communities (Blum et al., 1994; Institute of Medicine, 1994). Siegel and Raveis (1997) report that race or ethnicity combined with lower economic status appears to impact consistently a person's access to information, care services, and community-based organizations. One particularly haunting study provides evidence that some young African-American men and women who "despite, or because of, their daily confrontation with pain and suffering . . . deliberately sought HIV exposure" (Tourigny, 1999, p. 149).

More than 134,000 cases of AIDS have been reported among women in the United States (Centers for Disease Control and Prevention, 2001). Cases of AIDS in women in the United States are growing faster than among any other group (Cline & McKenzie, 1996b), with young disadvantaged women, particularly African-American women, being infected with HIV at younger ages and at higher rates than their male counterparts—seven times higher than young Caucasian women, and eight times higher than young Hispanic women (Chu, Buehler, & Berkelman, 1990; Michal-Johnson & Bowen, 1992; "National data," 1998). In the near future, women are expected to represent 30 percent of reported AIDS cases (Guinan & Leviton, 1995). More and more research indicates that infected women too often remain undiagnosed and, as a result, are neglected as targets for preventative information (Carver, 1993; Cline & McKenzie, 1996a, 1996b; Kistenberg & Shaw, 1993; Liu, Grove, & Kelly, 1997; Seals et al., 1995).

The "invisibility" of women in the AIDS epidemic is a sociopolitical construction of meaning in several ways (Cline & McKenzie, 1996a). First is the failure of providers to diagnose women with HIV:

*Until 1992, the Centers for Disease Control's diagnostic criteria failed to account for differences in how the disease manifests itself in men versus women. Further, practitioners, directly influenced by the scientific literature tend to misdiagnose women with HIV disease (Carovano, 1991; Wiener, 1991) as they do not "expect" women to contract HIV. (Cline & McKenzie, 1996a, pp. 366–367)*

A case in point is the story of Nicole, an interviewee in a study on women and AIDS (Liu et al., 1997). Nicole first displayed symptoms of the disease in 1982 but was not diagnosed until 1989. Even when she was hospitalized in 1987, doctors did not test her for HIV infection. In Nicole's words:

*Oh hell no. Do I fit the risk group? . . . The doctors kept saying when I went into the hospital, "No, not her, she's—look, she's white, she's been married for almost seven years, she's been with her husband for seven years, she has a child, the child is well. Her husband is well. They come from a good family," and uh, "No, it couldn't possibly be [AIDS]." What's funny is I'm dying. I'm on 100% oxygen, and I'm saying, "Hey guys in September of 1982, I had this flu." And I'm trying to tell them I was really sick initially . . . And I was not sick for two or three days; I was sick for weeks. I lost 30 pounds; I was so sick . . . Every gland in my body was swollen. There was a period of a week when I couldn't even walk . . . It was horrible. And I went into the emergency room three different times and they told me I had the 24-hour flu. And I'm going for three weeks! (p. 286)*

She finally had herself tested, and not only was she HIV seropositive, she was diagnosed with AIDS. On April 8, 1993, Nicole died of AIDS-related complications.

A second factor contributing to women's invisibility is the failure to treat women with HIV adequately. "Because of misdiagnoses and late diagnoses, women may not be treated adequately" (Cline & McKenzie, 1996a, p. 367). This certainly was the case for Nicole and other women, whose median survival rate with AIDS is much lower than it is for men (Lemp et al., 1992).

Finally, a third factor is the failure of women to see themselves as being at risk and, thus, not avoiding the greatest behavioral risks for HIV infection (Cline & McKenzie, 1996a, p. 366).

Once they do become infected, however, women too face the stigma. One young woman told AIDS activist Mary Fisher, "I wish I had cancer instead of AIDS. I could stand the treatments and the pain and my hair falling out. And I'm going to die anyway. But then, at least, my family wouldn't reject me. I could go home" (Fisher, 1995, p. 92). Still, without a doubt, individuals in the gay community remain the most stigmatized, silenced, and marginalized by the discourse surrounding this disease (Corey, 1996; Powell-Cope, 1995).

The socioeconomic layer of meaning undoubtedly influences the institutional/professional layer. Research, diagnosis, treatment, and education—all the work of professionals and the institutions that often control how these professionals work is interrelated and influenced by all other levels of the model.

## ◾ Institutional/Professional Layer of Meaning

The institutional/professional layer of meaning focuses on the meanings about AIDS that are held and communicated by health care organizations, federal and state governments, HMOs, and individuals in professions such as medicine, nursing, and social services.

At the broadest level, national and international organizations are responding to the alarming increase in infectious diseases such as AIDS. The U.S. Surgeon General, David Satcher, suggests that the rise in infectious diseases is linked to global travel; Senator Bill Frist (R-Tennessee), who is also a physician, states, "We can consider no site too remote, no person too removed, and no organism too isolated to affect our citizens" (Stamper, 1998, p. A11). Two prominent U.S. health organizations are focusing on this issue: The National Institutes of Health launched a $1.9 million program to provide infectious disease training for scientists in developing countries, and the CDC is working with the World Health Organization and other groups in 15 countries to establish a network for global surveillance and investigation of disease outbreaks (Stamper).

Because AIDS prevention depends on education, institutions and professionals are attempting to learn more about particular communities and their ongoing use of different channels (print and media) for knowledge about and discussion of AIDS (Engleberg, Flora, & Nass, 1995). One particular high-risk community being targeted for prevention messages is college students, who tend to engage in behaviors that enhance the risk of infection (sex with multiple partners and failing to use condoms) (Cline, Freeman, & Johnson, 1990; Sheer & Cline, 1994, 1995).

AIDS residential facilities are also being established in an attempt to treat those who are HIV positive as whole persons and to establish communities that can provide the support they need—but too often fail to receive—from families and friends. The Bonaventure House in Chicago, a residential facility for people living with HIV infection, opened its doors in 1989, offering services "which support and maintain the dignity of those being served without regard to race, gender, sexual orientation, religious beliefs, physical challenges, or income" (Adelman & Frey, 1997, p. 11). A study of an AIDS hospice revealed that the communicative practices of volunteers, including simply touching the person with AIDS, shaving them, or taking the time to talk about something unrelated to the disease, creates opportunities for entering the residents' world—for comforting them, for learning their needs, and for helping them through "the passage from this life to the next" (Kotarba & Hurt, 1995, p. 425).

Unfortunately, as we might realize from the meanings discussed in the ideological and sociopolitical layers, public health officials and other health care providers first approached AIDS solely as a biomedical phenomenon and failed to realize or address how culture, politics, and disease intersect (Dalton, 1989). People with AIDS also were often talked about and treated as suffering victims. Because of this, AIDSpeak was developed as a language of resistance by AIDS activists and individual patients to reject the "suffering victims" and "shattered life" stereotype. Instead, their goal was to develop a more vital perspective of AIDS as an opportunity to live life fully on a daily basis (Morris, 1998, pp. 212–213). What public health officials began to realize was that the disease needed to be considered from the perspective of those who were infected with and affected by HIV—at the ethnocultural/familial and the interpersonal layers of meanings.

## Ethnocultural/Familial Layer of Meaning

In the ethnocultural/familial layer of meaning, we consider the meanings of AIDS that derive from the cultural traditions, styles, customs, rituals, and values of everyday living, expression, and social interaction, which often are inculcated or learned through the family. In this layer, we learn that the ability of persons with HIV to cope with the disease greatly depends on the forms of support available from their family members and the multiple cultural communities to which they belong.

Some individuals can rely on networks of social support, including close friends, mothers, and romantic partners, to cope with emotional needs (Metts & Manns, 1996a). Most persons with AIDS, however, are not receiving the support they need. Too often, they are ostracized by family and friends, who because of the stigma feel fear, contempt, and other emotions and, thus, do not provide the support they would in the case of almost any other illness (Adelman & Frey, 1997).

The institutional/professional layer of meaning interrelates with the ethnocultural/familial layer in that through AIDS residential facilities, persons with AIDS gain the informal and formal social support processes they need (Frey, Query, Flint, & Adelman, 1998). Residents of such facilities report that because of the support they receive there, they engage in more healthy behavior, such as exercising, engaging in safe sex practices, and socializing, than they did before moving there (Frey et al.).

One of the most significant symbolic rituals associated with AIDS is the AIDS Memorial Quilt, which stitches into its fabric the names and lives of people who have died from this disease. It is immense, still growing, and cannot be experienced in one viewing:

> *The Quilt, in its communal spirit, enfolds everyone who feels moved in its presence. It creates a spontaneous bond among strangers who experience its power and recognize its assertion that suffering must be understood and respected as something other than a narrative of victimhood. (Morris, 1998, p. 213)*

Rewriting the narrative of suffering is also the goal of the activist group ACT UP (AIDS Coalition To Unleash Power), whose members *act up* deliberately and publicly (theatrical performances such as chaining themselves to government buildings or chalking outlines of the dead on the streets), thus challenging the public and institutions such as medicine, health care agencies, pharmaceutical companies, and even the church to think of suffering not just as a private affair but as social need to which we all must respond (Morris, 1998, pp. 214–215; see also Chapter 11).

The impact of the four layers of meaning discussed so far on communication in relationships is powerfully realized in both positive and negative ways. All four layers interrelate and reciprocally influence each other as well as the fifth layer of meaning—the interpersonal layer.

## Interpersonal Layer of Meaning

The interpersonal layer of meaning focuses on the dynamics of style, intimacy, emotion, and roles played out in human interactions surrounding AIDS. Wong-Wylie and Jevne (1997) cite five critical requirements in the communication between client and provider that contribute to a hopeful versus a hopeless interaction regarding AIDS: (a) being known as a human versus a patient (being known as a human allows for a relationship of caring, respect, and equal partnership); (b) connecting versus disconnecting (connecting means providers caring for, listening to, understanding, and supporting patients); (c) descriptive versus prescriptive (through description, providers encourage dialogue and use the layperson's language); (d) welcoming versus dismissing (providers are easily accessible and make the patient feel "special," "important," and "loved"); and (e) informing well versus informing poorly (providers communicate accurate, up-to-date information).

Barroso (1997) investigates long-term survivors, discovering what it means to "live well" with AIDS. Wilson, Hutchinson, and Holzemer (1997) reveal that AIDS survivors who are "living with dying" salvage quality of life from remnants. In a process of "struggling to keep on top," providers who work with family members of patients with AIDS do their best to provide physical, psychological, and social care. Mothers who are HIV positive struggle not only to face the stigma but also to engage in "defensive mothering," preparing their children for a motherless future (Ingram & Hutchinson, 1999). In the words of one mother, we see how the stigma complicates the urgency of her situation:

> *I have to give him everything that he will need to make it in this world, and I don't have much time to do that. I don't know how much time I have, but I know it's not enough. It's like I've got so much to tell him as I am dying. And nobody knows that I am doing it. I'm having to cram a lifetime of teaching him everything into such a short time, and I can't even talk about it. That's how crazy it feels. (p. 249)*

All the mothers in this study engaged in some form of defensive mothering that involved preventing the spread of AIDS, preparing their children for a motherless future, and protecting themselves through thought control. In what could be considered a form of defensive mothering, some HIV-positive mothers have created videotaped legacies for their children, answering the questions they knew their children would ask after they died (Barnes, Taylor-Brown, & Wiener, 1997). The videos allow these mothers to represent themselves in a way that the media might not and to comfort their children. In the words of one such mother, "if you ever get sad or lonely, and miss me, I want you to put your right hand on your left shoulder and your left hand on your right shoulder and pretend it is a hug from me" (Barnes et al., p. 25).

Caregiving during HIV infection is a significant dimension of the interpersonal layer of meaning. Because 80 percent of all people diagnosed with AIDS have been between the ages of 20 and 44 (Centers for Disease Control and Prevention, 2001), family members—particularly lovers—assume a caregiving role (Powell-Cope, 1995). Typically, research on caregiving focuses on the physical and emotional work of caring for an elderly family member from the perspective of a female caregiver. Gail Powell-Cope, a nursing professor, instead focused on the meanings that gay couples affected by HIV infection attribute to their circumstances and on the strategies they use to cope with transitions and loss, such as preserving independence and intimacy and developing acceptance of uncertainty and loss.

At this interpersonal layer, we learn of the rejection as well as the support and confirmation that people with AIDS experience in their relationships with others. We learn of the pain and suffering of living with AIDS, not just of the biological ravaging of the body but of the response by family and friends. Rejection by family and friends is not uncommon, as Bob explains:

> *I went to visit my brother during Easter vacation. He panicked when I told him . . . On Easter he went to his wife's family's house for dinner but didn't want me to go because he said they wouldn't understand. I spent Easter Sunday in a movie the-*

*ater alone. And when I told my mom I was HIV positive she said that it was about time [because I am gay]. She sees AIDS as a punishment for my lifestyle. (Metts & Manns, 1996b, p. 185)*

At the same time, some people experience a great sense of confirmation and support from family members, as Mark explains:

*I knew I had to tell my family. My brother was getting married and I had to go back east for the wedding. I told my mother over the phone and she said she would tell my father. We had a plan that if he wanted to disown me, she would just tell people that something had come up and I couldn't make the wedding. I am the oldest son and my dad didn't even know I was gay. When I arrived, I was stunned. There was a big banner across the house that said, "Welcome Home Mark." They all treated me like a king and so did the whole wedding party. (Metts & Manns, 1996b, p. 186)*

In these two drastically different accounts, we see that no one's story is the same—living with AIDS plays out differently in their interpersonal relationships as family and friends respond to their disease in both expected and unexpected ways.

Finally, as friends or family members of people with AIDS, we often don't know what to say or how to provide the support or comfort they need. Sociologist Carolyn Ellis (1995b) writes about one of her last interactions with her friend Peter, who eventually died from AIDS. At one point in their conversation over tea one afternoon, she looks at Peter, contemplating a time in her past when she was the caretaker for her partner Gene before he died from emphysema:

*I am not OF this scene. I am only visiting. I will leave it. Go back to normal. The word "normal" mocks me. Ha, ha. No this is not my life again. I am not taking care of a dying person. I am not dying. It will be your life again, some day. Death speaks inside my head . . . There is no way for me to make him feel better, nothing to say, no way to make something good out of his condition. Just watch what you say, I remind myself. (p. 78)*

In this story, in this interpersonal layer of meaning, we see how difficult it is to fathom suffering even when you have been there before. We also see how difficult it is to know what to say and how to say it.

These five layers of the Culturally Sensitive Model indicate the sources of meaning that underlie people's communication about AIDS. They offer sources of understanding for practicing cultural sensitivity in communicating about AIDS in clinical practice, health promotion, teaching health professionals, and empowering patient, family, and community members.

# PRACTICING CULTURAL SENSITIVITY

One useful way to think about practicing cultural sensitivity in the borderlands of our multicultural communities is to consider the dialectics of these intercultural interactions (Martin & Nakayama, 1999). "A dialectic is a tension between two or more contradictory elements in a system that demands at least temporary resolution" (Littlejohn, 1996, p. 265).[1] A dialectical perspective is crucial for understanding community in that "everyone who joins a group wishes to be both a *part* of the group and *apart* from it" (Adelman & Frey, 1997, p. 18; see also Tillich,1952). So, rather than assuming that people fit into one or another cultural community of health or illness, instead we may consider the fluctuating, interdependent, and complementary aspects of their interaction in any one or in multiple communities (Adelman & Frey; Martin & Nakayama, 1999; Yoshikawa, 1995). For example, people who are physically disabled by severe arthritis and have limited ability to walk may have a great need for both independence and dependence. Through their independence, their disability does not take priority in defining who they are. Simultaneously, through their dependence, they acknowledge that their disability is central to their identity, negotiating their dependence on others. Through their membership in both disabled and nondisabled cultural communities, they recognize and struggle with both their loss of control and their desire to control how they must depend on others.

We now turn to three specific dialectics that influence communication within a wide variety of cultural communities and that may play out differently in families, health professions, and health care settings (hospitals, hospice centers, and clinics). Communicating health and understanding in the borderlands of cultural communities depends on the interplay of (a) dialectics of biomedical selves and biocultural selves, (b) dialectics of humanistic knowledge and technological knowledge, and (c) dialectics of passive participation and active participation. Importantly, the differences we face in communicating should not be viewed as dualisms, emphasizing opposites in parallel, but as dialectics, emphasizing the interplay of opposites (Baxter & Montgomery, 1997, p. 328).

---

[1]For more discussion of the dialectical perspective, see Adelman & Frey (1997); Altman (1993); Altman, Vinsel, & Brown (1981); Askham (1976); Bakhtin (1986); Baxter (1988, 1990, 1991); Baxter & Montgomery (1996, 1997); Baxter & Simon (1993); Cissna, Cox, & Bochner (1990); Goldsmith (1990); Kanter (1972); Masheter & Harris (1986); Montgomery & Baxter (1998); Rawlins (1983, 1989, 1992); Rychlak (1976); Smith & Berg (1987); Werner & Baxter (1994); and Wilmot (1987).

## Dialectics of Biomedical and Biocultural Selves

The traditional ideology of health care treats disease mechanistically, as a biological problem to be viewed objectively and solved technically (Geist & Dreyer, 1993b, 2001; Waitzkin, 1979, 1983, 1991). Frequently, the multiple ideologies of the patients, families, and friends are not considered, negotiated, or solicited. The voice of medical science, focusing on biological concerns, often dominates in ways that suppress the voices of others, but their unique personal histories, family constellations, socioeconomic status, religious beliefs, and membership in particular cultural communities may be essential to their diagnosis, treatment, and care (Kar, Alcalay, & Alex, 2001a, p. 110). We see this so very clearly with the Hmong family and their American doctors, when the culture of medicine clashed with the culture of the Hmong in ways where these two forms of knowledge equally informed decision making. Failure to balance the dialectic of biological knowledge with biocultural knowledge, of our **biomedical selves** with our **biocultural selves,** can result in inappropriate assessment, treatment complications, and provider-patient miscommunication.

Research investigating the intersection of health and culture abounds with vivid examples of these challenges, of the successes and failures in negotiating understandings acceptable to both providers and patients. For Kleinman (1980), "medicine is a cultural system, a system of symbolic meanings anchored in particular arrangements of social institutions and patterns of interpersonal interactions" (p. 24). He uses the term *clinical reality* to describe health-related aspects of social reality—especially attitudes and norms concerning sickness and health, clinical relationships, and treatment or healing activities (p. 37).

Assessment is a clinical art that combines sensitivity, clinical judgment, and scientific knowledge (Anderson, Waxler-Morrison, Richardson, Herber, & Murphy, 1991). Rather than a clinical reality shaped by ideas like "taking the history" or "case management," health care providers negotiate a plan that is acceptable to both themselves and their patients. In this way, "a curative emphasis gives way to care, and attention turns to facilitating self-narratives that make sense of biographical turning points members of cultural communities experience in sickness and health" (Zook, 1994, p. 355). As a result, providers recognize that an important part of healing involves culture, not just biology. Improving our health condition is not simply "fixing" our disease but addressing illness as a rupture that disintegrates our embodiment of biological, psychological, social, and spiritual health (González, 1994; Zook).

This philosophy is well represented in Jane Delgado's (1997) book *Salud! A Latina's Guide to Total Health—Body, Mind and Spirit.* Delgado, who is president of the National Coalition of Hispanic Health and Human Services Organizations, suggests that we need to cultivate trust and respect for Latina women, not discourage their belief systems. In a review of her book, Condor (1998) describes how Delgado encourages the spiritual tendencies and personal instincts of Latinas as applied to health:

> *She said* consejos *(loosely translated to "the wisdom we gain from experiencing and living life") can be a powerful agent of healing. Everything from prayer to gut feelings to warding off the* mal de ojo *(evil eye) should be welcomed as part of the culture. (p. E-3)*

Delgado indicates that more and more health organizations are marketing to Hispanic communities. One such program is the Community Health Group Foundation of Chula Vista's *Salud, Divino Tesoro* ("Health, A Precious Treasure"). Geared toward both female and male Hispanic community members in San Diego County in California, it has the goal of minimizing the effects of diabetes and cardiovascular disease by using volunteer health educators who speak Spanish and by promoting free activities, such as neighborhood walking clubs or grocery store tours to select healthy foods (p. E-3).

Viewing cultures as dynamic and not as static, unified wholes means that variations exist among individuals of any one culture. Accordingly, health care providers need to assess each patient individually before deciding on a plan of care (Park & Peterson, 1991). Taking a more **holistic** approach, concentrating on an "individual's own experience and understanding of illness," may assist in this assessment (Littlewood, 1991, p. 1015). Providers should acquire a knowledge of the specific language of distress utilized by patients, and providers' diagnosis and treatment must *make sense* to patients, acknowledging their experience and interpretation of their own condition (Helman, 1990). Individuals from similar cultural groups often share sayings or idioms that express their perspective on situations, problems, and dilemmas (Zuniga, 1992). Providers may use these sayings in the form of anecdotes, stories, or analogies to build rapport with patients and to magnify the patient's need to make the changes recommended in a treatment plan (Zuniga).

One useful starting point for health professionals is training that assists them in examining their own cultural beliefs and values as a basis for understanding and appreciating those of other cultures (Gorrie, 1989). One such program at the University of Southern California offers a course in cross-cultural communication that sensitizes physician assistants to their personal biases and prejudices through videotaped mock interviews (Stumpf & Bass, 1992). Believing that self-awareness of personal discomfort can become a tool for promoting sensitive cross-cultural communication, the curriculum is based on the model "Differences + Discomforts = Discoveries" (Stumpf & Bass, p. 115). Critiquing the interviews, students are encouraged to investigate their own feelings of prejudice and bias and to use their sensitivity to discomfort as "a cue that they are perceiving a difference and to inquire further rather than seek safety in the harbor of fear and prejudice" (Stumpf & Bass, p. 115).

Training is not the only route for practicing cultural sensitivity in the dialectic of biomedical and biocultural selves. We can improve our health care competencies by balancing biomedical and biocultural knowledge. As health citizens, we take responsibility for talking with others, seeking advice and information, trying a home remedy, tracking our symptoms, and deciding what to do next. As health consumers and clients, we might purchase a healing product or make an appointment for a healing service (from conventional medicine or an alternative or coconventional therapy), yet retain our citizen role in evaluating our health and healing processes (Arnston, 1989).

Just as the biomedical and biocultural selves must be balanced in communicating about health and illness, humanistic knowledge must be balanced with technological knowledge if we are to enhance our understanding of cultural communities.

## ◼ Dialectics of Humanistic and Technological Knowledge

All cultures have knowledge and beliefs about health and illness that have been passed down from generation to generation (Galanti, 1997; Krajewski-Jaime, 1991). In the United States, the emphasis on technological progress and the biomedical model complicates the task of communicating to understand health based on knowledge gained from people and their cultural communities. A progressive ideology that elevates knowledge gained from technology over knowledge gained from listening to an individual's views has produced a society of experts who possess the technical knowledge, but not the social (and cultural) knowledge, and whose communication to the public places priority on the "body" and not the "person" (Hyde, 1990). This progressive ideology places great emphasis on the functioning and malfunctioning of people as human machines. One physician notes how this emphasis permeates medical education:

> Disease, we were told [in medical school] was caused by a malfunction of the machine, the body.... The emphasis began and ended with the body.... For this reason the modern medical model is called the molecular theory of disease causation.... (Dossey, 1982, pp. 6–8)

As a growing number of providers are discovering, however, this model does not account for parts of the human psyche that are most centrally involved in the cure of illness—namely, cultural variation in perceptions of what constitutes health, illness, treatment, and the appropriate interaction between provider and patient (Lowenberg, 1989; Morris, 1998; Needleman, 1985).

Many would argue, as Lowenberg (1989) does, that the single most overriding conflict in the health care system is the polarization between **humanistic knowledge** and **technological knowledge** in health care. Fisher (1986) suggests that cross-cutting all interactions between providers and patients is an ideology that supports the authority of the medical perspective and of technological knowledge over the patient's perspective and humanistic knowledge. Consequently, the asymmetry of power within medical relationships creates difficulties for patients from diverse cultural communities in discussing the problems of primary importance to them and in providing information that they see as being relevant (Fisher; Mishler, 1984).

Now more than ever, patients *and* health care providers are voicing their concerns with the inability of biomedicine to become attuned to the humanistic characteristics of patients, including the personal, social, and cultural composition of their lives. As a result, many are turning to alternative or traditional therapies, often called **complementary medicine,** in conjunction with biomedical therapies, often called **allopathic medicine.** With this in mind, consider how you might answer the questions in Theorizing Practice 3.4.

Allopathic medicine, with its reliance on technology, is referred to as modern, biomedicine, or conventional medicine. Generally, complementary therapies are referred to as traditional, folk, or **alternative medicine,** because many originated centuries ago from countries and traditions all over the world. Complementary medicine is an umbrella label for a wide variety of therapies, the assumption of which is that the mind and body are subtly interlocked and powerfully influence each other (Wallis, 1991). A partial list of such therapies includes acupuncture, biofeedback, chiropractic medicine, herbal therapies, massage therapies (such as shiatsu), homeopathy, aromatherapy, reflexology, and guided visual imaging (Center, 1998; Colt, 1996; Duerksen, 1997; du Pré, 2000; Wallis).

Clinics and hospitals across the United States are beginning to integrate allopathic and complementary medicine in their practices—thus integrating humanistic and technological therapies (Colt, 1996). Stephen Center, MD, a family and general practice physician who integrates both in his San Diego, California, practice, suggests that alternative medicine has moved from fringe to mainstream (Center, 1998). Describing the branches of alternative medicine, which he prefers to call complementary medicine because of his belief in the complementary nature of biomedicine and traditional medicine, Dr. Center emphasizes that complementary or alternative medicine is best used for conditions that are not as effectively treated using allopathic medicine, such as headaches, low back pain, or

## Remedies as Cultural Understanding

Most of us practice our own home remedies but without naming them as such. Consider a practice, ritual, or habit that you engage in at the onset of a flu or cold-like symptom. Then answer the following questions:

- How would you describe this remedy or behavior to someone else?

- Do you know anyone else who engages in this behavior?

- When or from whom did you first learn about this "remedy"?

- What do you think someone else would understand about you by knowing that you engage in this behavior?

- Have you advised others of this "remedy" when they experienced similar symptoms? If not, why?

Now talk with five people in your family about their health identity. Have them tell you what can be used to cure a stomachache, common cold, and so on. Create a chart of their health care issues and treatments. In one page, summarize what you have learned by considering your own cultural remedies with those of your family members.

chronic fatigue. Others agree, suggesting, for example, that "allopathy is clearly superb at dealing with trauma and bacterial infections. It is far less successful with asthma, chronic pain, and autoimmune diseases" (Colt, 1996, p. 39).

By combining complementary and allopathic medicine as integrative medicine, both patients and providers benefit. Dr. Tenzin Choedrak, a Tibetan doctor serving as the chief personal physician to the Dalai Lama, suggests that if we can combine the natural medicine of the Tibetan system with Western medicine, patients benefit from having more options.

> Choedrak said there are things his ancient system does better and things it can't do as well as high-technology medicine. The 38 clinics of his medical institute in India often refer patients to Western-style hospitals there for treatment of cancer, AIDS, diabetes and injuries, he said, while the hospitals send many patients with respiratory, digestive, kidney and liver conditions to the Tibetan Clinics. (Duerksen, 1997, p. B-1)

By using both forms of medicine in tandem, more and different types of information are available for diagnosis and treatment. That is, complementary therapies rely on data obtained with our own senses, while allopathic medicine relies more on data obtained with technology.

*In the Tibetan tradition, doctors use their own senses to run many of the same tests for which Western doctors increasingly rely on technology. As Choedrak demonstrated on the VA [Veterans Affairs Medical Center] patients, diagnoses usually are made by feeling the pulse, examining a urine sample, glancing at the patient's tongue and asking questions about behavior and history. (Duerksen, 1997, p. B-4)*

Dr. Deborah Hoffman, a third-year resident attending Choedrak's presentation, noted that Western doctors of generations ago had some of the same skills, but she suggests that today, "we rely on our technology so much that we've lost the art of basic physical diagnosis" (Duerksen, p. B-4).

An important part of that lost art is time with the patient. Technology becomes an interface that separates the provider and patient, leading us to become blind subjects of technological knowledge. Humanistic knowledge instead comes from participating in open discussion with experts and from the wisdom they gain from viewing the whole person, not just the biological symptoms as revealed in a technological assessment (Hyde, 1990). Appointments for complementary medicine typically last an hour or more, because therapists often ask open-ended questions about patients' lifestyle choices and emotional well-being to provide them with preventative care and long-term health maintenance (du Pré, 2000). In contrast, managed care has pressured allopathic physicians to see more patients in less time. As David Edleberg, a Chicago internist, points out, "I used to work for an HMO setting, which was like cattle-chute medicine. One patient every seven minutes and three examining rooms going" (Colt, 1996, p. 39). In this way, allopathic medicine places more emphasis on crisis intervention, where it is most successful, and less emphasis on prevention, healing, and lifestyle choices that promote healthy living.

The dialectic between humanistic and technological knowledge becomes more clear when comparing health care diagnostic and treatment decisions in different countries. Lynn Payer (1988), who investigated notions of health and sickness in Britain, the United States, France, and West Germany, indicates that "many of the medical mistakes made in each country can be best understood by cultural biases that blind both the medical profession and patients, causing them to accept some treatments too quickly and other treatments reluctantly or not at all" (p. 34). A few examples from Payer demonstrate the point vividly: (a) American doctors perform six times as many cardiac bypass operations per capita as English doctors; (b) low blood pressure is rewarded with reduced insurance rates in the United States, while in Germany, it is treated as an ailment; and (c) hysterectomies, which are performed infrequently in France, are the second most common major operation in the United States. These patterns may have changed over the years, but they still represent values, priorities, and actions that could contribute to cultural biases in diagnosis and treatment. They also show that the "range of 'acceptable' treatments for most diseases is much wider than that admitted in any one country" (p. 22). These cultural "blind spots" often relegate patients to a passive role in communicating about health, and they inhibit opportunities to discuss "alternative" diagnoses or treatment.

The challenge for providers is to engage patients in a way that emphasizes both humanistic and technological knowledge. By nature of their training, providers tend to be more comfortable discussing medical and technological knowledge, so training medical residents in patient-centered interviewing techniques is vital (Marshall, 1993). These include both open-ended interviewing techniques, in which patients are allowed to talk with providers about anything they want, and emotion-handling techniques, in which providers elicit and support the patients' expressions of emotion (Marshall).

An essential component of humanistic knowledge is an understanding of communication and emotion. The inherent inseparability of communication, emotion, and cognition is well documented (Andersen & Guerrero, 1998a, 1998b). Emotions are more than just affective or feeling states—they also contain cognitive, behavioral, and physiological components (Guerrero, Andersen, & Trost, 1998). Patients and providers bring their emotional states into their interactions, and this may affect how they behave toward one another, how they communicate their emotions, how they respond to others' expression of emotion, and how their emotions may be modified or changed during the interaction (Andersen & Guerrero, 1998b). Culture also affects emotional communication in that "we learn to have feelings and express them in manners that are consistent with our culture" (Porter & Samovar, 1998, p. 468).

One basic emotion, fear, is often a part of our experience with illness and disease. Communication scholar Kim Witte and her colleagues have developed the Extended Parallel Process Model to explain why fear appeals work—and fail—in public health campaigns (for a summary of this research, see Witte, 1998; also see our discussion of this model in Chapter 9). The model suggests that fear appeals work when people perceive a real threat or a negative consequence ("I could get skin cancer." "I could get pregnant.") and when they have strong efficacy perceptions—that is, when they feel able to perform a recommended response ("I can wear sunscreen." "I can use condoms."). Our membership in cultural communities may lessen or strengthen our perceptions of fear and our perceived efficacy. Consider how some cultural communities may not define negative consequences as threats or be capable of performing recommended responses because of cultural ideologies or familial beliefs and expectations. Witte, Sampson, Liu, and Morrison (1995) found that for members of collectivist cultures, fear appeals threatening one's family produced more fear than such appeals threatening the individual, which produced more fear for members of individualist cultures. In another study, Witte (1997) found that teen girls did not perceive "getting pregnant" as being a threat or a negative consequence:

> *According to these teens, far greater threats were "getting fat" or "losing friends." Thus the teens suggested that an effective pregnancy prevention fear appeal should threaten loss of friendship or weight gain as a consequence of sexual intercourse leading to pregnancy. (p. 436)*

Clearly, we have much to learn about emotion and communicating health in families, health settings, and public health campaigns. This knowledge may be vital in motivating people to enact healthy behaviors—and to do so competently through satisfying relationships with family, friends, and providers (Spitzberg & Cupach, 2002).

Undoubtedly, understanding health in cultural communities depends on both humanistic and technological knowledge. At the same time, however, tipping the scale toward one form of knowledge over another may influence people's active or passive participation in communicating cultural understanding.

### Dialectics of Passive and Active Participation

The very term *patient* is a problem-laden word. It denotes illness instead of health and recovery, and it connotes a stance of passivity or helplessness in which the person is a compliant recipient of medical directives—that is, **passive participation** (Sharf & Street, 1997a, p. 4). Instead, we need to redefine this role as including **active participation** "in activities focused on disease prevention, health promotion, and maintenance of physical, emotional, and spiritual well-being" (p. 4). In this way, a person with health concerns could be someone who "strives to form a more collaborative partnership with a physician or other clinician, taking an active role in his or her own medical care decision making" (p. 4).

Research provides some interesting examples of how providers and patients communicate to actively participate or control the interaction with one another. We tend to consider providers as active communicators "taking the history" and patients as passive communicators "responding to questions," but this is not always the case. Communication researchers Charlotte Jones and Wayne Beach (in press) explore the ways that patients seek assurance, solicit diagnostic information from physicians, proffer their own diagnosis, and generally attempt to become active collaborators with physicians during medical interviews. They found that while physicians accommodate patients by answering overt questions or cautiously confirming their lay diagnoses one-third of the time, more often they resist, ignore, or passively tolerate patients' solicitations for more information or a response to their statements. Not surprisingly, "physicians' actions do not yet reveal a proclivity toward 'partnership building' emphasizing joint participation and decision making during medical interviews." However, they suggest that by allowing patients and physicians to become aware of and educated about these interactional moments, both might become more adept at negotiating information and decisions as a collaborative endeavor.

In another study, aimed at understanding how patients and providers interact during medical history-taking, Beach and LeBaron (in press) reveal "how a patient and interviewer work together to adequately balance the patient's personal needs and emotional displays in the midst of moving forward with the 'official' medical agenda." Examining videotaped interactions between providers conducting patient health appraisal interviews, the researchers discover how providers solicit and attend to delicate moments when patients disclose their past experience with sexual abuse. These brief interactional moments reveal the patient's body not simply as a disembodied object for clinical attention but as one that receives immediate attention as an active collaborator. Providers delicately accommodate the patient's disclosures, "demonstrating interest in, appreciation for, and sensitivity about troubling topics." Clearly, empathic opportunities abound in provider-patient communication, but whether these communicative moments become resources for understanding and collaboration may depend on the active participation of both the provider and the patient.

From another perspective, it is important to realize that not all individuals or members of particular cultural communities seek a collaborative partnership with their providers. Often, cultural barriers to patient participation exist (Young & Klingle, 1996). Research indicates that "cultural forces can foster silent and submissive communicative behaviors that are not conducive to collaborative practice. Cultural norms influence an individual's ability to be assertive and his or her belief regarding the effectiveness of assertive communication" (Young & Klingle, p. 35). These researchers suggest that patient assertiveness training is not the answer. Instead, discussions with patients need to center on dialoguing in ways that make them feel comfortable and that help them to understand how their active participation improves health care delivery. At the same time, practitioners must not be positioned—or position themselves—as a passive or dehumanized authority but, instead, become active participants (Kleinman, 1988).

## SUMMARY

The collision of cultures in health care is inevitable as the borderlands between multicultural communities are crossed, fade, or remain rigid. Understanding communication is a critical bridge across, through, and even in eliminating these cultural borderlands. Developing cultural sensitivity necessitates communicating in ways that explore and acknowledge that illness is a biocultural construction. It also means that communicating health in cultural communities involves

> *initiating and sustaining fundamental changes at individual and societal levels. At the individual level, it requires changing personal lifestyle and risk behaviors that are deeply rooted in culturally conditioned beliefs, attitudes, practices, norms and patterns of personal relations (e.g., behavior related to food and nutrition, sex and reproduction, health care utilization, and personal safety). At the societal level, it requires changing cultural values, social norms, customs and practices, social organizations, and intercultural relations (including communication systems) that directly affect health-related behaviors and status. Finally multicultural communities [often] consist of minorities and high risk groups who are most likely to be poor, underserved, and powerless. Poverty, prejudice, and exclusion from social policy and governance that adversely affect their health and quality of life are major barriers to effective health promotion interventions in multicultural communities. (Kar, Alcalay, & Alex, 2001b, p. xi)*

We now know that a person's recovery "can be enhanced or hindered, depending on the communication that takes place between caregiver and patient" (Bowman, 1995, p. 2).

The power to make us sick or well "inheres not only in microbes and medications but in images and stories" (Morris, 1998, p. 36). A sick person can make a story out of illness as a way of trying to detoxify it (Broyard, 1992; Morris, 1998). Listening to patients' stories (Kreps & Thornton, 1992), soliciting their illness narratives (Kleinman, 1988), considering the poetics and politics of interaction (Geist & Gates, 1996), and building partnerships (Geist & Dreyer, 1993b; Jones & Beach, in press) will facilitate communicating health and understanding in our multicultural communities.

We all bring diverse and multiple beliefs and identities to our conversations about health and illness. Learning how to communicate our expectations and preferences and how to listen to individuals whose beliefs and identities differ from our own is essential if we are to live healthy and supportive lives.

Communicating in ways that enhance understanding from one community to the next is not a matter of learning everything there is to know about every other culture or the terrain of cultural geopolitics before providing or seeking care or support. It means accepting and seeking to understand the dialectics—the frictions and incongruities that we discover as we communicate at the edges, the shorelines, and the borderlands of cultural communities. It means practicing cultural sensitivity—communicating in ways that allow us to learn about health and illness as they are seen by other multicultural communities. Importantly, in this process, we must share and learn about our own and others' biocultural selves, respect both techno-logical and humanistic knowledge, and maintain active participation as we com-municate in our families, institutions, and cultural communities.

## KEY TERMS

borderlands

culture

communities

cultural communities

ethnocentrism

cultural sensitivity

layers of meaning

ideological layer of
meaning

sociopolitical layer of
meaning

institutional/professional
layer of meaning

ethnocultural/familial
layer of meaning

interpersonal layer of
meaning

stigma

biomedical selves

biocultural selves

holistic

humanistic knowledge

technological knowledge

complementary medicine

allopathic medicine

alternative medicine

passive participation

active participation

## DISCUSSION QUESTIONS

1. What about Lia's story do you find most fascinating?

2. What cultural communities do you have memberships in? Which one seems to dominate your thinking about health and illness?

3. Have you experienced collisions in two or more of your cultural communi-ties? How so?

4. Which layer of meaning in the Culturally Sensitive Model of communicating health do you find yourself negotiating either in times of health or in times of illness?

5. What did you learn about AIDS from this chapter that you didn't already know? Did the Culturally Sensitive Model help you to understand something about AIDS in a way you had not considered before?

6. After reading this chapter, how might you change your communication with either your family or your health care providers? Why? In what ways?

7. Under what circumstance would you be willing to engage in complementary or holistic medicine? Why, or why not?

8. In what ways do you think we all could do more to practice cultural sensitivity?

## INFOTRAC COLLEGE EDITION

1. Read the essay "Partnership for the Public's Health Report Places 'People at the Center of Public Health': Stories Show Partnerships Between Communities, Local Health Departments Making a Difference." Consider how these partnerships do—or do not—represent an effort to understand health in cultural communities. What cultural factors will be discovered through this process? How will the knowledge gained through these partnerships promote health care?

2. Look at the January 2002 issue of *Journal of Public Health Management and Practice*, which contains three articles about the politics of policy development in public health. Read each article, and then consider the following questions: How does cultural sensitivity play a part in public health campaigns? What strategies are used to gain knowledge about health issues in cultural communities? Based on what you've learned in this chapter, what seems to have been left out during the planning of these public health campaigns?

# 4

# Political Complexities of Medicine and Healing

Skin rashes, dry mouth, foul metallic aftertaste, numbness of the face, swelling of the limbs, fever spikes, headaches, dizziness, anemia, clinical depression, neuropathy so crippling that I could not type, so painful that the bed sheets felt like sandpaper, nausea so severe that I sometimes had to leave the dinner table to vomit, and diarrhea so unpredictable that I dared not leave the house without diapers.

These are some of the horrors that I have endured in the past 10 years during my fight for life against the human immunodeficiency virus [HIV]. But these ravages were not caused by HIV itself, or by any of the opportunistic infections that mark the steady progression of AIDS. Each of these nightmares was a side effect of one of the hundreds of medications I have taken to fight one infection after another on my way to a seemingly certain early grave.

Had you known me three years ago, you would not recognize me now. After years of final-stage AIDS, I had wasted to 130 lbs. The purple Kaposi's sarcoma lesions were spreading. The dark circles under my eyes told of sleepless nights and half-waking days. I encountered passages of time marked by medication schedules, nausea, and diarrhea. I knew that I was dying. Every reflection shimmered with death, my ghost-like pallor in the mirror, the contained terror on the face of a bus passenger beside me, and most of all the resigned sadness in my mother's eyes.

But still I was fortunate because along the way I rediscovered the ancient understanding of marijuana's medicinal benefit. So I smoked pot every day. The pot calmed my stomach against handfuls of pills. The pot made me hungry so that I could eat without a tube. The pot eased the pain of crippling neural side effects so that I could dial the phone by myself. The pot calmed my soul and allowed me to accept that I would probably die soon. Because I smoked pot I lived long enough to see the development of the first truly effective HIV therapies. I lived to gain 50 lb., regain my vigor and celebrate my 35th birthday. I lived to sit on the bus without frightening the passenger beside me.

Even at this stage of my recovery I take a handful of pills almost every day and will probably continue to do so for the rest of my life. While I am grateful for the life-saving protease inhibitor therapies, they bring with them a host of adverse reactions and undesirable side effects. Different patients experience different reactions, of course, but almost all patients experience some. Smoking marijuana relieves many of these side effects.

I am not one of the exceptional eight patients in the United States with legal permission to smoke marijuana. Every day I risk arrest, property forfeiture, fines, and imprisonment. But I have no choice, you see, just as I have no choice but to endure the side effects of these toxic medications. So many patients like me are breaking the law to enjoy relief that no other therapy provides.

I sit here, I believe, as living proof that marijuana can have a beneficial effect in staving off wasting. Every pound was a day. I figured that for every pound of body weight I could maintain, that was another day I could live in hopes that some effective therapy would emerge.

C.S. spoke at the Institute of Medicine workshop in Louisiana
about his use of marijuana first to combat AIDS wasting syndrome and later to relieve the side effects of AIDS medications.
(Joy, Watson, & Benson, 1999, pp. 27–28)

ost people would not suggest that C.S. is a criminal who belongs behind bars, but his story reveals the political complexities of medical marijuana. This controversial issue links the very personal and private with the public systems of health care, law, research, and activism.

**Practical politics** is the term used to describe the campaigns for California's Proposition 215, Arizona's Proposition 200, and Oregon's medical marijuana law, each of which aimed to legalize doctors' prescription of marijuana for medicinal purposes. Controversy arose and opinions were sharply divided when the California and Arizona propositions passed in November 1996, and again in November 1998 when Alaska, Colorado, Nevada, Oregon, and Washington passed state ballot initiatives in support of medical marijuana (Joy et al., 1999). Since then, seven other states have passed laws that permit physicians to prescribe marijuana for medical purposes or medical necessity as a legal defense: Connecticut, Louisiana, New Hampshire, Ohio, Vermont, Virginia, and Wisconsin (Joy et al., p. 17). Into the mix of voices for and against the propositions came differing opinions and powerful campaigns from groups in favor, such as the *New England Journal of Medicine* and the advocacy group Common Sense for Drug Policy, and from those opposed, including the American Medical Association and the advocacy group Partners for a Drug-free America.

The persuasive efforts of organizations with an interest in medical marijuana and the stories of people like C.S. reveal a wide array of contexts, complexities, and consequences of communicating the politics of health issues such as this. **Stakeholders,** such as doctors, patients, lawyers, educators, legislators, policy analysts, patient advocates, parents, law enforcement officials, school administrators, pharmacists, nurses, activists, federal agents, school officials, and drug company representatives, all share an interest in marijuana. Each stakeholder advocates slightly—or completely—different views on whether to promote or restrict its use as a medicine.

The debate over medical use of marijuana "is essentially a debate over the value of its medicinal properties relative to the risks posed by its use" (Joy et al., 1999, p. 19), but the complexity of the politics is revealed in the diverse issues raised. Some say, "Why not let sick people ease their pain by smoking pot?" Others believe that promoting medical marijuana could send the wrong message to young people, or that such use could become a stepping-stone to the use of other, more addictive drugs or, possibly, to the legalization of marijuana nationwide.

The politics become even more complicated when we get down to the basics and consider the difficulties in tracking doctors' oral and written prescriptions for medical marijuana or the time-consuming process of developing a system to document who has the right to use pot (for example, an ID card that individuals could carry to avoid arrest). When we consider who will plant, grow, cultivate, and sell marijuana, another set of political complexities are raised. For example, in Santa Rosa, California, 47-year-old Alan MacFarlane was arrested in May 1999 for growing nearly 100 marijuana plants, which he harvests to alleviate pain from his thyroid cancer ("Patient cleared," 2001). In January 2001, however, he was found not guilty. California's Proposition 215 permits the possession and cultivation of marijuana for medicinal purposes, but it does not provide any guidelines for how much marijuana can be cultivated, for where patients should obtain it, or for prescribing and distributing the drug.

The politics change considerably when we bear in mind the opinions of persons outside our national boundaries, in other countries and cultures, or when we look back historically at how this plant was viewed.

> *In colonial times [the cannabis plant] was commonly known as the hemp plant, while today in the United States it is commonly known as marijuana . . . Around the world, it is known by other names:* ganja *in Jamaica,* bhang *in India,* dagga *in South Africa, and* kif *in Morocco. The leaves and buds of the cannabis plant have natural therapeutic properties, which have been used for centuries in the treatment of numerous life- and sense-threatening illnesses. . . . In 1942 a film called* Hemp for Victory *was produced and distributed by the U.S. Department of Agriculture to encourage American farmers to grow cannabis for much-needed hemp products, particularly rope . . . [I]t was a patriotic duty for an American farmer to grow marijuana (hemp). (Mathre, 1997, p. 7)*

Mary Mathre, a nurse and an addictions consultant at the University of Virginia Medical Center in Charlottesville, offered this information in the introduction to her book *Cannabis in Medical Practice*. The authors in that edited volume suggest that the politics surrounding the "War on Drugs" in the United States has restricted accurate knowledge and distribution of information about the medicinal properties of marijuana for many illnesses, including AIDS, glaucoma, chronic pain, and seizure disorders.

At the same time, advocates for more research on the medicinal value of marijuana are not convinced that smoked marijuana has greater value than Marinol, the synthetic version (in pill form) of the naturally occurring THC (tetrahydrocannabinol) in marijuana that has been tested and approved by the FDA (Food and Drug Administration, but sometimes also referred to as the Federal Drug Administration). In contrast, Dr. Marcus Conant, a physician at the University of California, San Francisco, states:

> *The problem with Marinol is that it doesn't always work as well as smoking marijuana. Either you take too little, or 45 minutes later you fall asleep. Even though insurance will pay for Marinol—which costs about $200 a month—some patients spend their own money, and risk breaking the law, for the more effective marijuana. (Conant, 1997, p. 26)*

For some individuals, however, the issue is not whether marijuana has medicinal value but whether it meets today's standards of efficacy and safety.

*We understand much more than previous generations about medical risks. Our society generally expects its licensed medications to be safe, reliable, and of proven efficacy; contaminants and inconsistent ingredients in our health treatments are not tolerated. That refers not only to prescription and over-the-counter drugs but also to vitamin supplements and herbal remedies purchased at the grocery store. (Joy et al., 1999, p. 19)*

Yet no matter how sophisticated and advanced our synthetic drugs become, some people still seek out alternative, low-technology therapies (Joy et al.). In fact, the use of medical marijuana coincides with the trend toward self-help and "natural" therapies (Eisenberg et al., 1993, 1998; Purnell & Paulanka, 1998a), but of course, the benefits of any medicine must be weighed against the risks. In predominantly animal studies, marijuana's acute side effects have, in some cases, included impairment of attention, short-term memory, tracking, and coordination; chronic side effects may include harm to the pulmonary system (Grinspoon & Bakalar, 1997). As these authors point out, however, "not a single case of lung cancer, emphysema, or other significant pulmonary pathology attributable to cannabis use has been reported in the United States" (p. 250).

The political complexities of medical marijuana have far-reaching consequences for communicating about health and illness. First, the controversy has communicated a need for more information, leading health care providers, patients, researchers, and government agencies to collaborate on a research agenda. The benefits of medical marijuana as published in recent books and articles, including the 1999 report of research conducted by the Institute of Medicine, lead scientists to recommend more clinical research and development of a nonsmoked delivery system, such as an inhaler (Joy et al., 1999, p. 7). Second, if research continues to confirm the benefits of medical marijuana as recently described, communication with the general public will increase about its risks and benefits, new laws, and the enforcement of these laws. The health care system will necessarily devise the best ways to communicate this information to patients. Third, changes in health policy and law concerning medical marijuana will necessarily impact its presently unregulated, black market sale, pricing, and distribution. Fourth, whether we view medical marijuana as "smart medicine" (Conant, 1997, p. 26) or "a perilous path" (McCaffrey, 1997, p. 27), changes in attitudes, behaviors, and laws will affect how patients, their families, and medical professionals communicate about treatment options, risks, and benefits. Indeed, if more states adopt laws that permit doctors to prescribe medical marijuana, public health campaigns may change their focus concerning marijuana from "just say 'no,'" to "just say 'know'" (Mathre, 1999, p. 7).

This brief foray into the controversy surrounding medical marijuana reveals some of the political complexities involved with communicating about this topic. Talk with a friend about any other health or illness topic, such as sexually transmitted diseases, breast implants, prostate cancer, and so on, and you will find that political complexities abound. As we begin to share with others our own views on medical marijuana and other health issues, we often find that others see the topic from a different perspective. Based on how it has touched their lives personally or on what they believe to be true about the cultural community most affected, people take different or similar stands. As we read and talk more about any one particular health issue, we find that negotiating these politics can be a very different experience depending on our gender, race, ethnicity, or age. The politics of negotiating care in health care systems, both nationally and internationally, too often is complicated by the dominance of the biomedical model, the threat of litigation, or the power of large corporations to construct meaning and limit access to alternative points of view. Negotiating politics and transcending these imbalances means that we consider diverse voices, perspectives, and options. It means that as patients, family members, and health professionals, we must speak to the inequality, stigma, contradiction, and marginalization that we encounter when communicating about our own and others' health and illness.

This chapter defines politics and provides a brief historical look at the politics of the medical profession and how these dynamics have played out in a range of contexts. Often these politics directly affect who has access to care. We then consider the complexities of negotiating politics in three health care issues: (a) syphilis, (b) breast implants, and (c) prostate cancer. Finally, we close with an examination of the practical politics of addressing and transcending imbalances in communication.

## DEFINING POLITICS

*Was the government to prescribe to us our medicine and diet, our bodies would be in such keeping as our souls are now.*

(Jefferson, 1782, p. 264)

In his "Notes on the State of Virginia," Thomas Jefferson (1782), then the governor of that state, wrote of his concern that people's religious rights were being violated by oppressive laws. The statement quoted here reflects his concern that the politics of the time led the government to become oppressive and to keep people from enacting their religious freedoms.

While politics can restrict behavior, political action can bring about positive change. On the day that Hillary Rodham Clinton formally launched her campaign to become a U.S. senator from New York, she recalled a speech she made during her college commencement at Wellesley in 1969, stating that "I often return to one thing I said back then, that politics is the art of making possible what appears to be impossible. I still believe that today. We can do what seems impossible if we have the vision, the passion, and the will to do it together" (Humbert, 2000, p. A-2).

So why is it that when most of us hear the word *politics* we think negatively about forces that keep us from doing what we want to do—that more often we believe politics makes impossible what appears to be possible? Many of us find this especially true when it comes to communicating within the health care system, when seeking answers to questions about diagnosis and treatment. Issues related to employment, benefits, type of coverage, rules and regulations, and even just one-on-one time to communicate with our providers seems complicated and difficult to accomplish.

If politics is viewed as the forces that make things possible or impossible, how could the word be defined more specifically? **Politics** can be defined as the structure of diverse interests about a particular issue, or it can be defined as the process of communicating these interests. Politics as structure is represented in the position or authority people have regarding an issue (the authority of a physician, lawyer, or activist), how people view an issue (their philosophy or ideology), and their interests (or stakes) in that issue. Politics as process is represented in the ways that people communicate their interests, speak about an issue, try to persuade others to see their point of view, and make possible or impossible certain actions allied with that issue. Politics are never as simple as being for or against something—communication becomes instrumental in every aspect of almost any health issue as people take positions and communicate in ways that attempt to change others' points of view or to resist how their own positions are being characterized by others.

Consider the power of groups and corporations such as health maintenance organizations, pharmaceutical industries, medical professional organizations such as the American Medical Association, manufacturers of health care products, political action committees and lobbyists, and the FDA to define and to communicate their perspectives on medical and health issues. Let's look at one particular example where we learn about gender bias in clinical drug trials (Black, 2000).

In 1977, the FDA recommended that women with childbearing potential be excluded from FDA drug trials based on the risk—or potential risk—of toxicity from the use of investigative drugs (FDA, 1995). Thus, although both men and women who participate in clinical investigations may be at risk for adverse effects from experimental drugs, women were routinely excluded from these trials because of the potential impact on their reproductive status (possibly pregnant). In 1993, however, the FDA concluded that by excluding women from the clinical investigations, researchers were restricting the knowledge that could be gained about differences between men and women in their responses to the drug, potentially adverse effects of the drug, and appropriate dosages. The *Federal Register* (1997) describes the impact of the proposed amendment in this way:

> To identify such potential differences and to help refine labeling information, patient selection, and dose selection, the agency believes that it is important that those women who are likely to use an investigational agent [new drug] once it is marketed be included in clinical investigations that may identify potential gender differences. (p. 49951)

Discussions leading up to this very important change in 1993 revealed that the politics of this issue involved faulty assumptions on both sides: (a) that the costs of clinical investigations would double if parallel trials of men and women were necessary, (b) that women could not take steps to avoid becoming pregnant during drug trials, and (c) that protecting the fetus was more important than the knowledge gained from women's participation in the trials. In this example, we see that the politics surrounding the FDA drug approval process in the past restricted vital knowledge about how women might respond differently to a drug that had been approved by the FDA based on studies with men. The communication surrounding the politics leading up to the 1993 amendment of the FDA's position revealed faulty assumptions and the fundamental need for a change.

Interestingly, the NIH (National Institutes of Health) began monitoring the inclusion of women and minorities in all NIH-supported research during the 1980s (NIH, 1993). Then, in an amendment similar to the FDA's, they passed the Revitalization Act of 1993, which strengthened and revitalized its guidelines to require the inclusion of women and minorities in clinical studies.

Corporate domination leads us to take for granted what large corporations communicate and establish as "the way things are"—such as the safety of drugs approved by the FDA. Critical theorist and communication scholar Stan Deetz (1991) suggests that Americans believe society is democratic because we vote to elect our officials. Deetz argues instead that there is nothing democratic or participative about many of the daily decisions that most profoundly affect our lives, such as those concerning the technologies and products available to us and the working relationships among people. Critical theorists such as Deetz gather interpretive cultural data about language, motives, and actions and then make judgments about the power relationships that exist in organizations or society. Their research aims to unearth the deep structures of power and to discover details not only about what happens in the use and abuse of power in organizations and society but also *why* it happens.

**Power,** according to philosopher Michel Foucault (1977), is intimately tied to discourse—power cannot be established, consolidated, or implemented without the production, accumulation, circulation, and functioning of discourse. In his view, domination is built into the very understanding of the common activity, goods sought, or whatever forms the substance of a relationship. In this way, power is a pervasive, intangible network of forces that weaves itself into our slightest gestures and most intimate utterances (Burrell, 1988; Foucault). **Bio-power** is a term coined by Foucault (1978) that suggests we are all imprisoned within a field of bio-power (power over our bodies) even as we sit alone. And nowhere is bio-power more pervasive than when we find ourselves in the sick role, seeking professionals' expertise and advice. The power of medical discourse in this sense can become repressive and prohibitive as we, in our "diseased" condition, come under surveillance. We are classified and judged by standards of what is healthy, well, or compliant. We are monitored and assessed by clinical corporate-medical technologies. We are medicalized in ways that do not allow us to define our experience. The **body politic** is a set of communication routines where experts' knowledge of our bodies transforms us into objects of knowledge, and the support for those routines becomes the "political technology of the body" (Foucault, pp. 26–28).

Sociologist Jackie Orr (1993) invites us to consider what it means to resist the power of medical discourse to define our identities. She describes **writing the body** as a way of representing, talking, or expressing one's personal experience of illness without the domination, mediation, or rationalization of medical discourse:

> *When studying disease as a social thing we should remember that while disease may be constituted through the discourse of medicine, it is almost always also some "thing" outside its writing by a clinical gaze. This "thingness" of disease is not its natural or biological features but its particular relations to the scene in which it materializes as a form, a cultural, economic, symbolic, and gendered scene that includes, but is never restricted to the site of medical practices. (p. 452)*

As Orr points out, some diseases, especially "mental" diseases or disorders, may actually be forms of resistance, protest, or escape from uninhabitable social relations—they become a very real response to a profoundly social dis-ease.

In essence, politics as the structure of diverse interests or the process of communicating these interests can be understood in terms of both the power to define disease and the power to resist definitions of disease. In the following section, we turn to a brief, historical perspective of the politics of the medical profession, and we describe how some of these views have influenced the power exercised in the communication between today's providers and patients.

## ▓ Considering a Historical Perspective

*All disease is a socially created reality. Its meaning and the response it has evoked have a history. The study of this history will make us understand the degree to which we are prisoners of the medical ideology in which we were brought up.*

(Illich, 1976, p. 166)

Sociologist Paul Starr (1982) has written one of the most complete histories of the development of American medicine. He divides medicine's history into two movements: the rise of professional power or sovereignty, and the transformation of medicine into an industry. Starr calls into question the unchallenged authority and status of the medical profession. He begins by describing physicians' authority, which he believes lies at the heart of the therapeutic process. The concept of authority is one key to understanding how this history translates to a better understanding of the political complexities of communication in the provider-patient relationship.

The professional power of the medical profession lies in both its social and its cultural authority (Starr, 1982). For example, physicians exercise social authority when they control behavior by telling patients what to do about the illness they have diagnosed. Historically, this **social authority** or trust in the doctor emanated from a number of sources: (a) physicians' prestige and great social status; (b) "the halo of science," created through the public's increased respect for science and technological advancement; and (c) the media's depiction of doctors on TV and in movies (TV series such as *Dr. Kildare* [1961–1965]; *Marcus Welby, M.D.* [1969–1976]; and *Trapper John, M.D.* [1979–1985]) (Shorter, 1985; Turow, 1989). Physicians' social authority also extends to the medical hierarchy in that they tell nurses, technicians, and other subordinates what to do. Yet before they can recommend any action, physicians exercise **cultural authority** in communicating the meaning of reality for a patient. That is, when patients come to a physician, the physician has the cultural authority to interpret, diagnose, name, offer a prognosis, and suggest the treatment for a patient's condition. As Starr points out, "by shaping the patients' understanding of their own experience, physicians create the conditions under which their advice seems appropriate" (p. 14). Through their communication, physicians define a patient's reality and exercise both social and cultural authority. And that reality may feel as ambiguous and directionless as the cartoon on the next page exemplifies; for both physicians and patients, there may be a reluctance to confront bad news and to actually say the "C" word.

In essence, Starr (1982) does not question the essential value of physicians' authority in the therapeutic process, nor do we question the motives of physicians in making the most accurate diagnoses their expertise allows. Instead, Starr asks us to reconsider the history of the medical profession in light of the unquestioned power

*Reprinted by permission of Cartoonbank.com. © The New Yorker Collection 2000 John O'Brien.*

granted to physicians by American society. He asks us to think about, for example, how (a) historically, physicians have not always had this authority or status; (b) the medical profession is not as powerful in other societies; (c) only physicians in the United States have been successful in "resisting national insurance and maintaining a predominantly private and voluntary financing system" (p. 6); (d) in the twentieth century, physicians became prestigious, wealthy professionals who powerfully shaped the basic organization and financial structure of American medicine; and (e) physicians' professional power has begun to slip from their control, moving toward medical schools, hospitals, financing and regulatory agencies, health insurance companies, prepaid health plans, health care chains, and other corporations.

Starr (1982) provides an understanding of medicine as both a cultural and a business phenomenon. He reveals how the complexities of medicine in general, and of the doctor-patient relationship in particular, arise from political and economic interests and conflicts among a wide range of stakeholders, including governments, political parties, foundations, employers, unions, and voluntary agencies. Yet in providing medical care or in paying the costs associated with it, these stakeholders derive benefits, advantages, and authority to control the distribution, financing, and even the definition of health and illness.

Undoubtedly, in the past and more so in the present, medicine and healing are complicated by a wide range of politics that in many ways limit the communication between providers and patients. Medical historian Edward Shorter (1985) describes historical trends that he believes have negatively impacted the relationship between physicians and patients. First, the dominance of the biomedical model, with its disease orientation, leads medical students and physicians not to balance their knowledge of medicine with what they might gain by communicating with patients about the experience of illness. Shorter suggests that one-third to one-quarter of all diseases are psychological in origin and can only be cured through the therapeutic power of communication between physicians and patients. In his view, two things must happen for this therapeutic power to occur. First, the doctor must show an active interest in the patient, and second, the patients must have the opportunity to tell their stories in a leisurely, unhurried manner (p. 157). This strengthened emphasis on patients and their role and influence in health-related interaction was the focus of a special issue of *Health Communication* (Sharf & Street, 1997b). Take a look also at Theorizing Practice 4.1, and consider how Shorter's advice is not being followed in the dialogue between that provider and patient.

A second historical trend is physicians' increased reliance on drug therapy and patients' increased expectation for prescriptions. Even in countries that are medically less advanced, physicians and patients share a prescription-happy mentality, but a good deal of the medicines prescribed are useless for the ailment diagnosed (Shorter, 1985). For instance, since the discovery of penicillin in the 1940s, patients often demand antibiotics even when they are not appropriate. Today, overuse of antibiotics is contributing to a rise in dangerously drug-resistant bacteria.

Finally, a third historical trend is the pressure of time, in which physicians are limited in how long they can spend with patients. As writer and medical commentator Norman Cousins (1981) points out:

*Time is one thing that patients need most from their doctors—time to be heard, time to have things explained, time to be reassured, time to be introduced by the doctor personally to specialists or other attendants whose very existence seems to reflect something new and threatening. Yet the one thing that too many doctors find most difficult to command or manage is time. (p. 137)*

The historical trends and political complexities of medicine translate into subtle—and not-so-subtle—limitations on communication between physicians and patients. Pressures exist to focus on disease and curing rather than on the patient and caring, to "blindly" prescribe drugs rather than to teach preventive medicine and ways to avoid their necessity (Starr, 1982), and to limit the time available for communication between physicians and patients rather than to allow them the necessary time to develop a healing, compassionate relationship in which commu-

## The Human Dimension of Dialogue

Read the following dialogue between a medical resident and a mother, in which the resident tries to explain a possible defect in her child's heart.

Mother:    What would cause that hole in his heart?

Resident:   There's a little membrane that comes down, and if it's the upper chamber there's a membrane that comes down, one from each direction. And sometimes they don't quite meet . . .

Mother:    Oh.

Resident:   It's uh . . . one thing they never get SBE from . . . it's the only heart lesion in which they don't.

Mother:    Uh-huh.

Resident:   (*trying further to reassure*) The only thing you have to worry about is other babies.

Mother:    M-h'm

Resident:   Watch your Coombs and things.

Mother:    Watch my what?

Resident:   Your titers . . . Coombs titers.

Mother:    Oh yeah.

Discuss this dialogue, answering the following questions:

- How would you evaluate this dialogue?
- What seems to be missing?
- How might the resident's communication be adapted to include more of a human dimension?

---

*SBE* is subacute bacterial endocarditis, also called infectious endocarditis.

*Coombs titer* is a reference to the R. R. A. Coombs test for the presence in the blood of antibodies to one's own blood cells.

This dialogue, cited in Shorter (1985, p. 193), originally appeared in Korsch and Negrete (1972, p. 68).

nication is intensely personal and practical (Bulger, 1987, p. 123). As the next section reveals, contemporary scholars are much concerned with the impact of power and politics on health communication.

## The Politics of Medicine and Healing

*[W]e enable justice to achieve full equality by making the discriminations necessary to treat genuinely like cases alike and genuinely different cases differently.*

(Jagger, 1994, p. 252)

The politics of medicine and healing, as we've been explaining, has limited the communication that takes place in a range of contexts. Consideration of diverse points of view may be limited by the politics negotiated in these contexts, including medical settings where providers and patients interact (medical offices, hospitals, and clinics) or federal agencies where decisions are made about funding research (for example, the National Cancer Institute), the design of drug trials (for example, the FDA), or the development of public health campaigns (for example, the Centers for Disease Control and Prevention). We can see how the dominance of the biomedical model, the threat of litigation, or the power of large corporations to construct meaning or control access to alternative views may limit which voices are heard and what gets defined as important issues to be addressed.

Communication scholar and cultural critic Deborah Lupton (1994) challenges us to think about the interaction between providers and patients and the politics that impact their communication. Specifically, she considers how that language in the medical setting may benefit some people while discriminating against others. She asks, "In whose interests is the discourse operating? How does the use of language in the medical setting act to perpetuate the interests of some groups over others?" (p. 60). Lupton advocates a critical, cultural, and political approach to our understanding and practice of communicating about health and illness. She suggests that the struggles for power in medical settings can range from the communication surrounding the meaning of an illness and treatment experiences of an individual to the communication of those individuals, groups, or organizations that largely determine the information environment in which individuals make health decisions. By defining health not only as a state of physical or emotional well-being but also "as access to and control over the basic material and non-material resources that sustain and promote life at a high level of satisfaction" (p. 60), we see how essential it is to consider the political complexities of communicating about health and illness.

For critical scholars such as Lupton (1994), knowledge, discourse, and power are tied together intimately. Those with the knowledge also have the power to communicate in ways that may limit the voices of people based on their race, ethnicity, or gender. The predominance of a rational, neutral standard for comparing individuals who enter the health care system often renders those individuals powerless to define themselves or their conditions as unique, worth considering, or in being treated differently from what the standard prescribes.

The research of physician and critical theorist Howard Waitzkin (1985, 1991, 2000) and others (Waitzkin & Britt, 1989; Waitzkin & Waterman, 1974) elaborates how this power is enacted. In *The Politics of Medical Encounters,* Waitzkin (1991) describes three contexts or topics that become troublesome when they are raised in doctor-patient communication: (a) work-related problems, (b) family life difficulties, and (c) deviant activities or emotional problems. He found that when patients raise these topics, physicians become uncomfortable, because they feel these subjects are social rather than medical. In response, doctors tend to direct patients to conform to society's dominant expectations about appropriate behavior. He suggests that when communicating with one another—as patients acquiesce and doctors control—both face a **contradiction** between the professional commitment to help and medicine's limited ability to deal with contextual problems in individual or unique ways. Waitzkin argues that well-meaning physicians (and he includes himself in this group) communicate so that their medical ideology dominates the discussion of these three contexts, leaving patients unsatisfied that their individual health concerns have been addressed.

> *Seen in this light, doctor-patient encounters become micropolitical situations that reflect and support broader social relations, including social class and political-economic power. The participants in these encounters seldom recognize their micropolitical situations on a conscious level. To some degree, doctors and patients may experience frustration when contextual concerns arise and when they feel that their attempts to deal with them remain unsatisfactory. Yet even this discomfort is rarely mentioned as doctors and patients talk. (p. 9)*

As Waitzkin points out, even when people sense that the uniqueness of their contextual problems is not being considered, they feel they are not being treated fairly or equally, or they realize they are being discriminated against based on their race, sex, age, or disability, there exist subtle mechanisms of medical discourse that promote and reinforce their consent.

A recent survey of more than 6,000 adults focusing on patient-physician communication reveals that lower quality of health care is provided to minority Americans (Collins et al, 2002). Research to answering the question "Why?" leads us directly to communication: Minorities are more likely to forgo asking questions of their doctors, face greater difficulty in communicating with physicians, find it less easy to understand instructions from the doctor's office, are less involved in their health care decisions than they would like to be, and are more likely to feel that they are treated with disrespect. The study reveals that for almost every measure of quality of care, the experiences of whites and minorities are radically different. The difficulties minority patients face in getting the quality health care they need and in communicating with physicians are often related to political, cultural, and economic complexities. As Collins et al. reveal, barriers linked to language, literacy, and lack of health insurance must be addressed if we are to avoid the marginalization of minorities in health care delivery.

The political and cultural complexities of health-related communication in communities is the focus of research conducted by communication scholars Leigh

Ford and Gust Yep (in press). In their view, "the tensions between power and powerlessness, privilege and marginalization, participation and resistance" must be addressed through community-based health intervention if we are to correct the marginalization that often occurs in health care based on gender, race, ethnicity, social class, disability, and sexuality.

Rhetorician Michael Hyde (1990) provides a vivid example for the power of discourse, ideology, and consent in the **rhetoric** of medical technology. He coins the term **progressive ideology** to describe how people in our society tend to become blind supporters and subjects of technology—how we depend and put faith in an elite group of specialists solely because of their technical expertise. He is not suggesting that technology is bad and we should not rely on it. Instead, Hyde is suggesting that we discuss technologies and the information they provide. For example, one new technology for the treatment of infertility is a process of extracting eggs from one woman for donation to another who is no longer able to produce them. Several of these eggs are fertilized and then implanted in the womb of the woman who is infertile. As much as we can agree that it is a worthy goal developing technologies to help infertile couples to conceive a child, few people have discussed ethical decision making regarding the remaining, unused eggs.

We are only beginning to discuss, debate, and establish policy for the issues that arise as we begin taking advantage of these new technologies. As Hyde (1990) points out, in the case of medical technologies, "it is not the deficiencies of medicine that present the medical community with dilemmas, but the successes" (p. 120). Moral and ethical dilemmas arise as we discuss the appropriate uses of these technologies and the range of interpretations and possible actions that physicians and patients may want to take in response to the information these technologies provide. Clearly, such information presents an opportunity for patients to become active citizens who are involved in decision making and who concern themselves with rights, responsibilities, and their own competencies as they dialogue with providers (Rimal, Ratzan, Arntson, & Freimuth, 1997). A very current example is the scientific capacity to clone humans, in which our technical capacity is outstripping our moral resources and understanding of the implications of such a feat. Through this advanced technology, biomedical researchers and physicians possess technical knowledge, but without **public moral argument** and the active engagement of citizens discussing the very real implications of such technology, we may lack the practical and personal wisdom to make good decisions.

In the next sections, we explore three specific cases of the politics of medicine and healing and what it means to consider diverse voices, points of views, and options. First, we focus on the communication of stigmatizing messages in the politics of syphilis and privilege. Second, we explore the communication of contradictory information in the case of breast implants. Third, we consider how communication marginalizes survivors of prostate cancer. Finally, we close the chapter by discussing communication strategies for negotiating politics and transcending imbalances.

## COMMUNICATING STIGMATIZING MESSAGES: THE POLITICS OF SYPHILIS AND PRIVILEGE

*Why don't you do something to help us? We represent the lowest economic group . . . Give us jobs and decent homes, and we'll lo[wer] the V.D. incidence.*

Statement by an African-American leader in Chicago, 1937
(Poirier, 1995, p. 141).

Suzanne Poirier (1995), a professor of literature and medicine, provides a historical, rhetorical examination of the language, law, medicine, morals, people, and places of the 1937 Chicago Syphilis Control Program. Her interest in and decision to write about this topic came from the similarities she saw "between the issues surrounding the antisyphilis campaign of the late 1930s and the issues surrounding the treatment of AIDS and the HIV epidemic fifty years later" (p. 13). In Poirier's view, the story of the Chicago Syphilis Control Program "demonstrates that the complex interrelationships of individuals and circumstances can abet or confound any organization's 'best laid plans'" (p. 2).

The power of the Chicago Syphilis Control Program to stigmatize or privilege groups of people was apparent in the reporting of statistics, the execution of research studies, and the public health campaigns. For example, banned in the rhetoric of the Chicago Syphilis Control Program were any references to or discussions of race, making it impossible to create special educational programs or services tailored to the needs of any culturally identified people (African Americans, women, and so on). Yet at the same time, African Americans were stigmatized in discourse as "a notoriously-syphilis-soaked race" (Jones, 1981, p. 16) that refused to take the disease seriously and lacked the intelligence to follow the treatment regime (Poirier, 1995, p. 138).

Poirier (1995) provides another dramatic example of **stigma** and **privilege** in the discourse where "good" women who were the first to volunteer for syphilis testing were privileged and prostitutes who "should be isolated and kept under lock and key" (p. 151) were stigmatized. And what is more, as Poirer points out, no mention is made of the men who frequent houses of prostitution. Here she cites the language of Dr. Ben Reitman, who was active in the Chicago program and who used the strongest of language to describe whores as "women with pimps, they are vicious, antisocial and disease spreaders and they cannot be trusted to cease work while infected, they are not cooperative" (p. 151). He and others campaigned for mandatory testing not only of pregnant women but of any woman of childbearing age. Reitman advocated extensive control over the lives of infected women, suggesting that "every female with syphilis in the childbearing ages should be entered in a special book and the patient should be thoroughly supervised" (p. 152). As Poirier points out, the degree of control recommended for infected women was "not recommended for men with syphilis who might impregnate uninfected women" (p. 153).

Concluding her book, Poirier (1995) suggests that times have changed in that "a new emphasis on individual rights has created an environment in which law and policy receive careful scrutiny to detect bias based on race, gender, sexual orientation, or other cultural or biological situations" (p. 213). The striking similarities between the rhetoric of the Chicago Syphilis Control Program and the rhetoric of AIDS 50 years later, however, is a matter of concern:

> [E]arly media reporting and cultural studies of AIDS often drew comparisons with syphilis. Metaphors of plague and war have studded the rhetoric of both infections. Even though syphilis was curable in the 1930s, it was nevertheless repeatedly portrayed as a killer. Similarly citizens of Chicago in 1937 usually associated syphilis with illicit sexual "promiscuity" as well as sexual "liberation" in ways that foreshadow the associations that many people today make of HIV infection with the "gay liberation" of the 1970s. (pp. 213–214)

In Poirier's view, both syphilis and AIDS present epidemics of **signification** that are replete with fearful, moralistic language. That is, while both are diseases with physical symptoms, the language surrounding each illness signifies so much more—personally, culturally, and politically. Theorizing Practice 4.2 asks you to consider how the stigma Poirier describes in her research might be similar to the stigma that we may feel with other diseases.

We must take the time to critique and look "through" language to understand and address the rhetorical, medical, and moral dilemmas presented in the political complexities of disease. This is also the case with the contradictory information that has been communicated about breast implants, as the next section reveals.

## COMMUNICATING CONTRADICTORY INFORMATION: THE BREAST IMPLANT CONTROVERSY

*When I took off my lycra top in front of my bedroom mirror, I pulled it slowly over my shoulders—stretching and prolonging the ritual in an exaggerated fashion. Like the scene out of the movie, "Striptease," when Demi Moore seductively undressed in*

## Designing Health Messages Considering the Politics of Syphilis and AIDS

Suzanne Poirier (1995) states that

> it is the human responses to syphilis and AIDS and HIV that are timeless. Fear of disease and death, discomfort with discussing sexuality, distrust of people or groups whose culture or values differ from one's own—all of these elements unite the problems posed by syphilis in 1937 and AIDS more than a half a century later. These responses inform and shape the strategies, rhetoric, and policies that surround syphilis past and AIDS present. (p. 214)

Consider another disease that is prevalent today in our society. It could even be one that is not talked about openly or easily (anorexia, bulimia, alcoholism, or sexually transmitted diseases). Answer the following questions concerning just one of these diseases:

1. What parallels do you see in the language surrounding this disease with the language surrounding syphilis or AIDS?

2. How would you describe your own reaction or emotions regarding this disease?

3. How would you describe what you believe to be your own or others' fears about the disease?

4. What actions could individuals or groups take to alleviate fears and to create more awareness and understanding of this disease?

5. What audience or age group would be the best to target?

6. What type of message could be created to reach this audience?

7. How might the message be worded to reach this target audience?

8. Through what media should this message be communicated?

*front of her audience, I took off my bra in my own imaginary striptease. The words to Cyndi Lauper's song mesmerized me: "Time after time." For the first time, I could suddenly read the expressions on the men's faces seated in the front row of the dimly lit and dated strip bar. Instantly the scars stared back at me. Haunting me once again. A small, red gash with raised edges touched the margin to the right armpit. It claimed first rights to acknowledgment. Then, on closer inspection two much longer ones, about 2 to 3 inches, bordered the underside of each breast. Could men see it from the front rows, I wondered? Hopefully only from the fourth row back. But no matter how I slinked and shimmied across my imaginary stage setting, I knew the harsh shadows under tabletop lights would be clear. They explored the telling of a silent story about my breast implant rupture, now leaving me only the remnants of a partial mastectomy. Puckering above my indented right nipple was a third scar from yet another breast surgery, receding and since healed over. These scars replay themselves "time after time" whenever I undress. Tonight I am not feeling like the brave, new warrioress that I want to become. I am only feeling vulnerable. It is out of my vulnerability that my scars scream out. They want to tell my story to the girls who become young women, and to the young women who go on to nurse babies, to those who may fall prey to silicone and saline breast implants.*

Graduate student Marva, who had breast implants at the age of 27 but later had her implants removed (Smith, 2000).

*At that particular time, in retrospect, umh, a lot of people in my life were, I would say, shallow in appearance—in their perception of appearance. And the "perfect woman" . . . So, a lot of you know, in light conversation with friends—male and female—they were very much "Yeah. Go get breast implants." "Fantastic." "I hate women with saggy breasts." You know this and that. "I think it would be great!" You know, so a lot of it, they were very—in my perception—were shallow in the sense that they never gave it that extra thought of "What is it medically going to do to you as a person?" "What are the life-long ramifications that it's going to have?"*

Graduate student Anastasia, who considered but decided against having breast implants (Smith, 2000).

These stories reveal just two perspectives on breast implants. The political complexities of communication surrounding breast implant surgery are simply phenomenal. A wide range of opinions both for and against this form of surgery (either for cosmetic reasons or for reconstruction after breast cancer) are voiced by women, men, plastic surgeons, rheumatologists, representatives of corporations who manufacture implants, and the general media (newspaper coverage, documentaries, talk shows, public radio specials, and advertisements soliciting customers for the surgery).

Public health scholar Nora Jacobson (2000) tells us that "the history of breast implant technology is the story of the construction of many shifting political, social, and economic meanings" (p. 4). Tracing the 100-year history of this technology, beginning with the first implant in 1895, Jacobson describes how the contested realities surrounding breast implant surgery are represented in seven interrelated problems. Each problem involves different people who communicate divergent interests: (a) the health problem, (b) the suffering problem, (c) the bureaucratic problem, (d) the corporate problem, (e) the technical problem, (f) the legal problem, and (g) the body image problem (p. 10). For example, we learn conflicting information from the manufacturers and plastic surgeons seeking to ensure the continued availability of breast implants and from other physicians and activists seeking to restrict implants for health reasons. One of the best sources of information about the known risks from any type of breast implant is the FDA's status report on implant safety (FDA, 1997), which lists both the surgical risks (similar to other surgical procedures; for example, complications of general anesthesia, infection, abnormal bleeding, or clotting) and the implant risks (hardening of the breast due to scar tissue, leak or rupture, loss of sensation in the nipple or breast tissue, calcium deposits surrounding the tissue, shift from original placement, and interference with mammography readings, possibly delaying detection of breast cancer by "hiding" a suspicious lesion).

One facet of the controversy over breast implants is depicted in Theorizing Practice 4.3, which represents a case study of the increasing number of teenagers receiving implants. In 1998, 1,840 girls under the age of 19 had breast implants, which is up 57 percent from 1996 and 89 percent from 1992, with the largest percentage of surgeries being performed in California, Texas, and Florida (Warren, 1999). Even more alarming, breast implants have become a popular graduation gift to teenage girls (Dockrell, 2000, Iley, 2000; Ingrassia, 2000; O'Brien, 1999; Warren). Plastic surgeons suggest that communication is key in their decision to take—or to deny—a potential client. Dr. Gregory Borah, chief of plastic surgery at Robert Wood Johnson Medical School in New Brunswick, New Jersey, suggests talking with the teens to assess their physical and emotional maturity (O'Brien). He finds that although teens may be physically mature, they may be too psychologically immature for surgery; thus, his turn-away rate for breast implant surgery is twice as high for teenagers as it is for adults. Dr. Joseph Reichman, a plastic surgeon in Cherry Hill, New Jersey, indicates that a cardinal rule in his profession is to assess, after meeting with the patient, whether the teen has a minor physical problem that is causing a major emotional problem (O'Brien). If so, then he knows the teen will not be happy with the results, because the surgery just won't "fix" any emotional problem that was making her unhappy in the first place. Psychologist Alan Solomon, however, questions the wisdom of teens having breast implants no matter what level of maturity they express (Warren). He and others see media images of beauty as communicating a very narrow and limiting portrayal of body types, which leads teens (and surgeons) to tamper with young, developing bodies before they have a chance to mature.

No matter what stance they communicate about the controversy, surgeons, psychologists, parents, and teens clearly talk about identity and body image in making the choice to have—or not to have—implants (see Theorizing Practice 4.3). The formative life passages (discussed in Chapter 6) are times when teenagers are bombarded with images of "perfect" body sizes and shapes. The choices they make about risk-taking behaviors (drinking, smoking, drugs, or unprotected sex) and

## Should There Be a Law?

Read the following newspaper article, and discuss answers to the questions that follow.

### UK Doctor Says 15-Year-Old Too Young for Breast Op

LONDON, Jan 5 2001 (Reuters)—A 15-year-old British schoolgirl, offered breast implants as a 16th birthday present from her parents, has been told by surgeons that she is too young to undergo plastic surgery. Jenna Franklin, whose parents run a cosmetic surgery business, said an operation to increase her breasts would give her more self-confidence and make her happy with her body. But consultant plastic surgeon, Anthony Erian, who was approached by Martin and Kay Franklin to perform surgery on their daughter, said that Jenna—16 in August—was too young to cope with the implications of the controversial operation. "Breast augmentation is a good operation, it helps a lot of people," Erian told the BBC. "But I feel at 16 the breast isn't matured enough and that there are also a lot of psychological implications." Erian said that the family should wait until Jenna is 18 until deciding to go ahead with a breast enhancement. Jenna's parents said they were happy for their daughter to have the 3,250-pound [$4,875 at a 1.5 exchange rate], operation but added that they would respect Erian's advice. "If he says 16 is too young for Jenna to have the operation then we will respect that and she will have to wait until she is 18," Kay Franklin said. "I'm sure she may not be happy with that but if we were to do anything else then we wouldn't be responsible parents." Jenna is scheduled to appear next week on a Channel 4 documentary called "Perfect Breasts." (Reuters Health Information, 2001).

1. What "implications of the controversial operation" is Dr. Erian referring to?

2. How do you respond to Dr. Erian's statement that Jenna is "too young to cope" with the implications?

3. What is your response to the claim that increasing her breasts would give Jenna more self-confidence and make her happy with her body?

4. Would you be a supporter of Jenna in this situation? Why, or why not?

5. Do you believe that a law should be established for cases such as this?

6. What seems to be missing from all that is presented in this article?

cosmetic surgery (with the inherent medical risks) inevitably reflect their very real concerns about fitting in and wanting to be "normal." Our concern is that teens have the opportunity to communicate with others so they can learn diverse points of view and "write their bodies" in ways that do not require the risk of "unnecessary" cosmetic surgery.

The politics of health care, particularly for an issue such as breast implants, which affects mostly women, can restrict communication about risks through any number of means. First, women seeking advice from doctors about illnesses they believe are associated with their implants have been misdiagnosed, told they were crazy or going through menopause, or generally treated with indifference (Vanderford & Smith, 1996). Second, information about risks often is not readily available. For example, in August 2000, the FDA reported that more than 190,000 complaints had been officially received, which represents 10 percent of the 1.5 million women with breast implants (Zukerman & Nassar, 2000). In addition, although most of the public believes this controversy only concerns silicone and not saline implants, more than one-third of the official complaints involve saline implants, most of which have been sold in the last two years (Zukerman & Nassar). The suffering of these women is more than just their exposure to silicone or saline; it is their not being believed or supported by the people and the groups from whom they sought support. Illness narratives for silicone victims become moral and political accounts that indict powerful institutions they blame for their illnesses (Zukerman & Nassar). As Jacobson (2000) points out, women who suffer from silicone diseases experience wide-ranging symptoms similar to people with multiple chemical sensitivity and those exposed to toxic waste dumps.

The politics of breast implants cover a wide range of politics. While the FDA called for a voluntary moratorium on the use of silicone gel-filled implants in January 1992 because of safety concerns, by April 1992 they lifted the moratorium while suggesting limited distribution of the implants until clinical studies could be submitted and reviewed ("Breast Implants," 2000). Even today, questions remain about the safety of breast implants. While some studies reveal a clear link between ruptured silicone gel breast implants ("Fibromyalgia," 2001), there is "insufficient evidence to establish that either or both types of breast implants cause systemic health effects, such as autoimmune diseases ("Breast Implants"). At the same time, studies have confirmed that the primary safety issue with silicone implants are local complications such as rupture, pain, disfigurement, and serious infection ("Breast Implants").

Communication researchers Marsha Vanderford and David Smith (1996) take an in-depth look at the communication surrounding breast implants. Their research began as they were drawn into and learned more about the controversy among doctors at their medical school. Some plastic surgeons favored removing breast implants when women requested it, even though they did not see any medical benefit for the women. Other plastic surgeons disagreed, suggesting that unnecessary surgery puts patients at more risk than leaving in the implants. At the same time, a rheumatologist at the medical school—one of the first to speak out—communicated his perspective that a connection existed between silicone breast implants and connective tissue disease, prompting him to advise women not to have the surgery or, if they already had, to have their implants removed.

And so began an intensive study of communication and uncertainty surrounding breast implants. Vanderford and Smith (1996) interviewed 35 women who had undergone breast implant surgery and asked them to discuss issues related to the implants and health. They located articles on the subject from the past 30 years, searched newsstands each week for additional articles, and taped TV programs about the topic. TV coverage seemed to be instrumental in persuading women to consider the link between implants and their illnesses, particularly the 1990 interview with Connie Chung (see FYI 4.1 for a partial transcript of this program).

Nothing captures better the political complexities of this controversy than Vanderford and Smith's (1996) statement that believe each and every contradictory testimony they heard from women and physicians:

> We found it easy to identify with nearly everyone we talked to, regardless of their opinions and experiences. The women we interviewed seemed to be reasonable people. We believed them when they said they had suffered. We also believed those who had no trouble. We believed each group of doctors even when they disagreed with one another. Some of these people were angry and found some of the others unreasonable. Yet, each seemed sincere to us, convinced that their interpretations of experience were valid. All were seriously concerned and willing to help us. (p. 8)

Fifteen women in their sample provided stories of success and satisfaction with their breast implants. In their voices, we see an earnest desire to be heard and understood, as Vanderford and Smith capture well:

> The women we interviewed knew their value was not in their breasts, but their motives for implant surgery were compelling, nonetheless. Women who sought reconstructive surgery following mastectomies did not feel whole or normal until they regained the female appearance that disease took from them. Women who had augmentation surgery felt tangible pain as a result of being small-chested in a society where breast size matters. (p. 193)

The interviews also confirmed that 20 women in their study believed their implants caused health problems and, as a result, experienced a profound sense of loss and confusion. They experienced loss of physical strength and endurance and of social relationships as they became more exhausted and unable to participate in daily activities; in turn, this led to career and financial loss. Because of the proliferation of contradictory information about the health impact of breast implants, they all faced a frustrating search for diagnosis and relief.

That women seeking an explanation for their chronic pain and diminished lives were unsatisfied and disappointed when communicating with their doctors is unsurprising. Women were experiencing multiple symptoms that did not cluster together

**Transcript of Connie Chung Interview**

**December 10, 1990, 9:00-10:00 PM (CT), CBS-TV**

Connie Chung, Host: Most of us know little about breast implants. We have seen the ads; we have heard the rumors about which celebrities have them and which don't. But we don't know anything about the dangers. Since the early 1960s, some two million women have had breast implants. . . . The operation takes a few hours, and if all goes well, the implants should last a lifetime, at least that is what most women believe, but not the women we interviewed. In fact, it couldn't be further from the truth.

Dr. Douglas Shanklin (Pathologist, University of Tennessee at Memphis): Nobody came out and said, "We have an announcement to make. We're about to experiment on two million American women." But from a certain view, that's what's happened. We have done a large-scale clinical experiment on an unproven, probably unsafe medical device, which is placed inside the body where the body can react.

Chung: For almost thirty years, American women have been getting breast implants. An astonishing average of three hundred and fifty implant operations a day. But what's shocking is that these devices have never been approved by the federal government. Only now is the government looking at the dangers. For some women, it may be too late.

Judy Taylor (Breast Implant Recipient): I knew many women that have had implants, many women. And, you know, I've asked, How did it go? You know, were there any problems, you know, how does it feel? Do they hurt? And it was fine. I just didn't talk to the right women, the women that were sick.

Chung: Six years ago Judy Taylor received silicone implants after a double mastectomy. You thought everything was going to be just fine.

Taylor: And it was.

Chung: For how long?

Taylor: Approximately one year, and then I started getting sick.

Chung: What were your symptoms?

Taylor: It was flu-like symptoms: swollen glands, fevers, chills, sweats, sore throats, and many, many trips to the doctor. And I got more tired and more tired, and joint pain. And it was very difficult to go up and down a stair.

Chung: How long did this go on?

Taylor: This went on for almost five years.

Chung: Five years!

Taylor: Yes.

Chung: Doctors insisted she had a virus, until finally one physician told Judy her system was being poisoned. When the doctor told you what he thought was wrong with you, how did he explain it?

Taylor: He told me that I had silicone-associated disease. . . .

Chung: What did that mean to you?

Taylor: Absolutely nothing. You know, and . . .

*(continues)*

*(continued from previous page)*

Chung: It meant her implants would have to be removed, and when they were, what the doctor found surprised him. The implants were intact, but as this photo shows, silicone had leaked into the surrounding scar tissue of her breasts, and had traveled to her lymph glands.

Shanklin: Silicone gets right into the heart of the immune response system, and is processed in a way that causes the formation of abnormal antibodies.

Chung: And these antibodies, says Dr. Shanklin, not only attack the silicone, but can turn on the human system as well, causing the body to go haywire. Shanklin is a pathologist at the University of Tennessee in Memphis, where he has spent six years studying tissue from women with implants. He's found evidence of silicone in almost every part of the body.

Shanklin: I found it in the thyroid gland here in the neck. I found it in the spleen, which in most people is in the abdomen on the upper left side. I've seen it in the liver. I've seen it in the other lymph nodes in the body. . . .

Chung: Janice Buck (Breast Implant Recipient) is convinced that silicone is also at the root of her health problems. Eleven years ago, tumors in her breasts forced her to have mastectomies, breast implants. Today, she can barely walk. She's plagued with illness.

Buck: I suffer constant pain, constant pain and constant fatigue. I take a total of between four and five hundred dollars of medication a month to try to keep me going.

Chung: When the doctor told you that maybe it might be the breast implants, and that you ought to have them removed, what did you think?

Buck: I would've done anything if I thought it would help me get better, but it was probably the hardest thing I ever had to do, because it was so hard losing my breasts once, let alone having to lose them twice.

Chung: Sybil Golridge gave up on implants after five operations left her breasts mangled and infected. She allowed us to use this photo as a graphic example of her ordeal. Today, she's demanding that doctors warn women of all the dangers they may face.

Golridge: If every doctor would simply read the package insert to the patient, the woman would then have enough information to make her decision. Simply read the list of complications to the patient, and let her decide whether she wants to risk these complications. The complications they list are known. Just tell her what's there. She's not getting that information. Nobody's getting that information.

Chung: This is a typical insert that manufacturers include with their implants. It says that it's the surgeon's responsibility to tell the patient about any possible risks or complication. They include implant rupture, or tearing from excessive stress such as massage or vigorous exercise, silicone bleeding or leaking, and a warning that implants may cause severe joint pain, swollen glands, and hair loss. None of the women in this story had access

*(continues)*

in ways that allowed physicians to present a clear diagnosis, and "the temptation to avoid, ignore, or dismiss such patients can be significant" (Vanderford & Smith, 1996, p. 38). While physicians were describing silicone as an inert or motionless substance, women described silicone as "a living, growing phenomenon, uncontrollable, and

*(continued from previous page)*

to this information. That's because manufacturers didn't start disclosing it until five years ago. We spoke with more than 40 doctors around the country, and were surprised to learn that less than a third mentioned these complications to their patients.

Karen Valleya (Breast Implant Recipient): Had I known that these things could rupture, I would never have had this done, because I would've been afraid of leaking silicone.

Chung: Initially, when you had the implants, how long did you think they were going to last?

Valleya: A lifetime.

Chung: Karen Valleya is a nurse and mother of two. Before deciding on implants for cosmetic reasons, she had asked about the dangers. She thought she knew everything that could possibly go wrong. . . . When did you start noticing some problems?

Valleya: Six months after breast augments I started to experience extreme fatigue, fatigue to the point where I couldn't care for my children, mouth ulcers just eroded my mouth completely, fevers, pneumonia, chest pain, hair loss, bizarre skin rashes, and all of those things. And I just knew something was wrong.

Chung: Karen would later be diagnosed with a disease of the immune system called lupus, but there were other symptoms that no one could explain.

Valleya: I had leakage of a clear fluid from my right breast, and a lump there, and . . .

Chung: Leakage?

Valleya: Leakage from a nipple. I was absolutely shocked to find out that it was silicone that had been leaking out of me for two-and-a-half years.

Chung: And surgery confirmed what she had feared: the right implant had ruptured. Karen had them both removed. Karen, what are you left with now?

Valleya: I'm left with, you know, just about no breast tissue. I wear a prosthesis, just like someone with a mastectomy. . . . It's very difficult to tell people about what's happened to me, because I find it's somewhat embarrassing. Not that I did anything wrong, but just personal. But I feel that if someone doesn't speak out, and talk about this, I believe that there are probably many women like me, but how many want to tell the world this, you know. It's hard to do.

Chung: There are no statistics on how many women have become ill because of their implants. No agency, no study has kept track of them. While questions continue to be raised abut the safety of breast implants, only the state of Maryland requires doctors to inform their patients of all the known risks and complications. It took five years to get that law passed.

---

Taken from evidentiary disks/BMS 28413. Misspelled names are as they appeared in the transcript.

traveling throughout the body" (Vanderford & Smith, p. 49). The contradictions surrounded and debilitated women as they sought information and help.

One powerful source of information about breast implants was the news media. As Vanderford and Smith (1996) report:

*Magazine and newspaper headlines read: "Time Bombs in Breasts;" "The Implant Panic;" "My Breast Implant Disaster;" and "The Silicone Scare." TV anchors introduced stories with "Another health risk for women . . . ;" "Another disturbing medical story . . . ;" and referred to the "dangers of silicone implants." Between December 1990 and July 1992, the print and electronic news media told a public story about silicone breast implants: the women who had them, the plastic surgeons who inserted them, the companies who made them, the government agency that regulated them, and the scientific community that tested their safety. (p. 111)*

While women reported that they received most of what they knew about breast implants from the media, doctors were concerned that by sensationalizing the issue, the media had created unwarranted fear and worry for women with breast implants (Vanderford & Smith).

Physicians indicated how important it was for women to gain information from medical experts rather than relying on the media (Vanderford & Smith, 1996). Interestingly, however, good rapport and communication seemed to play a major role in how satisfied women were with their breast implants and their physicians. One plastic surgeon, who only had one of his patients ask for implant removal, wrote to 200 patients, making it a point to talk with them when the controversy hit the media. In his view:

*[p]lastic surgeons, when this first started, should have immediately contacted all their patients and said, "Gosh, there's this controversy and I really don't know what the answer is, but I want you to know that I'm concerned about your health and I want you to come in and talk with me about that. I'm going to keep you up-to-date on everything that we know. If there seems to be any problem whatsoever, I'm going to take your implants out and I'm not going to charge you." If we had done that, we would have as our allies a million women with breast implants. (Vanderford & Smith, p. 95).*

Being up front about the confusion and controversy was especially critical for physicians on this issue because of how scientific information played out in the media.

Vanderford and Smith (1996) describe a wide range of lessons for communicating about health by focusing on which characteristics of this issue made it controversial. First, because we take appearance seriously and act as if breast size matters, breast implants, as a product with high social value, raise public controversy and media attention. Second, controversy was raised because published studies presented contradictory information about the risks and benefits of implants. Third, news reports tended to focus more on the risks, but they were not as good at putting these risks in perspective regarding the likelihood of occurrence. Finally, media reports often mixed known risks (ruptures, leakage, and hardening) with unknown risks (autoimmune diseases and cancer) in ways that often convinced the public that breast implants caused cancer—even though there is unanimous agreement that cancer is not a risk.

What the authors conclude is that arguing science in the public arena is difficult, often because the horror stories get the most time, characterizing "women as victims, plastic surgeons as villains, and drug companies as profit-hungry big businesses" (Vanderford & Smith, 1996, p. 199).There are women who have been silenced, however, because of the contradictory information about breast implants and because of the stigma and marginalization they might feel in trying to find an arena for their voices and their pain. The same can be said for men who are survivors of prostate cancer, as the next section reveals.

## COMMUNICATING MARGINALIZATION: THE SILENT VOICES OF PROSTATE CANCER SURVIVORS

And the doctor said
I can see you're hurt
Just by looking at you.
Pain we can help.
But for hurt
There's nothin' we can do

(Connick, 1994)

Stigma, contradiction, and marginalization are all part of the communicative experiences of men with prostate cancer. Cancer of the prostate (a walnut-sized gland located in the front of the rectum, just below the bladder) is a diagnosis given to more than 200,000 American men each year (Korda, 1997). While one of every eight men is expected to contract the disease (Irwin, 1995), 80 percent of cases occur in men over the age of 65 (Poussaint, 1997).

The forces surrounding the politics of prostate cancer relate to what is possible—and what is not possible—to talk about as a survivor. As a culture, we tend to silence talk of sex and sexuality, particularly those voices of the elderly, who are often stereotyped as being asexual. Because this disease links older men with the loss of "sexual function," survivors find themselves doubly marginalized and voiceless when it comes to talking about their experience with the disease. Read the quote in Theorizing Practice 4.4, and answer the questions that ask you to consider the interrelationship between communication, fear, masculinity, and prostate cancer.

Communication scholar Michael Arrington (2000a, 2000b, 2002) has researched the experience of patients with prostate cancer and their attempts to

## Masculinity and Prostate Cancer

Read the quote below, and answer the questions that follow.

> Prostate cancer is the biggest fear of most men. It carries with it not only the fear of dying, like all cancer, but fears that go to the very core of masculinity—for the treatment of prostate cancer, whatever form it takes, almost invariably carries with it well-known risks of incontinence [inability to restrain natural discharges] and impotence [inability to achieve an erection and orgasm] that strike directly at any man's self-image, pride, and enjoyment of life, and which by their very nature, tend to make men reticent on the subject. (Korda, 1997, pp. 3–4)

1. Why should men concern themselves with prostate cancer when it is unlikely to affect them at all and, if it does, most likely not until their sixties?

2. While many men fear and even avoid the prostate cancer screening, which involves a digital rectal examination, most women are encouraged to and often undergo an annual pelvic examination for cancer screening. Why do you think this gender difference often occurs?

3. Men who are diagnosed with prostate cancer may be placed in the position of choosing between living with impotence or dying. Assuming that you choose to live, how would you redefine your life to live it to its fullest?

recreate and confirm their identities in the face of communication that silences their voices. Arrington (2002) suggests that scholars have overlooked the illness narratives of older men who find themselves at a loss in facing the stigma and identity changes that inevitably come with this disease. In his words,

> [a]s the academic and medical communities remain incognizant and negligent of survivors' experiences, the men are left to depend on news and entertainment media for validation of their experiences. Men whose stories do not match the handful of celebrity stories and dramatic television portrayals might never learn how to combat the stigma of prostate cancer. (p. 43)

The interest that elderly men may have in communicating their experience with prostate cancer is often limited by a body politic that leads physicians, partners, spouses, and even survivors themselves to become fearful, embarrassed, or ashamed to ask questions, provide information, and seek answers.

> Ironically, the taboo against inquiring into the sexuality of the elderly has become a self-perpetuating cycle. Older people are not asked about their sexual

*activity in surveys because everybody "knows" they aren't sexually active any-more. Because nobody asks, nobody learns otherwise, hence the assumption is thought to be correct. Doctors contribute as well. Many do not ask their patients about sexual problems and functioning because they fear embarrassing them. By such an obvious omission, doctors perpetuate the embarrassment. Because older patients are not routinely asked, they are often ashamed to bring it up. (Bland, 1997, p. 148)*

Arrington (2000b) learned firsthand about men's experience of marginalization and silencing by researching Man-to-Man, "a branch of the national social support group in which men and their significant others can share their experiences of prostate cancer with each other and gather information about the disease" (p. 3).

After attending 20 monthly meetings over three years, Arrington (2000b) was surprised that men rarely discussed issues related to sex or sexuality. Yet on further analysis, he found that the structure of the meetings, rather than the men's interest in discussing sexual matters, may have done more to silence this form of talk. Meetings were led by physicians, whose focus was on medical talk rather than on personal issues, which in turn led members' talk in breakout groups to focus on treatment decisions. When a new breakout group was formed to focus on psychosocial issues regarding prostate cancer, however, and was led by a psychologist, not a physician, roughly two-thirds of the men's conversations centered on sexual issues.

Analysis of group discussions in Man-to-Man revealed that members contested and revised the definition of sex that they inferred from society at large (Arrington, 2000b). One prominent theme was that these discussions confirmed *and* challenged definitions of "real" sex as spontaneous actions involving penile-vaginal penetration—anything else being phony or incomplete. A second theme was how men "negotiate sexuality with their partners in a wide variety of ways, ranging from abstinence to redefining sexual intimacy to seeking other forms of intimacy altogether" (p. 16).

Arrington's (2000b) observations of Man-to-Man meetings led to several important conclusions about the political complexities of communication. First, men clearly have been acculturated to accept erection as the essence of their sexual function, satisfaction, and the only prerequisite for sexual activity. With the opportunity to share different points of view, however, the men talked in ways to redefine their lives as sexual, sensual beings. Second, the shift in facilitators from physicians to psychologists was significant in opening up a space to talk about sex and sexuality. In this sense, psychologists engaged in the art of making possible what appeared to most men as being impossible. This change lessened the **marginalization** of certain topics of discussion, creating the opportunity to talk about physiological pain, psychological hurt, and emotional issues in general. A third, related conclusion is that physicians and patients typically do not discuss sex, despite research confirming that 91 percent of patients are willing to answer such questions from doctors (Andriote, 1998). Physicians' authority and silence on sexual matters often lead patients to feel marginalized, oppressed, and in the dark concerning their fears and experiences with sexual dysfunction. Arrington (2000b) concludes his research by asking us to attend to what is not said as well as to what is said. Group members in Man-to-Man never spoke about death and, therefore, faced a metaphoric "wall" that prevented them from grieving publicly or becoming aware of their own mortality.

We conclude this chapter by discussing the paths we might take in our communication with one another to negotiate politics and transcend imbalances.

## COMMUNICATING TO NEGOTIATE POLITICS AND TRANSCEND IMBALANCES

Wherever the art of medicine is loved,
There also is love of humanity.

Hippocrates[1]

The politics of medicine and healing can be the arts of making possible what seemed impossible *and* of making impossible what seemed possible. It is also more than that, however. Communication is central to the politics of negotiating identities, interests, and issues in ways that transcend stigma, contradictions, and marginalization. We need to consider the directions in which we are moving and continue to answer questions such as:

- What are we trying to make possible through our communication?

- Whose interests are at stake?

- What authorities must be challenged?

- What or who makes impossible what we thought was possible?

A significant key to answering these questions lies in the knowledge and understanding we can gain by seeking out and incorporating diverse forms of knowledge into our understandings of health and illness. Learning more about how the needs and interests of people may differ based on their race, culture, gender, sexual orientation, and age is a step in the right direction. In the *Handbook of Gender, Culture, and*

---

[1]Mencken, H. L. (Ed.). (1942). *A new dictionary of quotations on historical principles from ancient and modern sources* (p. 774). New York: Alfred A. Knopf.

*Health,* Eisler and Hersen (2000) suggest that the quality and effectiveness of disease prevention and health promotion depend on our understanding how "gender, ethnicity, age, and sexual orientation are related to health practices and outcomes" (p. ix). They cite several examples to illustrate the significance of this knowledge:

> [W]omen, more than men, appear more vulnerable to depression, eating disorders, and sexual abuse. Men are more likely than women to show high cardiovascular reactivity to stress and suffer more coronary artery disease, and Black men suffer from more cardiovascular disease and hypertension than White men. Cultural homophobia can cause gay men and lesbians to receive lower quality health care than other groups. Native Americans have very high rates of diabetes due to the prevalence of obesity and high fat diets. (p. ix)

Moving in this direction means researching and understanding how to address the various needs of diverse peoples as well as identifying the interests of social, cultural, political, economic, and institutional structures or stakeholders that may marginalize, discriminate against, restrict access, and/or fail to reach populations of people.

The book *Communication and Disenfranchisement* (Ray, 1996b) reveals how our interactions with family, friends, institutions, and messages from mass media influence our beliefs about acceptable identities, behaviors, topics of discussion, and expectations about who fits in, who controls resources, who makes decisions, and who sets the standards (p. xvi). At the same time our communication leads us to see people in situations different from our own as "others," we must recognize that

> [w]ith the roll of the die, with great abruptness, anyone can become "them". . . . We may find, after deciding to have children, that we are infertile. We may become suddenly homeless after leaving an abusive marriage, getting laid off, or working at a minimum wage job that does not cover our basic needs. We may find ourselves becoming suddenly disabled, diagnosed with HIV or AIDS, our child may contract cancer, or we may be diagnosed as terminally ill . . . It may happen to us or to someone we care about. (pp. xv-xvi)

The knowledge gained from this research moves us to see more clearly the politics of emotional and physical isolation, the magnitude of negative personal and societal messages, and the perpetuation of disenfranchisement and marginalization through communication. In addition, we gain an understanding of the power of communication to include, to empower, and to advocate for those persons and groups whose health care needs have not been considered or addressed. One such group is persons with disabilities who, through their own voices and experiences, provide knowledge about the obstacles they face—physically, emotionally, and legally—to make possible what others assume is impossible (Braithwaite & Thompson, 2000). Another such group is the elderly, who for a host of social, cultural, economic, psychological, and physiological reasons "are forced to adapt to what can be a cruel and unforgiving environment" (Nussbaum, Pecchioni, Robinson, & Thompson, 2000, p. xviii).

In addition, researchers and practitioners are insisting that more attention be paid to women's health care needs. The essays collected by Bayne-Smith (1996) take a comprehensive look at the health issues confronting women of color, and they help us to see how a woman's poor health often is the result of her environmental conditions of living, of the level and quality of her education, and of the norms that govern the gender roles by which she must abide. Similarly, Dan's (1994) collection of essays helps us to see how the erosion of women's access to food, shelter, occupation, and education results in the deterioration of their health. Finally, chapters in Parrott and Condit (1996) help us to evaluate women's health issues, identifying consistencies, inconsistencies, and highlighting gaps in research and our understanding of the messages communicated to women.

We must also incorporate technical and social knowledge with biological knowledge into our understanding of health and illness. One such example is the use of interactive technology to promote health (Rice & Katz, 2001; Street, Gold, & Manning, 1997). Interactive technology is

> computer-based media that enable users to access information and services of interest, control how the information is presented, and respond to information and messages in the mediated environment (e.g., answer questions, send a message, take action in a game, receive feedback or a response to previous actions). (Street & Rimal, 1997, p. 2)

While traditional media, such as brochures, videotapes, telephones, public service announcements, and professional consultations, are vital, interactive technologies allow messages to be individualized to meet personal as well as social needs. They also offer opportunities for individuals to become proactive, to make choices, to emphasize preventive care and wellness, and to access unlimited information, often from wherever they have access to a computer (Street et al., 1997, p. xii).

At the same time, we must consider the consequences of the Internet on health care. Communication researchers Ronald Rice and James Katz (2001) provide a collection of articles that explore peoples' experiences and expectations for the Internet and health communication. They discuss a variety of topics, including the quality of health information available via the Internet, the experience of online health communities, and policy, access, and privacy issues in using the Internet for heath care and communication. In the preface to that book, Steven Schroeder, M.D., who is also president of the Robert Wood Johnson Foundation, writes of the special burdens and questions raised by use of the Internet for health communication. One of the questions reveals how we have now made possible what we once thought impossible, but what are the consequences?

> [I]t is possible to transmit right from the home bedside to health center amazingly clear, live pictures of data from monitoring equipment and immediately bring back to the patient and family the voice and face of the health professional many miles away. But, what is the loss to the patient in terms of human contact? How do these gains and losses balance out? How acceptable are high-tech communications approaches to the elderly? The confused? How do we collect and disseminate best practices? (p. x)

As Rice and Katz confirm, communication technology must fulfill a need, but it must do so in a way that is "compatible with the predispositions, needs, and values of humans," including the "cultural and normative contexts of particular subgroups of society" (pp. 1–2).

The knowledge we gain from analyzing and understanding the political complexities of communication and health should move us to change policy. Personal stories can raise social awareness, de-stigmatize disease, celebrate survivors, commemorate the dead, *and* inspire or affect policy decisions (Sharf, 2000). Sharf's research on breast cancer demonstrates how survivors' biographies and narratives can become visionary, a catalyst to reform and political motivation. She cautions us, however, that "stories can make bad policy" if they become the only criteria we use for changing health policy. Rather, she recommends that recipients of illness stories, such as lawmakers and the general public, consider the following:

> In Aristotelian terms, the force of illness narratives is derived from pathos (emotional proofs) and ethos (character-related proofs). In order to use personal narratives as a means of affecting health policy, there remains the challenge to effectively combine stories with the other form of rhetorical proof, logos (logic, the rational). (p. 9)

Together, these forms of proof are integral to advocacy, and they help us to move forward in negotiating politics and transcending imbalances.

Finally, with these additional forms of knowledge, we can focus more on caring and stories along with curing. Associate professor of Medicine and Psychiatry at the University of Rochester, Anthony Suchman, M.D. (2000), talks about how the "thinness" of the traditional medical perspective, with its predominant focus on the physical dimension, creates physicians who are incapable of appreciating and responding to the patient's experience. Instead, he emphasizes the importance of communication in the patient-clinician relationship that requires physicians to let go of control and to focus on "being with" rather than on "directing." Physician Brian Campbell Broom (2000) agrees, stating that physicians have been trained to attach a diagnostic label to a patient's story and to focus on what the patient's story has in common with those of other people having the same diagnosis. Instead, physicians need to invite the patient's story to emerge through questions like, "Imagine for a moment that your illness (or symptom) is a communication from some deeper and wiser part of you. If this illness was a voice, what might it be saying?" (Suchman, p. 194). Communication is central to the art of medicine, and it is only through active participation and dialogue that providers and patients can learn what interests are at stake—and how to make possible what seems impossible.

## SUMMARY

Clearly, the political complexities of communicating medicine and healing focus both on making possible what seemed impossible and making impossible what seemed possible. Controversy, inequities, marginalization, stigma, power, privilege, and hope imbue and amplify the political complexities of communicating health and illness of any kind. Politics can be traced through the medical profession, both historically and currently, as patients and providers negotiate to address, transcend, and at times, maintain inequities. Stigma, contradiction, and controversy surround almost every illness or health topic, including syphilis, breast implants, and prostate cancer. Communication becomes both a source of information and a medium for reaching the wide range of stakeholders who have much to gain—and to lose—as the political complexities of medicine and healing play out.

## KEY TERMS

| | | |
|---|---|---|
| practical politics | writing the body | public moral argument |
| stakeholders | social authority | stigma |
| politics | cultural authority | privilege |
| power | contradiction | signification |
| bio-power | rhetoric | marginalization |
| body politic | progressive ideology | |

## DISCUSSION QUESTIONS

1. What sources have you relied on for knowledge about marijuana? What stakes or interests do these sources represent?

2. Can you identify a specific incident when you felt or witnessed the "body politic" in your experience as a patient? If so, describe it.

3. Have you noticed anything about the medical professions that makes them seem more business-centered than patient-centered?

4. If you had unlimited time to speak with your personal physician, what would you talk about?

5. Can you think of a moral or ethical dilemma that is raised by our use of technology in health settings?

6. Do you believe that technology has had a negative impact on communication in health settings?

## INFOTRAC COLLEGE EDITION

1. There are 191 citations for the key word search *politics of health*. Briefly review what you find, and summarize five key themes in this body of literature. In other words, what seems to be at issue? Then pick one of these themes and briefly summarize what the articles offer about addressing the issue. Consider what other key terms might offer sources related to negotiating the politics of medicine and healing.

2. In Charles Marwick's 2000 article, "New Center Director States 'Complementary' Agenda," we learn about the National Center for Complementary and Alternative Medicine, which has begun funding clinical trials of several alternative medicine treatments. What do you learn about the Center in this article? What surprised you about the Center? How would you describe the agenda the Center has set? From your own experience with alternative medicines, what could be added to this agenda? What else do you learn about alternative and complementary medicine from the other 55 citations on this topic?

# 5

## Beginning Life Passages

### The Sacred Birth

From the elation of three pregnancies and the devastation of three miscarriages I learned a great deal about what it means to feel silenced, both by others and by myself. I told everyone about the first pregnancy and felt numbed by the miscarriage. I wanted to talk about the baby—the name we picked out, the due date, how our life would have changed, and the devastation of our loss. But, no one let me tell my story; they summed it all up and closed the conversation by saying "lots of people have miscarriages" and "not to worry," that I would "get pregnant again." I told even fewer people about the second pregnancy, and then had to suffer the pain of telling close friends about the loss of a baby they didn't even know I had been carrying. By the third pregnancy, I was silent, hesitating to tell even my husband. To this day, many do not know of the third loss.

But the fourth was different. By then, I knew I had to stop being afraid to enjoy and share the excitement of my pregnancy, even if it ultimately meant the pain of having to share another loss. My friend Cristina told me that the number four is sacred—the four directions, the four seasons, and the four elements. I knew the fourth baby would live. I resisted the pressure I felt to silence my joy. I spread the word about the pregnancy—the baby was so very real. And so with gusto, my husband, J.C., and I prepared for the birth. We began attending a 12-week natural childbirth preparation course called the Bradley Way that encourages having an additional birthpartner for support. After agreeing that was what we wanted, we invited our friend and visualization guide, Linda, to join us in the miracle of our birthing journey. Together we began to learn about the process of birthing and what kinds of support are needed to manage the pain naturally. We learned about breathing, birthing positions, visualization, and stages—about the importance of walking, talking, and resisting the often unnecessary medical interventions that were sure to be recommended.

Our baby was due May 15, 1993, but my water broke March 29, 1993—six weeks early—a surprise to say the least. It was 3:00 a.m. and even though it might have been smarter to stay home until labor commenced, we couldn't stay home and contain our excitement. As nervous, first-time parents we grabbed our amazingly prepacked suitcase, checked into the hospital by 3:15 a.m., and called our close friend Linda right away. I was only three centimeters dilated, so I knew I had a long way to go to get to ten. We were moved to a birthing suite but everyone soon realized that my labor was NOT beginning. And the pressure began.

First was the pressure to have IV (intravenous) antibiotics. A nurse used scare tactics, telling us "the baby might die" if we resisted. But we knew from our research that the odds of that happening were small at this stage of delivery. We also knew that being immobilized by an IV would slow up the labor. We chose oral antibiotics and kept walking, walking, walking.

Next, I received a lot of pressure to take Pitocin, a drug to induce labor. Again, I resisted being immobilized by an IV and the unpredictability of an unnatural labor. We chose to wait and continue our walking, walking, walking. Ultimately, it was the natural methods of walking and using guided visualization that got the labor underway.

I ended up spending that night in the hospital. All three of us squished together on my single bed to watch the Academy Awards. Afterward, J.C. went home to get some rest for the big event and Linda stayed with me and began a guided visualization. She asked me for a focus for the visualization she would construct, and I told her about one of my favorite beaches in Hawaii, Lanikai (which means "heavenly water" in the Hawaiian language). So at 11:00 at night, with me comfortably tucked in my bed, Linda massaged my feet and described an incredibly relaxing and warming visualization that I believe helped induce labor and that returned to my consciousness time and time again during the hardest of labor contractions. By 3:30 a.m. (just four-and-a-half hours later) my labor began. It felt at first like severe cramps on one of the hardest menstrual cycle days imaginable.

Throughout the four-hour laboring process, I was pressured to stay confined to the bed for continuous monitoring of the baby's heart. To resist being immobilized by the lap belt monitor, we chose intermittent monitoring for five minutes at a time to assure us the baby's heartbeat was normal and kept up our walking, walking, walking.

We worked together beautifully as a team, envisioning, creating, and experiencing natural birthing at its best—soft lights, soothing music, and encouraging melodic voices. We allowed our informed resistance to unfold into strength, support, and spirit. Our baby, Makenna May, was born, 4 pounds 10 ounces, beautiful and healthy at 7:59 a.m. on March 30, 1993.

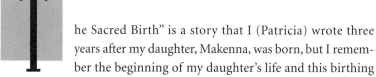

"The Sacred Birth" is a story that I (Patricia) wrote three years after my daughter, Makenna, was born, but I remember the beginning of my daughter's life and this birthing life passage as if it occurred yesterday. It truly was a fateful moment that changed our lives in powerfully moving ways.

The story represents one very significant beginning life passage—one that can be **life-affirming, life-challenging,** and **life-adjusting.** The communication surrounding pregnancy and birth can be life-affirming in that people talk about the anticipation of this new being and engage in a series of rituals and interactions with family, friends, and health professionals, all welcoming the child into this life. At the same time, even though we anticipate a positive outcome—a healthy baby and a healthy mother—pregnancy and anticipation of the birth can represent a life-challenging passage. Family, friends, even strangers may communicate "horror stories" of labor or traumas during infancy that make us consider what could go wrong. In some cases, interactions with health professionals during prenatal care, prenatal testing, and birthing may introduce information that "questions" the health of the baby or the mother. Pregnancy and birthing can be life-adjusting as people face the dilemmas of adapting to first-time parenthood or question what it takes to balance the needs of other children they may have. Yet for some people, communication may center on a multitude of other dilemmas, such as unplanned or unwanted pregnancies, abortion or adoption, giving birth to a disabled child, health complications during or after birth, and even a child's death, either at birth or during infancy. Communication surrounding these life passages is often complicated by the "loss of words" that people feel, not knowing the best way to support, guide, or comfort their friends and family. Pregnancy and the anticipated birth of a child is a *complex* beginning life passage that can be welcomed joyously, tentatively—or even fearfully. The communication surrounding this life-changing event can be positive or negative, affirming or threatening, but always complicated if the individuals involved feel very differently about the change.

Importantly, birth can be characterized as similar to a multitude of other beginning life passages that are also life-affirming, life-challenging, or life-adjusting. Both women and men face complicated issues concerning birth control, unwanted or unplanned pregnancy, miscarriage, infertility, or the dilemmas surrounding the birth of a disabled child. Beginning life passages are punctuated by communication with others about health care needs—our own, our families, our partners, and our friends—as we make decisions about having children, pursuing pregnancy after miscarriage, or the needs of any child we bring into our lives through birth or adoption. Understanding these life passages means recognizing how the messages surrounding these events, including the narratives that we ourselves construct during the passage, can lead us to affirm, challenge, and adjust our identities.

The communication surrounding children during their early, formative years is yet another series of beginning life passages. Such communication includes the resources and expertise that we seek and rely on to ensure a child's health, to prevent illness, and to promote the natural processes of growth and change that are central to each child's life experiences (for example, nutrition, safety, puberty, and menstruation). Beginning life passages draw our attention to the inevitable changes in communication and relationships as families and health care providers move through these affirmations, challenges, and adjustments.

Traveling through a beginning life passage significantly impacts our identities and how we communicate. We may feel that our identities are strengthened, questioned, celebrated, divided, solidified, or even transformed. We may find ourselves resisting identities imposed on us by others. For example, teenage mothers or fathers may communicate to celebrate their parenthood and resist the stigma associated with being teen parents. Women may communicate in ways to resist being defined only as a mother when they would like to celebrate many other aspects of their identities. A man, woman, or couple who decide not have a child often communicate in ways to resist the notion that they will remain unfulfilled if they do not become parents. Too often, people in our society communicate in ways that marginalize men and women who choose not to have children (Geist, Gray, Avalos-C'de Baca, & Hill, 1996).

These passages are times when we find ourselves being offered, offering, needing, or seeking health care services. Communicating during beginning life passages clearly raises personal complexities, especially when talking with others about birth stories, caring for children in health and illness, dealing with loss through miscarriage or the death of a child, living with infertility and its treatments, and seeking support for both celebrating life and mourning loss. Political complexities emerge as providers communicate contrasting views about diagnosis, treatment, and choices for caring and curing. Cultural complexities enter our communication when we consider how the five levels of the Cultural Sensitivity Model (see Chapter 3) play a role as individuals, families, friends, and providers communicate with us. As we face this broad range of complexities, we communicate to clarify health care needs, to soothe the pain that we may suffer, and to describe the joy or sadness that we feel as we face our changing bodies and lives. Inevitably, every beginning life passage is, simultaneously, an ending life passage, with all the accompanying transformations, ambiguities, and discoveries (for example, childless to parenthood, childhood to puberty, or menarche to menopause).

This chapter discusses a few of the beginning life passages by organizing them into three sections based on the central focus of communication and identity in each: (a) life-affirming, (b) life-challenging, or (c) life-adjusting. Inevitably, we touch on the personal, political, and cultural complexities of communicating health through each journey. We begin with the "Life-Affirming Passages: Communicating Through Pregnancy and Birth," then move to "Life-Challenging Passages: Communicating Through Miscarriage and Infertility." Finally, we consider "Life-Adjusting Passages: Communicating in Parenting a Disabled Child." (In Chapter 6, we move to "Formative Life Passages," discussing a few of the many experiences that can be part of adolescents' life experiences.)

## LIFE-AFFIRMING PASSAGES: COMMUNICATING THROUGH PREGNANCY AND BIRTH

*Birth stories are everywhere and nowhere. Seen in every movie theater but only heard in brief gasps of attention in grocery store lines or parking lots, inculcated in prenatal classrooms but shamed to the edges of conversation, birth stories permeate and haunt our everyday lives. . . . They rehearse the body politics at the heart of debates over reproductive technologies, genetic engineering, abortion rights, welfare reform, and custody law, signifying a contest of control over the meaning and value of giving birth of which they are, in turn, a vital part.*

(Pollack, 1999, p. 1)

Over the course of our lives we—or someone we know—will begin or face the journey of bringing a new human being into this world. This is a very complicated, painful, joyful, and confusing journey. A beginning life passage is necessarily a communicative process that, for most, is also a life-affirming passage. From the moment a woman tells just one other person she is pregnant, a man learns that he has helped to conceive a child, or a child is born, a journey of communicating health and identity begins. When pregnancy ends, never occurs, or results in the birth of a disabled child, or when a child dies early in life, our identities are challenged and powerfully impacted by the elations and devastations of these passages. As life goes on, the initial impact and communication surrounding these challenges wanes, becoming "background" to the other issues and events that occupy us.

Pregnancy and birth, while everyday occurrences, are also extraordinary experiences—personally, culturally, and politically. The personal experience of pregnancy and birth can vary dramatically depending on a woman's age, family support, marital status, cultural heritage, economic status, and even health insurance coverage. Cultural beliefs and practices regarding pregnancy and birth coincide and collide in hospitals, where most births in the United States occur. Without a doubt, politics abound regarding pregnancy, genetic testing, prenatal care, birthing practices, abortion rights, adoption, paternity, custody, and a range of other related issues.

Interestingly, the focus of communication changes during the course of this life passage. In many cases, the focus of talk during pregnancy is on the pregnancy. Once the child is born, the talk shifts to all the activities and behaviors of the child. It is not difficult to imagine a new mother or father talking for hours about little Jenny or Scotty—their cute looks, movements, sounds, and accomplishments. Many parents of newborns completely identify when another parent describes the sound of a baby's bowel movement as "an espresso machine." In some cases, however, friends who are childless, infertile, have older children, or are just not as interested in the topic of babies may find these conversations difficult, painful, or simply uninteresting. As a result, relationships often undergo a transition in that friends have less in common to talk about, spend less time together, and form new networks of friends who share their current interests.

The communication surrounding pregnancy can be joyous, complex, tentative, and in some cases, frightening. Consider the range of women who may discover today that they are pregnant: a teenager, a college student, a lesbian, a woman who just adopted an infant, a woman living in a shelter with her two other children, a woman with no health insurance, a woman who has experienced four miscarriages, a woman who has newly immigrated to this country, or one who has chosen single motherhood. Now consider who she will tell first about the pregnancy—if anyone. Consider too what makes communicating about each of these pregnancies different for each of these women.

Communication researcher Lisa Gates (1995, 1997) focuses her research on the birth stories that women tell and what these stories reveal about the communicative issues surrounding pregnancy and birthing. Writing about her own experiences with birthing and what she learns from interviewing other women about their stories, she discovers that

> [t]ales of childbirth, like male "war stories," stay with women their entire lives. Birth is not a discrete process beginning with the onset of labor and ending with the delivery of a baby. . . . My first birth involved numerous interventions: narcotic drugs, an epidural, an internal fetal monitor, an ultimate cesarean section, and more pain medication after birth. To this day, I still ask myself why I didn't say no to the proffered medication, and why I didn't request a longer trial of labor. . . . In this essay, I recount my own experiences along with the voices of other women to provide views of natural childbirth, why we want to do it, how we feel about our birthing experiences, and how we believe others see us based on our "radical" views. As I, and the other participants reveal, the desire to birth naturally is about women's efforts to reconnect heart, body, and soul as we make the transition into motherhood. (Gates, 1997, p. 187)

Akin to her own experience, the stories that Gates provides in her research indicate how many women, along with family and friends, communicate in ways to affirm their identities, dignity, and control over one of the most profound experiences of their lives (see FYI 5.1).

All the language or rhetoric surrounding pregnancy and birthing can be overwhelming. Information from medical professionals, birthing classes, friends, family, talk shows, and magazines may vary or even be contradictory. Because the complex communication during this beginning life passage is

> both a public event and a private experience, positioned at the interface between the biological and the social, the production of a coherent and continuous narrative may be difficult for a new mother to maintain. At times, she may feel that she has literally lost the plot of her story. . . . Some women may find that their experiences do not fit with their own or others' expectations. (Miller, 2000, pp. 321–322)

The **rhetoric** of this beginning life passage includes the symbols, metaphors, and language that shape what we "know" about pregnancy, childbirth, and the choices about health and care of a newborn. Information and views about this life passage are not transparent facts that are "out there" (Cheney, 1999); they are socially constructed through history and current practices. Pregnancy and childbearing, though intensely private life events, become a publicly defined **rhetorical situation** (Bitzer, 1968; Foss, 1989; Sharf, 1990) in which a diversity of information and

I (Eileen) was about five months pregnant with my first child. I was visiting my mother-in-law for the weekend and a neighbor, Marge, dropped by. Within 10 minutes, she, through no inquiry by myself or anyone else, began talking about her pregnancy with her first child (who was now in his forties). She began with conception, carefully detailed every month, included gory details of the delivery, and had little good to say about the experience. This took about 40 minutes. I tried to keep my eyes from glazing over, but it was hard. Just when I thought it was safe, she launched into her second pregnancy. Now I was getting worried; she had four kids. I was not interested in a blow-by-blow description of any of her children, nor did I want to hear her negative commentary. Frankly, I didn't care. Maybe that sounds selfish, but it's honest. I didn't care about her pregnancies, I didn't care about her deliveries, I didn't care about her complaints. If I had cared, I would have asked her. Interestingly, she never asked about my pregnancy or plans for the baby. She wasn't the first person to volunteer her "war" stories, and she wasn't the last. But this experience reinforced two things for me: First, if I see Marge walking up toward the door, head out the back way; and second, never assume that everyone wants to hear about my pregnancy or, later, everything my baby says or does. And if I act like they do, I will probably lose friends.

opinions are communicated to expectant mothers or parents about every aspect of this transition. In some cases, as revealed in FYI 5.1, the "war story" is told regardless of whether the expectant mother wants to hear it. The stories that anyone tells or the views they hold about birthing reveal much about their position, what they would like others to believe, and how critical their story is to their own identity (as a medical professional, mother, father, or family member). Remembering this allows us to see the rhetoric of birthing not only as communication designed to persuade but also as an invitation to dialogue with persons whose views may differ from our own and, thus, to create new meanings, practices, and discoveries about this beginning life passage (Foss & Griffin, 1995).

In the next section, we examine the rhetoric of birthing so that you may become aware of the diverse and, at times, competing views and prepare yourself to become a critical consumer of information when you or someone you know becomes an expectant parent.

## ◼ The Rhetoric of Birthing

This section explores the **rhetoric of birthing**. First, we take a brief historical look at birthing to see how this rhetoric includes three layers of stories that explain the event: (a) metanarratives (the culturally embedded expectations), (b) public narratives (medically, professionally, politically, and publicly defined), and (c) individual narratives (lay, informal, or personal) (Miller, 2000; Somers, 1994). We see too how a shift occurred when birthing moved out of the context of the home, with communication centered around the family and the event of birth, and into the context of the hospital, where communication centered more on the woman's body and the technologies needed to facilitate birth.

This history reveals how a life-affirming, mostly natural experience has been transformed into a pathology-based, medicalized problem that is tightly controlled by biotechnology. Although we must acknowledge how this shift has significantly reduced infant mortality rates and helped to save the lives of newborns who would otherwise have died, we should also consider how the transformation of this "natural event into a pathological illness model has repercussions for the ways in which women experience and make sense of the event" (Miller, 2000, p. 309). More importantly, this history is an invitation to consider the personal, cultural, and political complexities that are part of the context of birthing today. In this way, if and when the time comes for you to consider the kind of birthing experience that you would like to have, you will be in a better position to make an informed choice.

History plays a powerful role in the questions that are asked and the answers that are provided about pregnancy and birthing. History guides the development of norms and expectations, underlies the origin of rules within organizations, and suggests appropriate governmental interventions and policies (Parrott & Condit, 1996, p. 77). Without considering this history, people often are unaware of the options, issues, and opportunities that are not talked about as part of a hospital's standard operating procedures. Women and their families do have choices in how they compose and communicate throughout their pregnancy and birthing experiences. Narratives speak to these choices and represent consideration and dialogue about the wide array of decisions and varied viewpoints that are expressed in meta, public, and individual narratives.

Following this brief history, we discuss some of the choices surrounding birthing that women and their partners may consider. We explore the messages that people receive about these options and how their choices can be life-affirming regardless of whether they communicate in ways that embrace or resist the recommendations of the medical community—or other communities—involved in birth education. When you read about these choices, realize how often information is not available to pregnant women and their families, and you may then begin to understand why researchers believe not enough attention has been paid to the type and quality of messages that women receive about their reproductive health (Parrott & Condit, 1996).

## ▉ A Brief History of Birthing

A historical look at birthing in the United States reveals that in the eighteenth century, before the modern obstetric era, childbirth occurred at home. Neither health care providers nor pregnant women considered pregnancy and birth as a medical phenomenon that needed routine supervision (Oakely, 1984). Judith Goldsmith (1990), in *Childbirth Wisdom: From the World's Oldest Societies,* offers insight drawn from birthing traditions and practices around the world. In the preface to her book, she describes her exploration into prehospital, natural births:

> *I did not start out to compare traditional childbirth methods with modern. Like most readers of this book, I thought we were only too lucky to have entered the era of technologically-aided birthgiving. I hoped only that we "moderns" might be able to learn a few more interesting hints from our tribal sisters. But as I researched, I found quite the opposite to be true. In fact, women in traditional cultures were often wiser in their childbirthing and childcare customs: their practices aided the woman's and the child's bodies in their tasks rather than hindering them. For the most part natural processes were allowed to take their normal—and generally successful—course; interference was kept at a minimum. Simple techniques, which allowed the mother's body to perform without hindrance, helped as much or more than our highly technologized hospitals and medical specialties. (pp. xiv–xv)*

The wisdom gathered from other cultures and times has direct implications for communication. Up until the moment of birth, women continued to work and to interact, actually seeking out additional physical activity for the express purpose of stimulating labor. Although mothers gave birth without assistance, actually catching the baby themselves and holding it immediately, other women and children were present to offer encouragement as they walked and moved in ways that allowed gravity to facilitate labor, never lying on their backs as many women do in our Western culture. "Nowhere in the tribal world did a woman give birth among strangers. She carried out this intimate act among relatives and friends whom she knew well and trusted" (p. 25). We learn too that birth should not be a time of stress or abrupt change; that in most cultures, labor is relatively short (two or three hours) and generally very easy: "the mothers at no time showed signs of pain beyond acute discomfort. They groaned softly and perspired freely but seemed on the whole to give birth without difficulty" (p. 22).

A similar depiction of birth is offered by Fadiman (1997), when she describes what the birth of Lia Lee (recall from Chapter 3 the experiences of the Lee family) would have been like even today if she had been born in the highlands of northwest Laos, like her parents and 12 of her brothers and sisters:

*[H]er mother would have squatted on the floor of the house that her father had built from ax-hewn planks thatched with bamboo and grass. The floor was dirt, but it was clean. Her mother, Foua, sprinkled it regularly with water to keep the dust down and swept it every morning and evening with a broom she had made of grass and bark. She used a bamboo dustpan, which she had also made herself, to collect the feces of the children who were too young to defecate outside, and emptied its contents in the forest. Even if Foua had been a less fastidious housekeeper, her newborn babies wouldn't have gotten dirty, since she never let them actually touch the floor. She remains proud to this day that she delivered each of them into her own hands, reaching between her legs to ease out the head and then letting the rest of the body slip out onto her bent forearms. No birth attendant was present, though if her throat became dry during labor, her husband, Nao Kao, was permitted to bring her a cup of hot water, as long as he averted his eyes from her body. Because Foua believed that moaning or screaming would thwart the birth, she labored in silence, with the exception of an occasional prayer to her ancestors. She was so quiet that although most of her babies were born at night, her older children slept undisturbed on a communal bamboo pallet a few feet away, and woke only when they heard the cry of their new brother or sister. After each birth, Nao Kao cut the umbilical cord with heated scissors and tied it with string. Then Foua washed the baby with water she had carried from the stream, usually in the early phases of labor, in a wooden and bamboo pack-barrel strapped to her back. (pp. 3–4)*

After the Lees immigrated to the United States in the early 1980s, however, Foua instead gave birth to Lia "lying on her back on a steel table, her body covered with sterile drapes, her genital area painted with a brown Betadine solution, with a high wattage lamp trained on her perineum. There were no family members in the room" (p. 6). She did not experience the intimacy with her husband or with her newborn infant as she had back home in Laos.

Why would the experience of pain be so different in these traditional births versus those in modern hospitals? Rothman (1991) suggests that the medical management of birth actually contributes to the pain that is experienced in birthing, and that the reasons relate to communication:

*[First,] the lack of emotional support and the simple lack of distraction play a large part in the experience of pain. Before the pressures of the prepared-childbirth movement brought husbands into the labor room, laboring women were routinely left alone. Their only companionship might have been another laboring woman on the other side of a curtain. For many women, this is still the situation. A nurse will stop in now and again, but for hour upon hour the woman lies alone, with no one to comfort her, hold her hand, rub her back, or just talk to her, and nothing to do to take her mind off her pain. . . . Second, the physical management of birth in*

*hospitals may make it more painful. Confinement to bed prolongs labor, and the comparatively inefficient contractions in the horizontal position may make it more painful. When a woman is upright, each contraction presses the baby down against her cervix, opening up the birth passage. When she is lying down, the weight of the baby presses on the mother's spine, accomplishing nothing except to increase her discomfort. (pp. 80–81)*

Again, we see the significance of what is absent—communication. The emotional support provided through touch (the holding of her hand, the massaging of her neck or back) and talk (about anything) helps her to move through the pain.

Fifty years ago, the English obstetrician Grantly Dick Read (1944) called attention to the socioemotional context of birth:

*Civilization and culture have brought influences to bear upon the minds of women which have introduced justifiable fears and anxieties concerning labor. The more cultured the races of the earth have become, so much the more dogmatic have they been in pronouncing childbirth to be a painful and dangerous ordeal. This fear and anticipation have given rise to natural protective tensions in the body, and such tensions are not of the mind only, for the mechanisms of protective action by the body includes muscle tension. Unfortunately the natural tension produced by fear influences those muscles which close the womb and prevent the child from being driven out during childbirth. Therefore, fear inhibits; that is to say, gives rise to resistance at the outlet of the womb, when in the normal state those muscles should be relaxed and free from tension. Such resistance and tension give rise to real pain, because the uterus is supplied with organs which record pain set up by excessive tension. Therefore fear, pain, and tension are the three evils which are not normal to the natural design, but which have been introduced in the course of civilization by the ignorance of those who have been concerned with attendance at childbirth. If pain, fear, and tension go hand in hand, then it must be necessary to relieve tension and to overcome fear in order to eliminate pain. (pp. 5–6)*

Read captures the complex and often competing forces of nature and culture that he and others believe can be resolved through interaction, not through the "enforced isolation" that so many women experience. The "evils" of fear, pain, and tension imposed by cultural influences can be resisted through interaction between the birthing woman and the attendants or family members—communication is what reduces or eliminates fear.

The early beginnings of the personal, cultural, and political complexities surrounding pregnancy and birthing are captured in a wide array of books. One in particular, Ann Oakley's (1984) *The Captured Womb: A History of the Medical Care of Pregnant Women,* chronicles the gradual change in views about childbearing during the past 80 years. In the nineteenth century and before, communication with pregnant women focused on lifestyle advice and, for those who could afford it, monitoring of abdominal palpitation. By 1940, however, 50 percent of women gave birth in hospitals, and today, 97 percent to 99 percent give birth in hospitals (Nelson, 1996).

Why did this dramatic shift occur in birthing contexts? Why did women move from the natural setting of the home, attended by midwives and female relatives, to the more sterile setting of the hospital, attended by obstetricians and nurses? Included in the many reasons would be: (a) convenience, (b) insurance coverage, (c) the control of the American Medical Association over licensing of and practicing midwives, (d) the American faith in the "expert," and (e) women's desire to do what they are told is right for their babies (Sterk, 1996).

As early as the 1950s, the **natural childbirth** movement developed to resist the medicalization of childbirth and led some women to choose home births or birthing centers staffed by midwives, where they felt more in control over their lives and the circumstances of birthing and could more easily communicate their preferences for the birthing experience (Rothman, 1991). Natural childbirth is typically defined as an approach to birthing that is nontechnological (no drugs, no technological monitoring of the baby, no episiotomy), supportive (others comforting her, holding her hand, rubbing her back, talking to her to move through the pain), and affirming (the woman has more responsibility, autonomy, and control). (For definitions of terminology related to birthing, see FYI 5.2.)

Rothman (1991) provides a thorough history of maternity care and suggests that attempts to reform the medical management of childbirth came from diverse sources. In addition to Read (1944), another obstetrician, Ferdinand Lamaze (1956) of France, recommended childbirth education classes for women and their husbands to learn the mechanisms of labor, breathing, and relaxation. Obstetrician Robert Bradley (1975) developed a comprehensive program called "husband-coached childbirth," wherein he insists that medication of any kind is harmful to the laboring mother and the baby and minimizes the exhilaration of birth.[1] His program focuses on the entire nine months of pregnancy, with exercises to build the muscles needed in labor, diet recommendations, abdominal breathing, relaxation and visualization techniques, and recommended birth positions for effective breathing and pushing out the baby. La Leche League offers education on breastfeeding and the bond between mother and child. Frederick Leboyer (1975)

---

[1]Bradley's husband-coached childbirth has been criticized for denying the coach's (husbands or partners) personal experience and, instead, asking the coach to be the expert. In addition, some object to the emphasis on the sports metaphor (personal communication with Paaige Turner, communication scholar, November 30, 2000).

focused on the care that the newborn receives in the hospital. All these contributors to the natural childbirth movement offer a natural, holistic (biological, psychological, social, and spiritual), and interactional view of childbirth that differs from the typical obstetric education, which most often emphasizes a modern, technological, and disease-oriented view of birthing.

Today, although childbearing is defined as a pathology to be controlled and monitored by the profession of obstetrics, including prenatal testing, fetal monitoring, and sedation during labor (Goldsmith, 1990; Martin, 1987; Rothman, 1989, 1991), changes are facilitating communication and a more natural birthing experience. Birthing centers, staffed primarily by midwives, are being increasingly established. Some hospitals have created birthing suites that are designed to resemble bedrooms in décor, lighting, and music. Hospitals overall are now offering more alternatives for birthing, including being attended and coached by midwives and options for facilitating labor, such as birthing chairs, hot tubs, and shower facilities.

This more holistic view of birthing—and of the pain of birthing—fits with our emphasis in this book on moving beyond the biomedical model to one that embraces the psychological, social, and spiritual along with the biological. Research now documents that pain is not a sensation but, instead, is a perception that depends on the mind's active process in making sense of experience—thus, pain has historical, psychological, and cultural dimensions (Loeser, 1991; Morris, 1998; Price, 1994).

So, no matter what birth experience women and their families choose—natural or medicated; in the hospital, a birthing center, or at home; breastfeeding or bottle-feeding; circumcision or not; family members present or absent—options are available for negotiating a birth experience that takes advantage of the technologies available in modern medicine but is also a meaningful, life-affirming passage that fits with their personal, cultural, or even political beliefs. Feminist scholar Paula Treichler (1989) would agree, suggesting we have begun to challenge the medical model of birthing:

> Because childbirth is crucial [to a culture], a crisis in childbearing typically signals a crisis in culture. To study the cultural crises we may study the childbirth crisis. . . . What happens in a crisis is that contests for meaning are waged at every point, eventually dislodging the taken-for-granted and calling even widely accepted practices and assumptions into question. (pp. 425, 427)

This crisis is not one that doubts or questions the motivations of obstetricians to act in the best interests of their patients or the benefits of technology for patients and newborns who need such assistance. The crisis concerns the routine medicalization of women's natural experiences, in which technology and pain-relieving drugs are promoted and unquestioned, pregnancy is viewed as a service that medicine supplies rather than an activity in which women engage, and the routine treatment and monitoring of pregnant women shapes the choices they make about health care and birthing (Hyde, 1990; Riessman, 1987).

One particular area in which women and their families may discover this medicalization of experience involves the increased use of technology to monitor pregnancy. For example, sonograms (sound-wave pictures) performed as early as six weeks of pregnancy can indicate that the heart of a fetus is no longer beating, before a woman has any indication she may be about to miscarry. CVS (chorionic villus sampling), a blood test, and amniocentesis, a procedure for extracting amniotic fluid, provide information about the genetic makeup of the fetus and, thus, allow early diagnosis of chromosome abnormalities (for example, Down syndrome). Both procedures carry risks of fetal death, and if the test results confirm the presence of fetal abnormalities, genetic counseling often encourages women to terminate these pregnancies. For this reason, women often find themselves wrestling with information, options, and decision making that complicates and, in some cases, makes controversial their experiences with childbirth.

Rhetorician Michael Hyde (1990) suggests that medical experts should change their form of storytelling from an emphasis on technical knowledge (what technology does to the body) to social knowledge (what technology does to the person) by engaging in dialogue with patients about their values and morals. A patient's choice to use technology, therefore, is not a blind pursuit that assumes these innovations are inherently good or desirable for the patient, and individual narratives are not silenced by the privileging of public, technological narratives.

Perhaps some of the good sense that Hyde refers to can be found in considering a few of the messages women receive about their choices in birthing. As Oakley (1984) points out, "pregnancy and birth, like death, are bodily experiences which have different 'negotiated realities' in different cultures" (p. 276). In other words, women, their partners, and their families may want to learn what they can about birthing options and then communicate those choices to their medical providers, negotiating a birth experience that is compatible with the providers' expertise and with their own hopes and dreams surrounding this life-affirming event.

## ■ Communicating Life-Affirming Choices

At home and in hospitals, women are finding ways to communicate choices, enhance the life-affirming experience of birthing, and negotiate more control over their bodies and birthing through a diverse set of options. Communication researchers Helen Sterk (1996) and Elizabeth Nelson (1996) suggest that women and their families ask questions such as:

- Where do I want to deliver the baby (home, clinic, or hospital)?

- Who will attend the birth (physician, midwife, family members)?

- How will labor be managed (walking, showering, talking, visualization, medication)?

- How will birth be facilitated (induction, episiotomy, massage, walking, forceps, birthing chair)?

- Under what circumstances will a cesarean section be necessary?

- What environment will be created once the baby is delivered (low lights, soft music, presence of family members)?

Today, women and their families are seeking answers to these questions and discovering what their health plans, hospitals, and clinics offer. They are learning which of the standard procedures are essential for their unique situation. They are discovering a range of safe choices by taking childbirth preparation classes, and they are communicating those choices in creating birth plans, making birthing a family event, insisting on drug-free deliveries, hiring a doula (labor coach), birthing in water, walking throughout labor, and making informed choices about episiotomy, circumcision, and breastfeeding (Fitzsimmons, 1997, 1998; Gates, 1995, 1997; Hathaway, Hathaway, & Bek, 1989; Whitcomb, 1994).

While reading the following subsections, consider from whom you learned much of what you know about pregnancy and childbirth, and think about what these sources communicated to you regarding acceptable and unacceptable practices. This is not neutral information or "simple" choices. More often than not, this information is bound up in personal stories, cultural beliefs or myths, and the politics of what has been established as "the way it's always been done." Ask yourself "Why?" in relation to what you have decided is best for you or your family in regard to routine hospital procedures and breastfeeding.

***Communicating routine hospital procedures.*** One area in which women and their families can communicate their choices involves the **routine hospital procedures** during preparation for labor and delivery. In addition to the possible choices in each of the five following routine procedures, consider also the use of a **doula,** as described in FYI 5.3.

First, on their arrival at the hospital, women usually are "prepped," which typically means they are told to put on a hospital gown and then undergo a vaginal exam, an enema, and shaving of their pubic hair. More often than not, women are led through these procedures without being asked any questions, such as "Do you want to wear a hospital gown, or do you have your own to wear?" In addition, studies have not confirmed that all these procedures are necessary. For example, shaving the pubic hair has been justified by medical institutions as reducing the risks of infection, but research has not confirmed this. Nor has research confirmed that the enema reduces the risk of elimination during labor, the length of labor, or the incidence of infection (Enkin, Keirse, & Chalmers, 1989; Nelson, 1996). Some women are saying no to the enema and shave, bringing their own gown (made specifically for breastfeeding), and wearing their own robe to enhance their comfort.

Second, monitoring of the baby's heartbeat, either internally or externally, typically occurs at frequent intervals throughout labor. Each time such monitoring is applied to a woman, she must remain in bed near the machine with the external monitor strapped to her belly or the internal monitor attached, through the vagina, to the baby's head. In addition to contractions being much more painful lying down than when standing or walking around, research reveals no benefit from electronic fetal monitoring (Enkin et al., 1989; Nelson, 1996). Monitoring also restricts the communication and support that can be offered by family and

A *doula* has been defined as "a caring woman, experienced because of her own normal childbirth, providing constant reassurance, touch, and support throughout labor, delivery, and after the birth" (Scaer, 1993, p. 8). Doulas "mother the mother" (Fitzsimmons, 1997, p. E1). The doula does not replace the need for health care providers or the woman's partner; instead, she helps to communicate additional comfort in ways that make the partner feel less nervous and less responsible for everything a woman needs in birthing (Scaer).

Studies comparing hospital births with and without the use of doulas in Guatemala, South Africa, Finland, Canada, and the United States indicate that doula-assisted birth can dramatically improve outcomes (Fitzsimmons, 1997; Scaer, 1993).

A book about doulas reports significant findings in six separate studies (Klaus, Kennell, & Klaus, 1993). The presence of a doula reduces:

- The overall rate of cesarean section by 50 percent

- The length of labor by 25 percent

- Oxytocin use by 40 percent

- Use of pain medication by 30 percent

- The need for forceps by 40 percent

- Requests for epidurals by 60 percent

In addition, evidence is accumulating concerning the cost savings to hospitals resulting from the reduced need for these interventions (Scaer, 1993).

friends and, instead, focuses communication on the information that technology is providing.

Third, a wide variety of methods are used for inducing or augmenting labor, either because a woman is past her due date or is making little or no progress in labor. One method in particular, the use of intravenous drugs (Oxytocin and Pitocin), can be effective at enhancing contractions but, in some cases, can also produce unnaturally excessive contractions that might lead to cesarean section (Davis-Floyd, 1992; Nelson, 1996). In addition, administering the drug intravenously typically requires that the woman be confined to the bed, thus limiting her freedom to move about.

Fourth, use of a surgical incision to open the birth passage by cutting the perineum—an episiotomy—has also begun to be questioned (Davis-Floyd, 1992; Enkin et al., 1989; Nelson, 1996). Evidence does not confirm the purported benefits of an episiotomy in shortening the second stage of labor (by facilitating delivery of the baby's head and shoulders), nor is it easier to repair than random tears. Instead, an episiotomy is "associated with significant risks, including maternal blood loss, infection, and possible incontinence" (Nelson, p. 118).

Finally, a fifth routine procedure, used in the birth of a baby boy, is circumcision. In this surgical procedure, the sleeve of skin (the foreskin) that covers the head (glans) of the penis is removed (Wallerstein, 1990). Circumcision has been a routine procedure in the United States, though recently the rates of circumcision have declined. Even so, the United States is the only country in the world today where most male newborns are circumcised for nonreligious purposes (Payer, 1988; Wallerstein, 1982, 1990). Evidence continues to refute the list of reasons that have been used over the years to support conducting this surgery. Led by the American Academy of Pediatrics and the American College of Obstetricians and Gynecologists, parents are urged to communicate with providers, ask questions about this newborn surgery, and make their own choice (Wallerstein, 1982).

***Communicating about breastfeeding.*** Breastfeeding is one life-affirming choice that more and more woman are making—life-affirming for both mother and child because of the nutritional and immunological effects and the enhanced bonding between mother and infant. For these reasons, the American Public Health Association supports breastfeeding as the best food choice for infants. Among the reported benefits of breast milk are reduced percentage of infections (Beaudry, DuFour, & Marcoux, 1995), reduced infant illnesses (Wright, Bauer, Naylor, Sutcliffe, & Clark, 1998), reduced incidence of allergies (Saarinen & Kajosaari, 1995), reduced risk of breast cancer for both mother and female child as an adult (Freudenheim et al., 1994; Newcomb et al., 1994), reduced risk of juvenile diabetes (Verge et al., 1994), reduced postpartum stress for the mother ("Postpartum blues," 1998), and now, the discovery that breastfed children do better in school and score higher on standardized math and reading tests (Horwood & Ferguson, 1998).

*Healthy People 2010* recommends that mothers breastfeed until their infant is at least six months old ("Formula ads," 2000). Today, nearly 60 percent of new mothers choose breastfeeding over formula (Ryan, 1997). Breastfeeding is promoted by the American Academy of Pediatrics, the United Nations, the WHO (World Health Organization), and the U.S. federal government, all of which would like to raise that percentage to 75 percent and extend the recommendation from six months to one year (Fernandes, 1999). The greatest increases in breastfeeding have been discovered among women who are exposed repeatedly to public health campaigns promoting breastfeeding (Ryan). Women's exposure to formula ads, however, led them to give up breastfeeding earlier than they originally planned to ("Formula ads"). Promoting formula use to expectant mothers, distributing free samples, or using pictures that idealize bottle-feeding violates an international code of the WHO ("Formula ads").

Although information communicated from friends, mothers, and sisters are most likely to influence a new mother's choice of whether to breastfeed (Scripps Howard News Service, 1997), this decision is complicated by diverse and competing notions of motherhood, female sexuality, and morality. In addition to the cultural constraints on this decision are the politics of campaigns that communicate a mother is a "good" person if she chooses to breastfeed and a "bad" person if she does not.

As communication scholars Majia Holmer Nadesan and Patti Sotirin (1998) demonstrate, the U.S. Department of Agriculture's national "Breast Is Best" campaign and others like it construct contradictory messages about the value, status, and control of women's bodies. Nadesan and Sotirin suggest that "'Breast is best' is not a choice over whether to breastfeed or not, but an injunction to perform culturally authorized gender identities . . . [by casting] the decision to breastfeed as a dualistic choice between 'good' and 'bad' bodies, images, performances, and politics" (p. 230). Indeed, a woman and her partner may feel stigmatized by the decision, whether that decision is to breastfeed or not. Messages from family and friends also may communicate a sense that the mother should—or should not—breastfeed for reasons connected to personal, cultural, or even political belief systems. Read the two brief "nourishing" stories in FYI 5.4, and consider the varied and competing narratives impacting the communication and identities of both women and men surrounding this choice.

Women—or both women and men, as parents—choose which option is best based on a complex set of reasons, including time, bonding, work schedules, nutritional benefits, and opportunities for other family members to share in the feeding. Indeed, feeding an infant, who depends on others for food, is life-affirming regardless of whether that food comes from the breast or the bottle. Clearly, the decision to breastfeed is not a simple choice, as many public health campaigns imply. Instead, it is enmeshed in personal, cultural, and political complexities.


## ▨ Educating Ourselves

Some of the routine procedures described in this chapter have benefits and involve choices that women, men, and their providers make to ensure the health of the child and parents. It is essential, however, to recognize that options do exist, which may lead individuals to ask questions and discuss alternatives to these routine procedures. Women and men are becoming more educated about these choices, and they are communicating with providers who are willing to negotiate options with their patients. Yet at times, in their efforts to affirm their presence and participation in birthing, individuals find themselves needing to communicate in

### "Real Women Can": The Breastfeeding Backlash

Sixty years ago, breastfeeding was not a choice. One might've chosen a wet nurse, but breastfeeding was just not done. The recent variation on the wet nurse option was the invention of formula, which moms of the 1950s and 1960s, if they were "civilized," were expected to use. But now we have returned to breastfeeding and created a choice. . . . Ironically breastfeeding may not even feel like a choice for it can be so surrounded by pressure—the pressure of social stigma. This I didn't discover until I began to seriously think about having a baby. . . . "Are you going to breastfeed?" someone would ask a pregnant friend. His or her reaction was always one of horror if the answer was not a resounding, "Of course!" . . . So when I was asked the question, it didn't even cross my mind to say "Maybe." But secretly I worried. Could I do it? Would I hate it? Would it hurt? I couldn't discuss these fears during my pregnancy because I seemed to be surrounded by friends straight from the Mother Earth society. Not only did they worship breastfeeding, they discussed it in orgasmic terms. So I just got bigger, swallowed my concerns, read the book and went to nursing classes. . . . The voices of breastfeeding friends, of course, were also never far from my mind. Their implication was that if you cannot do something natural, it is because you are unnatural—too uptight, urban, plastic. . . . I dreaded their judgment. In retrospect, this seems incredibly insecure on my part. But I know many other women feel the same secret worry. This is the pressure . . . real women can!

Keren Giles (1998)

ways to resist the routine procedures, which often are offered—or even initiated— without discussion of other possible options.

Take a moment to examine the birth plan presented in Theorizing Practice 5.1. Consider the implications of this negotiated reality for the mother, the parents, and others participating in the birthing experience. Also consider how these choices might influence communication, and why this plan represents a life-affirming experience for those involved in the childbirth experience.

Most often, women and men learn about alternatives to a medicalized pregnancy and birthing primarily through childbirth education classes. One study, however, revealed how women in a mothers' and toddlers' playgroup discuss their own and others' health experiences, including pregnancy and delivery, physicians and

*(continued from previous page)*

## The First Lesson

When I hear Miranda laugh and see her enthusiastically shake the bottle of rice milk I've warmed for her, I can't imagine why I should deny her the happy experience of falling asleep in my arms as she nurses to sleep. As her father, this seems as close as I can come to sharing the nursing experience. I have seen my wife breastfeed Miranda before naps and bed to comfort her, as well as to feed her. The bottle allows me to develop a similar relationship as a nurturer and a nourisher. Occasionally I will offer Miranda (or sometimes she requests) a small bottle to console her when upset, or sometimes just to sit down for ten minutes. Most often when mom's away, a warm bottle and a baseball game conclude an evening of play, dinner, and bath. I love it when somebody gets a hit and Miranda will sit up, point at the TV and say, "Ball!" (without pronouncing the l's of course). Then she slumps back and resumes drinking her bottle. My pediatrician (who I like very much and agree with in most cases), his nurse, and my wife jointly concluded that a two-year-old sucking on a bottle was somehow a bad thing. The doctor told us to stop allowing Miranda the bottle at twelve months. I kind of nodded along with the whole thing at the time because I remembered my friend, Bonnie, being frustrated that her son was still drinking a bottle at two or three. I feel differently now and I can't remember why I thought a three-year-old or his parents would be embarrassed if he drank a bottle. Yet the question comes up constantly, "Are you still giving her a bottle?" It's the "still" I find questionable. My intuition tells me it's not time to wean her yet. Kathryn seems to have no intention of weaning her from breastfeeding either. Miranda didn't always nurse happily with either mother or father. Now that she does, it seems unfair to discontinue either breast or bottle without feeling that she is ready. . . . I can't begin to fathom what it might be like to feed a child that came from my body with my body fluids. But I also can't help but feel that the bottle lets me have a relationship with my daughter that I would not otherwise have. The fact that a device enables it does not diminish its depth.

Michael J. Nagro (1998)

---

hospitals, breastfeeding, illnesses and accidents, and diet and nutrition (Tardy & Hale, 1998a). This study revealed that conversations among women in the playgroup served the practical purpose of "cracking the code" of institutionalized practices as well as a "bonding" function.

Women also turn to newspapers and public health campaigns for information about pregnancy and childbirth, but research indicates these are not always the best sources of information. In a thematic analysis of 29 newspapers and their coverage of prenatal care from 1989 to 1993, Daniels and Parrot (1996) discovered that "newspaper articles overall offered a mediocre representation of prenatal care from a woman's perspective," often providing technical, confusing, and contradictory information (p. 231). They conclude that "too often, newspaper stories

## Constructing and Communicating a Birth Plan

Read the following birth plan. Make a list of questions you have about terminology, procedures, or rationale. Then create a second list of the implications of this birth plan for communication.

*Dear Obstetrical Staff:*

*We are writing to clarify what we desire during labor and the birth of our child. We have prepared for this special event through a 12-week Bradley Method childbirth preparation course. We anticipate following through with our plans to have a nonmedicated birth with minimal medical intervention.*

*Our desires for the natural birth of our baby are outlined below:*

1. *To have birth coaches present throughout the labor, birth, and entire postpartum period.*

2. *To have no routine "prep" (i.e., NO intravenous access and NO fetal monitoring).*

3. *To have no stimulants (such as Pitocin) to induce or speed up labor.*

4. *To have no sedative, tranquilizer, pain medication, or anesthesia administered OR offered.*

5. *To allow the membranes to rupture in their own time.*

6. *To allow for the choice of position during labor and birth, including walking around and showering as necessary.*

7. *To keep the perineum intact, and to use perineal massage to avoid an episiotomy.*

8. *To avoid the use of forceps or vacuum extractor.*

9. *To breastfeed the baby immediately after birth. The baby is to receive NO bottle-feeding in the hospital. Any and all feeding is to be handled by mother and father.*

10. *To cut the cord ONLY after the placenta has been delivered and after it has stopped pulsating without human intervention (cord is NOT to be milked).*

11. *To have the baby with us at all times following birth until release from the hospital.*

12. *To have NO vitamin K shot administered to the baby.*

13. *To have NO silver nitrate or erythromycin put in the baby's eyes.*

14. *To have NO circumcision if the baby is a boy.*

15. *To have the baby bathed with water only.*

16. *To have the option of early discharge (2–12 hours following the baby's birth).*

*Should complications arise, all procedures must be discussed and approved by both parents.*

functioned as a springboard for guilt and paranoia, rather than confidence and competence" (p. 231).

In another study of efforts to promote prenatal care, Parrott and Daniels (1996) found that none of the campaigns "are directed at promoting the practice in terms of benefits for the pregnant woman," and they did nothing to dispel myths and misinformation about pregnancy and prenatal care (p. 17). They recommend that a model of pregnancy care must encompass more of a woman's social network and "include differences among women—adolescents, rural women, high risk women, and others" (p. 217). One such study investigated the childbirth beliefs, practices, and experiences of Korean women who had immigrated to the United States (Park & Peterson, 1991). These researchers found, as other studies have, a need for developing Korean-language pamphlets about the U.S. health care system and community health programs along with a bilingual pamphlet of medical terms. Health care providers need to visit patients often to discuss their health care needs and to ensure understanding.

These studies all indicate the need to develop a more systematic approach to communicating information that is life-affirming for both mother and child and that meets the needs of the diverse beliefs and practices of our population. In *Evaluating Women's Health Messages,* communication researchers Roxanne Parrott and Celeste Condit (1996) suggest that not enough attention has been given to the quality of messages that women receive about their reproductive health care. Their book explores the historical, political, and practical issues in communicating about topics such as abortion, contraception, and drug and alcohol abuse in pregnancy, birthing, and prenatal care.

As is all too clear, pregnancy and childbirth can be one of the most affirming life passages. Equally, however, this time can be life-challenging and life-adjusting. In the next two sections, we move to a set of beginning life passages that, although predominantly challenging, can also be considered life-affirming and life-adjusting. Specifically, we look at the communication complexities surrounding miscarriage and infertility as well as giving birth to a disabled child.

## LIFE-CHALLENGING PASSAGES: COMMUNICATING THROUGH MISCARRIAGE AND INFERTILITY

*After my third miscarriage, I heard something that I had never heard before. A dear lady said, "Diedra, God made that baby and he wanted you to bear that baby, but he wanted that baby in heaven for himself. He had this beautiful child and he wants to raise the baby himself. You can see the child when you get to heaven." It was such a positive outlook because so many people had been telling me, "Oh, it was a boy and you can't carry boys" or "Oh it was probably good because it would have been deformed." So I felt like I was always making bad babies. There's something wrong with this baby, and "it's a really good thing that it didn't get born." Very few people said, "It was a perfect baby and it's in heaven because God wanted that baby." I grasped on that one. After going through it three times, I like that. I liked that a lot.*

Diedra, after her third miscarriage (Ross & Geist, 1997, p. 177)

*For my first D & C's [dilation and curettage], my in-laws sent beautiful bouquets of flowers. They were wonderful, just wonderful. My husband's mother even offered to come down and help out. It was such a wonderful surprise that she could understand. It said to me, "You have a right to grieve, to be in pain." On the last miscarriage, we didn't tell anyone. So I came home and there were no flowers, no phone call. By not sharing, we cut ourselves off from our support.*

Emily, after her third miscarriage (Ross & Geist, 1997, pp. 179–180)

*I remember people saying that I was young and could have more children. People said that something was wrong with the baby. One friend even said, "Your kids would have been too close together in age and it would have been too hard on you." All I wanted to hear was that they were sorry and that they were there for me. It made me feel like this baby didn't matter. Like this baby was just a process and not a person. Even the doctor, when I asked him whether it was a boy or a girl that I had lost, looked at me like, "What the hell is wrong with you? Have you lost your mind?" He made me feel so stupid, like "What difference does it make? It's gone."*

Alexandra, after a miscarriage (Ross & Geist, 1997 p. 177)

These three voices represent the types of communication that many women experience after miscarriage (Ross & Geist, 1997). We know that most often family and friends intend to provide support, but often without realizing it, they speak in ways that minimize the emotional effect of miscarriage (Elkin, 1990) or that diminish the significance of the loss (Bansen & Stevens, 1992). People communicate in ways that fail to address a woman's deeply felt grief, and most often, they do not take the time to ask or listen to what she wants to talk about—usually the "baby" she had hoped for (Allen & Marks, 1993; Bansen & Stevens; Ross & Geist).

In contrast, some men and women may not experience the same level of grief. They do not necessarily take the loss lightly, but they do not view it as a life-defining event. Instead, they may see the miscarriage as a natural event that is relatively common, and so they focus their energies on the future and a subsequent pregnancy. Thus, they may choose not to communicate a great deal about the loss. In some situations, these individuals may feel stigmatized by others who communicate in ways that suggest they "should" feel intense grief and make their loss a public narrative. Instead, the individual or couple may choose to not communicate or to grieve privately, personally, and in a symbolic way.

## Communicating the Loss Symbolically

Some people search for specific and personal ways to communicate their feelings of loss and grief—planting a tree, naming the unborn child, or gathering family and friends to celebrate what might have been the child's birthday. In this way, a beginning passage such as miscarriage can be both life-challenging and life-affirming. When I (Patricia) experienced a series of miscarriages once again after the birth of our first child, my husband, J.C., and my daughter, Makenna (then age two), and I planted a palm tree in our front yard. After digging the hole, we placed Makenna's placenta in the ground as nourishment for the tree. We told Makenna that a part of her would always provide nutrients for the tree in memory of the babies we lost through miscarriage. It was a special ceremony that helped all of us to talk openly about our losses and to grieve in a powerful way.

Another avenue for affirming the loss is through writing. Communication scholar María Cristina González (1997) wrote a poem about her experience with miscarriage:

> There must have been a place
> deep within
> that held the oceans of my love for you
> and when you died
> it burst.
> how else explains the endless tears?

Along with creating personal rituals for grieving, individuals who experience miscarriage may need to seek emotional support by communicating their loss in an organized support group, such as Empty Cradle.

## Communicating Support

Empty Cradle is a nonprofit, national support group with local community affiliates that sponsor monthly meetings to offer **emotional support** for parents who have experienced the loss of a baby through miscarriage, stillbirth, or infant death. In addition, they offer emotional peer support by telephone to bereaved families and a lending library devoted to loss of a baby. In their monthly newsletter, Empty Cradle describes their meetings as an opportunity to share experiences, information, and friendship. Guest speakers touch on any number of related topics, including "Grand-parents' Grief: A Double Hurt," "Facing Grief in the Workplace," "Grieving the First Few Months," and "Helping Other Children in Your Life Understand Why Your Child Died." The newsletter publishes brief articles about grief, healing, and community outreach. In addition, it includes a "Remembrance" section, publishing the names of babies lost; a "Congratulations" section, for babies born after the experience of loss; as well as poems and stories dedicated to the little ones lost.

## ▇ Communicating Stigmatizing Messages

When these losses occur, especially if a woman or a couple have no other children, individuals often face stigmatizing messages concerning their infertility and child-lessness (Avalos-C'de Baca, Geist, Gray, & Hill, 1996; Geist et al., 1996). Even people who choose to remain without children experience these same **disenfranchising messages**—messages from "the media, the church, from the legal system, from the government, from the health care system, and frequently from the couple's own family and friends" (Geist et al., p. 160).

These messages may focus on negating a person's sense of masculinity or femininity, emphasizing their inability to live up to familial or religious obligations. Friends and family members often communicate in ways that upset the individuals who need their support, unintentionally making them feel even more stigmatized and isolated. The potential support from religious institutions and their members is often negated by the strong emphasis of most religions on childbearing. Professionals in the medical community also unintentionally communicate stigmatizing messages in their medicalization of infertility and the treatment of infertile individuals as being "diseased." As a result, the voices of men and women who experience the pain of infertility often are silenced.

## ▇ Communicating Men's Stories of Infertility

More recently, research has been focusing on male infertility (Glover & Barratt, 1999) and on men's perspectives about it—their anxieties and frustrations about being unable to produce a child (Mason, 1993; Webb & Daniluk, 1999). In an interview study of men's experiences about their own infertility, Mason (1993) offers the voices of those who describe how they felt after receiving the news and of some who focus specifically on communication issues:

> I remember a friend of mine at college got his wife pregnant and he said it was great to find out he wasn't shooting blanks. That was the first time I thought con-

*sciously about my ability to be a father. I didn't think much more about it until we started trying for a baby. I didn't know a lot about sperm and I remember thinking my test results were quite good even though I had hardly any sperm. (pp. 77–78)*

*I felt like an outcast, a failure. All around me there were pictures of happy families, so I felt incomplete. There was an awful feeling of being different from everyone else because I wasn't like all the smiling men you see with their children. (p. 97)*

*You really feel left behind when other people start having children. The biggest thing is the awful loneliness it causes. You see more and more friends get pregnant and have children. Their lifestyles change and they mix with people who have children. I think they also feel guilty and uncomfortable when they are with you because they know you want children so much, so there's this barrier between you. They avoid you because they don't want to hurt you and they disappear into the woodwork not because they don't care, but because they can't cope with your distress. (p. 96)*

*I felt cut off from other people and ashamed of the infertility label. I knew of no other men in the same boat as me so there was nobody for me to talk to. On reflection I think all the messages were inside me and not coming from people round me. When I did tell people they were generally sympathetic. (p. 136)*

*They [friends] used to ask me why I had stopped drinking and smoking, so I told them I was infertile and was trying to do something that would improve my sperm. People, particularly men, seemed to almost ignore what I said and pass over it quickly. In the end I tried to avoid saying anything because I felt uncomfortable about the whole subject and so did my friends. (p. 134)*

*To start with I felt infertility was just my problem. I had all these raw feelings and became very selfish and bitter trying to cope with them, particularly the first six weeks after the diagnosis. It helped when I talked to my wife, but the feelings of loss didn't come out until about six months later. I remember lying on the bed, saying I really wanted to be a dad. Everything seemed too unfair, I just broke down and cried. That was a release. These softer feelings of grief had been pushed to the back of my mind because I was so cross about my infertility. When the feelings came out I started to feel better though the problems were still there. (p. 141)*

*There were good things about what happened and it wasn't all bad. It was a problem we worked on together and this brought us closer together. Our relationship became stronger because we found out more about each other and our different needs. We had to become much better at communicating with each other. (p. 98)*

Infertility is a challenging beginning life passage that leads men to feel grief and loss, powerlessness and lack of control, inadequacy, isolation, and betrayal in

## Reproductive Technologies

The introduction to the book *Reproductive Technologies* (Wekesser, 1996), published in a series called "Current Controversies," states that "about 8.5 percent of U.S. married couples are infertile [and] reproductive technologies . . . are allowing hundreds of families each year to have babies. But the miraculous new techniques have raised troubling questions about medical science's increasing ability to tinker with biological processes" (p. 13). Read the following description of reproductive technologies from Wekesser, then consider the five controversies she offers that follow. In teams, select a position either for (affirmative) or against (negative) one of the resolutions. Research your position, and be prepared to debate that position in class.

**Reproductive technologies** refer to a wide range of procedures, including:

**Artificial insemination:** Sperm is artificially introduced into the uterus; has been used for years and is probably the simplest of the reproductive technologies.

**In vitro fertilization:** Pioneered in 1978, involves fertilizing an egg with sperm in a Petri dish, then transferring the embryo into the woman's uterus for gestation.

**ARTs (assisted reproductive technologies):** Involves surgically removing eggs from a woman's ovaries and using a variety of techniques to achieve pregnancy.

**ZIFT (zygote intrafallopian transfer):** Entails putting the embryo into one of the woman's fallopian tubes (tubes that conduct the egg from the ovary to the uterus) and then allowing it to travel to and implant in the woman's uterus.

response to the discovery they were responsible for not being able to father a child (Webb & Daniluk, 1999). In one man's view, "I think the biggest thing that we've had to work though as a couple and me as a person is just learning to live with it. Because it changes everything . . . being infertile changes everything" (Webb & Daniluk, p. 19).

Men in both these studies (Mason, 1993; Webb & Daniluk, 1999) reported that they worked through a solution to their problem and resolved the challenge they first faced either through in vitro fertilization, adoption, or by learning to live life without the prospect of having children.

### ■ Considering Reproductive Technologies

The health care system plays a powerful role in communicating options for infertile couples. As Theorizing Practice 5.2 reveals, however, the reproductive technologies available to infertile men, women, and couples are fraught with controversies.

(continued from previous page)

**GIFT (gamete intrafallopian transfer):** Involves placing the sperm and the un-fertilized egg into the fallopian tubes, which is followed by conception and im-plantation in the uterus.

**Zona cracking or drilling:** Cutting the outside of an egg and inserting a single sperm, thereby causing fertilization. The embryo is then implanted in the woman.

> Which technology someone chooses largely depends on the cause of their infertility. For example, women with blocked fallopian tubes may utilize in vitro fertilization to become pregnant. Men with few or weak sperm may benefit from GIFT, ZIFT, or zona drilling. Women who want to experience pregnancy, childbirth, and parenting without the involvement of a man may choose to become artificially inseminated with sperm from a donor. Similarly, a man who wishes to be a father without being a husband may find a surrogate [woman who is willing] to be artificially inseminated and to bear a child" (pp. 13–14).

*Resolution 1:* Reproductive technologies are beneficial.

*Resolution 2:* Postmenopausal women should become pregnant.

*Resolution 3:* Surrogate motherhood is beneficial.

*Resolution 4:* Reproductive technologies result in unethical treatment of embryos.

*Resolution 5:* Reproductive technologies should be regulated.

When a couple fails to conceive or give birth, medical professionals are the ones who speak of hope by offering alternatives for treating infertility. The traditional medical model leads medical professionals to treat infertility like an illness. Patients who often are not really ill, who have no physical symptoms, but instead hold the desire to have a child are subject to a highly technological industry of diagnosis and treatment (Greil, 1991). The solutions offered by most medical professionals focus on the technical aspects of infertility, often ignoring the social, emotional, and cognitive aspects (Greil; Phoenix, Woollett, & Lloyd, 1991; Stanton & Dunkel-Schetter, 1991).

Being treated for infertility has a profound impact on a couple. They often feel powerless, as if they have turned over their lives to physicians (Abbey, 1992). Relational difficulties are not uncommon as couples experience emotional and psychological stress (Daniluk, 1988; McEwan, Costelli, & Taylor, 1987); challenging personal, interpersonal, and ethical dilemmas (McDaniel, Hepworth, & Doherty, 1992); as well as dysfunctional and unsatisfying sexual relations (Link & Darling,

1986). The family system is, in a sense, dismantled from without by professional experts as the couple seeks guidance in exchange for the commodified goods and services of infertility treatment (Deetz, 1992). Not surprisingly, in the process, these men and woman may experience depression (Hynes, Callan, Terry, & Gallois, 1992), stress (O'Moore & Harrison, 1991), lowered self-esteem (Abbey, Andrews, & Halman, 1992), and feelings of loss of control over their everyday lives (Daniluk, Leader, & Taylor, 1985).

Infertility research, both medical and psychological, has focused predominantly on the biology and voices of women. Frequently, women and their bodies are also the first target of diagnosis and treatment (Becker & Nachtigall, 1991), in some cases without even checking the sperm count of the husband (Corea, 1985a, 1985b). As McDaniel et al. (1992) point out, "it is not unusual for a poorly trained physician to schedule advanced infertility treatments—even surgery—on a woman without first checking her partner's sperm count" (p. 114). Low sperm count, one of the principal causes of infertility, has been understudied, and surprisingly, the U.S. federal government does not include men in its national fertility survey (Faludi, 1991). Overall, we hear women's stories about the pain of infertility, medical research focuses almost entirely on women, and when a couple has trouble conceiving, as mentioned, most often the diagnosis and treatment focuses on women (Geist et al., 1996). In actuality, however, infertility can be attributed to women in 50 percent of cases, to men in 40 percent, and to both in 10 percent (DeWitt, 1993; Geist et al.).

The medicalization of reproduction is one and the same with its industrialization. It has become "an enterprise of mass production, supervised by trained specialists, dependent upon expensive and sophisticated equipment, and managed according to principles of rational efficiency" (Greil, 1991, p. 37). In 1997, more than 71,000 cycles of in vitro fertilization and other ARTs (assisted reproductive technologies) were performed in the United States, with only one out of every four attempts resulting in a baby (Pappert, 2000). In addition, now that fertility drugs have been shown to significantly increase the risk of ovarian cancer, the U.S. Food and Drug Administration requires many, such as Pergonal, Clomid, and Gonal-F, to include a warning about this risk (Pappert). In addition, because the use of fertility drugs often leads to multiple births, parents are faced with the dilemmas of high-risk births, congenital abnormalities, and abortion decisions in the case of too many fetuses (Meckler, 1999). In the United States, ARTs have been at the center of "Senate hearings, consumer legislation, lawsuits over everything from false advertising to risky medical procedures to the misuse of embryos, and investigations into the practices of dozens of clinics and doctors" (Pappert, p. 45).

For the approximately 20 percent of American couples who are infertile, this is a crisis with no resolution (Butler & Koraleski, 1990). The inability to conceive and to bear children is a deeply serious psychological event. For many, it means not achieving one of life's milestones, and it symbolizes a failure to live up to one's own or others' expectations (Butler & Koraleski; Pines, 1990). And for many, the only resolution is communicating to negotiate an empowered identity using any number of avenues, including continued hope through alternative medicine, infertility clinics offered by traditional medicine, adoption, or participation in groups such as the National Association for the Childless, RESOLVE, or Empty Cradle.

At the same time that controversy has surrounded the development and use of reproductive technologies, these innovations have helped some couples give birth to the child they have dreamed of. In addition, other technological advances have contributed to decreased infant mortality rates and the survival of premature babies, who in the past might not have lived. For example, now babies born as early as 19 weeks may survive because of a technology enabling them to breathe using a liquid (Adler, 1998).

Undoubtedly, other types of communicative challenges enter people's lives when they begin the life passage of becoming parents. For some new parents, that challenge begins immediately, when they discover that their newborn child is disabled. In the next section, we offer a life-altering passage through the story of one young couple whose son was born with congenital heart disease.

## LIFE-ADJUSTING PASSAGES: COMMUNICATING IN PARENTING A DISABLED CHILD[2]

*[On] April 17, 1988, Staci Zwann wrote in her journal, "Zachary Mandel was born at 12:40 a.m." Labor was long, lasting 21 hours. Through the waxing and waning of contractions, the pain and the waiting, Staci told herself, "It's all going to be worth it."*

*But a nagging thought plagued her. "Something is wrong . . ." Suddenly, as if her body had decided labor had lasted long enough, it ended abruptly and Zachary Mandel was born. With her husband Monte at her side, Staci welcomed her son early that Sunday morning.*

*The staff at Luverne Community Hospital began the routine birth procedures— make sure the baby breathes, turns pink, [and] if necessary, suction fluids from the baby's nose and throat. Staci and Monte were elated. A son. Their firstborn. So many hopes and dreams and plans they had for this child.*

---

[2]The authors would like to express their sincere gratitude to Staci, Monte, and Zachary Zwaan for sharing their stories.

*But he didn't turn pink. He didn't cry. The suctioning device did not reach into his nose. Dr. Larry Lyon called on the Sioux Valley Hospital newborn team to examine the infant. The team arrived and had no explanation for the problem. They took Zachary to Sioux Falls. By 2 p.m. the baby was on his way to the University of Minnesota Hospital in Minneapolis for examination of birth defects.*

*Staci wrote in her journal, "I was so out of it. It didn't really sink in until that night that my baby was gone. . . . It was hard being in the hospital and hearing all the babies crying."*

*Soon Monte and Staci learned their son had holes in his heart between the right and left ventricles. Rather than efficiently circulating blood to his body, the heart pumped it back and forth between ventricles. The left pulmonary artery, rather than being hooked up to his left lung, floated toward his arm. The artery that was connected to his lung was pumping too much blood and overstressing the lung that did work. He began having seizures and was unable to suck. A blood clot developed in the working lung.*

*On April 26, when Zach was nine days old, Staci wrote, "We got to hold Zach today for the first time since he was born. When we put him back in his bed he started to seize (have seizures) real bad. It was so awful to see him do that. I cried."*

*On May 4, Zach had his first major heart surgery. Surgeons connected the misplaced pulmonary artery and placed a band around the main pulmonary artery of his heart to slow the flow of blood to both lungs.*

*"They try to prepare you for what you are going to see when your child comes back from surgery," Monte said. Six pound Zachary was surrounded by 12 IV poles including two central lines into his navel, a respirator, a chest tube, and IVs into his head.*

*Staci wrote, "It was so hard seeing our little boy go through all that. It hurt so bad. Monte almost fainted."*

*At three weeks of age, little Zachary's trials, and those of his parents, had only begun.*

(Winter, 1991, p. B1)

Throughout this life-adjusting beginning passage, Staci kept a journal documenting her emotions, conversations, and hopes. From all her writings, interviews with local journalists, messages that she and Monte communicated in a TV broadcast about their challenge, and even the annual Christmas letters, it is clear they have faced—and are still facing—one of the biggest adjustments in their lives. All the circumstances surrounding this life-adjusting event present Staci and Monte with

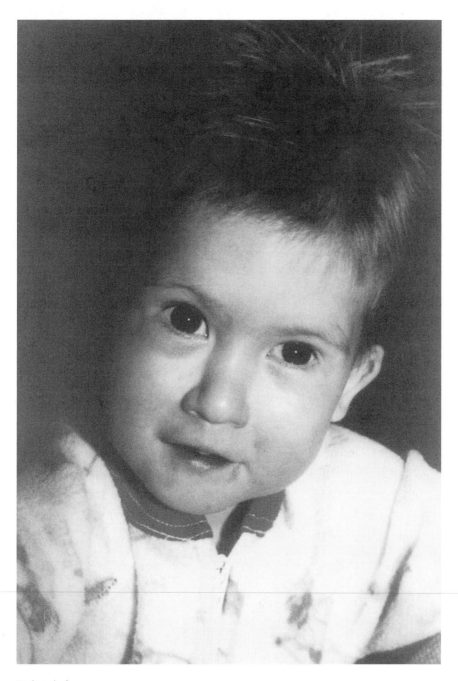

Zachary before aneurysm surgery.

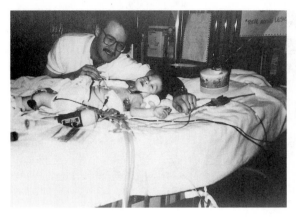

Zachary with his dad, Monte.

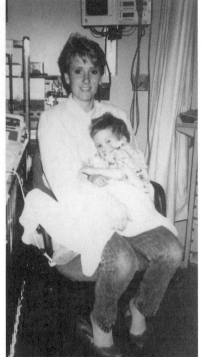

Zachary with his mom, Staci.

communicative challenges that complicate, threaten, and strengthen their identities, their relationship with one another, their efforts to communicate with providers, and especially, their efforts to communicate with Zachary.

## ■ Communicating Decisions

One of the most urgent communicative adjustments for Staci and Monte is the need they now have to engage in a continuous decision-making process. Both must negotiate with providers on a moment-to-moment basis, and with each decision comes an adjustment to its implications. Staci describes the heart-wrenching series of events that providers continuously updated them on throughout their ordeal: "It was one thing right after another, whether it was an infected line, or drug withdrawals, or seizures, or whatever, it was always something, one thing after another" (Children's Miracle Network, 1992). Monte speaks to the difficulty in considering what doctors described as a questioning of, and an adjusting to, a fine line:

*The doctors said that and I can see it's a very fine line to draw. They (the doctors) always want to continue to try to help Zachary. And sometimes that gets a little frustrating because they don't know, well, "Are we really helping him or are we prolonging the agony?" (Children's Miracle Network)*

Complicating the decision-making process further is the intermixing of **technical decisions** with **moral decisions** about what is right and fair for their son. And these communicative dilemmas continued through the first four years of Zachary's life, as he survived 18 surgeries, including a heart transplant and aneurysm (a weakening of a portion of a blood vessel) surgery. Staci tells us:

*I can remember he had his aneurysm on his aorta, I said "No way!" With what this kid has already gone through, why now would he have an aneurysm? He must want to go. This must be his way of telling us he's got to go. He wants out. And he still made it through that! You know, he was down seven minutes and he still lived through that. (Children's Miracle Network)*

Clearly, Staci was trying desperately to connect with and tune into her son's needs and wants. Each new challenge required adjustment. Staci and Monte had to adjust to what they faced concerning Zachary's condition and the best ways to communicate with Zachary to help their son adjust to living in the hospital. Even when a child is this young, evidence reveals that such adult-infant interaction can have a powerful impact on medical outcomes (Thompson & Gillotti, 1993).

### ▓ Communicating Support

Even the closest bond between parent and child and effective communication between parents and providers, however, cannot prevent the unexpected outcomes of surgery. During the procedure on November 30, 1992, to remove the aneurysm from Zachary's chest wall, the aneurysm ruptured. For seven minutes, Zachary was without a heartbeat or blood pressure as doctors tried to stop the bleeding. Soon after the operation, the family knew their son had suffered brain damage. Staci describes what it felt like to bring Zachary home from the hospital on January 9, 1993, the first time he had been home since April 1992:

*That first two weeks we were home were so sad because it's like, it's like losing a child, it's like a death basically because this happy little boy we had last year and then we came home with this physical being that doesn't recognize you, doesn't know how to love you . . . [and] who would never say "mommy" again. (Children's Miracle Network, 1992)*

After this dramatic turning point in Zachary's health, both parents and child had to adjust their lives to the lost capability of using words to communicate their feelings with one another.

Often what parents in this situation need most is to communicate authentically with providers, families, and friends about the realities of the new challenge and their fears. Yet too often, this type of communication is silenced:

> Stories with dire conclusions are often simply prohibited, either by doctors who warn prospective mothers off anecdotes and lore for fear of panic or noncompliance or by the generations of mothers who think they're doing newcomers a favor by not revealing the "secret." Another friend related how comforted she had been by a labor nurse's story of living through her infant's congenital illness and death at six months. The nurse was fired soon after, apparently for sharing this story with other women whose bodies and lives similarly ached with the possibility of telling this story themselves. (Pollack, 1999, p. 5)

Although Staci and Monte faced quite a number of situations in which communication with providers was not what they had expected, Staci indicated that in their communication, for the most part,

> you could tell they [the providers] really cared about Zach and about us. They, you know, thoroughly talked about what their procedure was going to be and what they were going to do and made it very understanding. They would stay and visit with us for a long time. You know, it wasn't a quick come in, tell us what we're going to have done and then leave the room. . . . It was just a very good experience. (personal interview)

Once they returned home, their support came primarily from the 24-hour nursing service that Zachary needed to survive. Staci points out that although family and friends have always been concerned and caring, they don't understand why Staci and Monte can't "just bring him" to a gathering.

By December 1999, the family still found life an adjustment, with Zachary now age 11 and his two sisters, Mackenzi and Chazni, 6 years old and 2 years old. Staci and Monte wrote in their Christmas 1999 letter:

> Zachy is 11 years old already. He has had an outstanding summer and fall. He hasn't been sick since May. Thank the Lord! He goes to school every day from 8 to 5, to Sioux Falls on a bus. He does well there. We feel so blessed he is so happy. He still doesn't talk or eat. But he's come a long way. We saw his cardiologist in August, and it's been seven years since his heart transplant and they don't feel he'll reject at this point, but now has a bigger risk of a sudden heart attack or cancer from the drugs he takes for his transplanted heart. He is such a sweet boy, I wish you all could expe-

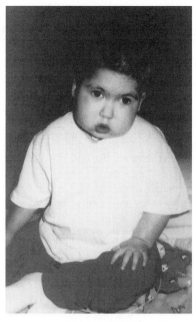

Zachary at age 12 with his sisters, Mackenzi (7) and Chazni (3).

Zachary: After aneurysm surgery.

*rience the different kind of joy he gives us. Having a disabled child brings a whole new perspective on life and challenges your heart in ways you can't even imagine. We thank God every day for our precious time with him. We still have up to 16 hours of nursing a day, which is also a challenge. We are in the process of placing Zach in a home in Luverne, either by himself or with another boy. This has been the hardest thing for Monte and I. We have cried and prayed a lot about this. We are so fortunate that our community offers such services. If they didn't we wouldn't move him out of our home. But we feel he'll benefit in some ways. We will still be his mommy and daddy and will never stop loving or caring. We just won't have him sleeping here and won't have any more caregivers in our home. We need some privacy. We need to be able to experience some normal things with our girls that we can't because of the constant care that Zach needs. As a mom, it rips at my heart, but I know I'm still his mom and love him so much. We will be judged, but we will have to overcome that because we have given him a lot and will continue to.*[3]

Throughout these continual adjustments and heart-wrenching experiences, Staci and Monte found that it was often difficult to communicate with family and

---

[3]Used by permission of Staci Zwaan.

friends who "have no idea what it is like." And although they may try to explain and their friends and family want to understand, Staci believes that "you can never make people feel or understand what you are going through."

## ■ Communicating with Children

One communication dilemma that Monte and Staci have had to adjust to more recently is explaining to their girls the struggle to care for Zach and the decision to move him to the home where he and another disabled boy will live and be cared for:

> *I decided I couldn't handle this anymore. I couldn't handle dealing with the nursing care company. I couldn't handle people in my home anymore. I am so tired of it. My girls don't even know any different. When Mackenzi and I have talked about it—she's six—and when we have talked and discussed about, just about Zach moving out, and about moving into a home, she says, "Well, why mom? No way. He can't live some place else." And when I try to explain to her that we'd like to get away from having caregivers in our home, she says, "Well, so what. Let 'em be here." You know, she doesn't even know the difference of whether or not they are in our house all of the time. (personal interview)*

For Staci, the move will give her the freedom to be a good mom to her girls, to have friends over for dinner, and to do activities spontaneously, without the constant adjustments needed to care for Zach. The comfort to their hearts is knowing that if not for their total devotion to Zachary, their son would not be here today.

Yet it is not always easy to convey to Zachary's sisters the toll these adjustments take on the family. Because they have never known a life apart from these adjustments and the burden of caring for Zachary is not directly theirs to bear, they do not perceive the situation as their parents do. Staci and Monte cannot always find the words to explain Zachary's illness to his younger sisters. Communication researcher Bryan Whaley (1999) discusses how the clinical literature offers strategies for explaining illness to children, including monitoring word choice, using figurative language, and being accurate. He points out, however, that we have failed to assess how effective these strategies have been, and that we have failed to consider "what children want and need to know (as determined by them) regarding their illness . . ." (p. 190). Researchers focusing on the nature of children's explanations reveal that children desire reassurance (Furnham, 1994; Whaley, 1994, 1999). Rather than technical reasons for their illness, children prefer that adults' communication focus on what is termed a **normalcy explanation:**

> *Explanations that foster reassurance—expressing the normality of illness—appear to address children's emotional and cognitive needs. By framing an illness as a normal course of affairs, children get the sense that their experience is typical. As*

*such, their illness is understandable and manageable. This communicative process appears to best reduce children's anxiety and uncertainty. (Whaley, 1999, p. 191)*

In this sense, what we learn from children is that an effective explanation of "illness" may not include any explanation of the actual disease but, instead, reassurance about what is happening in their lives. Zachary's sisters needed the reassurance that he would still be their brother and that they would still see him whenever they wanted.

## SUMMARY

Life-affirming, life-challenging, and life-adjusting passages prompt us to consider revisions in our communication and identity. Communicating through beginning life passages impacts our identities and the support we may need to face the dramatic changes they produce in our lives. Often the stigma and pain that we experience silences the stories we have to tell about our experiences with birthing, infertility, and managing life with a child who is disabled. At the same time, communication can be affirming as we adjust to any beginning life passage. At times, we may communicate in ways that hold onto "the way we were," but at the same time, we may struggle with how to behave and talk with this changing identity. This is especially the case for adolescents as they transition from children to adults and face a multitude of physical, emotional, social, and spiritual changes—as the next chapter, "Formative Life Passages," reveals.

## KEY TERMS

| | | |
|---|---|---|
| life-affirming | rhetoric of birthing | disenfranchising messages |
| life-challenging | natural birth | reproductive technologies |
| life-adjusting | routine procedures | technical decision |
| rhetoric | doula | moral decisions |
| rhetorical situation | emotional support | normalcy explanation |

## DISCUSSION QUESTIONS

1. Why do you think birth stories have become "war stories"? What less violent metaphors might we use to describe this beginning life passage?

2. What role can communication play in helping women and their families to negotiate a birthing experience that interfaces the benefits of traditional with those of modern birthing practices?

3. Although women are often at the center of birth stories, what vital roles do men play in this life-affirming passage?

4. How are the communicative challenges of coping with infertility and miscarriage similar or different for men and women?

5. How might communication in a social support group provide a different kind of comfort than family members can when a woman, man, or couple experience miscarriage or infertility?

6. What factors complicate communication between providers and parents of a newborn child who is disabled?

7. What seems to be the biggest source of strength for Staci and Monte in their efforts to adjust to the circumstances surrounding Zachary?

8. What communication complexities surround Staci and Monte's decision to place Zachary in a special home that can meet his needs?

### INFOTRAC COLLEGE EDITION

1. Read the 1996 article by Turnbull et al., "Randomised, Controlled Trial of Efficacy of Midwife-Managed Care," and then summarize the focus of this study and the method used to conduct this research. Be sure to examine the types of questions that were asked of the participants. What does the article state as the value of midwives in managing health services during pregnancy and birth? In the end, what does the article conclude about the satisfaction of women who worked with midwives? Brainstorm a list of the ways that communication is central to managing this type of health service.

2. In Bernice Lieberman's 2001 article, "The Unmet Need," we learn about a men's group that meets regularly to provide an opportunity for men to talk about their infertility. Describe what you learn from this article about male infertility and the value of communication for men in the group.

# 6

## Formative Life Passages

### A Missing Father

It was the first year of high school and baseball season was about to start. I had just gotten over a severe case of the chickenpox when I got a phone call from my uncle. After a moment of small talk, he mentioned he had some bad news. The bad news was that my father had been in a fatal car crash while drinking and driving. I hung up the phone in a state is disbelief and shock, thinking this phone call must have been a dream. What was I to tell my mother and sister? I suddenly felt as if I was a different person. My role in the family had changed from a happy-go-lucky teen to a father figure for my sister and the man in the house for my mother. I realized I had to be strong even though I wanted to be weak. I kept asking myself, "What do I tell my friends? My father was a drunk and died doing something stupid!" I then realized I would use his bad judgment as a motivator for others not to follow his footsteps. I reversed the stigma of my father's young death to teach friends about the severity of driving while under the influence. To my surprise, his death brought all kinds of support. However, this support was a short-term patch for something I have to live with for the rest of my life.

MIKE TYLER, a junior in college

### Goodbye

What do you do when your best friend calls you to tell you goodbye? Ever have to drive to a friend's house at two in the morning to try and convince her to unlock the door to the bathroom she's in? To sit on the other side and tell her that she's good enough to continue living? To wait on the other side knowing she's swallowed a bottle of aspirin and you need to get her to the hospital? To cry with her? Tell her you love her?

You finally get her out and into the car. You drive her to the hospital and check her in for an attempted suicide, overdose. She gets her stomach pumped. She wants to leave the hospital and tries, [but] she doesn't get far.

You leave the hospital, go home, try to sleep, wonder what will happen to your friend. Will she be able to survive and continue on? She's tried before. What happens if she tries again? How many times will she try? Will she ever succeed? What happens if she succeeds? Why does she do this? I hope you never have to deal with this type of goodbye.

Kerri Weir, a junior in college

Children and adolescents are people without the life experience of adults, but like any person, they move through beginning life passages and into formative life passages, experiencing profound and formative biological, psychological, social, and spiritual changes. On a day-to-day basis, they interact with "authorities" (parents, teachers, health professionals, grandparents, older siblings), family, and friends in diverse contexts (home, preschool, school, clubs, athletic teams, homes of family and friends, providers' offices) who offer advice and support or, in some cases, communicate mandates concerning healthy and unhealthy behaviors. As they grow, children and adolescents may find themselves considering, resisting, and learning from the stories that others offer concerning what is "good for them" and what is "the best medicine."

Even though we have titled this chapter "Formative Life Passages," it cannot capture the expansive array of experiences and messages that form, shape, and mold young people—who they are, their understandings, and the questions they have regarding their health. Instead, we want you to consider just a few of the contexts or circumstances surrounding health or illness that may be part of young people's experiences. We want you to glimpse the stories they have told about how they communicate health. The voices of young people provide insight regarding the information they have learned about health and illness, their thoughts and feelings, and how communication has invalidated or excluded their views. Their identities are powerfully and subtly embedded in their ideas of how the world is and how they are "supposed" to live their lives, including their conceptions of health status and medical care.

Think back to all the changes you have experienced from childhood until now. Consider how communication with friends, parents, siblings, and even yourself (through journals or other forms of expression) figured prominently in your efforts to make sense of and come to terms with your changing identity. Then take a moment to write the story asked for in Theorizing Practice 6.1.

In this chapter, we touch on some of these changes, and we ask you to consider how your own experiences have mirrored or differed from those of the young people featured here. We begin generally, with communicating a sense of self, but then move specifically to particular changes, events, or behaviors that are part of young people's formative life passages, focusing in particular on communicating about sexuality and risk-taking behaviors.

## COMMUNICATING A SENSE OF SELF: THE EMOTION OF CHANGE

*"Instability of self-image, interpersonal relationships, and mood . . . uncertainty about . . . long-terms goals or career choice. . . . The person often experiences this instability of self-image as chronic feelings of emptiness or boredom."*

*Isn't this a good description of adolescence? Moody, fickle, faddish, insecure, in short, impossible.*

(Kaysen, 1993, pp. 152–154)

In this passage, Susanna Kaysen, who at 18 was committed to a psychiatric hospital, reads about her diagnosis, "Borderline Personality," from the *Diagnostic and Statistical Manual of Mental Disorders* (American Psychiatric Association, 1987). *Girl, Interrupted* is the memoir she wrote 25 years after the 2 years she spent in

---

**THEORIZING PRACTICE 6.1**

### A Formative Life Passage

Each person goes through an array of formative, health-related life passages that have tremendous impacts on who they are, what they know and believe, and who they become. Write a story about your experience with just one of these formative life passages, and feature the communication that occurred as you moved through it and how this one experience affected who you have become.

---

that psychiatric hospital as a teenager. Both the book and the movie of the same title attempt to capture how our definitions of sane and insane, of well and mentally ill, vacillate over time and through the different life passages we travel.

**Formative life passages** for young boys and girls often revolve around their emotional expression, self-esteem, and body image. Communicating feelings is considered to be a significant aspect of both mental and physical health (House, Landis, & Umberson, 1988; Pennebaker, 1995). At the same time, self-esteem is considered to be a critical indicator of mental health (National Advisory Mental Health Council, 1996). In addition, body image has a major influence on self-esteem and great significance to young people in a culture like ours, which is preoccupied with physical appearance, especially as it is communicated through the media (Kolb & Albanese, 1997; Shaw & Waller, 1995; Strasburger, 1995).

One qualitative study asked 209 fifth, eighth, and twelfth graders to respond in writing, "using their own words," to questions about emotional expression, body image, and self-esteem (Polce-Lynch, Meyers, Kilmartin, Forssmann-Falck, & Kliewer, 1998). The results revealed that boys restrict emotional expression from early through late adolescence, but girls increase emotional expression during the same period. The researchers suggest that "[l]ater in life, males' emotional restriction may render them more susceptible to health problems because their bodies unconsciously do the 'emotional' work for them in the form of medical problems such as ulcers, high blood pressure, heart problems" (p. 1039).

The voices of male adolescents reveal that they are confused and struggling with the "emotional stuff," and that they have clearly been socialized to believe the outward display of emotion is not acceptable. They learn that it can lead to peer rejection and that the social support they may seek in communicating these emotions may not be provided. Polce-Lynch et al. (1998) suggest we need to help boys and men to "develop the vocabulary to 'live in' the emotional world, and we need to reward—rather than punish—appropriate healthy emotional expressiveness in school, family, and professional relationships" (pp. 1039–1040).

Their study also reveals that female more often than male adolescents cited overall looks and specific body parts (hair, face, smile) as a source of feeling good about the self (Polce-Lynch et al., 1998). Both males and females, however, indicated that how they look has a great impact on how they feel about themselves ("When I look good, I feel good." "When I look bad, I feel bad"). Polce-Lynch et al. suggest that images of what "looks good" are perpetuated by the media, and that boys and girls are

*vulnerable to the mass media because they do not think about the messages communicated to them. Therefore, unless children and adolescents are taught the importance of—and how to—deconstruct mass media (TV/MTV, commercials, advertisements, etc.), this aspect of culture will largely remain an unconscious influence on body image, allowing media's influence to be all the more insidious. (p. 1040)*

These researchers also suggest that we must begin by raising consciousness about how unhealthy gender stereotypes are perpetuated in the media. (Theorizing Practice 6.2 considers specifically how men and women are depicted in music videos.) They conclude by summarizing what many of the youth in their study communicated: that relationships matter, as does being productive and involved in healthy activities.

**Adolescence** (ages 10–19) is a developmental period of "accelerating physical, psychological, social/cultural, and cognitive development, often characterized by confronting and surmounting a myriad of challenges and establishing a sense of self-identity and autonomy" (DiClemente, Hansen, & Ponton, 1996, p. ix). It is a time of change, self-consciousness, and search for identity (Tiggemann & Pennington, 1990). It is a time when young people's communication often shifts more exclusively to their friends. It is a time when communication with others becomes restricted as young people grapple with a range of developments—becoming more independent, making sense of the profound physical changes that their bodies are experiencing, and feeling more interested in the opposite sex.

What happens during this formative life passage we call adolescence "is to a large extent defined by the culture in which one lives, by the expectations society places on its young" (Robbins, 1998, p. 47). Some cultures engage in ceremonies

---

**THEORIZING PRACTICE 6.2**

### Depictions of Men and Women in Music Videos

Communication researcher Sut Jhally (1987, 1995) has produced two films (*Dream Worlds: Desire/Sex/Power in Rock Video* and *Dream Worlds 2: Desire/Sex/Power in Music Video*) that dramatically reveal how MTV music videos construct a negative image of men and women and both depict and naturalize violence against women.

In the next few days, watch five different music videos, and write down the images of men and the images of women that you see. Then consider the following questions:

1. What roles or "characters" do men play in the videos?

2. What roles or "characters" do women play in the videos?

3. What relationships between men and women are represented in the videos?

4. What solutions are offered for dealing with conflict or difficult situations?

5. What objects or symbols are represented as vehicles of or avenues to these solutions?

6. How might these depictions of roles, relationships, solutions, or symbols contribute to unhealthy or destructive interaction?

---

or rituals to help ease the emotional upheaval of this passage; others merely expect the child to become an adult without support or assistance. In this complex and confusing time, young people try out new behaviors and try on identities; teenagers look, feel, and sound differently than they did just a short time ago (Robbins). Traveling through puberty, adolescents experience a number of physical changes that clearly influence how they communicate with others—and how these others communicate with them.

**Puberty,** as defined in social science terminology, refers to "the biological changes that lead to reproductive maturity," (Lee & Sasser-Coen, 1996, p. 30) and adolescence is the "contextualized social/interpersonal period of the life-course surrounding puberty bridging childhood and adulthood" (p. 30). This time in a young person's life (usually around 12 years old for girls and 14 years for boys) is loaded with cultural meanings about gender and sexuality, and it is a time when they experience an abundance of physical, social, emotional, and spiritual changes. "Puberty is the most rapid period of human growth outside of neonatal growth and adolescents struggle to integrate these new bodies into their selves" (Martin, 1996, p. 11). Because many adolescents have their first experiences with sex during puberty, sexual well-being and overall well-being are intricately connected (Laumann, Gagnon, Michael, & Michaels, 1994). As children, they are trying to construct adult selves, and their feelings about their bodies and their sexuality play a significant role in their feelings of agency—the feeling that they can will things and make them happen, and the feeling that they can give expression to their experience (Aptheker, 1989; Benjamin, 1986; Martin).

Adolescents engage in narrative work to reconcile their contradictory feelings, to balance what happens to them both with what they hoped would happen and with what they have learned is "supposed to happen," to grapple with the sense of loss of their childhood, and to maintain a continuity of self despite physiological, cognitive, and emotional change (Levy-Warren, 1996; Martin, 1996). Here is how 15-year-old Nicole describes puberty:

> I didn't know what it [puberty] meant. So am I supposed to be like a woman now? Or what? It seemed so awkward to be like a little girl with breasts, I couldn't have both, but I didn't want to be a woman, but like, I didn't, it didn't feel right to me. It felt really awkward, but there wasn't anything to do about it. (Martin, p. 19)

In contrast to girls, who move into puberty with ambivalence and anxiety about their new bodies, most boys talk about how much older and more adult they feel and, with that, how much more independent and autonomous they have become (looking older, voice changing, and shaving). The following voices of adolescent boys reveal these sentiments (Martin, 1996):

*I was glad when I finally got taller and older. Being older you just get to do more, go out and stuff. (Joe, a 15-year-old boy) (p. 19)*

*It was about seventh grade [when my voice changed], I remember it changed pretty early, actually because, umm, all my teachers would say I was talking real loud, and I wouldn't notice it, and I told my mom, and she said, well it's probably 'cause my voice is changing and sometimes I'd pick up the phone and people would think it was my dad for a second. . . . I felt more grown up. When I went on vacation, I could pass for an older age or something. I thought that was kind of cool. Some people just thought I was older. (Brad, a 15-year-old boy) (p. 47)*

*I tried it in seventh grade and I just shaved right here, sideburns, you know. Now I don't shave that much, maybe once a week or something. No one told me or helped me. I did it just to feel kind of grown up, to kind of pretend. Kind of an ego booster I guess. (Brent, a 15-year-old boy) (p. 47)*

Young women also talk about the anxiety and frustration concerning the messages they begin to receive as they develop breasts. The boys notice, make comments, and judge them. Parents also notice, and they begin communicating warnings about boys and sex.

*I was self-conscious [when I developed breasts]. I still am. I don't know. It's just the boys. Some of them, how they react and stuff, just like if you're bigger you're better and stuff like that, some of the boys. I know some. It's aggravating. (Wendy, a 16-year-old girl) (p.31)*

*When I started to get them and now that I have them, I wish I didn't have them. . . . well, I'm just, I mean, I am self-conscious about my chest. I wish I was little again where you know, no one really worried about it and guys didn't really care as much and all that stuff. You know now it's the first thing they check out. (Jill, an 18-year-old girl) (p.32)*

*My father, just . . . Well, they both just told me to like to look out and not to put up with anything and stuff like that. You know to be careful you know, stuff like that. (Amanda, a 15-year-old girl) (p. 33)*

One researcher suggests that the developing female breast as a visual cue of puberty is at the center of a **body politic,** placing young women in the position of internalizing—and resisting—the messages that objectify their breasts (Lee, 1997). Another author suggests that breasts are never innocent:

*The sexualization of "innocent" parts of the body takes place primarily through the generation of meanings around them, the bundling of signs into a referential system. Female breasts are never innocent, their socialization takes place at the very moment they appear—a moment that also signals the entry into adulthood. (Haug et al., 1987, p. 139)*

When asked how she felt about her developing body, 24-year-old Robin stated:

*Awkward. I mean it was round the time when I was wearing a bra and some of us were and some of us were not wearing bras, and some of us, you know, were wearing bigger bras than others. And there was this whole bra-strap thing, you know, where boys would come and snap your bra strap or they would feel your shoulder to see if you were wearing one. There were lots of jokes made and rumors that this person stuffs her bra and this person doesn't even have anything, she doesn't even wear one. It was such a big deal. It was ridiculous. (Lee, 1997, p. 466)*

Young women talk about **menstruation** in some of the same ways they talk about the development of breasts—as ambiguous, confusing, and embarrassing. *Menarche,* the onset of menstruation, is just one of many changes that girls experience at puberty, but it is also one of the most significant markers or transitions. Menarche is "simultaneously feared and revered, considered to be magical, contaminating, and dangerous" (Lee & Sasser-Coen, 1996, p. 20). Across almost every culture, talk of menstruation is secretive, emotionally laden, shame-filled, and bound into the politics of the female body (Lee & Sasser-Coen; Thorne, 1993). When girls or women talk about their first blood, we gain insights regarding the impact of this transition on their views about their bodies, their identities, and how they resist—or comply—with the negative discourse that often surrounds menstruation (Lee & Sasser-Coen). Jessica, a 56-year-old white woman who grew up in Germany, describes the way women help other women:

*That was my support system, all of us girls talked and shared among ourselves. We would always tell each other we were having our period. And we talked about if we had cramps or how uncomfortable it was. We talked to each other about the length of our periods because we had varying lengths. We talked like how often we had to change our pads. . . . Once one of our teachers was having her period and somehow her pad became unhooked and it was really obvious, it was just poking, kind of poking way out (laugh) and she was busying lecturing. . . . So one of the girls wrote her a very nice little note and handed it to her. (Lee & Sasser-Coen, p. 178).*

Sarah, a white woman in her forties, describes her "resistance to the negative discourses surrounding menstruation" (p. 179):

*Every month I felt dirty, until age 17 when I became pregnant. Five years of feeling humiliated, different and afraid. When I became pregnant I was happy. I was looking forward to a baby—and also nine months of being smell-free "down there." It was only after my child was born that I realized this was a beautiful gift I had. I began to feel better about being a woman! I made a vow that I would explain menstruation to my children—girls or boys. I wouldn't let them become another victim. Along with this positive information, why there is a lack of education, the horror stories, and lack of understanding the natural processes of a woman's menstrual periods were explained to both my children. Two boys! (p. 180)*

One other natural and inevitable journey for young people is their first experience with sex. This process of sexual development can be viewed as an awakening of sexual identity and an unfolding of intimacy expressed through sexual behaviors (Porter, Oakley, Guthrie, & Killion, 1999), as the next section considers.

## COMMUNICATING SEX EDUCATION

Educating young people about puberty, sexuality, menstruation, and pregnancy is essential during these formative life passages. Now more than ever, we are considering what schools and parents should be communicating to children about sex. Experts may disagree about the who, what, and when questions of communicating this information, yet most would agree that parents and teachers play a significant role in this process. Parents clearly have the first opportunity to communicate with children; however, parents may also be embarrassed, hesitant, misinformed, or simply unwilling to talk frankly with their children (Daniels & Hoover, 1974; Roberts, 1980). Family communication can serve as a significant role model for adolescents and enhance both their reasoning and their decision-making skills (Booth-Butterfield & Sidelinger, 1998). One study indicated that the quality of parent-adolescent communication affected adolescents' sexual intentions and behaviors. In other words, the teens "with higher sexual abstinence values tended to have higher communication quality with their parents about sexual issues" (Miller, Norton, Fan, & Christopherson, 1998, p. 43). Another study indicated that young people reported infrequent communication with parents about sex and rated parental communication about sexuality as unwanted and inappropriate; teens see this type of information as part of their personal domain and not appropriate for parents to discuss (Rosenthal & Feldman, 1999).This study does, however, suggest that for parents to be effective communicators, they need to give more attention to the following:

*We will only understand parental-adolescent communication about sexuality if we think of sexuality in differentiated ways. That is, the area of sexuality may not be one unified domain but may consist of a variety of different domains including, for example, physical developments, dangers of sexuality and perhaps psychological or interpersonal issues. Second, adolescents are not passive recipients of parental messages and to understand whether parental communication is effective we must focus not only on the amount of communication, but whether the young person feels it is appropriate or important that his or her parent deals with a given topic. (p. 837)*

These findings clearly indicate that parents "need to learn how to provide the right amount of the right information at the right time" (Rosenthal & Feldman, p. 849).

Specifically, information about sex and sexuality needs to be less clinical and biological and more subjective and experiential (Martin, 1996). Like many other parents, I (Patricia) have read that the "best" time to communicate about sex and sexuality is when your child raises the questions. I have also learned that you don't have to decide what is too much or too little information—if you listen to your children, they will either keep asking questions or tell you they have learned enough for today. For example, when my daughter Makenna was seven, she once asked me right after her nighttime story, as I was shutting out the light, "Mommy, can I get pregnant sitting next to a boy?" I knew this was one of those "opportunities" that I didn't want to miss, so I sat down on her bed and talked with her candidly about how when she became older, she would need to make decisions about who she wanted to make love with, and that it was her decision and one she needed to be comfortable with. I tried to blend this relationship issue with biological information, using the correct terms, such as *vagina, penis, egg,* and *sperm,* in describing sexual intercourse and pregnancy. At that moment, it was clear to me that Makenna was asking questions not only to understand the words and the biological processes she had heard about from conversations at school, but that she wanted to talk about how she felt about this topic and what it meant for her communication with boys at school.

Undoubtedly, teens gain information about sex and sexuality from many sources beyond their families. The media, for example, have a profound influence—from billboards to TV commercials (Greenberg, Brown, & Buerkel-Rothfuss, 1993; Haffner, Kelly, & Bozell, 1987; Kinder, 1999). Regardless of the source, however, what seems to be essential is to teach *sex* education in the context of *gender* education (Martin, 1996). For example, Kendra criticizes what she has been taught:

*Women are taught really confusing messages about their own sexuality and we're supposed to be either this wild sex symbol, like crazy body and man's wildest fantasy or else like completely rigid and like have the guy like show us our sexual body or something. . . . I know girls who really liked a guy and really liked what they were doing and would've felt comfortable doing what they were doing, except they had all these messages in their head and like "You should be saying 'no' more," and "You should be hard to get," which is ridiculous. (Martin, p. 123)*

Tracy and other adolescents suggest the need to learn less about physiology and internal organs and more about relationships and emotions. They feel they would learn more from sex education through a discussion of what boys are like and how they behave:

> They just taught, they didn't really teach, well yeah, they taught sex. Like VD and stuff like that. . . . Maybe they could've stressed more, talked about relationships or something. 'Cause when I started high school I had no—I don't know what they could teach—but I had no clue of what boys were like, you know, how they are. (Martin, p. 125)

Some adolescents suggest they might learn more from a sex education class with just boys or just girls, so that they would feel more comfortable asking questions and talking about their own experiences. It has also been suggested that we consider the value of older peers, siblings, and other family members in communicating their more grounded, experiential knowledge to younger people as opposed to simply adults communicating to adolescents (Martin). This is especially important in terms of sex education in the school system.

Although controversial, many believe that sex education in the schools needs to be improved along lines similar to those suggested for parental communication. Sociologist Michele Fine (1988) studied sex education in New York City schools and found that it does little to enhance the development of sexual responsibility in adolescents. In fact, most sex education in public schools promotes a discourse of female victimization, authorizes suppression of talk about female desire, and privileges married heterosexuality over all other sexual practices (Fine). There clearly are exceptions to these results, however. One text designed to help parents answer questions about sex and sexuality suggests that a parent's personal views might cause difficulty in answering a child's question of "Can a woman have a baby if she isn't married?" (Uslander & Weiss, 1975). That book states that some parents might suggest it is wrong, difficult, or not a good idea, but that parents with a more open attitude toward sex may answer the question this way: "Yes, a woman certainly *can* have a baby if she isn't married and there's nothing wrong with it. . . ." (p. 49) Sex education that takes into account the need to change some of these stereotypical meanings and discourses about sexuality can serve an important function—bolstering boys' and girls' self-esteem, body awareness, and positive and healthy views of sexuality.

One vital area of sex education is **safe sex** talk. A wide variety of media campaigns and educational programs are designed to persuade individuals to use condoms each time they have intercourse to protect themselves against pregnancy, transmission of HIV, or contracting other sexually transmitted diseases, such as genital herpes, gonorrhea, or syphilis. Cooperation among partners in following this advice depends crucially on communication, but as many people have realized, it isn't always easy to talk about this issue (Adelman, 1992; Edgar, 1992; Metts & Fitzpatrick, 1992). Communication researcher Mara Adelman (1992) sees a dilemma in much of the research investigating communication between partners about condom use—that it focuses on safer sex communication as a form of negotiation which is explicit, persuasive, and controlling. In her view, when sexual partners construct their intentions, strategy, and planning before they engage in sex, their talk is structured and organized out of context. Then, when the couple enters the context of sexual intimacy, they may be faced with obstacles or resistances to the communicative plan because of arousal as well as social tensions or relational concerns.

Instead, Adelman (1992) suggests that because sexual activity tends to be improvisational, suspended, and unpredictable, a more powerful and practical metaphor is one of safer sex as play:

> I use the term play to include a variety of communicative verbal and nonverbal exchanges that interactants find amusing (e.g., verbal play such as jokes, punning, storytelling, rhyming, metaphors, baby talk, personal idioms, role-playing; nonverbal play such as mock fighting, object play, hand games). (p. 72)

Adelman suggests these metacommunicative frames help intimate partners to accomplish serious business in their relationship through improvisational adaptation in the context of sexual interaction. Adelman and two of her colleagues have even developed a video entitled *Safe Sex Talk* (Adelman, Moytl, & Downs, 1988), which includes role-played safer sex discussions between sexual partners. For example:

F: Right, and I want to think about using . . .

M: One of those.

F: I really do.

M: A . . . a raincoat (smiling up at her). Is that what you're driving at?

F: Yes, a glove.

M: (laughing) I have one of those (they kiss, then the male looking mischievously at the female). I have a whole box of them.

F: You do?

M: Pristine, unopened box. (kiss) We could use (kiss) every single one of them. (Adelman, 1992, p. 82)

Joking in this scene releases tension, serves as verbal foreplay, and diminishes inhibitions to talk about safer sex. In this way, each of us, in our intimate interactions, frames our sex talk in ways that sustain healthy passions. In addition, playing with safer sex may help young people to avoid the dilemma facing more and more teens—teenage pregnancy.

Undoubtedly, teenage pregnancy is a concern when you consider statistics about teenagers' experimentation with sex: (a) once every 10 seconds, a teenager has sexual intercourse for the first time (Children's Defense Fund, 1994); (b) nationally, 25 percent of 15-year-old girls and 27 percent of 15-year-old boys already have had intercourse (Porter et al., 1999); and (c) over one-half of all males are sexually active by the age of 16 or 17 (Sells & Blum, 1996, p. 17).

Advertisements on TV selling pregnancy tests simplify this complex moment in most women's lives. In addition, these commercials often depict a young couple in their twenties, delighted to discover that they will have a baby. Indeed, this sometimes is the case, but pregnancy may be a more complicated issue when the circumstances are not as depicted on TV. When the plastic stick reads positive, questions that have personal, cultural, and political implications abound. These commercials don't present the image of two 15-year-olds flipping back and forth through a medical index, trying desperately to determine if they might become teen parents. These commercials don't let us hear their voices, barely audible, speculating what their parents will say or do if the young woman is indeed pregnant. The confusion, panic, sense of hopelessness, guilt, and doubt are not captured in most depictions of this turning point in a young person's life.

Each year, about 900,000 American teenagers become pregnant ("Pregnant facts," 2000, p. F6). European countries and Canada have a better record of preventing teen pregnancies than the United States, not because teens are less sexually active in those countries but because they have better access to counseling and birth control ("Pregnant facts").

Controversy abounds as the problem of teen pregnancy is addressed through a wide variety of campaigns, including those promoting abstinence, distributing birth control pills and condoms, and sending messages promoting "safe" and "protected" sex. France's national campaign, addressed to adolescents through radio and TV ads, promotes contraceptive use and asks teens to be responsible ("Pregnant facts"). In contrast, the predominant message in the United States of "abstinence only" is often criticized for not promoting communication: "Basic communication should improve. 'Abstinence only' campaigns claim the moral high ground, but they also discourage meaningful public debate and ignore the reality of many adolescents' lives" (Pregnant facts," p. F6). There are some exceptions, however. A full-page ad by the California Wellness Foundation (1997) in the *San Diego Union-Tribune* was designed to raise awareness about the causes and consequences of teen pregnancy by sharing the views of researchers, counselors, and teenagers (see Theorizing Practice 6.3). Unlike other campaigns, this ad also suggests that the best approach to communicating about unplanned teenage pregnancy is to explore

## Speaking about Teen Pregnancy

Speaking about teen pregnancy. *Reprinted from the 1997 Public Education Campaign, The California Wellness Foundation Teenage Pregnancy Initiative. Courtesy Public Media Center.*

*(continued)*

(continued from previous page)

Read the ad, and answer the following questions:

1. Which voice stands out for you? Why?

2. Are any voices missing? If so, whose?

3. If you were to revise this ad, what would you change or include?

4. Do you think this ad will reach teens? Why, or why not?

5. Through what other forms of communication might we reach teens?

a wide range of answers for helping adolescents to grow up healthy and safe, including listening to the voices of teenagers. In the year 2001, the U.S. teenage birthrate declined to the lowest ever reported (Wilke, 2002). The drop in teen births is attributed to (a) fewer teens having sex, (b) more teens using contraception, (c) a vigorous national campaign to prevent teen pregnancy, (d) more attention to girls' sports and education, and (e) more mothers and other female role models who demonstrate the payoffs of a good education and solid working skills (Wilke, A12). While this is good news, there remains great concern about the high number of births to single girls and the continued focus of teen pregnancy as a sex problem rather than what many see as a major social and economic problem (Wilke, p. A12).

Clearly, it is vital for family planning practitioners and clients to be partners in discussions about selecting birth control methods that satisfy the clients' needs and to which those clients can be committed. One group of researchers studied the communication between family planning providers and clients at such clinics in Kenya to explore whether they were able to create this partnership (Kim, Odallo, Thuo, & Kols, 1999). Unfortunately, they found that providers dominated the conversation in most counseling sessions, and that clients rarely took an active role. Their results suggest that the approach providers take to communicating with their clients—whether in Kenya or the United States—must focus on: (a) building rapport and showing that they care; (b) personalizing the information, tailoring their talk to a client's individual situation and needs; (c) rewarding clients when they participate actively by providing positive reinforcement; and (d) asking open-ended questions that encourage clients to speak more freely (p. 16). These results have implications for communicating with clients of every age, but they are particularly important for teens, who often find it difficult to communicate with their parents about sex, sexuality, and pregnancy.

Similar results were found in a U.S. study, which stated that there is a "disturbing lack of communication between physicians and their patients" (Romney,

1999). The telephone survey of more than 2,200 women found that at their last health care visit, only 35 percent of respondents were counseled on birth control options, 30 percent were counseled on STDs (sexually transmitted diseases), 27 percent were asked about their sexual history and sexual practices, and only 8 percent discussed emergency contraception. Alina Salganicoff, who is the director of women's health policy for the Kaiser Family Foundation, states, "We are taught to be good patients. A good patient is a compliant patient. And people are taught that the doctor knows the right thing to do" (Romney). This failure to communicate can "mean the difference between a wanted, welcome pregnancy and an unintended one, between proper prenatal care and no care at all, or between awareness of a sexually transmitted disease, like HIV/AIDS, and ignorance" (Romney).

Most would agree on the importance of communicating to teens the need to wait before having children, but it is not unusual for people to communicate, to just about anyone, what they think is the "best time" or the "wrong time" to have children (Kelleher, 1998a, 1998b). In fact, newlyweds often say that one of the most annoying personal questions they are asked, even on their wedding day, is "When are you going to have kids?" Later in life, if women or men choose not to have children, they often are stigmatized by comments from family and friends, inquiring about how or why they would make that choice (Faux, 1984; Landa, 1990; Lisle, 1996; Morell, 1994). Ironically, the silence that surrounds the topic of teenage sexuality, pregnancy, and abortion stands in stark contrast to the unrestricted communication that appears to be more prevalent among adults. Instead, teenagers are often on their own in their experimentation with sex and other risk-taking behaviors; the next section explores some of the health campaigns designed to communicate with teens about risk-taking behaviors.

## COMMUNICATING ABOUT RISK-TAKING BEHAVIORS

Formative life passages for young people may also include their first ventures into **risk-taking behaviors**. In fact, the greatest threat to an adolescent's health is from their own risk-taking behavior (DiClemente et al., 1996). Therefore, along with their healthy, natural exploration of communication and identities, adolescents face increasing threats to their health and well-being—from tobacco use, disordered eating, alcohol use, drug use, suicide and suicidal behavior, unintentional injury (car accidents, drowning, sports, firearm use), delinquency, adolescent violence, teen pregnancy, and sexually transmitted diseases (DiClemente et al.). In one study of male and female undergraduates, risk-taking behavior, such as reckless driving, substance abuse, and risky sexual behavior, correlated with high **sensation seeking** (Wagner, 2001). Sensation seeking can be defined as the need for varied, novel, and complex sensations and experiences as well as the willingness to take physical and social risks for the sake of such experiences (Zuckerman, 1979).

Many health campaigns have been developed to address the at-risk behaviors of adolescents. Over the years, campaigns have attempted to educate adolescents by raising their awareness of the potential negative consequences of at-risk behavior or by developing their social skills to "just say no." Yet research is revealing that education may not control—or even predict—behavior, because many adolescents see themselves as being immune to illness and disease (Hochhauser, 1988). These findings suggest that telling adolescents to "just say no" may have the exact opposite of its intended effect. Critics of the campaign suggest that it "was single focused and failed to take into account the complexity of behavioral patterns and the multiplicity of influences on behavior" (DiClemente et al., 1996, p. 415) (see Chapter 9 for a more complete discussion of this campaign).

Normal adolescent development of egocentrism—an overall focus on the self emerging at all transition stages of cognitive development—actually leads adolescents to *not* feel at risk or vulnerable (Elkind, 1967, 1978; Greene, Rubin, Hale, & Walters, 1996). Clearly, however, some adolescents are, in fact, at risk as they begin to experiment with drinking and smoking. In addition, some adolescents may become vulnerable to poor eating habits—or even to eating disorders—as they become consumers of TV advertising.

## Communicating about Unhealthy Eating Habits

People's healthy and unhealthy eating habits are formulated in childhood. Although these habits can—and do—change throughout our lifetime, often the habits established early on can be linked to poor nutrition and obesity. In fact, research indicates a relationship between TV viewing and unhealthy eating habits: the more TV children watch, the more likely they are to select unhealthy foods. In addition, children who prefer to eat unhealthy foods are more likely to believe that the unhealthy foods are actually healthy (Signorielli & Staples, 1997). The findings may have direct relevance to the growing problem of obesity in general, and of overweight children in particular, in U.S. society—first, because the 20 hours on average per week that children spend watching TV could be spent in more energy-intensive activities; second, because watching TV is associated with snacking; and third, because the myriad unhealthy food messages found in both TV commercials and entertainment programming influences children's (and adults') choices of foods (Dietz, 1990).

What is needed are healthier TV messages and parents becoming aware of what and how much TV their children watch, educating children about what constitutes a healthy diet, and increasing children's awareness of how what is offered in advertising may not be healthy (Signorielli & Staples, 1997, pp. 298–299). Without such interventions, unhealthy eating habits can easily lead to obesity. Adolescents who are obese have an increased risk for a variety of medical conditions, and because thinness is admired in Western culture, especially among adolescents, these young people often are stigmatized as well (Ponton, 1996).

In addition to images of unhealthy eating, TV and advertising offer not only unhealthy but unrealistic images of acceptable body shape and weight (Grogan, 1999). In Western, affluent society, slenderness generally is associated with happiness, success, youthfulness, and social acceptability (Grogan), while excess flesh is associated with low morality, reflecting an inadequacy or lack of will (Bordo, 1993). As they go through puberty, many young girls and boys become dissatisfied and uncomfortable with their bodies, making them especially susceptible to these messages and images of unrealistic body weight and appearance. Dieting is more common for girls than for boys, but boys' images of adult males as being slender and muscular is something they strive for through exercise and dieting (Grogan).

Mild forms of disordered eating can become more risky and severe if preteens and teenagers restrict their food intake regularly by dieting or developing eating disordered behaviors such as anorexia nervosa and bulimia nervosa, as described in the next section.

### ■ Communicating Through Control of Food: The Appetite as Voice

*In the spring of 1986, at the age of 15, I invited bulimia to come live with me. She never moved out. Sometimes I tuck her deep in my closet behind forgotten dresses and old shoes. Then one day, I'll come across her—as if by accident—and experience genuine surprise that she remains with me. Other times, for a few days or perhaps a week or month, she'll emerge from the closet to sleep at my side, closer than a sister or mother would.*

*This is our story.*

(Tillmann-Healy, 1996, p. 76)

And so begins the story that communication researcher Lisa Tillmann-Healy tells about her ongoing struggle with a severe eating disorder, bulimia. Her story takes us close to her life—and to all the ways that this unhealthy behavior is communicated and kept secret from both friends and family members. Before we hear the stories that Lisa and others have to tell about this risk-taking behavior, however, let's define a few terms.

**Anorexia nervosa** is a form of disordered eating in which a person either restricts food intake or engages in purging (bulimia; discussed later). The disease is characterized by (a) refusal to maintain a normal body weight, (b) intense fear of becoming fat when one is actually underweight, (c) body weight dominating self-evaluation, (d) denying the seriousness of the current low body weight, and (e) the absence of at least three consecutive menstrual cycles (Ponton, 1996).

**Bulimia nervosa,** another form of disordered eating, is characterized by episodes of binge eating (lack of control in eating large portions of food) that are followed by efforts to prevent weight gain, such as "self-induced vomiting, misuse of laxative, diuretics, enemas, and other medications; fasting; or excessive exercise" (Ponton, 1996, p. 84). Although many of us engage in binge eating on occasion, this practice becomes a disorder when the binge eating and purging occur, on average, twice a week for two months or longer (Ponton).

History professor Joan Jacobs Brumberg (2000), who has thoroughly researched the history of anorexia, tells us that anorexia nervosa was named and identified in the 1870s almost simultaneously by medical men in England, France, and the United States. Although anorexia nervosa is a relatively modern disease, female fasting is not a new behavior.

Brumberg (2000) finds a long history of food-refusing behavior and appetite control in women, dating back to the medieval world. In her view, anorexia is a cultural artifact, defined and redefined over time and, thus, implying important continuities in female experience across both time and place. She suggests that the real question to ask is "Why is it that women and girls in certain cultural systems and historical epochs become susceptible to particular forms of exaggerated behavior centered on food?" (p. 7). To answer this question, and to consider the responsiveness of disease to cultural settings, Brumberg states that

> *we must look beyond the doctors, diagnoses, and therapies to the patients themselves. People express both physical and psychic discomfort in myriad ways, depending on their gender and age, their class, their ethnic origins, their worldview, and a host of other cultural variables. (p. 8)*

Labeling the appetite as voice, Brumberg suggests that

> *[t]oday's anorectic is one of a long line of women and girls throughout history who have used control of appetite, food, and the body as the focus of their symbolic language. . . . Because food was a common resource in the middle-class household, it was available for manipulation. Middle-class girls, rather than boys, turned to*

*food as a symbolic language, because the culture made an important connection between food and femininity and because girls' options for self-expression outside the family were limited by parental concern and social convention. In addition, doctors and parents expected adolescent girls to be finicky and restrictive about their food. Young women searching for an idiom in which to say things about themselves focused on food and the body. Some middle-class girls, then as now, became preoccupied with expressing an ideal of female perfection and moral superiority through denial of appetite. (pp. 5, 184)*

So what do the voices of girls and women suffering from eating disorders tell us? In just a few stories, we can learn.

### Aimee

*The sense of accomplishment exhilarates me, spurs me to continue on and on. It provides a sense of purpose and shapes my life with distractions from insecurity. . . . I shall become expert [at losing weight]. . . . The constant downward trend [of the scale] somehow comforts me, gives me visible proof that I can exert control. (Liu, 1979, p. 141)*

### Lisa ("The First Time")

*I kneel in front of the toilet bowl, afraid yet strangely fascinated. As I stare at my rippling reflection in the pool of Saniflush-blue water, my thoughts turn to an article in the latest* Teen Magazine *about a young woman who used vomiting to control her weight. It sounds repulsive in light of my experiences with the flu and hangovers. Still, I want to try it, to see if I can do it.*

*I place the shaking index finger of my right hand to the back of my throat. I hold it there for five or six seconds, but nothing happens. I push it down further. Still nothing. Further. Nothing. Frustrated, I move it around in circular motions. At last, I feel my stomach contract, and this encourages me to continue. Just then, I gag loudly.*

*Shhh.*

*Footsteps clonk on the linoleum outside the bathroom door, and I immediately pull my finger out of my mouth.*

*"Lis?" my father calls. "You OK?"*

*"I'm fine, Dad," I answer. "Playing basketball tonight?"*

*"Yeah, and I'm late."*

*I hear him pass through the dining room and ascend the stairs.*

*Listening closely for other intruders, I gaze into the commode, determined to see this through. The front door slams as my father exits, and I return to my crude technique. Again my stomach contracts. When I feel my body rejecting the food, I move my hand aside to allow the smooth, still-cold liquid to pour out of me—a once perfect Dairy Queen turtle sundae emerges as a brown swirl of soft-serve ice cream, hot fudge and butterscotch, and minute fragments of chopped pecans.*

*Again and again, 20 times or more, I repeat this until I know by pushing on my stomach that it is satisfactorily empty. My pulse races.*

*I am 15 years old. (Tillmann-Healy, 1996, pp. 86–87)*

### Kate

*For myself, and I think it's probably true for a lot of people who go through this [bulimia], you're not gonna be able to face the issue and deal with it until you can say it out loud. To somebody, even if it's to your own face in the mirror. But until you can hear the words actually come out of your mouth that "this was a painful thing for me." Or if you have really negative feelings about some member of your family that you think God's gonna strike you dead if you say it out loud. I think that before you can stop stuffing down inside you symbolically with the food, you actually have to physically—you're doing something physical to keep it inside you so you have to do something physical to get it out. So saying exactly what it was, I think you have to do that . . . I actually a couple of times went to the cemetery and said it out loud up at my father's gravesite. . . . I would actually go and have conversations with him about things that were going on in my life at that time that, if he were alive, I would wish I could say to him. So I would go up and do that. (Reindl, 2001, p. 203)*

In these and other stories we see the complexities of communicating—and of not communicating—when girls and women suffering from eating disorders struggle for a sense of self. In this way, they step out of their role as censor or judge and begin to communicate a sense of connectedness with their feelings, instincts, needs, and desires (Reindl, 2001).

## Communicating about Alcohol

Alcohol abuse, like eating disorders, is also a serious risk-taking behavior that can claim adolescents lives, not only through accidents but also through the suicides that may occur while under the influence of this drug (National Clearinghouse for Alcohol and Drug Information [NCADI], 2001). Almost all adolescents experiment with drinking as a way to help them feel less inhibited, make friends, or let off steam. As mild as this sounds, however, alcohol abuse affects more than 4.6 million adolescents a year, with accidental deaths, homicides, and suicides being the three most prevalent forms of mortality associated with this at-risk behavior (Windle,

Shope, & Bukstein, 1996). In fact, 20 percent to 35 percent of suicide victims have a history of alcohol abuse or were drinking before their suicide (NCADI). **Binge drinking,** which is defined as five or more drinks on a single occasion, is on the rise among adolescents, and this is associated with other problems as well, such as poor school performance and difficulty in getting along with family (Windle et al.).

Not surprisingly, alcohol abuse continues to be a problem as young people move on to college, where the associated negative consequences include sexual assaults, unsafe and unplanned sex, driving while intoxicated, automobile accidents, arrest, and use of illegal drugs (Dorsey, Scherer, & Real, 1999). In their study of college drinking, communication researchers Dorsey et al. found a significant relationship between excessive drinking and the social networks of the students. One of the "most powerful and least surprising findings was the significant relationship between Greek membership and excessive drinking" (p. 329). Another significant finding was that talking with friends about certain topics (effects of drinking too much, participating in casual sex, binge drinking, using a controlled substance, physical violence or fighting, and unwelcome sexual advances) also correlated with excessive drinking. Their findings reveal how dramatically students' communication within their social networks can influence at-risk behaviors such as alcohol abuse. As they point out, we need to learn more about the forms of communication in social networks that can assist college students in resisting potentially dangerous behaviors.

Analysis of fraternity drinking stories reveals that members of this culture frame excessive drinking as a positive, functional, and even necessary activity (Workman, 2001). Group interviews conducted by communication scholar Thomas Workman with 17 fraternities revealed emergent themes of "drunk stories," including the adventure story (drunkenness as risk taking), the stupid story (drunkenness as entertainment), the naked or puking story (drunkenness as physical exploration), the regretted-sex story (drunkenness as a sexual trap), and the college story (drunkenness as contextual behavior). One example of a stupid story reveals how "notorious" drunks are outlandish, tolerated, and amusing. In the telling of these stories, the narrators frame the drunken behavior as entertainment yet add commentary that indicates the behavior is "seen by the culture as extreme" (p. 435).

A:        Some people are a little more prone to do stupid things.

B:        Coming home from the bars one night, walked by the Union when there was construction being done and the Caterpillar was sitting open and this other guy got in it and drove it home.

C:        He used like a mailbox key to turn it on. It worked! He was drunk and I can't believe he made it home without hitting anything.

B:              That is a stupid drunk.

Interviewer:    It's not like anyone says, we can't let this guy get drunk again?

B:              No, no. (Workman, p. 435)

What is problematic is that drinking stories such as this "prohibit critical self-reflection on what is obviously a dangerous set of behaviors. Drinking stories not only limit individual and group reflection of potential danger, but they also serve as a form of protection against counter messages about drinking" (p. 442). Although there were also "tragic" stories of injury and death, these stories were not told and retold, because "they would bring everybody down" (p. 442).

## ▓ Communicating about Smoking

In addition to experimenting with alcohol, most adolescents try smoking, another at-risk behavior, as a way of taking on a new identity and responding to pressure from peers to smoke. Research shows that individuals who eventually become habitual smokers typically start before the end of high school (Johnston, O'Malley, & Bachman, 1994), but what parents, peers, and the media communicate about the at-risk behavior of smoking may have a powerful impact on initiating, continuing, or ceasing risky behaviors. One study, for example, found that children in third through eighth grades have lower rates of smoking intention and initiation when their nonsmoking *or* smoking parents engage in antismoking socialization (Henriksen & Jackson, 1998). In other words, if parents play an active role in communicating knowledge, attitudes, and skills that prepare children to resist smoking, then these children are less likely to smoke or to express an intention to begin smoking.

One group of smokers on the rise is Americans who do not continue their education beyond high school (Sengupta, 1996), but how do we reach them? What we are learning is that antismoking media campaigns must be diverse and not focus only on the harmful effects of smoking. These messages are effective for at-risk adolescents, but they are not as effective when targeted at current smokers—who are already aware of the negative health consequences (Sengupta). Instead, messages communicated to less educated smokers must stress the importance of a healthy lifestyle in general and of the power they have to improve their own health. The American Lung Association's "Freedom from Smoking for You and Your Family," which is aimed at blue-collar workers, focuses on quitting skills and motivation to quit (Abrams & Biener, 1992).

Smoking, excessive alcohol consumption, disordered eating, and unhealthy eating habits are just a few of the risk-taking behaviors that can be a part of formative life passages. Clearly, we need to carefully consider how communication from friends, family members, authorities, and the media may promote, discourage, and even ignore the risk-taking behaviors of adolescents.

## SUMMARY

This chapter has explored some of the formative life passages through which young people travel, and we have learned about some of the biological, psychological, social, and spiritual changes that they experience in the process. Clearly, a key to sustaining health for adolescents is communication with peers in their social network, with parents, and with teachers. Adolescents are also surrounded by messages from advertising, TV, music, and many other forms of media that promote both healthy as well as unhealthy behaviors. Young people need to become critical consumers of these messages so they can sort out what is essential for maintaining their health throughout their lives. In the next chapter, "Sustaining and Enduring Life Passages," we explore some of these other contexts for communicating health.

## KEY TERMS

formative life passages

adolescence

puberty

body politic

menstruation

safe sex

risk-taking behaviors

sensation seeking

anorexia nervosa

bulimia nervosa

binge drinking

## DISCUSSION QUESTIONS

1. When you think about your past or recent formative life passages, which ones stand out in your mind? Why?

2. What formative life passages are not represented in this chapter? What should be discussed about these passages?

3. For many teens, formative life passages are associated with pain, embarrassment, or confusion. Considering your own experiences, which one person or one event stands out in your mind as having helped you to feel less pain, embarrassment, or confusion?

4. If you had the opportunity to talk with a young teen who trusted and felt comfortable talking to you, what would you say to support and guide this person through any one of these formative life passages?

5. As a college student, you or your friends may have engaged in some of the risk-taking behaviors discussed in this chapter. If you were to design a health campaign to reach someone like yourself or your friends, what messages would that include? What forms would these messages take?

6. Do young people in our society experience moralistic language concerning their "unhealthy" behaviors? What specific examples come to mind?

**INFOTRAC COLLEGE EDITION**

1. Providing adolescent health care means focusing on the biological, behavioral, emotional, and social forces that influence adolescent health and well-being. Robert W. Blum's 1990 article, "Adolescent Medicine," describes what adolescents need in health care programs. Read this article, and create a list of the basic health care needs of adolescents. Describe the ways that communication can be critical in addressing these health care needs.

2. Using the subject search index, locate sources focusing on *puberty*. Summarize the types and content of the sources that are listed. Summarize one of the articles that you see as related to the emotion of change. Summarize a second article that indicates how the experience of puberty may be different based on your membership in different cultural communities. Finally, summarize a third article that captures how puberty is linked to other formative life passages, including risk-taking behaviors.

# 7
## Sustaining and Enduring Life Passages

The telephone rang . . . It was my husband, asking me to prepare a lunch and deliver it to him at his workplace. . . . Quickly, I put together a rudimentary lunch, and went to my car. I hesitated for a moment, confused on exactly how to place both my purse and the lunch container on the seat beside me. After some juggling, I backed the car from the driveway. As I drove to Jack's office, I noticed a strip shopping center, new to me. It was strange I had not noticed this mall previously. I traveled this route frequently. I passed the street leading to the off-site, and drove several miles down the road before realizing my error. No doubt the new shopping center had thrown my judgment off, I mused, and turned around to retrace my steps.

Near the driveway leading to my husband's office, I observed a fire station which was also new to me. That would be a good landmark to guide me to the company entrance in the future.

Jack saw my car approaching and came out of his building to greet me. Accepting the lunch with thanks, he leaned against the car.

"Jack, when did they build that new strip shopping center on Kirkman Road? Funny, but I don't remember it being built, and it is already open for business."

Jack frowned thoughtfully, then shook his head.

I continued, "Oh, well, I'm glad to see the new fire station near your entrance. It will give me a good landmark."

Jack laughed and again shook his head. "Diane, that station has always been here," he chided. "Even before my building was built!"

I suddenly became irate. I started the car, and began to pull away from Jack, who leaped from his position leaning against the vehicle.

"Whoa! What's your rush?"

I braked, staring before me in confusion. Where was the exit?

"Jack," I asked shakily, "How do I get out of here?"

DIANE FRIEL McGOWIN, before being diagnosed with
Alzheimer's disease at the age of 45 (McGowin, 1993, pp. 5–6)

e can all share the terror and frustration that Diane felt in this experience. Clearly, it was the beginning of life-altering events that would significantly affect her sense of self, her relationships with others, and the remaining story of her life.

Life challenges are inevitable for all of us, and while we hope that most are wonderful, we are also bound to face some that are devastating. In part because today we're living longer and being diagnosed earlier, we are likely candidates for many illnesses. For example, the American Cancer Society predicts about 1,268,000 new diagnoses of cancer in 2001 (American Cancer Society, 2001), and by 2050, the National Alzheimer's Association predicts that 14 million Americans will test positive for Alzheimer's, compared to only four million today (Schwartz, 1999). How we adapt to these turning points in our lives is central to our well-being and to our physical and mental health. None of us can be prepared for the dramatic changes that would invade Diane McGowin's life, but nothing about Diane makes her any different from the rest of us. As she observed:

> At one time, I had managed a law office. At one time, I had been a legal assistant, conducting research, traveling to court, doing administrative work, delegating duties to others, and overseeing office procedures. At one time, I had acted as hostess on behalf of the senior partner of my law firm at a dinner party honoring the governor. At one time, I had an IQ of 137. (McGowin, 1993, p. 31)

We are all vulnerable to the curves that life throws our way, and as we continue to live longer (reaching a record high of 76.9 years in 2000) (U.S. Department of Health and Human Services, 2001), we are much more likely to live those extra years with chronic health problems. How will we communicatively adapt to and renegotiate our relationships with others throughout these changes? How do our relationships communicatively sustain us and help us to endure as we age?

In this chapter, we examine some of these issues and their impact as we deal with health changes throughout our life span. We identify many of these behaviors, and we emphasize the role of communication as a mediator of much of our health. Specifically, we discuss several health-challenging contexts, including mental (depression), physical (blindness), and social (aging) health turning points, and then focus on coping strategies. We begin by considering life-altering health challenges in general and then focus on specific examples.

## LIFE-ALTERING HEALTH CHALLENGES

Lyons, Sullivan, and Ritvo (1994) define **chronic illnesses** and **disabilities** as

> *conditions that result in moderate to severe restrictions in physical functioning and the performance of social roles related to work, leisure, family, and friendships. The term* chronic *signifies a long-term condition encompassing a course that may be stable, unpredictable, or progressive. (p. 5)*

Examples of chronic illnesses include Alzheimer's disease, arthritis, blindness, cancer, cardiovascular disease, diabetes, multiple sclerosis, depression, bipolar disorder, schizophrenia, eating disorders, and posttraumatic stress disorder. Some are also now calling AIDS a chronic, rather than terminal, illness given how many people are now living much longer after being diagnosed (Perloff, 2001, p. 124).

Once we are diagnosed with an illness or experience a traumatic life event, its seriousness, prognosis, and debilitating potential shifts our identities toward disenfranchisement—to someone now on the societal margins, perceived as being unable to participate in life as before (Ray, 1996b). We are now stigmatized, with the degree of stigmatization being proportional to how taboo our culture considers the illness or experience.

Goffman (1963) talks about **stigma** as "an attribute that is deeply discrediting" (p. 3). Stigma divides people into two groups, those who are acceptable and those who are not, which results in a superior-subordinate relationship. Stigmatizing others helps us to keep our own identity intact: as long as we are not "like" them, it will not happen to us. For example, persons with AIDS are stigmatized because of some of the ways in which AIDS is transmitted. Victims of sexual assault are also stigmatized, often blamed, and revictimized. The key is that we blame victims for their own misfortune, hoping to make ourselves invulnerable in the process. We think, "If I'm not gay and not an intravenous drug user, I can't get AIDS," or "If I don't wear a short skirt and spaghetti-strap top, I won't get raped." These thoughts may temporarily comfort us, but they are illusions. We have all read about—or even known—someone just like us who got AIDS or who looked and dressed like us and was raped. The data don't bear out our illusions either. We know, for example, that in the United States, close to 800,000 cases of AIDS have been reported to the CDC (Centers for Disease Control and Prevention) through December 31, 2000, and about 40,000 new HIV (human immunodeficiency virus) infections are reported each year to the CDC (2001), and that one in four women experience rape or attempted rape by the time they are in college (Botta & Pingree, 1997). As our population ages and medical advances continue, more and more of us will face our own or a loved one's chronic illness.

We would all prefer that bad things only happen to bad people, but we are all susceptible. Chances are great that, at some point, our day-to-day lives and relationships will be disrupted and we will experience various degrees of emotional and physical upheaval. How we manage this upheaval and balance our relationships in the process is the focus of this chapter.

## MANAGING OUR RELATIONSHIPS

Even in the best of times, developing and maintaining relationships can be difficult. When we or our loved ones face illness or disability, our relational equilibrium is thrown into imbalance, and we must renegotiate, either explicitly or implicitly, our relationships. As Lyons and Meade (1995) observe:

> Superimpose the additional complexities of illness, and people must navigate carefully over particularly strange and foreboding relational terrain . . . threats to social identity, performance of roles, and hopes for the future . . . each party in the relationship asks, "What will life be like for me in this relationship and for us?" (p. 186)

With the introduction of new health problems, we *remodel* (Lyons & Meade) our lives and relationships, making substantial lifestyle changes because of illness or disability. The unpredictability introduced by chronic illness (as in conditions such as arthritis, multiple sclerosis, or bipolar disorder) creates the need for **chronic adaptational activity** (Lyons & Meade). We continue to adapt as our illness or disability improves, maintains, or worsens.

In the next three sections, we discuss depression, blindness, and aging as exemplars of life-altering conditions involving mental, physical, and social health. We focus on the communication ironies and realities that are both caused by and manifested within these conditions.

## Depression

Health-related life-altering events are not limited to or independent of emotional illnesses. Depression has no age boundaries, and the devastation that it leaves in its wake is all-encompassing and difficult to understand for those who have never experienced it. About 10 million Americans—roughly three percent of the U.S. population—suffer from depression, and women are diagnosed with depression at least twice as often as men (Kettl, 1999). Research on communication and depression has not received much attention. Among communication researchers, Chris Segrin and Mary Anne Fitzpatrick (1992) have done the most work in this area and have found, for example, that in marriages with more verbally aggressive wives, husbands are more depressed.

Despite depression being so widespread (just in January of 2000, 840,000 prescriptions were written for Prozac and 847,000 for Zoloft) (Galewitz, 2000), clinical depression—and virtually all mental illnesses—remains a taboo topic in our culture. We still stigmatize people who admit to having this or other mental illnesses. We tend to blame them for their illness, believing that if they would just pull themselves up by their bootstraps, they would be fine. Making "them" different from us gives the illusion of invulnerability, but it is just an illusion. Any of us may face a mental illness, leaving our intimate, work, and even casual relationships impacted and tested.

Several communication-related issues surround depression. Persuasive evidence supports a biological cause, but most mental health professionals agree that communicative aspects are involved as well. Here we discuss three: (a) communicating from the depressed person's perspective, (b) the impact of labeling mental illness, and (c) the importance of supportive communication.

***Communicating from the depressed person's perspective.*** A major clinical depressive episode is difficult to imagine for those who have never experienced it. Being clinically depressed is different from being "down" or "blue." William Styron (1990), an award-winning author, says the word "depression" does not adequately describe how it feels:

> When I was first aware that I had been laid low by the disease, I felt a need, among other things, to register a strong protest against the word "depression." . . . I would lobby for a truly arresting designation. "Brainstorm," for instance, has unfortunately been preempted to describe, somewhat jocularly, intellectual inspiration. But something along these lines is needed. Told that someone's mood disorder has evolved into a storm—a veritable howling tempest in the brain, which is indeed

*what a clinical depression resembles like nothing else—even the uninformed layman might display sympathy rather than the standard reaction that "depression" evokes, something akin to "So what?" or "You'll pull out of it" or "We all have bad days." The phrase "nervous breakdown" seems to be on its way out, certainly deservedly so, owing to its insinuation of a vague spinelessness, but we still seem destined to be saddled with "depression" until a better, sturdier name is created. (pp. 36–38)*

Clinically depressed people have described feeling a downward, black spiral that they feel powerless to stop. Many feel they do not have an adequate vocabulary to describe their experience, and that others who have not been through it cannot possibly understand their depths of despair. Styron (1990) describes how he felt in the throes of his major clinical depression:

*The pain is unrelenting, and what makes the condition intolerable is the foreknowledge that no remedy will come—not in a day, an hour, a month, or a minute. If there is mild relief, one knows that it is only temporary; more pain will follow. It is hopelessness even more than pain that crushes the soul. (p. 62)*

When in the eye of the depression, sufferers can see what is happening, but they cannot intervene. Their ability to communicate with others is severely impeded as they face the paradox that they

*greatly desire connection while they are simultaneously deprived of the ability to realize it. Much of the depression's pain arises out of the recognition that what might make one feel better—human connection—seems impossible in the midst of a paralyzing episode of depression. It is rather like dying from thirst while looking at a glass of water just beyond one's reach. (Karp, 1994, p. 343)*

Hopefully before it reaches this point of crisis, others have observed troubling nonverbal behaviors, such as increased isolation, withdrawal from social events, and decreased communication with others, and will intervene on behalf of the depressed person. In FYI 7.1, we list the criteria that psychiatrists follow to determine if a person is depressed.

***Depression as a label.*** Experiencing a major clinical depression changes not only your life but your identity as well. Now you are one of "them." It was more than 30 years ago (in 1972) that Thomas Eagleton was the vice-presidential running mate of George McGovern. The media exposed Eagleton's treatment for clinical depression, and despite McGovern's initial (in his words) 1,000-percent support, Eagleton was removed from the ticket. Today, Tipper Gore, wife of the 2000 presidential candidate Al Gore, has spoken publicly on her bout with depression. This suggests progress toward destigmatization, but it is also worth noting that Gore's depression

A. Five (or more) of the following symptoms have been present during the same 2-week period and represent a change from previous functioning; at least one of the symptoms is either (1) depressed mood or (2) loss of interest or pleasure.

Note: Do not include symptoms that are clearly due to a general medical condition, or mood-incongruent delusions or hallucinations.

(1) depressed mood most of the day, nearly every day, as indicated by either subjective report (e.g., feels sad or empty) or observation made by others (e.g., appears tearful. Note: In children and adolescents, can be irritable mood)

(2) markedly diminished interest or pleasure in all, or almost all, activities most of the day, nearly every day (as indicated by either subjective account or observations made by others)

(3) significant weight loss when not dieting or weight gain (e.g., a change of more than 5% of body weight in a month), or decrease or increase in appetite nearly every day. Note: In children, consider failure to make expected weight gains.

(4) insomnia or hypersomnia nearly every day

(5) psychomotor agitation or retardation nearly every day (observable by others, not merely subjective feelings of restlessness or being slowed down)

(6) fatigue or loss of energy nearly every day

(7) feelings of worthlessness or excessive or inappropriate guilt (which may be delusional) nearly every day (not merely self-reproach or guilt about being sick)

(8) diminished ability to think or concentrate, or indecisiveness, nearly every day (either by subjective account or as observed by others)

(9) recurrent thoughts of death (not just fear of dying), recurrent suicidal ideation without a specific plan, or a suicide attempt or a specific plan for committing suicide

(American Psychiatric Association, 1994, pp. 320–327)

was caused by the near-fatal accident of her son. (See Chapter 9 for more information on the political ramifications of Gore's public admission.) No mention was made of a specific cause for Eagleton's depression, but much was said about his receiving ECT (electroconvulsive treatment). Many laypeople can understand the devastation Tipper must have felt, but ECT, despite significant advances in this procedure, scares most people and suggests the person must have been *really* sick to require such drastic treatment.

Labeling depression as a mental illness can be stigmatizing to sufferers as well. Psychologist David Karp (1999) reports interviewing Karen, a 24-year-old graduate student who had been hospitalized for clinical depression. She comments on being labeled as mentally ill:

*I think of it less as an illness and more something that society defines. That's part of it, but then, it is physical. Doesn't that make it an illness? That's a question I ask myself a lot. Depression is a special case because everyone gets depressed. . . . I think that I define it as not an illness. It's a condition. When I hear the term illness I think of sickness . . . [but] the term mental illness seems to me to be very negative, maybe because I connect it with hospitalization. . . . (p. 85)*

Karen also notes the impact of the depression label on her identity:

*You know, I was a mental patient. That was my identity. . . . Depression is very private. Then all of a sudden it becomes public and I was a mental patient. . . . It's no longer just my own pain, I am a mental patient. I am a depressive. I am a depressive (said slowly and with intensity). This is my identity. I can't separate myself from that. When people know me they'll have to know about my psychiatric history, because that's who I am. ([roman] as in original; p. 83)*

Karp (1999) suggests identity turning points as a way to categorize redefining identities that are experienced by people suffering with depression:

1. *A period of* inchoate feelings, *during which they lack the vocabulary to label their experience as depression.*

2. *A phase during which they conclude that* something is really wrong with me.

3. *A crisis* stage *that thrusts them into a world of therapeutic experts.*

4. *A stage of* coming to grips with an illness identity, *during which they theorize about the cause(s) for their difficulty and evaluate the prospects for getting beyond depression. ([roman] as in original; p. 86)*

In stage four, depressives still identify themselves from the mental illness perspective. Even if the episode passes and no depression is experienced for a long time, however, it takes a while to trust this new normality and to shift from depressive being the primary—and often singular—self-identifier to being just one of many aspects defining the self. For Karen, it took several years:

*A couple of years ago, three years ago, four years ago, I would feel a need to tell people about it because I still felt depressed, because I still felt mentally ill. But now I no longer see myself in that way. I'm other things. I'm Karen the grad student. I'm Karen the one who loves to garden, the one who's interested in a lot of things. I'm not just Karen the mentally ill person. (p. 85)*

Labeling depression as an illness may cause us to view sufferers as victims of a biochemical imbalance and, therefore, as passive, helpless, and absolved of inappropriate behaviors and responsibility (Karp, 1999).

***The importance of supportive communication.*** Social support is extremely important for people experiencing depression. This can be difficult for others, because during this time, the support is not likely to be reciprocal. Depressives are self-focused and likely to lack the energy to be an active member of a relationship. As Styron (1990) observes, however, it made a huge difference to him during the throes of his depression:

> *During the same summer of my decline, a close friend of mine—a celebrated newspaper columnist— was hospitalized for severe manic depression. By the time I had commenced my autumnal plunge my friend had recovered . . . and we were in touch by telephone nearly every day. His support was untiring and priceless. It was he who kept admonishing me that suicide was "unacceptable" and it was also he who made the prospect of the hospital less fearsomely intimidating. (pp 76–77)*

Styron was fortunate to have this friend, but often, this is a time when the energy needed to communicate even about mundane matters is too straining. Paradoxically, when those with depression most need interaction, they are least able to initiate or engage in it.

One of the most devastating outcomes of depression is suicide (Kettl, 1999). The number one protection against suicide is integration in a social network. This may be through a formal support group, with a therapist, or informally among friends and family. Being connected to others, having them to talk to, significantly decreases the risk of suicide. Take a look around your classroom, your dorm floor, or where you work. Suicide is the third-leading cause of death among 15- to 24-year-olds (after car crashes and homicide) (CDC, 2002). And for every one who succeeds, 100 to 200 try—and those who try are likely to try again (Cantor, 1999). At the other end of the age spectrum, depression accounts for 60 percent to 75 percent of suicides in people 75 and older. White males over the age of 80 have the highest suicide rate of all Americans, at six times the national average (Saenger, 1999). It's impossible to stop a determined person, but we can still be aware of—and respond to—any verbal and nonverbal clues someone may give about their inner turmoil and intentions (see FYI 7.2).

Current research suggests that mental illness results from a combination of biological, environmental, and communicative influences. It may be acute or chronic, and most mental health practitioners recommend a combination of drug and talk therapy. One major concern of both practitioners and patients is that most health insurance plans now cover only a limited amount of therapy, usually

1. A recent loss and apparent inability to let go of the grief.

2. A change in personality, becoming sad, withdrawn, irritable, anxious, tired, indecisive, or apathetic.

3. A change in behavior, such as inability to concentrate or loss of interest.

4. Lowered interest in sex.

5. Expressions of self-hatred.

6. Change in sleep patterns.

7. Change in eating habits.

8. Making direct statements about committing suicide, such as "I just need to end it all."

9. Making indirect statements about committing suicide, such as "You won't have to worry about me anymore."

10. Making final preparations, such as writing a will, giving away possessions, repairing poor relationships, or writing revealing poems or letters.

11. A preoccupation with themes of death.

12. A sudden and unexplained show of happiness following a period of depression.

13. Marked changes in personal appearance.

14. Excessive risk taking and an "I don't care what happens to me" attitude.

Adapted from http://www.befrienders.org/suicide/warning.htm and
http://www.suicidology.org/index.html.

about 20 sessions. Practitioners argue that for many sufferers, longer-term therapy is critical, but if patients can't afford it on their own, they must stop prematurely. Others warn that our society's reliance on a quick fix, as exemplified by the many psychotherapeutic drugs now available and in use, is dangerous (Kramer, 1993). The politics of these arguments get played out by many, including drug companies, psychiatrists, and insurance companies.

While we don't know exactly what causes mental illness, we do know that when it occurs, whether as an acute or chronic episode, relationships and interactions are dramatically altered. The same is true for other life-altering experiences. In the next section, we shift our focus from mental to physical health as we discuss a sudden onset physical disability (blindness).

## ▩ Blindness

Over the past four years, I (Eileen) have had the good fortune to know Heather Reich, a graduate student at Cleveland State University. Heather is in her early forties and was originally an RN (registered nurse). She has had diabetes for most of her life, and in 1992, because of complications from surgery, she completely lost her sight. Heather has kept a journal since becoming blind and generously shared it with us. Throughout this section, we hear her voice as she struggles, comes to terms with, and struggles some more with her traumatically altered identity. We turn to Heather's words as she faced the beginning of her blindness:

> *Several days earlier it had been Thanksgiving and I watched the young woman that I was disappear in front of my failing eyes. I was getting ready to go out and had a pretty new dress from Anchorage [Alaska] (my last pretty dress that I could verify) and had to kneel on my bathroom sink in order to see any of my face to put make-up on. All that was left was a small oval surrounded by blackness. I looked at what was left and wanted to cry out, "Don't go and leave me alone in the dark. I will miss you too much," but I disappeared anyway.*

From this moment on, Heather was no longer just a wife, mother, and RN; she was a blind wife, blind mother, and blind RN. She was forced to grapple with the impact of her blindness on these roles. She had to adapt her old roles to accommodate her blindness. It was impossible to continue working as an RN, and in her late thirties, she made a dramatic shift in her professional identity from RN to returning college student.

Obviously, our introduction and adjustment to a sudden-onset disability or chronic illness is traumatic. DeLoach and Greer (1981) suggest a **three-phase model of adjustment to disability.** We can also apply their model to those adjustments faced by the family and friends of that person. The reactions of the newly disabled and of their family and friends mutually impacts their relationships and identities.

The first phase, *stigma isolation,* refers to the initial period of adjustment, when we believe we are being treated in ways that are separate from our disability. At this point, we may be in denial and unwilling to acknowledge we are any different than we were before. Or, we may accept our altered identity, but friends, family, or strangers may treat us in stereotypic ways, avoiding or ignoring us and refusing to treat us as persons first (Braithwaite, 1996) and as disabled second. For Heather, this type of treatment is very frustrating:

> *I have so much isolation and very little privacy. I tend to feel disconnected from other people since being blinded because I don't see them approaching, can't make eye contact. I have trouble knowing if my points are understood; with all of this I am isolated. Yet I have no privacy because people grab me, feel they have the right*

Heather, Chuck, and Jep. *Photo reprinted with permission from Heather Reich.*

*to touch me without permission and do so even after my protestations. That, cou-*
*pled with being spoken to as if I was developmentally delayed, makes me feel like*
*much less than a whole person, more than mere blindness.*

These behaviors define the disabled person's identity as one of dependence, defeat, and victimization. This can be further exacerbated by perceptions in the medical community, as Heather observed:

*I was told by one eye surgeon that to have a patient go blind is like losing a patient*
*for other specialties. They look at blindness as a defeat to their professional abili-*
*ties. If they look at blindness as equivalent to the death of a patient, how can they*
*ever communicate anything positive to the newly blinded?*

The medical community may view the newly disabled as having a chronic medical condition rather than as having a new physical characteristic that needs to be incorporated into, rather than overtake, their identity. For example, when Heather asked her doctors why they didn't recommend a cane and rudimentary rehabilitation when she first became blind, they said:

*if they tell patients to learn those skills, the patients lose hope and believe the doc-*
*tors have given up on them. So instead they initially told me I would have the*
*hardest year of my life and just rely on my husband and take his hand if I needed*
*to go anywhere.*

In the second phase, *stigma recognition,* comes an understanding of how we are different because of our disability. At this point, we begin developing ways to deal with our changed identity and begin assimilating into a new culture. Out of desperation, Heather initiated this turning point:

> *I was trapped at home in a three-and-a-half story townhouse alone all day with no vision, no cane, no training, and no real information or hope. One day, almost out of my mind with frustration, I called the telephone operator and told her I was recently blinded and needed the number to anywhere that could help. She gave me the number to the National Federation of the Blind (NFB). They sent me a cane and made arrangements for Chuck [Heather's husband] and me to come to Baltimore to visit the national center. It was the first time I spoke to other blind people, and they explained blindness matter-of-factly. They told me blindness was just another physical characteristic and would someday become nothing more than a sometimes nuisance, not a handicap. For the first time I saw blind people work and travel on their own. They gave me a mobility lesson right down their back hall.*

The third phase, *stigma incorporation,* occurs when we integrate our changed identity into our self-definition. We develop coping strategies and learn to adapt and to function successfully. Communicatively, we develop strategies that enable us to function in the dominant culture. For Heather, her primary coping strategy is humor:

> *I took a couple of courses at a community college to see if my mind did in fact still work. The "powers that be" had a security guard silently (so they thought) follow me to keep me safe (I would mention to him that his shoes squeaked and his change jingled). He finally quit following me when a woman came up to me and shouted, "Do you know where you are?" and I replied, "Yes, I did, was she lost and did she need directions." The security guard laughed and told someone on the radio I was fine and he was going elsewhere.*

Heather realizes, however, that her humor may be offensive to a well-meaning person offering help. She recognizes that still-unresolved issues are behind her sometimes caustic or rude reactions to others, but she emphasizes the importance of being treated as a competent person. In response to suggestions that she wouldn't mind able-bodied people trying to help if she accepted her blindness, Heather's reply underscores the importance of how others react to her:

> *It's a civil rights issue. Rosa Parks accepted that she was black. She just didn't like sitting at the back of the bus. I tried to explain that being blind I could handle. It was the way I was treated.*

After becoming disabled, we enter a foreign land, one not of our own choosing, and we must learn its symbols, language, expectations, and meanings in the midst of our fear and anguish. Immediately, we become members of a new **speech community,** where we must learn new norms regarding the type, content, and interpretation of acceptable communication (Labov, 1972). We must learn a new language, new terms, and a new physical environment and develop new relationships as we attempt to juxtapose our former and new subcultures. These may be sudden and dramatic or subtle and gradual adjustments that take place over time, and some of us will be more successful at making these adjustments than others.

Some communication scholars describe persons with disabilities as members of a distinct culture. Communication researcher Dawn Braithwaite (1996) suggests that persons with disabilities constitute their own culture because "they hold a set of beliefs about themselves as disabled and as distinct from the larger nondisabled society and they share common communicative codes, or sets of communication strategies used to communicate with able-bodied others" (p. 457). While there are **co-cultures among persons with disabilities** (based, for example, on the type of disability), all persons with disabilities share certain common experiences and marginalization by living in an able-bodied world (Braithwaite). Few people who are blind or visually impaired consider themselves a completely separate culture, but they do use cultural practices enabling them to function in a sighted world (Smith & Kandath, 2000). The cultural perspective provides a useful framework, but in reality, there has to be some sense of bonding that forges and maintains these co-cultures. From the perspective of a person who is blind, this doesn't necessarily happen, as Heather explains:

> *I keep hearing about what a sense of community the deaf have established. The blind have very little that is comparable. I believe the commonality in using sign language provides the common ground, much more than with Braille. You must use some sort of sign language if you are to be understood in some verbal synonym. But a blind person can be understood with the spoken word and the computer is being used as a replacement to Braille. Yet by having these commonalities with the sighted world, there is less of a need for a sense of isolated community. I do believe blind people need community; it's just very hard to find. There is competition on who is a good blind person, who is functioning like a sighted person, who acts blind, etc. There is enough discrimination from external sources that we as the blind population don't need to add more to ourselves.*

People who experience sudden-onset disabilities are thrust into a new world in which relationships and communication are suddenly and dramatically changed. The sharp contrast between our old and new selves highlights our differences. When the onset is gradual, however, we are often less aware of these changes until we examine them retrospectively. Mental and physical changes caused by aging are one area in which onset is often more imperceptible. As we discuss in the next section, we are often unaware of how we have adapted to new roles, communication, and physiological changes as we age.

## Aging

In 1968, Paul Simon wrote a song called "Old Friends." In it, he describes two shriveled old men, wrapped in overcoats, sitting on a park bench, contemplating being 70. During our teens and twenties, and even during our thirties, it's often hard to imagine being 70 or older. Fortunately, today Simon's description is not an accurate portrayal of the aging population. In fact, life expectancies for people born in the year 2000 are expected to reach a record high of 76.9 years (U.S. Department of Health and Human Services, 2001). Not only does the "graying" of America promise us a greater likelihood that, at some point, we will be caregivers of spouses or elderly parents, it also promises a greater likelihood that we will develop some combination of illnesses.

As we age and lose some of our physical, emotional, or mental abilities, we may find ourselves becoming more dependent on others. Our roles in relationships with significant others and friends inevitably change, and we are forced to renegotiate and internalize new identities. It is useful to consider this process under the framework of **integrated health theory,** as posited by communication researchers Bruce Lambert and colleagues (1997).

According to Lambert et al. (1997), we experience health when our self-image, our social image, and our behavior are aligned (see Theorizing Practice 7.1). As we

Even though suffering with many symptoms of Alzheimer's disease, Paul Berlin is able to participate in a family celebration. *Photo by Ruth Zittrain.*

---

**THEORIZING PRACTICE 7.1**

## Aligning Our Health Images

Our health self-image is impacted not just from our observations of others but from the messages that we receive both interpersonally and through mass media.

1. What does a "typical" person in their twenties look and act like? In their forties? Their sixties? Seventies? Eighties? On what are you basing these impressions? Think of two interpersonal messages you have heard or observed and two messages from the media for each of these age groups.

2. For all these age groups, bring in two examples of each from the mass media. For each age group, have one example that portrays that age group positively and one that portrays it negatively.

---

age, we are forced to reconcile our images and behaviors with our shifting realities. This can be very difficult, especially in our youth-oriented culture. For those who are less willing to accept growing older, gray hairs and wrinkles sends some straight to the beautician or cosmetic surgeon, while others run to the drugstore for hair dyes and face creams. We may deny that our bodies and abilities have changed, so we become weekend warriors, spending Saturdays and Sundays playing tennis, softball, basketball, or jogging, and then returning to work on Monday nursing various tendon and muscle injuries. Others may accept changes as a natural part of aging. At some point, we usually juxtapose our memories of what we could do with what we can do now and modify our self-image, social image, and behaviors. We begin a workout slowly, we stretch and warm up longer, and we come to respect—or at least coexist with—the changes in our bodies. We realign how we see ourselves, how others see us, and how we act based on those perceptions.

In other words, we feel healthy when we are physically and mentally able to participate in the activities that we want to participate in, and we compare our abilities to others and assess the quality of our health based on those comparisons. For example, I (Eileen) attend a free-weights class twice a week, walk a couple of times a week, and feel pretty healthy. My 80-year-old mother-in-law and her 85-year-old boyfriend, however, go polka dancing every Sunday with a 70+ year old crowd. Unlike many of the regulars, my mother-in-law and her boyfriend don't dance every single dance. Compared to the nonstop dancers, they feel less healthy and out of shape. None of their peer friends or family go dancing, however, much less engage in any regular exercise, so compared to these sedentary folks, they feel that, especially for their age, they're in very good health. The fact that they can be so active, especially compared to similarly aged and even younger family members and friends, enhances their feelings of good health. For me, any beliefs I had about feeling healthy were put to rest when I went polka dancing with them—and was out of breath before I was a quarter of the way around the floor, while they danced several songs in a row. Compared to my friends who exercise sporadically, I feel moderately healthy, but compared to the 70+ polka crowd, I feel like a slug. This experience caused me to re-evaluate my self-image to being barely in shape, my social image from reasonably athletic to flabby, and my behavior from occasional exercise to a more stringent routine—or at least thinking about a tougher routine. My new goal is to make it at least halfway around the dance floor before I'm 55!

The alignment between our self-image, social image, and behavior shifts over time. *Resistance* refers to any factors that threaten this alignment. We resist changes in image and behavior that run counter to how we've always seen ourselves, been seen by others, and behaved. The more aspects of our images and behaviors that are affected, the greater our resistance. As we age, these changes are more gradual. We notice that we can't shop as long as we used to, prefer doubles to singles tennis, sleep less or more fitfully, can't eat rich foods without repercussions, or can't read without glasses. Any of these alone may be annoying but not particularly noteworthy. Then, one day, we receive an AARP (American Association for Retired People) discount card in the mail and realize that we are aging.

These examples emphasize the interdependence between our health and our identity as well as how we must reconcile our past and current circumstances when we face life-altering situations. So, for example, elderly people who never drove much and always counted on others to provide transportation are likely to be less resistant when told they should no longer drive at all. Elderly people who always viewed themselves as independent and highly functioning, however, are likely to have a much stronger reaction. At stake is not only the actual act of driving but also their entire sense of who they have become and where they are headed. They have to engage in maximum reconstruction of their private and public identities and the accompanying behavioral changes. Many of us will experience this reconstruction firsthand as we watch our parents age. In the following section, we focus on these changing relationships and issues of intergenerational communication.

***Changing relationships and intergenerational communication.*** In her book *How Did I Become My Parent's Parent?*, Harriett Sarnoff Schiff (1996) refers to **chadults** as "adults whose parents are still living" (p. 1). She discusses the changing roles and identities of parents and adult children as their parents' aging takes its physical, emotional, and mental toll.

It may begin suddenly, with a parent having a stroke or heart attack, or it may be gradual, with changes barely noticeable in day-to-day interactions. We may

June Ray and Jim Feehan dancing the polka. *Photo reprinted with permission from June Ray and Jim Feehan.*

notice our parents paying less attention to detail, wearing dirty clothing, not keeping their home clean, becoming highly anxious and fearful, or becoming confused or forgetful. It is common for chadults to deny these changes, wanting to believe that their parents are able to control their behavior. These warning signs should not be ignored, as they may signal serious health conditions that require diagnosis and treatment and impact our quality of life and our communication patterns.

In most cases, care providers for the elderly will be significantly younger and have little in common with the people they treat. This communication between people of significant age differences is called **intergenerational communication** (Bergstrom & Nussbaum, 1996). One factor that seems to impact significantly on intergenerational communication is **ageism.** Ageism occurs when the elderly are communicated with based on stereotypes rather than as individuals. It used to be common for elderly parents to live their later years with family members. This was possible because many women did not work outside the home and were able—and expected—to provide this care. Grandparents, adult children, and grandchildren shared this experience and saw the aging process as a natural progression of life. Today, however, this kind of care is less common. With more than 50 percent of married women now in the workforce, elders who require more care are more likely to be placed in a care facility. In addition, many of our elderly are able to care for themselves or need only moderate help, so they can maintain more independence by living in assisted-care facilities, an option not available in the past. It is not uncommon, then, for people to have had little or no contact with the elderly.

Our stereotypes of the elderly impact our communication with them by essentially setting up a self-fulfilling prophecy: if we expect older adults to be incompetent in their self-care or thought processes, we are likely to treat them in ways that foster this dependency (Ryan & Butler, 1996). Research has identified the two interaction styles of *independence-ignore* and *dependence-support* scripts between older people and their partners:

> On a behavioral level, the dependence-support script is characterized by pronounced tendency of social partners to support, foster, and actually demand dependent behaviors without considering the competence level of the older person. The independence-ignore script signifies that independent behaviors are not attended to and, instead, are actually discouraged. (Baltes & Wahl, 1992, p. 221)

It may be, then, that older people not only get positively reinforced for being dependent on others but are ignored or actively discouraged from continuing any independent behaviors. This impacts their communication as well. The greater the discrepancy between the older person's actual communicative competence and our negative expectation of that person's competence, the more likely we are to use, for example, baby talk, patronizing speech, simplified speech, or talk about the older person to a third party while they are present. We accommodate in order to meet our perception of the elderly person's needs or style. It is interesting, though, that both interaction styles treat the elderly in a negative manner. We suggest considering *independence-support*, in which social partners support the elder's independent behaviors, as a more positive style of relating to the elderly.

Scholars Nikolas Coupland, Justine Coupland, and Howard Giles (1991) describe **communication accommodation theory** as people's tendency to mirror each other's communication styles to show liking and respect. *Convergence* occurs when both parties communicate using, for example, similar gestures, paralanguage, and vocabulary. *Divergence* takes place when one person communicates differently than the other, such as by speaking very fast while the other person speaks slowly. Divergence may be perceived negatively, suggesting that the people speaking are socially distant and may not understand or like each other. For example, a family member who asks a doctor to explain alternative treatments may find that the doctor speaks rapidly and uses medical jargon. The family member may converge by also using jargon and speaking quickly to accommodate the doctor's style, or the family member may diverge from the doctor's style by asking the doctor to explain what each medical term means, subsequently slowing down the doctor's speech.

It is also possible to overaccommodate, responding in an exaggerated way to a perceived need. You may have heard people speak to an elderly person in a slow, patronizing voice. The elder mirrors this speech style, which initiators see as reinforcing the elder's slow, patronizing speech, so they increase their accommodation, leading the elder to further accommodate, and so on. If this happens often, elders may start to believe that they are unable to understand regular speech and then behave accordingly (Ryan & Butler, 1996).

Ageist stereotypes may also affect communication among older patients and health care providers. **Geriatric medicine** is a relatively new field, although some medical schools have added programs or courses in this area. Doctors certified in subspecialties of internal medicine (for example, cardiovascular disease, gastroenterology, hematology, or rheumatology) can earn a certificate of added qualifications in geriatric medicine by passing an exam offered by the American Board of Internal Medicine. Many elderly are comfortable with the primary care physician they've been using, however, or they can't find geriatric specialists in private practice. This leaves them using internists or general practitioners who have no special training in providing health care to the elderly. Because they lack this expertise, physicians may confuse normal aging processes with their own ageist stereotypes, speak to their patients in demeaning ways, miss important diagnoses, and not be up-to-date on the latest advances in treatments. For example, general practitioners are less likely to recognize and treat depression in their elderly patients, and when they do, they typically treat it with antidepressant drugs. Unfortunately, however, they are unlikely to be up-to-date on geriatric drug dosages, side effects, and interactions with the myriad drugs that the elderly often take. They also may not fully appreciate that many elderly patients have good reason to be depressed, having lost family members and friends, their independence, and their physical or mental competence (or both) and finding themselves face-to-face with their own mortality. Medication alone does not take away the pain of losing a spouse of 50 or more years. Instead, it may trivialize their despair and cause them to spend their final years in psychic pain (Blazer, 2002).

As a culture, Americans do not revere our elderly. We are uncomfortable with watching people age and facing our mortality. The huge cosmetic surgery industry attests to our preoccupation with looking young. Rather than valuing the elderly for their wisdom and life experiences, and seeing their lined faces and sagging skin as tributes to their years, we tend to dismiss their reminiscing and stories as repetitive, boring, or irrelevant. It is often only after they die that we realize we have lost

**THEORIZING PRACTICE 7.2**

## Interviewing the Elderly

Interview an elderly person. This can be a relative or a friend. If you don't have access to a relative or friend, visit an assisted care facility or local nursing home, and ask the director if you could spend some time talking with a resident. Your goal is to help them to tell their story. Include these questions along with others that you develop:

1. Tell me what things were like when you were growing up. What was your childhood like? Where did you go to school? What do you remember about your school experience? Who were you best friends? Did you keep these friendships into or through adulthood? What did you want to grow up to be when you were a child? Did you do this? Why, or why not?

2. Who was the most colorful relative you remember from your childhood? Tell me about this relative.

3. What were family holidays like? Christmas? Thanksgiving? Fourth of July? Passover?

4. When you think about your life, what are three of your most memorable experiences? What made them memorable?

5. What do you think of the current state of the world? What do you think of the new technology and how it's changing our lives?

6. What do you think about kids today? Do you think they have it harder or easier than when you were growing up? Why, or why not?

7. How has your communication with family members and friends changed over the years? Which of these have been good changes? Which have been bad changes?

8. Is there anything that you regret?

9. What has been the best period (or periods) of your life? Why?

a vital link to our past. As you complete Theorizing Practice 7.2, think about your own ageist beliefs and how they impact your view of the elderly, how you communicate both with and about them, and how you view your own aging.

While significantly more money is now being spent for research and treatments for many of the illnesses we've discussed, we cannot yet count on cures. What we can do, however, is engage in health-related behaviors that may postpone some of these problems and, at the least, maintain our physical and mental well-being so that we can better dodge or cope with life's various slings and arrows. One of the more effective coping strategies is social support. In the next section, we discuss the importance of communicating support and how social support can buffer our stress when we face life-altering health experiences.

## ∫ OCIAL SUPPORT

Much of **social support** is communicative, whether verbally or nonverbally. We like our worlds to be orderly and predictable, and we assess and evaluate our lives in ways to maintain that predictability. Communication scholars recognize that support is particularly important during times of stress and uncertainty, when we feel a lack of personal control, and this uncertainty is a key characteristic we experience when we or someone we care about is ill.

There is no question that social support has both a direct and indirect effect on our physical and mental health. By direct effect, we mean that social support in general tends to help us maintain or enhance our physical and mental health. By indirect effect, we mean that social support also acts as a buffer between a stressful situation and our physical and mental health. It is this function as an indirect effect that we focus on here. When we are faced with a stressful situation (such as illness), how does supportive communication help us to cope?

Communication researchers initially conceptualized supportive communication as interaction that reduces uncertainty and increases perceptions of personal control for the person receiving the support (Albrecht & Adelman, 1987). This conceptualization does not take into account, however, situations in which, for example, reducing uncertainty is impossible or undesirable (such as telling a person how long they have to live). Sometimes we can predict general behavior patterns, but we cannot predict who in particular will respond in these ways. Recently, for example, a 9-year-old boy inexplicably drowned at a summer camp near Cleveland. A newspaper article focusing on how his family is coping quotes another father who lost his son in a similar way several years ago:

> *Dr. Alan E. London, a Cleveland Clinic pediatrician whose own son died in a similar accident three years ago, said the Steins could count on two things: Some friends will drop away. Some people will make excruciating remarks. ("Losing a son," 2000, p. A10)*

After only a month since the death, the victim's sister said she had already experienced both these behaviors ("Losing a Son"). In times of crises, it is not uncommon for some "close" friends to become distant—and for some former acquaintances to become close. What appears to be certain is that relationships will change. What is uncertain is exactly how and with whom.

Uncertainty can be a stressor even when it centers around a positive health event, such as a terminal illness that goes into remission. All of us, of course, would wish for this outcome, but it may be simultaneously distressing. Communication scholars Dale Brashers and colleagues (1999b) interviewed people who are HIV-positive or have AIDS who had once resigned themselves to death but now, because of new treatments and discoveries, find that they may live. This *revival*—a change in health status from dying to living with a chronic illness—while certainly welcomed, also required redefining their identity. Some had accepted their impending death, quit their jobs, reconciled with family and friends, and lived what they thought were their final days. There was no uncertainty; they knew they would be dying soon. Now, they find that their death may not be impending—and they are thrown back into uncertainty. Will the new medications work? If so, for how long? What will be the quality of life? While none of us would refuse this reprieve, we may find our reactions to be more complex than we might initially think. One again, we are required to renegotiate our identities and social roles, interpersonal relationships, and orientation to the future.

Uncertainty is not always negative, however. For example, there is uncertainty about how quickly a person will decline if they have a degenerative illness like Parkinson's, Alzheimer's, or multiple sclerosis. While there may be certainty about the eventual outcome, functioning relatively well for a while may allow these people and their families to be in a conscious state of denial about their illness. It may increase our appreciation of the person and magnify their current abilities by the constant realization that they could rapidly decline at any time. Often this enables people to resolve old conflicts, share their feelings, and take care of important business (such as legal documents and living wills) while they can still make their wishes known. An "I love you" takes on poignant significance as our awareness increases that they may not understand those words tomorrow.

Health problems, by their very nature, increase uncertainty and shake the orderliness and predictability of our lives. Communication scholars Austin Babrow, Stephen Hines, and Chris Kasch (2000) developed **problematic integration theory** as a way to think about the relationship between social support and managing uncertainty in health/illness situations. Illness upsets the equilibrium of our life, forces us to redefine who we are, and heightens our stress levels. What becomes critical is not that uncertainty and the resulting stress exist but, rather, how that uncertainty is managed. We have to determine the probability of certain outcomes and our evaluation of how desirable these outcomes are. We try to integrate high probabilities to lead to desirable outcomes. Whether the uncertainty is reduced, maintained, or increased depends on our ability to assess the support recipient, the situation, and our ability to use appropriate communication skills (Babrow et al.). Depending on this assessment, support may function in different ways.

## Functions of Support

Generally, there are four distinguishable functions of support. *Emotional support* allows people to vent their feelings, share personal concerns, and feel safe. One specific type of emotional support is comforting. Comforting, as studied by communication scholars Brant Burleson and Daena Goldsmith (1998) refers to verbal and nonverbal communication that attempts to lessen or alleviate someone's emotional distress. Although their work has not specifically focused on the health communication setting, their research suggests that the most comforting messages seem to be those that focus on the topic of concern rather than on providing solutions or minimizing, denying, or avoiding the topic, describing and explaining the topic, and being sensitive to the needs of the recipient (p. 254). *Appraisal support,* sometimes combined with emotional support, provides us with positive information about ourselves and reinforces our sense of self-worth. *Informational support* gives us helpful data or knowledge, while *instrumental support* provides actual help, such as driving someone to his or her appointment, cooking his or her meals, or cleaning his or her house. Sources of support include spouses, romantic partners, parents, children, siblings, friends, health care professionals, and various media.

The extent to which each type of support is helpful varies by the needs of the person receiving it and the status of their health concern. For example, someone just diagnosed with cancer is likely to be stunned and may benefit most from emotional support. We also know, however, that patients who are given bad news don't hear what is said immediately after the news is delivered. As the shock subsides, they may find informational support more useful as they try to decide which treatment protocol they will use. Once they begin treatment, such as chemotherapy or radiation, instrumental support is likely to be more helpful. The neighbor who brings over dinner, the spouse who drives the kids to their activities, the friends who come to clean the house or mow the lawn are all helping to relieve the burden on the family.

Under ordinary circumstances, there is an underlying assumption of immediate or delayed reciprocity of support as a process that develops over time. You expect that if you drive a friend to the airport, they will do the same for you in the future. However, illness may preclude the possibility of reciprocity. The terminally ill friend will not be there to support you down the road. The sibling who is suddenly paralyzed may no longer be able to provide support in anticipated ways.

As an illness progresses, support attempts are likely to become more complicated. One study found, for example, that for patients with recurrent breast or gynecological cancer, support from family and friends appeared to increase the amount of pain the patients could tolerate (Rummans et al., 1998). As pain increases, however, it is likely that patients may become more withdrawn and isolated, and friends may withdraw when patients can no longer participate in regular activities.

Providing support does not appear to differ based on gender. Research suggests more similarities than differences in how men and women provide support (Goldsmith & Dun, 1997). Despite the proliferation of popular press books that characterize men and women as aliens from different planets, such as those by John Gray and Deborah Tannen, research suggests that rather than men being from Mars and women being from Venus, "men are from North Dakota and women are from South Dakota" (Wood & Dindia, 1998, p. 32).

We want to suggest a fifth function of support: *unconditional listening*. It is important that the person being supported is also heard. Social support functions in this way to give voice to a person's story. Being heard and validated, talking about our uncertainties and fears, often provides much comfort when we are in situations where we feel powerless or frightened. It allows us to write—and revise—our story in our own way and to have that story heard. James Pennebaker (1995) has done a great deal of research that shows talking about traumatic events has a positive effect on negative health outcomes while not talking about them can lead to destructive physiological illness.

The importance of telling our stories has been underscored in research done by myself (Eileen) and several colleagues involving adult survivors of incest. Communication plays a large role in survivors' lives: it was the messages from their perpetrators that functioned to silence them. Imagine the power of the messages recounted by several adult survivors of incest:

### Marsha (Abused by Her Father):
*He (perpetrator) said if I told, I would destroy the family. That he would go to jail and I would have to live with strangers. (Ray, 1996b, p. 282)*

### Michelle (Abused by Her Father and Uncle):
*My mother was furious. She just kept saying, "You're lying. You've always been a liar. You just want to get attention. I won't let you ruin our lives with your lies." (Ray, 1996b, p. 284)*

These powerful messages worked and kept many children quiet. And as they grew up, many experienced difficulties with relationships, substance abuse, and both physical and mental illnesses. They had internalized their perpetrator's messages, and for some, it was not until they confronted their abuser in person that they began to heal. As one survivor states:

*Just last weekend I went and confronted him [my father] about it. He did not deny it for a minute. He said he was really sorry and it was the worst thing in his life and he said that he had been proud of most things he had done but that it [the abuse] just canceled all those things out. He said it wasn't my fault; girls are supposed to do what their fathers tell them. (Ford, Ray, & Ellis, 1999, p. 146)*

For others, talking with people who have had similar experiences can be more helpful: "A lot of my friends have had the same thing happen to them. That's how they became my friends. . . . We've been able to talk about it openly to each other" (Ford, Ray, & Ellis, 1999, p. 153). And for others, just having someone (not necessarily a therapist or trained mental health professional) listen to their story in a nonevaluative way is especially validating:

*Very few people have ever believed me—so I went into the interview expecting the same negative response I've received several times. Beth [the interviewer] obviously believed me! WOW! That felt great! I feel very good about it [the interview]. It helped me because it had been a long time since I shared that much of my story in one sitting. I've been able to get more in touch with my feelings associated with my story. It also helped just to have someone listen and believe me. (Varallo, Ray, & Ellis, 1998, p. 263)*

Telling our story to trusted others and receiving unconditional support in our regular interpersonal relationships is one way that we can find and use our voice. Sharing our stories with people who have had similar experiences can be helpful. These people are often found in formal support groups or structures designed to attract them. These groups and settings can provide support in different ways than friends and families can, as we see in the next section through Gilda Radner's eyes. (Gilda was one of the original Not Ready for Prime Time Players on *Saturday Night Live* and is also mentioned in our preface.)

### Formal Support

Formal support occurs in situations specifically developed to bring people, often strangers, together with others like them and to share common experiences and information. Support groups exist for victims, friends, and family of almost any illness or trauma. You read about some support groups for parents who experienced miscarriages in Chapter 5. In her book about her battle with ovarian cancer, comedian Gilda Radner (1989) discussed the services offered at The Wellness Community, a cancer patient support program:

*Amazingly, everything was free. There were group therapy sessions that met for two hours a week, available at many different times during the week, called "participant groups." These groups were the only Wellness Community activities that required a commitment. They were facilitated by licensed therapists. Everything else was on a drop-in basis, including instruction in guided imagery and visualization and relaxation three nights a week. There were group sessions for spouses or family members of cancer patients, nutrition and cooking discussions, lectures by doctors, workshops on anger management, potluck dinners and parties, therapy through painting, vocalizing, improvising— all techniques that would help in stress management and improve the quality of someone's life. (p. 140)*

For those suffering from an illness, the support group can give them a place to fit in and to be treated more normally. For example, I (Eileen) once attended my dad's Alzheimer's support group meeting with him. Eight men at various stages of the disease were there. The first part of the meeting included the facilitator talking about current events while soliciting comments from the men. A few participated, but several said nothing and looked distant. I got the impression that they had no idea what was going on. Their next activity was (semi-ballroom) dancing. My father had raved about this woman who led the dancing. She visited the group throughout the year and had been a professional dancer in New York. She played music of their era and took turns bringing each man up to dance with her. Much to my amazement, all the men came alive. When they danced, they were smiling; they were clearly engaged. It was an incredibly poignant experience. Each man was spoken to as an adult, verbally reinforced for any attempts to participate, and nonverbally touched and hugged. For the rest of the meeting, the men were more energized. Here, they had a respite from their home and spouse, where they were men who happened to have Alzheimer's rather than Alzheimer patients who happened to be men. And the respite wasn't just for the men. These group meetings, which take place three times a week, give their care provider some time off and a chance to return to their noncaregiver role.

Clearly, support groups help others to see that they are not alone and that others share their frustrations and feelings. It is impossible, for example, to truly understand the experience of chemotherapy unless you have been through it. Gilda captures the critical role of communication, again discussing The Wellness Community:

*If indeed God created the world and then left us on our own to work things out, then getting together with other people to communicate is what we should be doing. I learned at The Wellness Community that that is the most magic thing we have, our ability to open our mouths and communicate with each other. (Radner, 1989, pp. 140–141)*

For family members, support groups can be a double-edged sword. While they can provide valuable information and empathy, they can also show frightening glimpses of what is to come. Participants need to determine which aspects of a support group are helpful at what time. We may be ready for information about new treatments or doctors, but not about caregiving to someone in the late stages of the illness. Both the ill person and we, as their families, may want to know that we are not alone, but not what we are likely to face as the disease progresses. Over time, however, these groups provide new friendships, networks, and levels of relationships that would otherwise not be available. Once again, Gilda describes her experience:

> *My next treatment, when I felt,* Ooh, I hate this, I want to run away, let me get out of this, *I just thought of all those faces at The Wellness Community. People who have become friends, all at different stages of cancer, all fighting, all different, some with hair, some with clumps of hair, some with radiation burns—how brave we all are together. I just felt them all around me and it made me be braver. The same way people in gangs can do things that the individual could never do alone, the gang of us fighting cancer makes us all stronger. Sometimes I imagine all their little faces inside my body shaking their fists at the sky, rallying against our common enemy—cancer. (Radner, 1989, p. 148)*

It should be noted that what seems to be most important is not how much support we receive, but how much support we believe is available and accessible when we need it. Support providers may be family and friends but also what are known as weak ties—people we do not have an ongoing relationship with, such as acquaintances, caregivers, or coworkers (Granovetter, 1973). With the influx of technology, especially the Internet, we have more support available to us than ever before. Through e-mail, we have access to long-distance supportive ties with family, friends, and strangers. **Interactive technology** allows people, through computers and modems, to access medical advice and information, medical libraries, research protocols, databases, as well as virtual support groups and laypeople's stories of their medical experiences (Street & Rimal, 1997). In a study of the Breast Cancer Listserv, an information and support group on the Internet, the online group was compared to face-to-face support groups (Sharf, 1997). The Internet group had the advantages of being available at all times, with the probability of a rapid response, accessibility regardless of geographic location, the likelihood of connecting to others with very similar circumstances (for example, men with breast cancer being able to communicate with one another), as well as the ability to enlist the expertise and resources of a larger number of participants. Conversely, keeping up with the large volume of daily e-mail might be a disadvantage for some people, as might the lack of visual and tactile communication (Sharf). While there are many questions about privacy, accuracy of information, and ethical concerns, it is clear that the World Wide Web has dramatically changed how we communicate health.

## SUMMARY

Throughout our lives, we will face many life-altering health experiences. In this chapter, we have focused on communication issues central to mental, physical, and social health concerns. These issues are critical for those experiencing an illness and for those providing their care. As our health waxes and wanes over time, we want our verbal and nonverbal communication needs to be met and our behaviors as providers to be appropriate; however, this is probably overly idealistic. In reality, we are all dramatically changed by life's events and not always able to do or say the right thing. We can only hope to have the necessary education, skills, and abilities to endure and sustain us—as well as those we care about—as we navigate our lives.

## KEY TERMS

chronic illnesses

chronic disabilities

stigma

chronic adaptational activity

three-phase model of adjustment to disability

speech community

co-cultures among persons with disabilities

integrated health theory

chadults

intergenerational communication

ageism

communication accommodation theory

geriatric medicine

social support

problematic integration theory

interactive technology

## DISCUSSION QUESTIONS

1. What does it mean to say that people with chronic illnesses (mental, physical, or both) are stigmatized? How might the view of people with disabilities belonging to co-cultures or different speech communities increase or decrease how much the disabled are stigmatized?

2. What are some advantages and some disadvantages of interactive technology for people who are ill? For their caregivers?

3. Choose a physical or mental illness. How does problematic integration theory provide a framework to make sense of it?

4. What are some of the impacts likely to be felt by people who are HIV-positive or have AIDS and by their family and friends when they experience what

Brashers et al. (1999b) call a revival? What are some of the uncertainties that emerge for them? Could a revival actually be a stressor and have a negative impact? If so, how?

5. What are some ways in which communication accommodation theory and intergenerational communication might lead to a decrease in ageism?

## INFOTRAC COLLEGE EDITION

1. Read Jane Glenn Haas's 1994 article, "John Folcarelli Defies Grip of Alzheimers, But It Has Stolen His Independence." How is his experience similar to or different from what you know about Alzheimer's disease? Would you want to know if you had an Alzheimer's gene? What might be some advantages and disadvantages of having that knowledge? What might be some useful communicative strategies for dealing with a person who has Alzheimer's? What kind of verbal and nonverbal communication might be most helpful for the caregiver?

2. Read the 1997 article by Ana Veciana-Suarez, "Families Coping with Mental Illness Find Help from Support Groups." Tie in issues related to communication and social support from the chapter and class discussion. Can support groups impact people negatively? Give examples.

3. Read Myrne Roe's 1996 article, "Depression Affects Not Only Its Victims But Also Their Family and Friends." Discuss different ways communication among family members and friends may be affected when living with a person suffering from depression. How might family or friendship networks change or adapt over time? What are some communicative strategies that might help depressed persons and their families?

# 8 | Ending Life Passages

As comedians have often said, none of us is getting out of here alive. Right now, approximately 2.3 million people in the United States die each year, and by 2030, that number will have increased by about 30 percent (Newman, 1997). Obviously, death is the one thing we all have in common, regardless of our race, gender, socioeconomic status, geography, ethnicity, culture, and any other demographic category. Each of us is going to die, and each of us is going to experience the death of someone we are close to. Talking about it, however, has always been difficult in our culture.

The term **death anxiety** refers to our difficulty in talking about and facing our own mortality. For some, even thinking about it can set off an anxious reaction. For example, as I (Eileen) have been working on this chapter, I've been reading quite a bit about death and dying. I generally find the topic interesting, but I also find it very anxiety provoking. I've regularly experienced physiological sensations such as a tight chest, difficulty swallowing, and a general sense of discomfort. These sensations have varied depending on which topic I focused on. When writing about suicide, I often reacted anxiously, I believe because of experiencing the suicide of a friend when I was a teenager. Reading about the terminally ill certainly humbled me, but it didn't provoke the same physical or emotional sensations. Reading about what happens to the body after we die (which I ended up not including here) really set me off—almost to a panic response.

We tell you this for several reasons. First, you may find yourself having both affective and physiological reactions as you read this chapter (and others). If so, pay attention to these responses. You are definitely not alone. Second, your views about death are highly influenced by how the topic was addressed in your family of origin. Was it talked about in general? If someone you were close to died, did people help you to talk about it? Was it a sudden death, or was it a long, protracted illness? Were there any rituals that helped you?

Our purpose in this chapter is to recognize how cultural values are embedded in how we "do" death, in how we talk—or don't talk—about death, dying, and issues that surround it. Thus, our focus is not just on interpersonal issues, such as what to say to a terminally ill person, whether doctors should tell patients they are dying, how we can comfort a grieving family member or friend, or how we face our own mortality. Our focus is also on a broader, societal level, considering, for example, organ and tissue donation, advance directives, and the functions of obituaries.

We begin by examining the many metaphors that are used when we talk about dying and how these metaphors may function. We then discuss a range of communication issues, beginning with the breaking of bad news, continuing through the dying process, and ending with communication among survivors and others after the death. To focus on many of the related communication issues, this chapter looks at the dying process that occurs during a chronic illness rather than a sudden death. We chose this emphasis because we wanted to highlight the effects of communication during the dying process, when health care providers, family members, and friends can communicate with the dying person, whether to ask for treatment decisions, to resolve conflicts, and/or to say good-bye. Sudden death robs us of these possibilities.

Talking about death has always been taboo in our culture. Different religions and ethnic groups have very different ways of dealing with—and of talking about—death and dying. None of these is wrong. They all function to help people grieve and find comfort. Our goal here is to help bring death to center stage. And we're sure, by now, you're just dying to read on.

# THE MANY METAPHORS OF DEATH AND DYING

*The sheer number of metaphors we use in reference to human mortality is an index of our cultural discomfort with the topic. In fact, one would be hard-pressed to find a type of reference to death in this culture which is both frequently used and without metaphoric content. Rarely is death called by its own name.*

(Sexton, 1997, p. 337)

In our culture, talking about death is taboo. We use the word as a euphemism for nonfatal actions, such as "I'm dying to see that movie," or "Wear your coat or you'll catch a death of a cold," or "You were dead right about that proposal." We rarely, however, use the word when actually talking about the subject. It has such a harsh sound to it. Instead, we use **metaphors for death and dying.**

Clearly, cultural differences are involved. In the United States, we may *be gone, have passed, passed away,* or *been lost.* During a sabbatical in New Zealand, I (Eileen) was struck by how, in regular conversations, New Zealanders used no euphemisms when talking about a dead relative. For them, no one is *lost* or *gone.* They are *dead,* and no attempts are made to soften the reality of death through their choice of words. While that may sound harsh to us, some other non-U.S. cultures take a more direct approach to labeling death and dying, as one oncologist suggests:

> The most common metaphor I hear clinicians use when speaking to nonmedical personnel and families is "lost." "We lost the patient," or "We attempted resuscitation, but lost him anyway." When I first came to this country this struck me as rather odd. I wanted to say, "Well, we didn't really lose your husband. We know where he is, it's just . . . he's not breathing there anymore." (Sexton, 1997, p. 339)

Several thanatology (death) experts contend that "more is better." In other words, we need to talk more—and often—about death and to treat it as a normal part of the life cycle (Kubler-Ross, 1969; Nuland, 1995) rather than cloak it in euphemisms and metaphors. Those in the medical profession, for example, often use specific metaphors as their own language. One example is the word *code.* Patients in the throes of a life-threatening emergency are "coding." A *code blue* means that someone is having a heart attack, while a *code yellow* means there is a fire in the hospital. The *code team* is responsible for performing CPR on patients who have stopped breathing. The term *code* is often used as a verb as well, such as "The patient in 3A coded this morning."

Medical staff also may use metaphors or gallows humor as coping mechanisms. For them, *circling* suggests the image of vultures flying around a dying person, waiting to attack the body. Patients who suddenly lose their vital signs *crash,* much like a vehicle running out of control. PBAB refers to *pine box at bedside,* and patients may *croak, kick the bucket,* or simply be *gone.* We're usually not told where they've gone or how they got there, but we know they are no longer "here"—and that they won't be back. Once the departed moves to the funeral home, they may be located in the *reposing* (embalming) room or the *slumber* (visitation) room, or they may undergo *calcination* (cremation). We are buried in *caskets,* not *coffins;* we are taken to the cemetery in *coaches* or *professional cars,* not *hearses;* we are laid to rest in an *interment space,* not a *grave;* the dead are *loved ones,* not *corpses;* particular corpses are referred to by their name; and cremated *ashes* are *cremains* (Mitford, 1998). And when we're finally buried, sleep metaphors abound: we are *laid to rest, put to sleep,* or simply *sleeping.* As a hospice social worker notes, however, these metaphors can have a long-lasting—and potentially traumatic—impact:

*It never surprises me when children in this culture are afraid to go to sleep. So many times, we use references like "Grandma went to sleep, and didn't wake up," or "Grandma is resting now." In fact, it amazes me that children ever go to sleep at all after hearing things like that. But really, it's just the most common thing I hear parents tell their children. (Sexton, 1997, p. 342)*

On the other hand, these metaphors often serve useful functions. They may help us to face our own mortality or the death of someone we love. They can provide comfort. By listening to the dying, we can take our cues as to which metaphors are helpful and which may not be. It is this **reflexivity** (Miller & Knapp, 1986), or reacting on the spot to the patient's lead, that is important. The experience of one hospice nurse, interviewed by M.C. Ray (1997), reminds us to follow the lead of the patient:

*I remember my early days of hospice nursing, when we used to sit around self-righteously saying, "When someone dies, we should say so. We need to use the word 'death' as professionals as often as we can, so the world will catch up with us and become more accepting." But now I have more life experience than I care to admit. And we were wrong back then. For instance, there's a patient I cared for just last month. She had cancer for eight years before she came into hospice, and she was one of the most accepting people I've known. She was very comfortable talking about her death; we talked about it more frankly than I do with most patients. But I never heard her use the word "cancer" and she never once said anything direct about dying. She called it "my problem" and she talked about "not being around." That's as close to saying it as she got. It would have been stupid of me to go shouting the words "cancer" and "death" in every conversation. Normally I do use those words but with this patient, I just called it her "problem" too. (pp. 82–83)*

What is important is to be aware of our use of metaphors, why we choose to use them, and that they do not necessarily get in the way of what needs to be said or done for the dying or the survivors. As Sexton (1997) comments, "It is not the fact that our perceptions are altered by our metaphors that makes them potentially dangerous; it is that we are too often unaware of this alteration" (p. 344).

# TALKING ABOUT DEATH AND DYING

Throughout the rest of this chapter, you will read the words of two very special individuals. The first is Lisa Hearey. In November 1998, the Cleveland newspaper, *The Plain Dealer,* ran a posthumous, daily, 26-article series on its front page

Lisa and Clem Heary (left) and friends. *Photo reprinted with permission from Erica Goldfarb.*

("Losing Lisa," 1998) about Lisa, who provided a reporter and photographer with unrestricted access to her and her family during the last four months and for a full year after she died. Lisa Hearey was 39 years old when she was diagnosed with two very rare cancers, carcinoma of the appendix and adenocarcinoid of the appendix, both of which had metastasized throughout her abdomen. She was married to Clem and had three young sons, C.J., Michael, and Christopher. According to the articles, Lisa had several motivations for providing this access: (a) she was angry about the limited medical research to help her and others with rare diseases, (b) she was obsessed with the fear that her children would not remember her or how hard she fought to stay alive for them, and (c) she hoped to help others confront their own fears about dying. She died on October 28, 1997, at the age of 41.

The second person is Katherine (Kay) Smith, whose story is told by her daughter, Barbara Verlezza. Kay was diagnosed with PSP (progressive supranuclear palsy) in 1995; this followed several years of symptoms and incorrect diagnoses. PSP is a rare neurological disorder related to Parkinson's disease that affects middle-aged adults and the elderly. Symptoms include stiff limbs, imbalance, problems walking, and limited upward and downward eye movements. The disease progresses over time and, in its advanced stages, leaves people bedridden or in wheelchairs

Barbara Verlezza (left), Kay Smith (right), and granddaughter Allegra. *Photo reprinted with permission from Barbara Verlezza.*

and unable to swallow or speak ("Statement of," 1998). You may have heard of PSP following the diagnosis of the late actor/composer Dudley Moore. Kay underwent various treatments, but they were not successful. She began to show signs of illness in 1986, but she was not correctly diagnosed until 1995. She spent the last several weeks of her life in hospice, with her husband, Barbara, or Barbara's sister by her side the entire time. She died on December 10, 1998, at the age of 75. Barbara was very excited to share her experiences through interviews with Eileen, both to describe one of the most meaningful experiences of her life and to help dispel our taboo of talking about death.

It is important to realize that both Lisa and Barbara's willingness to candidly tell their stories about death and dying is a relatively new phenomenon. In fact, death as a topic of study and understanding only gained visibility when Elisabeth Kubler-Ross (1969) published her book, *On Death and Dying,* which was based on interviews with 200 terminally ill patients. Since then, we have seen significant cultural shifts in communication by medical professionals regarding terminal illness as well as in the communicative needs of patients and their families. It is still difficult, however, to tell people that their future has been dramatically altered. What we are told, how we are told, and by whom we are told impacts our reaction and decision making from that point forward.

# THE BEGINNING: BREAKING BAD NEWS

*Communication with the terminally ill is a complex matrix in which wrenching emotion, unrestrained urgency, unrelenting pain, and complicated information are fused. Issues are more often ambiguous than clear; decisions are more often perplexing than simple.*

(Addington & Wegescheide-Harris, 1995, pp. 267–268)

The need to **break bad news** is not restricted to those with chronic or acute illness. Buckman (1992) defines bad news as

*any news that drastically and negatively alters the patient's view of her or his future. This definition implies that the 'badness' of any bad news depends on what the patient already knows or suspects about the future. In other words, the impact of bad news depends on the size of the gap between the patient's expectations (including his or her ambitions and plans) and the medical reality of the situation.* (p. 15)

Obviously, this includes a terminal illness or sudden death. It also includes any condition that may not result in imminent death but signifies a continuous deterioration or disability at some level, an irreplaceable sense of loss and grieving for what is being lost, and an unavoidable confrontation with our own mortality (as discussed in Chapter 7). In this chapter, we focus on telling bad news related to death and dying.

As a culture, Americans generally adopt a "more is better" orientation. We want more information about our illness, our treatment options, and our care provider's background. We may gather that information interpersonally, from family, friends, or acquaintances, or we may gather information using mass technologies like the Internet. Today, it is not uncommon for patients or families, after hearing the bad news, to actively seek information and to become educated health care citizens. If the physician is less than candid, these families will likely find out through their own research.

In the United States, it is now the norm for patients to be told a terminal diagnosis, but this was not always the case (Long, 1997). It used to be the norm for doctors to avoid talking about the diagnosis and prognosis, assuming that patients didn't really want to know, that knowing might make the patients passive and resigned to dying. This norm also reflected the health professionals' own discomfort in talking about death. Keeping the prognosis a secret, however, can be extremely stressful for patients, their families, and their health care providers. Today, most doctors openly tell patients and families a terminal diagnosis

(Thompson, 1989). This helps the health care providers as well, who report higher job satisfaction when they can talk openly with terminally ill patients and their families (Parry, 1987).

Only recently, however, have some medical schools started including how to deliver bad news as part of their curriculum. At the University of Illinois at Chicago, for example, where I (Barbara) used to teach in the medical school, medical students are not only exposed to presentations on the topic but also practice "bad news conversations" with simulated patients, who are trained to provide feedback following the experience. More medical schools are now including these skills as part of their curriculum, but it was not very long ago that medical students were only given broad generalities, such as "Be sensitive when talking to family members," and had to find practical resource books on the subject in local bookstores rather than in their academic classes (see, for example, Leash, 1994).

Obviously, it is difficult to tell a person that they are going to die. Nurses tend to be better at telling this news (Field, 1989), but most patients would rather find out from their physician (Helm & Mazur, 1989). In fact, patients who feel that their doctor effectively communicates with them about their illness have a better reaction to the diagnosis (Jacobsen, Perry, & Hirsch, 1990), react more positively, and accept the diagnosis more readily. For many patients, fear of abandonment by their physician is a primary concern (Dunphy, 1976), so it is important that physicians remain communicatively close as their patients approach death. This need was underscored by one of Lisa's experiences with her oncologist, Dr. Streeter. Toward the end of Lisa's life, she yearned to hear from her doctor. It was clear to her family that Lisa felt a strong connection to Dr. Streeter and needed to say goodbye to her. Several phone messages were left, but the doctor never returned their calls, a cause of great anger among family members. Theorizing Practice 8.1 looks at determining such information needs and repercussions.

While telling someone bad news is difficult, hearing it is equally hard for the patient and their loved ones. Buckman (1992), writing for health care professionals, does an excellent job of describing one reason for this:

*Bad news causes pain to the person hearing it, and as health care professionals we naturally find the act of inflicting pain unpleasant. Furthermore, in most of our training we are taught to relieve pain, and if it is necessary that we inflict it (during surgery, for example), we are accustomed to giving an anaesthetic or analgesic to minimize or remove it. Unfortunately, there can be no anesthetic that removes the pain of hearing bad news—the patient has to be awake and mentally competent in order to understand the situation. For us to consciously inflict pain on a conscious patient seems to upset the normal rules of our relationship with the patient, and [this] is one reason we often try to avoid it. (p. 18)*

## Determining Information Needs and Repercussions

Imagine you have been diagnosed with a terminal illness. Would you want to know? Would you want your family to know? If so, would you want them to know before or after you were told? Would you want the doctor's best estimate of how much time you had left? What might be some of the pros and cons of having this information?

Typically, once the bad news is broken, little else the physician says is heard or processed. The patient is in shock, overwhelmed with emotions. Patients experience multiple fears when told they have a life-threatening illness. They fear the physical symptoms or disability their illness may cause, dementia, side effects, being a burden on their family, and financial losses. Health care providers should recognize that breaking the bad news, difficult as it is, may be the easier task facing the provider. Responding appropriately once the patient starts reacting requires more complex skills (Gillotti & Applegate, 2000).

A caveat, however, is necessary. There are cultural differences regarding the openness of diagnosis. Not all cultural groups subscribe to open discussions about fatal diagnoses and impending death between patients and health care providers. Some prohibit these conversations, designating a senior family member, such as the oldest son or brother, to participate in such discussions and to be the chief decision maker. In Japan, the tradition has been nondisclosure or actually lying to patients. While there has been some change toward disclosure, clinical practice has not caught up to this attitude shift (Long, 1999). Although the trend has been toward more disclosure, some health care professionals still grapple with ethical dilemmas related to sharing full medical information with their patients (Purtilo, 1999). Clearly, however, once this news is shared, patients' relationships with their family, friends, and health care providers change. They must renegotiate their roles, adapt their stories, and enter a new relational territory that comes with no road map.

# THE MIDDLE: AFTER THE DIAGNOSIS

*I want to share my symptoms with my family. I want to tell them what this disease feels like, in and on my body. And it isn't always because it hurts. Sometimes I want to talk about it because it fascinates me, all these changes. But I don't always mention things. I'm never sure if they think I'm being informative or if they think I'm just complaining.*

Incurable cancer patient (M. C. Ray, 1997, p. 22)

For the terminally ill, communicating about their feelings after the diagnosis may be difficult, especially if this kind of communication was difficult before. Contracting a terminal illness may exacerbate already fragile relationships and strengthen already strong ones. Communication also is affected by how much pain the dying feel, medications, the extent of withdrawal by friends and family members, if they are spoken to in a condescending manner, or if they are excluded from interaction when they are physically present. Feeling devalued and not treated as active and contributing, the dying often experience a **social death** before their physical demise (Doka, 1989), as others experience *anticipatory grieving*.

The isolation and exclusion that are likely to result from these behaviors can add to patients' feelings of increased loss of control over their body and abilities as they become more dependent on others for care. Sensitivity to interaction also heightens, because patients, "fearing abandonment by others and that they are abandoning others as terminality approaches, are extremely sensitive to the slightest hesitation from interactants" (Thompson, 1996, p. 391). It is easy to understand how feeling a lack of control is salient to the terminally ill. Interestingly, however, research suggests that even when patients are asked to make decisions about different aspects of their care, they still complain that they have a lack of control (Pepler & Lynch, 1991). This may indicate a frustration with their inability to control what really matters—the course of their illness.

## ▪ Awareness Contexts

Obviously, different people are comfortable with different levels of disclosure and communication. Glaser and Strauss (1966) identify four **awareness contexts** for the terminally ill. The first, *closed,* is characterized by patients having no knowledge that they are dying. The second, *suspicion,* is characterized by patients guessing that they are dying. The third, *mutual pretense,* occurs when both those dying and those around them pretend that the patients will not die. There is no communication about death, and future plans are discussed as though the patient will be alive. There is much small talk, and all parties work to make the situation appear normal. Glaser and Strauss note that this behavior is common even among spouses, with only 35 percent of couples in which one partner was terminally ill saying they had expressed awareness of their plight. Another 34 percent of couples reported that one of them had expressed awareness but the other denied it. The fourth context, *open,* occurs when the impending death is acknowledged by all involved. Research suggests that survivors have an easier—though still difficult—adjustment after the death when it was discussed openly (Glaser & Srauss).

Some patients reveal they know the prognosis but do not tell their relatives, because the patients don't want to upset them. These same relatives also often know the prognosis but don't mention it for the same reason. No one wants to upset anyone else. Instead, tiptoeing around the subject can add further to the patient's sense of lack of control. Not only can they not talk honestly (should they choose to), but they cannot say their farewells, something most dying patients want to do (Kellehear & Lewin, 1988–1989). In addition, what remains of their waning energy gets devoted to keeping the secret. It is the old "there's an elephant in the living room" game: everyone sees it but walks around it and pretends it isn't there. Rifts don't get mended, good-byes don't get said, reconciliations don't take place—and the elephant just gets bigger and bigger.

## ■ The Five Stages of Dying

In addition to the possible complications already discussed, the terminally ill may progress through various stages once told they are dying. Kubler-Ross (1969) identified five **stages of dying:** (a) denial, (b) anger, (c) bargaining, (d) depression, and (e) acceptance. She emphasized that these stages were descriptive, however, not prescriptive. Stringent adherence to these stages is not likely. Instead, both dying persons and their families may experience some (or all) of these stages, in no particular order, and may revisit them. For our purposes, these stages provide a framework for understanding the complexities of feelings that many terminally ill experience.

*Denial.* Denial includes thoughts like "No, not me, it cannot be true," underscoring the shock, disbelief, and high anxiety the person feels. Kubler-Ross (1969) found that almost all her interviewees used denial during the first stages of their illnesses or after confrontation, but it also occasionally appeared later on. She observed, "Denial functions as a buffer after unexpected shocking news, allows the patient to collect himself [sic] and, with time, mobilize other, less radical defenses" (p. 39). She also believed that any dialogue with patients about their impending death should only occur when initiated by patients—and that they must be terminated when patients choose to do so. Thus, patients may exit denial for a while and talk openly about their dying, then return to denial. Kubler-Ross also believed that talking about death and dying should take place while patients are still relatively healthy—as long as patients want to talk about it.

Denial can also be seen in those close to the patient. In Lisa's case, Clem's denial was evident when her oncologist said, "No one has survived this cancer. There is no known cure. You have six months to live." From that point on, Clem's reaction was, "This cannot be. We are not giving up." It should be noted, however, that denial is not always negative. In Clem's case, for example, his refusal to accept Lisa's death sentence motivated him to actively search the Internet and to enlist the help of friends and family in medicine. As a result, they found a doctor who was willing to try an experimental treatment, which achieved a brief remission. When Lisa's tumor returned, Clem again searched for new treatments. Two months later, the same oncologist told Lisa and Clem, "You have days, maybe weeks left." It was at this point the denial ended, and they called in hospice. When Lisa was still alive three months later, however, her denial may have turned to potential hope as she began a new three-month round of chemotherapy.

***Anger.*** Anger takes place when patients ask questions like "Why me?" In this stage, interviewees were filled with anger, rage, envy, and resentment that they were facing death while others were healthy. They may be hostile toward loved ones in particular and to the world in general. This can be a very difficult stage for family and care providers, because the patient's anger is often projected and displaced onto them, which can set up a negative spiral. Caregivers and family members may take the patient's hostility personally, even though it has little to do with them and everything to do with all that the patient is losing. If this anger is taken personally, however, caregivers and family members are likely to respond by shortening their visits, avoiding the patient, or getting into arguments over irrelevant issues. In turn, this increases the patient's anger as that very anger continues to keep people away.

***Bargaining.*** Bargaining includes thoughts such as "If I'm allowed to live, I promise. . . ." During this stage, interviewees appeared to be progressing toward an acceptance of their death. Usually, their first wish was for an extension of life, followed by wishing for relief from pain or discomfort. They may secretly pray for a reprieve from death, if only long enough so they can share in a special occasion like a wedding or a birth. As Kubler-Ross (1969) observed, bargaining is actually an attempt to postpone death that often offers a "prize" for good behavior, sets a self-imposed deadline (for example, just until the wedding or the grandchild is born), and includes an implicit promise that they will not ask for more if this postponement is granted. Typically, of course, these promises are not kept. Bargains made privately with God usually make some altruistic promise. During this stage, Kubler-Ross found that communication with the patient, once again, was very important. As she noted, "Psychologically, promises may be associated with quiet guilt, and it would therefore be helpful if such remarks by patients were not just brushed aside by the staff . . . he [sic; staff] may well wish to find out if the patient feels indeed guilty for not attending church more regularly or if there are deeper, unconscious hostile wishes which precipitated such guilt" (p. 84).

*Depression.* Depression focuses on despairing thoughts such as "It's really going to happen to me, and I can't do anything about it." In this stage, patients cannot deny their illness. They may need surgery, chemotherapy, or radiation; have more symptoms; lose more weight; have less energy; and feel worse physically. There is a great sense of loss, not only physically but possibly also financially, and in some cases, there is also loss of employment. As Kubler-Ross (1969) reminds us, however, this grief is necessary for patients to experience if they are to prepare themselves for death.

The terminally ill may experience both reactive and preparatory depression. A *reactive depression* occurs in response to a particular event, like the death of a loved one, and can be dealt with best by eliciting the cause and then helping to rid the unrealistic guilt or shame that often accompanies it. With *preparatory depression,* however, the loss is not related to some past loss but, instead, results from impending losses. In this type of depression, encouragement and reassurance are less meaningful than validating patients' sorrow to help them with their final acceptance. As opposed to reactive depressions, during which patients can be quite talkative, preparatory depressions are characterized more by silence. Patients with preparatory depression can often be better supported through nonverbal communication, such as touch or just sitting with the person.

*Acceptance.* Acceptance, the final stage, includes thoughts like "I'm ready." At this point, patients are very weak and tired, sleep much more, and tend to become passive. Ideally, they have had sufficient time and help to work through the previous stages and are not depressed or angry. This stage is also characterized as almost devoid of feelings. As patients let go, they may no longer want visitors. They may not want to talk. As in the previous stage, nonverbal communication is likely to be more helpful than verbal communication. For Kay, for example, singing was extremely beneficial, as Barbara observed:

> We sang to her a lot, and we found that that was incredibly comforting to her and they confirmed that with her vital signs. Everything would just drop . . . with the singing they could stave off two hours of pain medication, with the singing they found there was absolutely no discomfort. Two hours we could go with singing.

### ■ Family as Primary Caregivers

It is not uncommon for family members to become primary caregivers, at least during the earlier stages of the illness. While both men and women take on this role, research—and the popular press—suggest that women are more likely to provide this care, even when the relative is an in-law. While there are many sociological and cultural explanations for this gender role difference (see, for example,

Wood, 1994), for many women, this burden is added to an already overfull schedule of working outside the home and then working a **second shift,** caring for a spouse and children after returning home (Hochschild, 1989). Under the best of circumstances, this is a stressful situation. Add in the responsibility of caring for a dying relative, and it is not surprising that relationships are often severely strained.

Some positive changes also may increase the family's stress. After watching their loved one suffer, perhaps the family has adjusted to their relative's dying, but few illnesses progress in a straight trajectory. The dying person may suddenly experience renewed energy and become more mobile and animated. Or, the illness may not progress as quickly as expected, so that new patterns of communication have time to emerge and become the norm. This gift of time may allow families to tie up loose ends, repair relationships, and spend quality time together. When this reprieve ends, families may choose to help their loved one die with the help of hospice.

## ▨ Hospice: Meeting the Needs of the Dying

If a person has been diagnosed as terminally ill and with less than six weeks to live, **hospice** is an option to consider. Doctors often have difficulty suggesting hospice, however, because it clearly communicates that there is no hope for recovery. Family members also often have difficulty in considering hospice for the same reason. As a result, while the provider and family dance around the issue, time is running out, and the patient's last days may be filled with pain and loneliness. Hospice provides what is often called a "good death."

Hospice is relatively new in the United States. It was not until 1963, when Dr. Cicely Saunders, the founder of St. Christopher's Hospice of London, gave a speech at Yale University that death and dying became open topics for discussion in this country. In 1974, eleven years later and spurred on by the publication of Kubler-Ross's *On Death and Dying* (1969), the first hospice in the United States, Hospice of Connecticut, opened its doors (Paradis, 1985).

The goal of hospice is to provide palliative (or comfort) care rather than curative care. When there is no hope of recovery, the focus shifts from curing patients to helping them live their final days as fully, as pain-free, and as lucidly as possible. Hospice is more than a physical place, however. It is a philosophy that views death as a natural, final stage of life. When there is no hope of cure, hospice helps to ease the dying person's physical, emotional, and spiritual pain. As Stoddard (1992) says:

*People in hospices are not attached to machines, nor are they manipulated by drips or tubes, or by the administration of drugs that cloud the mind without relieving pain. Instead, they are given comfort by methods sometimes rather sophisticated but often amazingly simple and obvious; and they are helped to live fully in an atmosphere of loving-kindness and grace until the time has come for them to die a natural death. (p. 14)*

Whether in the person's home, in a home-type setting within a hospital, or in any other physical setting, hospice provides care for the whole patient. The orientation is one that emphasizes the importance of communication. Typically, a health care team works together to manage the patient's needs. Physicians, nurses, aides, social workers, and volunteers visit the patient and teach family members to care for their loved one. Effective communication, both among the health care team and with the patient and their family, is essential. In fact, hospice workers are often excellent models of good communication with dying people. Unlike many doctors and nurses, who tend to withdraw from their dying patients, hospice workers are there to spend time with and to comfort, both verbally and nonverbally, dying persons and their loved ones. With so much to recommend it, it may strike you as surprising that hospice has only recently gained some "stature," as evidenced by the fact that some insurance plans now reimburse at least some of its costs.

Interestingly, the intensity of interaction between hospice staff and patients has resulted in an acute awareness of attempts by patients to communicate in ways that are not always easy for others to interpret. Some hospice workers have identified a common theme that they call nearing death awareness.

## ■ Nearing Death Awareness

Miller and Knapp (1986) found that, when communicating with dying patients, it is best to be reflexive—in other words, to follow the patient's lead regarding what topics to talk about. As the illness progresses, patients' communication likely is affected by their illness, their medications, or a combination of both. Understanding what patients need and are trying to communicate may be difficult, especially as they report occurrences that seem unlikely to those around them. Nonetheless, supporting and validating a patient's experience is important. Kay's daughter, Barbara, observed, "There were times my mother would talk to people in the room that weren't there. I really believe she had one foot in one place and one foot in the other. I truly believe that."

This type of communication is called **nearing death awareness** (Callahan & Kelley, 1992), and it is based on the experiences of hospice workers with many terminally ill patients. Callahan and Kelley suggest that the dying do communicate their needs, feelings, and desires, but that we also need to know how to listen and what to be aware of. As they observe:

*Nearing death awareness reveals what dying is like, and what is needed in order to die peacefully; it develops in those who are dying slowly. The attempts of dying people to describe what they are experiencing may be missed, misunderstood, or ignored because the communication is obscure, unexpected, or expressed in symbolic language. (p. 13)*

Thus, comments or gestures made by the dying person may be interpreted as nonsensical, confusing, hallucinatory, or the result of either medication or mental confusion. Based on this interpretation, others respond to the dying patient with frustration, annoyance, condescension, or increased medication, all of which distance them and further isolates the patient. Essentially, everyone stops listening to the dying person. As Barbara observed, "I think most of the time people thought that my mother was far more demented than she was. They just didn't understand her communication." In Kay's case, however, Barbara found meaning in her mother's behavior:

*When I had my first alone talk with her, where I said good-bye my first time . . . she said to me, "I want to fly. I want to fly like a bird." I woke up one morning in the hospital, 4 or 5 in the morning, and she was flying. She was lying in bed with both arms raised in a diagonal, with this look of euphoria on her face. So I went over and I got as close as I could and I laid across her arms and put my hands on hers and we flew together and the look on her face was so amazing and she could never tell me more about that.*

Callahan and Kelley (1992) identify two themes in dying patients' communication. The first includes patients' attempts to describe what they are experiencing while dying. The second includes their requests for something they need for a peaceful death. Whether it's visions of deceased loved ones or religious figures or being given permission to die, the key is to not label patients as either disoriented or crazy but, instead, to recognize what they are trying to tell us. By acknowledging and understanding nearing death awareness, patients can teach the rest of us how to die.

These themes are clearly evident with both Lisa and Kay. In Lisa's case, Clem was unwilling to give Lisa permission to die. To others, he seemed to be in denial, supporting Lisa's decisions to continue treatment even after they were told she had only weeks or days to live. Finally, after pressure from his sister, Clem conceded. Though difficult, the impact on Lisa was evident:

*Clem went home at lunchtime and walked upstairs to his wife, who had not come downstairs since her return from the hospital five days earlier. She was lying in bed, on the side closest to the door, facing him when he came in. He lay down next to her, pressing his chest against her back and wrapping his arms around her.*

*"I've been thinking about what you said to me last night," he said, and he started to cry. "You can go, I can let go. I will be fine, the boys will be fine. You don't have to worry about me or them. It's OK to go."*

*Two hours later, Lisa got out of bed. She stepped tentatively, her feet virtually colorless and splayed duck-style as she slowly made her way down the stairs, carrying her stomach bag in one hand, the morphine pump in the other. Everyone—her parents, her sister, her friend—looked surprised to see her.*

*A half-hour later, propped up in bed, she smiled and her eyes widened. "I'm not worried about Clem anymore," she said. She nodded her head for emphasis. "Really, I'm not worried about Clem. He's going to be fine."*

There was a similar concern for Kay, but it took a hospice social worker to call it to the family's attention:

*A social worker came in [at hospice], a wonderful woman who was very insightful and she was the one who finally sat down with my father. She felt that my father had to verbally, as well as in his heart, tell my mother that it was ok to go. Because she was not dying, she was hanging on and nobody could get it. They kept saying, "Does she have unfinished business?" And we kept saying no but then we realized she did. It was dad. I believe she really was afraid to leave him and he didn't want to let her go. And we didn't realize that he was hanging on so much.*

Some of Kay's behaviors could have been interpreted as hallucinatory and bizarre. Barbara and other family members, however, were able to interpret those behaviors in a soothing and helpful way. Barbara tells of one example that stood out, the butterfly balloon:

*The other thing that we did every day, we would call it taking the butterfly out of retirement. My sister had brought in the most amazing balloon, it was about three feet across, it looked like stained glass and it was a butterfly and we would actually have to put that away. My mother got so worked up over that butterfly. She would get completely lost in it. We had to put it away because the first day, we let her have it for almost four hours and you couldn't communicate with her when she had this butterfly in any way, shape, or form. It was an inflated balloon, see-through like stained glass, on a ribbon. It was the most beautiful balloon, everyone commented on it. This was an extraordinary balloon. And my mother, we would let her go flying. She would get so lost in this balloon and she would begin to perspire. First she would hold it, she would constantly pull it down and let it go to fly up. She would talk about it—just get a little sound or a word or groan out—she would just stare at it and would be gasping and the first night, after the fourth hour, that's when we knew that we had to do this a little bit in stages. She began to pull at this and she was perspiring and actually almost hyperventilating. She could not go to sleep if the butterfly was in her vision. So at that point, we would retire the butterfly . . . she seemed to accept when we would retire it. We would bring that butterfly out many,*

*many times in intervals through the day and night over the next two weeks. For my mother, if the balloon was there, you were not there. We would help her but there was no acknowledgment and even as she could not grab it anymore, sometimes you would see her fingers try to and we'd realize she wanted to let it flip so we would do it for her. And eventually we would just put it in her eyesight and she would stare at it. When she had her butterfly, that was her drug, that was her time that she flies. And we felt that she always was going to that other place and she always looked so content and happy. She wasn't on any medication until the last Tuesday night and she died on Thursday. So eight days, plus the two or three prior days in the hospital.*

When Barbara was interviewed, Kay had only been dead a month. As she reviewed the experience, Barbara found herself moved, humbled, and a changed person:

*My biggest impression of this entire process [Kay's dying] is that this is all so big. This death thing is so big. But it all comes down to detail and minutiae, the last look, the tiny teaspoon of pudding, the last breath. It all is about details. The last bath. And not in a bad way. It's about paying attention to every word and story that you tell because this thing, this dying process that is going on and you can't stop this current, it's so big and so vast in contrast to all these little tiny things you're dealing with and feeling every moment. And that to me, that contrast, is still so huge because it all became about minutes with mom, seconds, and the last this and that. . . . All those things mean so very much. It's so big and it's so full of so many people and yet it's such a lonely endeavor. And I have to say, looking back a month after my mom's death, it has real beautiful aspects to it. . . . This is it, this is the last big dance and you either join in or you lose this incredible experience.*

While Barbara and Clem actively participated in their loved one's process of dying, both had very different experiences. After the death occurs, survivors are simultaneously faced with overwhelming emotions of grief, comforting memories, possible regrets, and the pragmatic concerns of making arrangements for their loved one. In the aftermath of the death, numerous additional communication issues arise. In the next section, we focus on several of these concerns: organ and tissue donation, writing obituaries, and talking both among and with survivors.

# AFTER THE DEATH: COMMUNICATING AMONG AND WITH SURVIVORS

There are many possible ways to organize this section, but our rationale is based on when, in relation to a death, most people find themselves faced with the concerns discussed here. The first two, organ and tissue donation and writing obituaries, usually require communication among survivors, and they typically take place immediately before or soon after a death. Communication between survivors and others (those not family and close friends) more often occurs after the death, during the memorial service or funeral and the grieving period. Each is often a daunting—and painful—hurdle for the newly grieving to face. Everyone grieves in a highly personal way, but patterns can be found that reflect individual family differences and embed our cultural norms and values surrounding communication about death.

## ◾ Organ and Tissue Donation

When loved ones die, it is often difficult to make sense of their deaths. This is especially true if the death was sudden or the person was young. One way to help survivors deal with their loss is through organ and tissue donation. In these cases, once a person is pronounced brain dead, healthy organs or tissue are removed and transplanted into suitable patients. Because many people do not make their wishes about donating their organs or tissue known in their advance directives (discussed later in this chapter), survivors are often left with this decision.

Deciding to donate a loved one's organs is often gut-wrenching for the family, but organs are desperately needed. Currently, about 79,000 people are waiting for some type of organ transplant, but, for example, only 11,684 organs were retrieved in 2000. As of 2000, approximately 52,000 Americans are waiting for new kidneys; however, only about 13,000 received kidneys in 2000 (United Network for Organ Sharing, 2002). About 60 people receive organ transplants every day, while an average of 16 people die daily because of an organ shortage ("Organ donation," 2002). More than half of all potential organs are lost because the deceased person's family either declines to donate (MacPherson, 1996) or is not even asked or identified as being willing to donate (Shelton, 1996). The difference between the number of potential and actual donors results in those patients waiting for transplants having a one-in-three chance of dying before an organ becomes available. There are a number of reasons for this problem, and many of them center around communication.

Organ donation begins with healthy people thinking about their own wishes should this situation ever arise. You may have first thought about organ donation after hearing public service announcements or when you got your driver's license. It's much less likely that you have been asked your donor status in your doctor's office; however, attempts are being made to change this. Following the lead of the Texas Medical Association, the American Medical Association has begun the "Live and Then Give" program to increase organ donation by 20 percent in two years. This program asks physicians to make a commitment to speak to their patients about organ donation during a normal medical interview and to encourage their own families and staff to become donors ("Talk to," 1998).

Once you decide to be a donor, you need to complete and sign (with witnesses) an organ donor card. Discussing your wishes with your doctor, family members, and friends is also critical. You may feel uncomfortable bringing the subject up, because most people don't want to entertain the possibility of this situation arising some day. One Gallup Poll (1993) found that while 85 percent of Americans surveyed said they support the concept of organ donation and 90 percent believe transplants are not experimental, only 79 percent said they would personally accept a transplanted organ. In addition, only 28 percent carried a signed-and-witnessed donor card, and only 27 percent of those who didn't said they would be willing to sign one. Not only is signing an organ donor card important, so is making sure that your next-of-kin are aware of—and agree to carry out—your wishes. Some communication researchers have focused on designing messages that will persuade people to carry organ donor cards. For example, they've found that prior thought and intent about organ donation plays a significant role in determining how willing people are to sign an organ donor card, and that narratives are more persuasive than statistical evidence in convincing those who are willing to sign donor cards (Smith, Morrison, Kopfman, & Ford, 1994). They've also found that willingness to discuss organ donation with family members also affects people's decisions to donate (Kopfman, Smith, Ah Yun, & Hodges, 1998).

On the other hand, you may find yourself having to decide whether to donate a loved one's organs. Probably the greatest challenge to increasing the number of available organs is acquiring consent from the families. Once a patient is declared brain dead, next-of-kin are asked for permission to donate the deceased's organs. This is the typical scenario—even when the deceased had signed an organ donor card. As a result, less than half the families asked about organ donations give permission, which is not difficult to understand given the enormity of their situation. As Weber (1994) states:

> *The families, confronted with what is usually a sudden, unexpected death, must quickly grasp the enormity of the tragedy, then draw on their deepest reserves to allow unknown individuals to benefit from their loss. Those family members who are aware of the deceased's prior wishes are much better prepared to make this decision. Yet very few people discuss organ donation with their loved ones.*

The problem is not always with the families, however. In some states, hospitals are not required to ask families for permission. Because they cannot use organs without permission, potential organs remain unused. New York recently passed a law making it mandatory that all families be approached. States that require asking have seen donor figures increase by more than 25 percent in the first year (Mullally, 1997).

In addition to this advance discussion, those seeking donation must first allow the family to come to terms with the death of their loved one. For some, what is meant by the phrase *brain death* is unclear. Weber (1994) again notes that 20 percent of Americans believe that brain death can be reversed and that 16 percent are not sure. Thus, families may become suspicious that those seeking the organs are "jumping the gun," that the person is not really dead and could still be revived. In addition, it is important for families to understand that, to be eligible as a donor, the patient's heart must be kept beating after brain death occurs. One suggestion is that telling the family of the death and asking for organs should be separate conversations, allowing time for the former to sink in. Another suggestion is to use appropriate terminology. Transplant teams refer to *harvesting* the organ, but grieving family members may find the thought of their loved one being "harvested" offensive.

Another concern for health care workers seeking organs is their goal to not add to the family's grief. For many families, however, donating their loved one's organs helps them to make sense of the death and aids in their grieving. For example, one study of organ donor families found that 96 percent felt the donation was a positive that came out of the death, and 89 percent said they would make the same decision again (Weber, 1994).

What we don't often hear about organ donation is the perspective of the organ recipient. You first met Heather Reich in Chapter 7. Here, she shares her thoughts and feelings while awaiting a pancreas transplant (she had already received a kidney from her brother):

> *The experience of receiving a cadaveric organ transplant is one of conflicting emotions. My first reaction was one of shock; no matter how you prepare, the call is a surprise. Then utter joy and elation. After the shock wears off comes the realization that someone has died.*
>
> *I felt deep sadness for the young man who lost his life and curiosity about the loved ones left behind. I knew that he was in the Navy, and being a military wife for almost 20 years I wondered about a young wife and children. The faces of many of the young women, children, and mothers of sailors, who would stand with me on piers waiting for ships to return flashed in front of me.*
>
> *Then I wept. The magnitude of the gift fully hit me, the enormous generosity, courage, and love it took to transcend what must have been devastating grief and think of the lives of suffering strangers. It was one of the most deeply spiritual moments of my life. After these moments of holy awe and humility, I became energized and got busy with the details of going to Washington, DC, for six weeks (for the transplant surgery). I felt as if my life was beginning again, a life without the further complications of diabetes.*

It was not only Heather who got a new lease on life from this gift. She discusses some of the other recipients:

*This tragedy changed the lives of three people, as two others received kidneys from this young man. One man had waited two years for his transplant and the other eight years. We had all suffered and were so grateful for the second chance for life.*

One year after receiving the pancreas, Heather's kidney failed and was removed. Five months later, her transplanted pancreas failed and had to be removed. Heather poignantly describes her grief:

*When I realized I was losing the pancreas, I again thought of the young man and his brave family. I cried for us both. I felt we were both dying again. I had thought of him in moments of thanksgiving for beautiful days without insulin, for being able to have ice cream on a hot summer night, and the larger joys of thinking of being there for my daughter's children and the ability to plan a future with my husband. The liberating joy, just simple joy, that I had been missing since the complications of diabetes began to take a hold of my life and humanity.*

After waiting 11 months, Heather received a second kidney. She is continuing her graduate studies (where she almost always sets the curve), maintains her wonderful sense of humor, and is enjoying life once again.

On a practical level, it is clear that communication issues are central to the success of organ donation programs. A summary of several programs includes a number of communicative and behavioral steps:

*If you want to donate any or all of your organs or tissues, carry a signed and witnessed donor card. Discuss your wishes with family, your physician, and friends. Put your desire in writing as well. Talk to your family members to find out their wishes for organ donation. Encourage them to carry a card and make their wishes known to others too. Have a signed, witnessed power of attorney and living will and make sure your family, physician, and friends know your wishes. (Adapted from "Organ donation," 2002)*

## ◼ Obituaries

Our obituary is one of our last pieces of public communication, a cultural ritual that allows us to publicly memorialize someone. **Obituaries** are usually written with input from family and friends. While many opt for the brief version, which gives basic demographic and burial information, others make more elaborate choices. We can consider obituaries as one measurement of our life's achievement. As such, they mirror our cultural norms and values. Reflecting our traditional differences, a study of obituaries in two newspapers from 1992 to 1993 found that women had significantly fewer and shorter obituaries than men (Maybury,

1995–1996). The study also found that women had the longest obituaries when they were the relative of a famous man.

Most of us never read the obituaries in the newspapers. Those who do may find that others think they're odd or obsessed with death. Obituaries can be very interesting, however. Many times, they are called Death Notices and simply provide information such as the person's name, age, vocation, cause of death, survivors, and date and time of the funeral or memorial service. Some mention a person's religious orientation, tell humorous anecdotes, discuss the deceased person's jobs or hobbies, or give a chronology of the person's life. They can even be wonderfully entertaining, providing insight into that person's life and uniqueness. These obituaries not only provide information but serve as tributes to the person and their survivors and give a flavor of the deceased person's personality. In Theorizing Practice 8.2, we ask you to consider your own obituary.

As Clem found after speaking to a newspaper obituary reporter, however, it can be very difficult to compose a fitting tribute in the midst of your grief:

> *I talked to that guy [the reporter]. That was hard. What do you say about somebody? Particularly when he said, "Sounds like all she had time for was work and kids." Whoa. There's a summation for you. [chuckle.] Nothing against him. It's just sleep deprivation. I wanted to say, "Hey buddy, this woman ran an operations center that did 1.2 billion dollars in mortgages in nine months. More than any other mortgage center in all of California." [pause.] "Like I said, I'm just tired."*

### ■ Talking with the Survivors

Although Americans, as a culture, are not good at talking about death, we do have a formal vocabulary for labeling our experiences. For example, when we experience the loss of a loved one, we are *bereaved*; we find ourselves in a mental state of distress in reaction to our loss as we *grieve*; and we *mourn* according to culturally prescribed and accepted time periods and behaviors as we express our grief. The extent of our grief varies depending on the situation and the person, but people with stronger and larger support networks adjust more easily than those who are not as tightly linked to others.

Not everyone, however, can share their grief and count on the support of others. This is especially true when the person lost was part of a marginalized group. When the death is of someone our culture does not value (for example, a gay partner), it is difficult for survivors to publicly share their loss, to mourn, or to get social support. This **disenfranchised grief** (Doka, 1989) makes the grieving process even harder. For others, such as the elderly, they may experience *bereavement overload* (Kastenbaum, 1995). As we age, we lose not only our strong, healthy bodies and sharp minds but

## Considering Our Obituary

Write your own obituary. How would you want to be remembered? What would you consider your accomplishments, unique characteristics, and meaningful relationships? Would you include a picture? Why, or why not?

also many of the loved ones and friends we would share these losses with (Kastenbaum). The losses continue to mount. A similar experience has been shared by friends of gay men who have died of AIDS. During the peak of this epidemic, it was not uncommon to attend at least two or three funerals a week, week after week. One of my (Eileen's) friends said that he buried at least 150 friends. After a while, he became numb, went through the motions, and could not remember most of the funerals.

Obviously, the bereaved need our support, but we are often at a loss for words for survivors when someone has died. For many of us, there was little—or no—discussion of death among our families when we were children. Research shows, however, that our attitudes about death are often similar to those of other family members, and that they are often shaped through nonverbal communication, such as silence, general impressions, and what is *not* said when a death occurs (Book, 1996). Our resulting awkwardness in communication may cause us to avoid survivors at a time when they need us the most.

Several things, however, are usually not good to say:

*One of the most thoughtless things you can say to a parent is, "God needs another rose for his garden." Worse is the comment, "At least you have other children." (M. C. Ray, 1997, p. 71)*

*There is one condolence letter I will never forget. The person wrote, "Your father is so much happier now that he's in heaven. He's with his Maker, where he always wanted to be." That letter disgusted me. My father was agnostic, maybe even an atheist. I don't think he even believed in heaven. And I know for certain he wouldn't be happiest there. He'd much rather be with his buddies in the club house, drinking a beer after 18 holes of golf. She should have left her "God" out of my condolence letter. (M. C. Ray, 1997, pp. 73–74)*

While the quotes above were not appreciated by those family members, others might find them very comforting. As always, in order to communicate competently, we need to analyze our audience and use a message that is appropriate to them. Often the most comforting message may be sharing memories of the deceased, listening to survivors talk about their loved one, or giving the survivor a hug. FYI 8.1 provides suggestions from a Michigan hospice for communicating with a grieving friend

1. Don't worry about what to say. Just being there shows you care. Don't feel you have to have answers. Just be a good listener.

2. Talk about the deceased—anything you know about them, such as what they said or did. It helps the grieving persons to keep them closer.

3. Call often. Especially after the first couple months. Their energy level may be too low for them to make the effort even though they may need to talk.

4. Send cards even weeks after the funeral. They are always helpful, and there is a disappointment when they finally quit coming.

5. Do visit in the home after the funeral service is over, but stay just a short while. Grievers need some privacy.

6. If you want to do something with or for the bereaved, give him or her an option. Some days they just can't cope with "something to do."

7. Don't avoid the person when you see them for the first time after the funeral. Go up to them first.

8. Try not to look startled when the bereaved mentions the deceased. Let him or her talk about the deceased loved one as much as they like.

9. Don't try to get the mind of the griever off of a loved one. That is impossible for a long time if the relationship was close. Remember, the hardest thing for the bereaved is to see life going on.

10. Don't make small talk. Talk about what is uppermost in the griever's mind.

11. Don't be uneasy if you cry and the bereaved doesn't. A person can only cry so much. The hurt is still there.

12. Don't talk about what the deceased might have been spared by death. Those thoughts bring no comfort.

13. Don't remind the person of what they have left, such as other children. At the time, all the bereaved can think of is what he or she has lost and the feeling that there is no future. The deeply grieved does not want to think about tomorrow.

14. Things you could do to be helpful: grocery shop; go to the library; harvest garden; mow lawn; prepare hot meal; babysit; clean house.

15. If they have children, invite them to spend time with your children. If the children have lost their father, it would be wonderful if another man would spend some time with them also. He could include them occasionally when he does something with his own kids.

16. Don't assume the deeply bereaved is "over it" in just a few weeks or even months because they are going on with routines. Grief takes much longer, and people can pretend to be doing much better than they really are doing. Share your love, your time, and most importantly, your prayers.

From Arbor Hospice brochure, Ann Arbor, Michigan.

## Communicating with Survivors

If you have experienced the death of a loved one, think about what people said or what you found supportive. Were things said or done that were unsupportive? Did this change over time? For example, did people say things to you soon after the death that made you angry but that, several months later, would not have upset you? Why might this happen?

If you have not had this experience, interview someone who has, and ask them these same questions.

As a class, put together a list of supportive and unsupportive messages and behaviors you have identified. What are their similarities? Their differences? Are there consistent changes over time? If you were teaching the general public how to communicate with survivors, what advice would you give them?

or relative, and Theorizing Practice 8.3 asks you to consider communicating with survivors. These communication behaviors are especially important later in the grieving process after the funeral is over, when everyone has gone home and the survivors must return to their daily lives.

Up to this point, our focus has been on understanding communication issues related to the actual process of dying. Several communication issues, however, should be addressed long before then, when we are still healthy and of sound mind. We now shift our focus to communicating our wishes for treatment if we become unable, physically or mentally, to make those wishes known at a later time.

# MANAGING OUR OWN END-OF-LIFE CARE

*[M]echanistic biomedicine in which the pursuit of cure reinforces an illusion that our lives can be indefinitely extended by means of continuous high-tech repairs. . . . In effect, patients and doctors collude in this fiction. A strong presumption throughout medical education was that all seriously ill people required vigorous life-prolonging treatment, including those who were expected to die, even patients with chronic illness such as widespread cancer, end-stage congestive heart failure, and kidney or liver failure. It even extended to patients who saw death as a relief from the suffering caused by their illness. Death is a scandal in postmodern times partly because it unmasks the illusion that we can live forever.*

(Byock, 1977, pp.15, 26)

**FYI 8.2**  KEY LEGAL CASES FOR THE RIGHT TO END LIFE-SUSTAINING TREATMENT

While the prospect of death may seem distant for most college students, these two precedent-setting cases involved young people. Karen Ann Quinlan was 21 and Nancy Cruzan was 26 when they were catastrophically injured. Both cases had a major legal impact on who could decide when to end life-sustaining treatment in the absence of the patient's advance directive.

**The Case of Karen Ann Quinlan**

Karen Ann Quinlan was the first modern icon of the right-to-die debate. The 21-year-old collapsed after swallowing alcohol and tranquilizers at a party in 1975 and ceased breathing for at least two 15-minute periods. As a result, she suffered severe brain damage and, in the words of the attending physicians, was reduced to "a chronic persistent vegetative state" in which she "no longer had any cognitive function."

Accepting the doctors' judgment that there was no hope of recovery, but frustrated by the doctors' refusal to remove the respirator (since her brain activity still enabled her to be considered "alive"), her parents sought permission from the courts to disconnect the respirator that was keeping her alive in the intensive-care unit of a New Jersey hospital.

The trial court, and then the Supreme Court of New Jersey, agreed that the respirator could be removed and Karen Ann Quinlan allowed to die. It was argued that the parents had Karen's best interests in mind and knew of her fundamental values. The court stated that "if Karen herself were miraculously lucid for an interval . . . and perceptive of her

*(continued)*

Medical care in the United States has traditionally followed the biomedical model, which emphasizes treating the disease as something that is separate from the emotional and social life of the patient. The goal is to cure the disease, and the death of a patient is considered to be failure. Several movements are challenging this model, however, as evidenced by the best-seller *Final Exit* (Humphry, 1991), which promotes **rational suicide,** and the more than 100 suicides assisted by Dr. Jack Kevorkian (in jail as of this writing for actually administering a fatal dose and capturing it on videotape). It is beyond the scope of this chapter to address the ethical questions underlying these issues. Communicatively, however, the attention paid to them in the media has led to more open discussion and evaluation of our values related to end-of-life concerns.

**Advance directives,** as the name implies, are decisions that a person makes regarding his or her health care in advance of a situation occurring where she or he is no longer capable, physically or mentally, of making such decisions. As it has become common for people live into their eighties, there has been a sub-

*(continued from previous page)*

irreversible condition she could effectively decide upon discontinuance of the life-support apparatus, even if it meant the prospect of a natural death."

The respirator was disconnected, but in a final twist, Quinlan kept breathing. She remained in a coma for almost 10 years in a New Jersey nursing home until her death on June 11th, 1985.

### The Case of Nancy Cruzan

Nancy Cruzan, 26 years old, was severely injured in an automobile accident in 1983 and lapsed into a persistent vegetative state. After a number of years, it was clear to all concerned that she, like Karen Ann Quinlan, would not emerge from this condition.

Her court-appointed guardians requested that the tube-feedings that kept her alive be discontinued. The administrator at the state-owned hospital where she resided objected, however, and a state court concurred. The court argued that Nancy Cruzan was not in a 'terminally ill condition' and that, without clear and convincing evidence that she had authorized the termination of life-sustaining treatment, the state can require its continued use. Because such evidence was lacking, the hospital continued to tube-feed the patient.

The U.S. Supreme Court upheld that a state has the right to insist on a patient's actual intent and that each state remains free to set its own standards in such cases. Nevertheless, after the U.S. Supreme Court's decision, the Cruzan case was again brought before the state courts, and this time, it was not impeded. Despite objections from Right-to-Life groups, the tube-feedings were stopped. Nancy Cruzan died on December 26th, 1990.

---

Information from http://www.who2.com/karenannquinlan.html and http://www.lcl.cmu.edu/CAAE/80130/part3/cases/Cruzan.html; downnloaded on June 16, 1999.

---

sequent rise in the incidences of cancer, dementia, heart disease, and other illnesses. The explosion of new technologies also now enables people of all ages to be kept "alive" by machines—sometimes for years. The emotional and financial costs to the family, not to mention the loss of dignity by the patient, are enormous.

It has only been since the mid-1970s that we have we examined the implications of using this technology. For example, the question of whether to keep alive through artificial means a person who is in a vegetative state has led to much public debate and legal changes, initiated by the landmark cases of Karen Ann Quinlan and Nancy Cruzan, as described in FYI 8.2.

None of us wants to end up like Karen Ann Quinlan or Nancy Cruzan. While we cannot control our illness, we can control how we want to be treated if we are dying. It is essential that we clearly communicate our **end-of-life (EOL) decisions.** Communication scholars Stephen Hines, Austin Babrow, Laurie Badzek, and Alvin Moss (1997) define an end-of-life decision as *one in which a patient (or legally authorized surrogate) facing the progression of an incurable medical condition (a) refuses or consents to or (b) withdraws from or continues a life-sustaining treatment that may result in or perpetuate a significant reduction in the patient's quality of life. (p. 200)*

These decisions are best made when we are healthy, well-informed, and actively involved in deciding which treatments are acceptable. It is usually uncomfortable to bring up the subject of our possible demise. There is never a good time, in advance, to broach the subject. It doesn't add to the ambience at parties, ball games, or shopping. It is even difficult to talk about when we find ourselves actually faced with the situation. In their study of dialysis patients, Hines et al. (1997) found that both doctors and patients were likely to avoid talking about needed life-sustaining treatment until they absolutely had to. They also found that EOL discussions between doctors and patients centered on treatments to sustain life and did not include allowing life to end as a possible choice.

So, it is critical that we communicate, both verbally and in writing, with our health care provider and our family through advance directives. For example, your hospital chart can be labeled DNR (Do Not Resuscitate), so that if you go into heart failure, no attempts will be made to revive you. Advance directives such as living wills and durable power of attorney let your physician know at what point you want your treatment stopped and if you want your organs or tissue donated. Most Americans have not completed a living will or durable power of attorney, however, much less even talked about their wishes with their health care provider or loved ones, leaving their fate up to others (see FYI 8.3 and 8.4 for examples).

Interestingly, when asked, many people are definite about their wishes, often using the vegetable metaphor to reflect their distaste for dependency on others. In one study, Long (1997) found that many people were quite clear on what they desired. As a 62-year-old police officer hospitalized for cardiac testing said:

*If I was in a state of [being a] vegetable, I wouldn't desire to continue if I had the choice. If I'm in a coma, don't pull the plug, or if it's a stroke, because you don't know. But if I'm brain dead, then it's worthless. If the brain is dead then the soul is gone. (Long, p. 18)*

A woman in her fifties commented:

*If I'm a vegetable, forget it. Don't put me on a machine. I wouldn't know what I'm doing anyway. I won't recognize anyone. You see people on TV where the family comes to visit and the person doesn't even recognize them. It's sad. (Long, p. 19)*

Another concern that Americans have is with the cost of prolonged life. Here again, the issue of quality of life is raised, as is the concern with being a burden to family. As one man, a retired, 65-year-old industrial worker, observed:

A Living Will is a document that allows you to direct the medical care you would receive if you were to become terminally ill and unable to make your wishes known or become permanently unconscious.

A terminal illness is one from which your doctor has determined you have no reasonable chance of recovery. If you should be terminally ill *and* unable to tell your physician or family what you want done, by having completed a Living Will you could make certain that your wishes would be followed regarding the medical care you receive.

If you are in this situation, a Living Will can give your doctor the authority to withhold all life-sustaining treatment, *INCLUDING* artificial nutrition and hydration if they are not needed to provide you with comfort or relief from pain. Artificial nutrition and hydration is the replacement of your body's fluids and nutrients through intravenous "feedings." A Living Will would *not* allow your doctor to discontinue "comfort care."

There are four important *limitations* to the Living Will:

1. It does not apply if you are able or will be able to speak for yourself.

2. It does not give the physician authority to withdraw "comfort care." Comfort care would include any medical or nursing procedure that lessens your pain and doesn't simply postpone your death.

3. It does not give your physician the authority to withdraw nutrition or hydration if you are permanently unconscious *unless* you indicate that this is your wish on the Living Will form and it was determined that they were not needed to lessen your pain or discomfort.

4. If you are pregnant, it does not allow life-sustaining treatment to be withdrawn if doing so would terminate the pregnancy. The exception would be if two physicians determine that the fetus would not be born alive.

A Living Will cannot become operative until your attending doctor is told about it. It is not necessary to go through any court procedure before the Living Will becomes effective. However, before the instructions are carried out, the attending physician must determine that you are no longer able to make informed decisions on health care and a second physician must agree with the diagnosis that you are either terminally ill or permanently unconscious. To verify that you are in a permanently unconscious state, one of the physicians must be a specialist in an appropriate field. If you draft both a Living Will and Durable Power of Attorney for Health Care, the Living Will would take precedence over a Durable Power of Attorney. You may revoke a Living Will at any time and in any manner.

---

From *Ohio's Living Will: A Guide to Ohio's Living Will* by the Ohio State Bar Association and Ohio State Medical Association, August, 1991, p. 1.

When you complete a Durable Power of Attorney for Health Care, you are naming a person to act as your attorney-in-fact to make health care decisions for you if you become unable to make them for yourself.

This attorney-in-fact has the power to authorize and refuse medical treatment for you. This power is not limited to situations in which you are terminally ill or permanently unconscious, but generally includes all medical treatment decisions. However, this power is only effective if you are not competent or able to make health care decisions for yourself.

There are five *restrictions* to the authority of the person who would act as your attorney-in-fact:

1. The attorney-in-fact cannot order that life-sustaining treatment be withdrawn from you unless you are in a terminal condition or a permanently unconscious state, two physicians have confirmed the diagnosis and your attending physician has determined that you have no reasonable possibility of regaining decision-making ability.

2. The attorney-in-fact cannot order the withdrawal of any treatment given to provide comfort or relieve pain and not just postpone death.

3. If you are pregnant, the attorney-in-fact cannot order that life-sustaining treatment be withdrawn if doing so would terminate the pregnancy unless there is substantial risk to your life or two physicians determine that the fetus would not be born alive.

4. The attorney-in-fact cannot order that nutrition and hydration be withdrawn unless you are terminally ill or permanently unconscious and two physicians agree that nutrition and hydration will no longer provide comfort or alleviate pain. If you want to give your attorney-in-fact the power to withhold nutrition and hydration if you become permanently unconscious, then *you must indicate this on the appropriate section of the Durable Power of Attorney form.*

5. If you have previously given consent to treatment (before becoming unable to communicate), your attorney-in-fact cannot withdraw your consent unless your condition has changed and the treatment is no longer of benefit or the treatment hasn't proven effective.

A Durable Power of Attorney goes into effect when your attending physician is told about it. It is not necessary to go through any court procedure. Before the attorney-in-fact is granted authority under the Durable Power, the attending physician must decide that you are unable to make health care decisions for yourself.

Once it is determined that you are unable to make these decisions, your attending physician may assume that your attorney-in-fact is speaking for you and follow his or her directions.

You may revoke a Durable Power of Attorney at any time and in any manner.

From *Durable Power of Attorney: A Guide to Ohio's Durable Power of Attorney* by the Ohio State Bar Association and Ohio State Medical Association, August, 1991, p. 1.

*I had a friend who keeled over in the street. He was brain dead and put on machines for five days—and didn't die for another three days. A helicopter took him to the hospital. They charged his poor widow $3500. I don't want this. I have already talked with my wife and family. (Long, 1997, p. 17)*

This concern was reiterated by others. According to another man, a 55-year-old diemaker who was admitted to the hospital for possible insertion of a pacemaker, "I wouldn't want my family wiped out financially. I don't want their quality of life destroyed by me being hooked up to machines" (Long, p. 17). A 63-year-old former steelworker with severe heart disease and arthritis said, "I don't want to be a burden on anybody. If I'm in the shape I can't take care of myself, I don't want to go on" (Long, p. 17).

Once a person is seriously ill, it is often too late to ask for their wishes. Instead, we need to talk—when we are healthy—about our wishes if we are ever being kept alive by technology or become terminally ill (see Theorizing Practice 8.4). The

---

**THEORIZING PRACTICE 8.4**

## Writing an Advance Directive

Give some thought to issues that you need to consider in writing an advance directive, and then answer the following questions:

1. Under what circumstances do you think your advance directive would be needed?

2. What do you consider to be "heroic measures"?

3. Under what conditions would you want heroic measures to be used? Are there some measures you approve of and others you do not (for example, hydration, artificial nutrition via feeding tube, respirator)?

4. When would you want these measures not to be used, to be used, or to be used and then withdrawn?

5. What do you consider to be "comfort care," and at what point do you want only that (for example, sedation, pain relief)?

6. Who do you want to make these decisions? Consider several people, because your first choice may die before you. Do you want an individual or a group of family or friends making the decision? If a group, how should conflicts be resolved? Are there any family or friends you do not want involved in the decision-making process?

Discuss your decisions with those close to you, and give a copy of this to your physician, family, and friends. Remember to revisit your choices periodically, so that you can update the advance directive to reflect changes in your preferences and in medical technology.

---

burden should be shared with health care providers. Discussion of advance directives should be initiated by doctors during well-care visits, when you are healthy and in a good state of mind, rather than being left to a last-minute, death-bed task. Once you enter a hospital, it is often a bureaucratic chore punted to a hospital admitting clerk rather than a thoughtful discussion among family, friends, or persons hired to keep your best interests in mind.

## SUMMARY

Throughout this chapter, we've identified important communication issues that affect those who are dying as well as their health care providers, family members, and friends. We've also underscored the importance of making decisions about concerns such as organ donation and life support and of communicating those choices, both informally and formally, to the appropriate people.

While our specific personal choices will vary, in the end we all want to be treated with dignity and respect and to be listened to throughout any illness we may incur. If we cannot control the course of our illness, we at least want to control any aspects of the process that we can. It comes down to feeling like we matter, that we make a difference in people's lives, and that, after our death, we will not be forgotten. With that in mind, it is fitting that we end this chapter with the poignant tribute paid to Lisa Hearey by her friends and neighbors:

> He [Clem] cried as he held a single sheet of cream-colored paper. "This went to everyone on the street. Boy, does this make me cry."

> "Lisa Hearey passed away this morning . . ." the notice began. "To honor Lisa's life, spirit, strength and smile and to express our sorrow . . . a group of neighbors have chosen to light a luminaria each night for seven nights."

> The flier included instructions on where to pick up the luminarias and when to light them.

> That night, at 10 p.m., virtually every front stoop on Grenway Rd. glowed with the light of a candle set inside a paper bag. Clem stood on his front lawn, looked up and down the street and cried.

> "Lisa would have loved this."

## KEY TERMS

| | | |
|---|---|---|
| death anxiety | reflexivity | awareness contexts |
| metaphors for death and dying | break bad news | stages of dying |
| | social death | second shift |

| hospice | obituaries | advance directives |
| nearing death awareness | disenfranchised grief | end-of-life (EOL) decisions |
| | rational suicide | |

## DISCUSSION QUESTIONS

1. Think about your family. How was death talked about when you were young? Was it discussed openly or never mentioned?

2. Have you experienced the death of someone close to you? How was that treated? To what extent did you talk about it? With whom? Who initiated the talk, and how? How has this approach to death impacted you as an adult?

3. What are some rituals that your family follows when someone has died? What are the origins of these rituals? Are they religious, unique to your family, or community based? What are the functions of these rituals, and how successful are they?

4. Imagine that you only had six months to live. How would you spend this time? What are some things you would definitely not do? Who would you spend this time with? Who would you tell? Why? Who would you not tell? Why not? What, if anything, would you do to put your affairs in order?

5. What are some ways that we, as a culture, view death through our institutions, such as schools, churches and synagogues, and courts? How have these views changed over time or been sustained through these institutions?

6. How has the increase of available weapons, drive-by shootings, children murdering children, and other cultural changes affected our view of death?

7. What were your thoughts about dying when you were in elementary or junior high school? In your opinion what do today's students think about death?

## INFOTRAC COLLEGE EDITION

1. Read Michael Betzold and David Zeman's 1994 article, "Kevorkian Ordered to Stand Trial; Medical Panel Barely Recommends Legalizing Practice," and Juliet Wittman's 1997 article, "Our Health Care System Fails the Dying." What are the key issues regarding assisted suicide? What is the role of communication regarding this issue? Consider communication within the contexts of a patient's family, a doctor-patient relationship, as well as some of the ramifications for our society.

2. Read Juliet Wittman's 1995 article, "In the Face of Death, Truth Matters." What is your reaction to this article? If you had an incurable illness, would you want to know? If so, how much would you want to know, and whom would you want to give you the information? Who else would you want to know? Would you tell family members, or would you want someone else to tell them? If someone, who? What are some advantages and disadvantages, for you and for others, of having this information?

3. Read Avery Comarow's 2001 article, "Transplant to a Friend," and Nancy Scheper-Hughes' 2001 article, "The Organ of Last Resort." What are your reactions to these articles? Would you offer a kidney or part of your liver to a friend? To a family member? Why, or why not? Would you sell your kidney or part of your liver to a hospital to be used for someone needing the organ? If not, why not? Would this ever be acceptable? Can you think of any situations when you might change your opinion?

# 9

# Using and Evaluating Health Information

Nancy Weston, an attractive young woman with long, blond hair in her mid-thirties, is a wife, working artist, and mother of two young children. Following several months in which she has experienced puzzling symptoms that include painful back spasms and nausea, Nancy is told by her gynecologist during a routine pelvic examination that an abnormal growth is on her ovary. Further testing and biopsy reveal that she has an early stage, malignant ovarian tumor. She has received some information about her condition from her doctor, but as the impact of this alarming diagnosis sinks in, she goes to the library to seek further information on her own.

This is the basic plot of a continuing narrative that was featured from 1990 to 1991 in a popular prime-time TV dramatic series, *thirtysomething*. The show was a unique effort to explore in depth the multifaceted experience of living with cancer, a challenging task for entertainment programming (Sharf & Freimuth, 1993). Viewed in retrospect, the show is now a piece of TV history—and certainly today, Nancy would be searching the Web rather than a library microfilm machine. Still, this experiment in following a fictional TV character with a life-threatening disease over the course of a calendar year, even at the risk of frightening away viewers, remains a noteworthy example of using popular media to teach the public about a health issue. Although many viewers chose not to watch this difficult subject matter, a sample of those who did reported that Nancy became a role model—for both positive and negative ways of handling this situation (Sharf, Freimuth, Greenspon, &

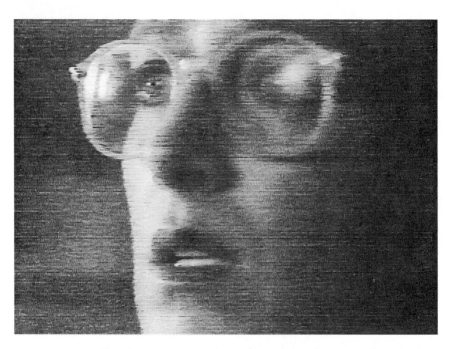

Nancy Weston searches microfilm for information about ovarian cancer. *Reprinted by permission of MGM Studios and Patricia Wettig.* © *1989 MGM Studios Inc. All rights reserved.*

Plotnick, 1996). For this reason, it is interesting to take note of Nancy's responses as she perused the literature to find out more about ovarian cancer.

The photograph catches Nancy with an extremely worried expression as she scans articles on microfilm. As she speeds through reel after reel, she sees pictures of tumors, titles of articles such as "The Role of Chemotherapy," "Surgical Treatment," and "Washing Cancer Away," as well as isolated words, such as "pain" and "fears." Soon the words and images blur together. With her face illuminated by the light from the microfilm machine, Nancy is so totally absorbed by what she reads that she is visibly startled by the voice of a librarian letting her know that her time is up on the machine. By this point, Nancy's distraught appearance shows that the information she uncovered has overwhelmed her. This episode conveys a strong message to viewers that an unguided search for medical information can be confusing or even terrifying.

A similar scenario is depicted in the feature-length movie *Lorenzo's Oil*. This film tells the true story of Augusto and Michaela Odone, whose young son Lorenzo was struck by ADL (adrenoleukodystrophy), a steadily degenerative and ultimately fatal disease of the central nervous system. Rather than stand by passively and observe this impending disaster, the Odones—neither of whom had a medical background—decided to become as knowledgeable as possible in the hope of discovering something that would save their boy. During a poignant scene in the library, Augusto—much like Nancy Weston—was devastated by his initial foray into the literature on ADL, learning that Lorenzo's terrible prognosis would include a horrifying array of symptoms, including blindness, muteness, dementia, and spastic movements—as well as death within two years. Overcome by panic and grief, a weeping Augusto collapsed on a stairway outside the library. This courageous father returns to the library repeatedly, however, encouraged by a helpful librarian and determined to search for any research that will get his family beyond this seemingly hopeless situation. It is through his dogged, widespread search of basic science and clinical literature that Augusto, indeed, uncovers information that leads Michaela and him to formulate a theory that eventually results in production of a dietary oil that not only has helped to partially reverse Lorenzo's severely degenerative condition but has proven to be a cure for other children with ADL. After this movie, viewers can't help but be impressed with the positive power of information (not to mention hope and personal tenacity).

Considered in juxtaposition, the episode of Nancy Weston's pursuit of data about ovarian cancer and the unfurling story of Augusto Odone's quest for research findings that shed light on ADL illustrate the basic tension underlying the conception of information, which is the basis of this chapter. Health-related information can empower or overwhelm the person who seeks it. Its resources may enable individuals to take action and to move forward; conversely, its complexity may mystify and promote psychological paralysis. In the stories of both Nancy and Augusto, as each becomes more knowledgeable about the medical problems they face, challenges arise about both the extent to and the ways in which nonprofessionals can apply their expertise. (In *thirtysomething*, over time Nancy Weston also learns a great deal about her disease and uses that knowledge in coping with the many problems incurred by her illness.) Information is integral to the process of quality decision making, relationships between practitioners and patients, the legal-ethical principle of patient autonomy and the practice of informed consent, and public health undertakings. An emerging concept that refers to the competency of citizens to use information as a way of maintaining or improving well-being is **health literacy,** defined as "the degree to which individuals have the capacity to obtain, process, and understand basic health information and services needed to make appropriate health decisions" (Healthy People 2010, 2001).

In the following sections, we explore three fundamental attributes of health information: (a) quantity and quality, or how much and what is to be communicated; (b) foundational values, which underlie and shape health messages; and (c) accessibility, in terms of who is privileged through their ability to acquire information and, likewise, who is marginalized because they have been denied information. All these factors contribute to the dynamics of understanding and assessing health-related issues. For each attribute, we first review questions that tend to pose serious and, at times, conflicting considerations for people attempting to participate responsibly in their own health care, maintenance, and prevention. Next, we examine a specific communicative situation that exemplifies each of these questions as they play out in context. In the remaining sections, we raise some functional and practical consequences pertinent to the issues of decision making and confidentiality that arise from communicating health information. Before we go further, however, Theorizing Practice 9.1 helps you to recall your own health information-seeking experiences.

# QUESTIONS OF QUANTITY AND QUALITY

Because health information is such a broad topic and affects many aspects of our lives, this section focuses on two issues with significant consequences for how we learn about health issues and participate in medical interactions. As consumers of products and services in the health care marketplace, we receive a variety of health messages via media headlines, recommendations from providers, discussions with family and friends, advertising campaigns, and the World Wide Web. Knowledge can be helpful, even empowering, but sometimes the sheer volume of information may seem overwhelming. Informational content may lead to confusion, because the data we receive may be contradictory or health advice may change within a short period of time. In still other instances, the available health information that we seek to answer our questions and concerns may seem distressingly inadequate. Questions of legitimacy and validity may be raised about the sources or the kinds of information conveyed. In this section, we explore how such issues arise in some familiar health care circumstances, posing challenges as we strive to be discerning and knowledgeable health citizens.

## ▣ Dilemmas in Health Education

How much information is enough? What kind of information is appropriate? These questions have been raised repeatedly by individual health professionals and health agencies, who traditionally have carried the responsibility for educating patients and the public about a variety of topics, including specific diseases, medications, and desirable lifestyle changes. The answers to these questions are not so clear-cut, unfortunately, and they may require judgment calls about the **adequacy of health information** that might not equally satisfy all the parties involved.

For example, when a physician prescribes a medication, there is a professional expectation that the doctor will explain to the patient how to take the drug and about its possible side effects, though such conversations do not uniformly occur.

## Personal Information Seeking

It is no coincidence that Nancy Weston and Augusto Odone intensively search for medical information after they are confronted by a personal health crisis. This crisis or **critical incident** prompted a need to know that would enable each of them to take a more active role, whether in care of the self or a significant other.

Several communication theorists have described such personal turning points in varying but related terms. Anthony Giddens (1991) describes "fateful moments . . . when individuals are called upon to make decisions that are particularly consequential . . . for their future lives" (p. 112). Patricia Geist and Lisa Gates (1996) refer to moments of crisis in health care when one's personal voice or identity must be recovered after difficult medical encounters in which institutional policies and structures dominated over interpersonal relations. Eric Zook (1994) speaks of "ontological ruptures" (ruptures of being) during which "we become fully aware of the tenuousness with which ourselves and our world is bound" (p. 364).

Consider a critical incident in your own life during which you experienced a fateful moment, rupture, or need to recover your own identity (or that of a loved one) in a way that led you to seek information you did not have before. Examples of such events include a death, serious illness, or disability in the family; a birth; a weight loss or weight gain; or an episode of depression.

- What kinds of questions did this crisis raise for you?
- What sources of information did you seek?
- Who or what hindered your search for information?
- Likewise, who or what helped you find out what you wanted to know?
- In what ways did your situation change after you gained more information?

According to one study of family physicians' conversations in which they are prescribing medications, the fact that patients frequently don't fill their prescriptions or don't take their medications as prescribed may be attributed to doctors neglecting to provide key data, such as explicit instructions, benefits as well as side effects, and cost issues (Parrott, 1994). Think about instances in which you have been prescribed antibiotics to take over a ten-day period. Did you continue the medication for the entire time, even if you were feeling better after five or six days? If you stopped early, did you think any serious consequences might occur from skipping the last few days? What did you do with the remaining prescription? Did you think it a good idea to take it at another time, when you might be suffering with similar symptoms? Did you pass the "extras" on to a friend who was sick?

In recent years, patients have received additional information about medications from printed inserts in the package from the drug manufacturer or the pharmacy as well as from comments by the pharmacist. Should the consumer be forewarned of every side effect that has ever been reported with use of this substance? What if some of those side effects are much more common, say, occurring in 28 percent of those who have taken this medicine, versus relatively rare effects, say, occurring in only 1 percent of patients? Does knowing about potential side effects before taking the medicine better prepare an individual to respond quickly if unintended harm should occur, or does it psychologically predispose an individual to experience an unintended harm? Are both scenarios possible? If consumers are told all the possible—albeit unlikely—side effects, how many will avoid taking substances that are likely to help them? Physicians and pharmacists are responsible for overseeing possible interactions among prescription drugs, but who should be responsible for overseeing possible interactions between prescription and over-the-counter medications or dietary supplements? All these questions factor into the process that physicians, pharmacists, and drug companies use in determining how to supply medication information.

Let's now turn to a different sort of question of quality, that of what kinds of information are regarded as privileged and significant and, conversely, what kinds are devalued and why.

## ◼ Challenges to Expertise

Clearly, physicians as well as other health care and public health professionals possess specialized knowledge needed by **laypersons** (nonprofessionals). What is not so clear, either to practitioners or to citizens, is that laypersons bring their own type of expertise to the health care encounter. That is, each of us is an expert in knowing things such as how we've experienced symptoms, how well we can tolerate certain medications and other forms of treatment, what the stresses and resources are within our particular lifestyles, how we combine medical advice with that from other sources of information, and so forth. Also, many times people have already formulated their own ideas about the cause of symptoms before going to see a health professional. These ideas may be based on cultural concepts and folklore or on personal reasoning, and they are referred to as **explanatory models** (Kleinman, 1988; Kleinman, Eisenberg, & Good, 1978). This type of personalized information, which can be supplied only by the individual patient or health citizen, has implications for both diagnosis and treatment, and is essential to the success of any so-called expert plan for health prevention or medical treatment (Sharf, 1984). Rarely, however, are laypersons credited—by themselves or by health professionals—for contributing or even having such expertise.

The consequences of not acknowledging the information that individuals have to contribute to a medical encounter can be quite significant. For instance, the explanatory models of patients are often very different from those of clinicians. They can be so different, in fact, that communication researcher Brent Ruben (1990) asserts caregiver-patient relationships may be thought of as a form of intercultural communication, with each party bringing distinct language, rules, values, symbols, interactional patterns, and so forth to the clinical encounter. Until these explanatory models of what causes ill health—and what should be done about it—are articulated and the differences between them negotiated to the satisfaction of both parties, the likelihood of a patient following professional recommendations is much diminished. In one case study, an overweight, middle-aged man suffered from severe, chronic pain in his legs after surgery on a herniated disc in his spine. When he complained to his family doctor about the pain, which he described as "shocky" and "nervy" (especially when he touched metal or wool), the doctor emphasized the need to lose weight, which would in turn lessen the burden on the patient's legs. In contrast, the patient referred several times to his belief that he had "some kind of electricity" running through him, which had perhaps occurred during a nerve conduction test performed on him in conjunction with the surgery. Based on a videotaped conversation between the two, it appeared improbable that the patient was convinced weight loss would eliminate the pain (Sharf, 1990).

An interesting illustration of the problem of devaluing patient input occurs routinely within the medical record system. For the past 30 years, health professionals have been taught a system of collecting and recording "patient data" known as SOAP notes. SOAP is an acronym that stands for: (a) Subjective, or what the patient says about the illness or medical problems; (b) Objective, or what the physician, nurse, physical therapist, or other health professional reports in terms of observations, test findings, and laboratory results; (c) Assessment, or what the health professional surmises about the patient's prognosis based on the first two categories; and (d) Plans, or what the practitioner intends to do or recommend in terms of further treatment. The **subjective-objective dichotomy** as seen here is a telling indication of how patient input is viewed in the clinical context. As physicians William Donnelly and Daniel Brauner (1992) observe, subjectivity connotes insubstantiality or something that exists only on a mental basis, whereas objectivity signifies something that exists in reality and that has physical substance. They argue that by labeling the statements of patients as subjective, this personally based information is perceived as less scientific, more biased and irrational, and hence, less valued than the input of the clinicians. Furthermore, in labeling the statements of health care workers as objective, their subjectivity and, thus, their humanity is obscured. This last element is important to understand, because it underscores that even with quantifiable information, such as a blood test result or a cardiogram, the meaning or significance attributed by health professionals to that set of numbers—

as well as their thoughts regarding what should be done about the conditions those numbers represent—are also subjective interpretations.

The point is that significant information may be based on verifiable, external evidence or on experiential, anecdotal reports. An aspect of subjectivity is present whenever interpretation is required, whether by the practitioner or the layperson. All these types of information have value in problem solving and decision making related to health issues, and all should be treated as valid.

One context in which the experience of nonprofessionals has been recognized as a sort of distinct expertise with particular import is that of support groups organized around a particular illness, such as epilepsy (Arntson & Droge, 1987) or hemophilia (Scheerhorn, 1997); a psychosocial issue, such as coping with Alzheimer's disease within a family; or the promotion of healthy lifestyles (Brennan & Fink, 1997). In these groups, people often discuss and deal with problems that may be outside the expertise of medical professionals (Sharf, 1997). Though not often officially recognized as such, expertise among nonhealth professionals based on life experiences qualifies as a valuable and widely used source of health information.

Debates concerning the rights of citizens to information about their own health and about what constitutes adequate information have historical roots that have shaped contemporary law, medical ethics, and communicative practices. The next section provides a case study of one such debate: informed consent.

## ■ Case Study: The Process of Informed Consent

Concerns about informational quantity and quality are pertinent to the topic of **informed consent,** which refers to patients having adequate information and understanding to make a reasonable decision whether to accept treatment proposed by a medical practitioner. At its roots, informed consent is a legal concept that has gradually developed since the early twentieth century through several precedent-setting court cases. These cases involved patients who had suffered negative results from medical or surgical procedures and who formally complained they had received inadequate information from their physicians before those procedures. Through these cases, a pattern was established of linking patients' rights to self-determination regarding their bodies in response to the questions of if and how they had been informed by their doctors. Of particular importance to the modern-day concept of informed consent were three specific court decisions.

In 1957, in *Salgo v. Leland Stanford, Jr., University Board of Trustees,* the patient, Mr. Salgo, claimed that his surgeons had not warned him of possible risks from an operation that left him paralyzed. In a written opinion, the judge stated that a physician violates the professional duty to a patient if that physician withholds the necessary facts for "intelligent consent" of the patient (Katz, 1984, pp. 61–62).

In 1960, in *Natanson v. Kline,* Mrs. Natanson, who suffered from breast cancer, sued her radiologist for negligence in treatment and failure to provide information about therapeutic hazards after she suffered severe injuries (burns and destruction of her ribs) from cobalt treatments. In an appeal decision, the Kansas Supreme Court stated that physicians have the obligation to disclose—and to explain in simple language—the nature of a patient's ailment, risks of treatment, and possible alternatives.

Finally, in 1972, in the most explicit landmark case, *Canterbury v. Spence,* Mr. Canterbury sued his physician for negligence and failure to warn him about risks after becoming paralyzed following spinal surgery. The court ruling specified that doctors have "the duty to warn patients about risks" and, further, that "true consent to what happens to one's self is the informed exercise of a choice, and that entails an opportunity to evaluate knowledgeably the options available and the risks attendant upon each" (Katz, 1984, p. 73).

In addition to the legal requirement, informed consent should be perceived as a functional communicative practice. People must have sufficient understanding, based on information and dialogue, to make a reasonable decision whether to accept or refuse a professional recommendation, such as whether to have surgery or a medical procedure, or a professional request, such as whether to participate in a clinical trial. Courts of law can mandate the general content—but not the process—necessary to achieve such understanding. In clinical parlance, doctors-in-training are often instructed "to obtain" informed consent from a patient (or, alternatively, "to consent the patient"), as though consent is a thing to be plucked or handed over from another person. In fact, "the thing" is the patient's signature on a preprinted consent form. To fulfill the spirit of the legal conditions set forward in the court cases cited earlier, however, the understanding that should precede the signed (or unsigned) form entails having a conversation in which a health professional explains a medical procedure in terms that are comprehensible to a layperson who, in turn, feels free to ask questions and to register concerns. In other words, a person's decision to give—or to withhold—consent for treatment should be the result of a communicative event in which information is exchanged and meaning is created between a health care provider and the patient. Again, however, how much specific information is required for any one person to make such a decision is variable, a unique negotiation between the participating individuals. At minimum, the conversation should describe the suggested procedure, the purpose of the patient taking part in this procedure, the alternative options available (including no treatment at all), the comparative potential benefits that may result from each, and the potential harms that may result from each. FYI 9.1 provides a relatively simple medical consent form along with several related issues to consider.

Here is a standard consent form for a common procedure, an appendectomy, that includes the use of anesthesia. Perhaps you have signed off on a similar document.

- As you read over this consent form, what questions and concerns does it raise in your mind?

- What further information, if any, would you like to have before signing the consent form?

HOSPITALS

DISCLOSURE AND CONSENT MEDICAL AND SURGICAL PROCEDURES

TO THE PATIENT: You have the right, as a patient, to be informed about your condition and recommended surgical, medical, or diagnostic procedure to be used so that you may make the decision whether or not to undergo the procedure after knowing the risks and hazards involved. This disclosure is not meant to scare or alarm you; it is simply an effort to make you better informed so you may give or withhold your consent to the procedure.

I voluntarily request Dr. _____ as my physician, and such associates, technical assistants and other health care providers as they may deem necessary, to treat my condition which has been explained to me as: _____

_____

I understand that the following surgical, medical, and/or diagnostic procedures are planned for me and I voluntarily consent and authorize these procedures:
  APPENDECTOMY

_____

I understand that my physician may discover additional or different procedures than those planned. I authorize my physician, and such associates, technical assistants and other health care providers to perform such other procedures which are advisable in their professional judgement.

I (DO) (DO NOT) consent to the use of blood and blood products as deemed necessary. I understand that no warranty or guarantee has been made to me as to result or cure.

I certify this form has been fully explained to me, that I have read it or have had it read to me, and that the blank spaces have been filled in and that I understand its contents.

DATE _____     TIME _____

_____          _____
PATIENT SIGNATURE (or RESP. PARTY)            RELATIONSHIP TO PATIENT

WITNESS:

_____          PLACE PATIENT LABEL HERE
SIGNATURE

FIGURE 9.1  Generic hospital consent form. *(continues)*

*(continued from previous page)*

DISCLOSURE AND CONSENT MEDICAL AND SURGICAL PROCEDURES (Continued)

I authorize the taking of medical photographs for medical education and record purposes with the understanding that my identity will be protected. I expressly release ALL SAINTS HEALTH SYSTEM, its personnel, and my physician(s) from any liability arising from this authorization.

Just as there may be risks and hazards in continuing my present condition without treatment, there are also risks and hazards related to the performance of the surgical, medical and/or diagnostic procedures planned for me. I realize that common to surgical, medical, and/or diagnostic procedures is the potential for infection, blood clots in veins and lungs, hemorrhage, allergic reactions and even death. I also realize that the following risks and hazards may occur in connection with this particular procedure: **NOT REQUIRED BY STATUTE** _____

_____

I consent to the disposal by hospital authorities of any tissue or parts to be removed. I have been given an opportunity to ask my HEALTH CARE PROFESSIONAL about my condition, alternative forms of anesthesia and treatment, risks of nontreatment, the procedures to be used and the risks and hazards involved, and I believe that I have sufficient information to give this informed consent.

I understand that anesthesia involves additional risks and hazards but I request the use of anesthesia for the relief and protection from pain during the planned and additional procedures. I realize the anesthesia may have to be changed possibly without explanation to me.

I understand that certain complications may result from the use of anesthesia including respiratory problems, drug reaction, paralysis, brain damage or even death. Other risks and hazards which may result from the use of general anesthesia range from minor discomfort to injury to vocal cords, teeth or eyes. I understand that other risks and hazards resulting from spinal or epidural anesthetics include headache and chronic pain.

I have been given the opportunity to ask questions about my condition, alternative forms of anesthesia and treatment, risks of nontreatment, the procedures to be used, and the risks and hazards involved, and I believe that I have sufficient information to give this informed consent.

I certify this form has been fully explained to me, that I have read it or have had it read to me, that the blank spaces have been filled in and that I understand its contents.

DATE _____     TIME _____

_____     _____
PATIENT SIGNATURE (or RESP. PARTY)          RELATIONSHIP TO PATIENT

WITNESS:

_____     PLACE PATIENT LABEL HERE
SIGNATURE

In addition to considerations of what and how much information to include within health messages, there is an added complexity of which and whose ideas of worth both shape and are reflected in those communications. In the following section, we look to the values incorporated within health information.

## QUESTIONS OF VALUE

When information is communicated, decisions are made about what (of the total body of health-related knowledge) to tell, to which audiences, and how to tell it. Data derived from research and applied to health problems—despite the frequent desire to imbue it with a halo of scientific objectivity—emerges from a context of social patterns, political motivations, and cultural beliefs. In other words, information is not value-neutral. Underlying and shaping health messages are **foundational values**—principles that define what is right or wrong, good or bad, and desirable or undesirable. Our values are at the core of our relatively stable, firmly held health beliefs (for example, the position that stem cell research must be continued for its potential to save or improve countless lives vs. the conviction that harvesting fetal cells for research is immoral) as well as our more transitory attitudes about current issues (for instance, would you rank bioterrorism as our most significant public health priority? Gun violence? Obesity?). In the mid-1980s, after it was discovered that HIV could be transmitted through sexual contact, impassioned public debates went on throughout the United States about how explicitly sexual practices should be addressed—if at all—in media messages designed to educate the citizenry. In some social circles, even mentioning the word *condom*, let alone showing how to use one properly, in brochures or public service announcements was shocking. In such disputes, the underlying values of propriety and decency came into conflict with those of candor and the wish to save lives.

In discussions between providers and patients, the value-laden issue of **quality of life** is frequently at stake in terms of how best to manage a health condition. Physicians can offer information and advice about treatments that may extend life or reduce risk. In communication surrounding medical decision making, however, there are frequently uncertainties and difficult trade-offs to be considered. Men who discover they have prostate cancer through PSA (prostate-specific antigen) screening may undergo surgery—along with impotence and years of concern about the possibility of recurrence—yet whether this prompt treatment affects their mortality from the disease is questionable. Premature babies can be delivered and kept alive at many weeks of gestation earlier than would have been the case a decade ago, but these children risk potential problems of impaired eyesight and pulmonary function as they grow up. FYI 9.2 illustrates the lifestyle and health issues involved with one particular value-related point of view.

---

**FYI 9.2**     **VALUES IN THE NEWS**

What image do you have of men who smoke cigars? As you read through the following article, keep in mind our claims that (a) information is not value-neutral and (b) underlying health messages are foundational values. This brief report on the health dangers of cigar smoking summarizes the results of a scientific study that quantified the correlation between number of cigars smoked daily with an increased risk of cancer, heart disease, and pulmonary disease. At a more subtle level, the article illuminates the strategy of public health officials to link the currently fashionable practice of smoking cigars with the negative sentiments and penalties currently associated with cigarettes.

Thursday, June 10, 1999       The Dallas Morning News       9A

# Cigars linked to higher disease risks

*Boston Globe*

A California study has found that regular cigar smoking significantly increases risks of heart and respiratory disease and some cancers, and raises fears that cigars and alcohol together may be a particularly hazardous combination.

The findings add weight to research indicating that smoking cigars is far from safe—something that may not be recognized by the many who have been making cigars fashionable in recent years.

Most of the increased health risk was found in men who smoked five or more cigars a day. Only 17 percent of the study subjects smoked that heavily.

"Thus our findings should not be generalized to people who smoke cigars infrequently," the report said.

Most worrying of the findings is the apparent synergy between cigar smoke and alcohol, creating higher risks than either by itself.

"The popularity of cigar bars where both cigar smoking and alcohol consumption are encouraged arouses special concern with respect to the public health," commented Dr. David Satcher, the U.S. surgeon general, in an editorial published in Thursday's *New England Journal of Medicine*.

The study of 1,546 cigar smokers and 16,228 nonsmokers showed that cigar smoking raised a man's risk of heart disease and certain cancers by as much as twofold. Although significant, the hazard is much less than from cigarette smoking, which increases risks 1.5 to three times for coronary heart disease, nine to 25 times for emphy-

sema and related lung diseases, and eight to 24 times for lung cancer.

Dr. Satcher, in the accompanying editorial, called for raising federal taxes on cigars, which now are much less than for cigarettes, and said that warning labels similar to those on cigarette packages should be required for cigars. "It is critical that cigars not be construed as a safe or less costly alternative to cigarettes," Dr. Satcher wrote.

Thursday's report is from a study by Dr. Carlos Iribarren and colleagues at the Kaiser Permanente Medical Care Program in Oakland, Calif. They drew their subjects from a group of 17,774 men, ages 30 to 85, who were enrolled in the health plan. Of the men who smoked cigars, 76 percent smoked fewer than five a day and 17 percent smoked more than five daily.

("Cigars linked," 1999).

- Do you find yourself advocating a particular point of view as you read the report?
- Are there certain words that jump out at you?
- What questions, if any, does this article raise for you?

---

Certainly, the social and political climate at any particular point in time helps to determine the value orientation of a health message—or even if information is conveyed at all. Drawing on your own experiences, consider some of the following questions that may illustrate this point:

- Are problems with alcohol abuse presented as a sickness that should be treated medically or as a character defect and, thus, preventable through self-control? How about problems with drug abuse? Are these presented differently than those connected with alcohol? Are addictions to "street" drugs portrayed differently than addictions to prescription medications? Do you even hear about the latter? If not, why?

- What do you recall learning about mental illness? Do you hear as much about mental diseases as about physical diseases, such as heart disease or diabetes? Through which media are messages about mental illness conveyed (conversations with your physician, movies, TV talk shows, or gossip among friends)? Would you classify a condition such as anorexia nervosa as a physical or a mental ailment? What was your experience learning that someone you know had a mental condition, such as depression? What were your initial reactions, and how did that knowledge affect your relationship with that person?

- What difference has former Senator and presidential candidate Bob Dole becoming a spokesperson for erectile dysfunction (or ED, as we have learned from his public service announcements) made to your own under-standing of sexual dysfunction? What are the pros and cons of celebrities lending their name and face recognition to particular diseases or health is-sues? How have the media ads for the drug Viagra affected your perceptions of the problem? Why do you think this topic received comparatively little public attention before this time?

In reflecting on these instances concerning substance abuse, mental illness, and sexual dysfunction, value-related considerations about moral character, personal credibility, public shame, and societal priorities surface as factors that greatly influence the communication of health information. Health communication scholar Nurit Guttman (2000) has conducted an extensive meta-analysis of how values function in a variety of public health campaigns. Her results emphasize not only the importance of values in this context but also their "hidden" nature. Values are frequently concealed from conscious awareness due to subtle tactics used by campaign creators and unquestioned assumptions on the part of recipients. She cautions us to be alert to issues such as:

- Why particular health goals have been chosen.

- How claims, representations, and arguments are embedded within health messages.

- How health problems are defined (for example, a biomedical vs. a socio-economic explanation of the cause).

- What the values are of those proposing a health intervention, and what the values are of the target audiences for that intervention.

- What the values are that underlie the evaluations conducted of health campaigns.

- What the social and political circumstances are that may favor the implementation of certain interventions over others.

- Who is likely to benefit and who is likely to be disadvantaged as a result of choices made in health messages and interventions.

To better understand the crucial role of values, let's further explore communication in practice concerning illicit drugs.

## Case Study: Drug Abuse Campaigns

The impact of illegal, addictive drugs such as cocaine, heroin, and ecstasy has evolved into one of the biggest social and health problems in the United States, affecting an estimated 14 million users as well as their loved ones, colleagues and employers, crime victims, and the tax-paying public (Office of National Drug Control Policy, 2000). (The specific information cited on drug abuse prevalence is taken from slide number 18 in a Power Point presentation entitled "Data snapshot: Drug abuse in America [March 2002]," which is linked to this Web site. The specific slide referenced within this presentation is entitled Summary of Current Situation: National Household Survey.) Illegal drug abuse correlates with a variety of societal ills, such as prostitution, unemployment, and AIDS (acquired immunodeficiency syndrome). It is the basis for crimes ranging from international smuggling to local peddling of drugs to minors, from armed robberies to domestic violence. A fortunate minority of people with substance addictions may be helped to recovery through the limited public and private treatment programs that are available; many more will continue their addictive behaviors while jeopardizing jobs, endangering families, and even risking imprisonment and accidental overdose.

At issue in our discussion is the emphasis given to public information campaigns about drug use, both in this country and in Canada. In doing this comparison, the concept of national and cultural values is highlighted. In the United States, public communication campaigns have been focused largely on the notion of **abstinence,** especially in messages targeted to children, teenagers, and young adults, to persuade them not to start or "get hooked." The essence of such thinking was epitomized in the campaign endorsed by First Lady Nancy Reagan during the early 1980s. Her simple, personalized slogan—"Just say no"—was easily understood and remembered, and it became very popular. A similarly memorable, uncomplicated message from the Partnership for a Drug-Free America was a televised public service announcement with three sentences: "This is your brain" (visual image of an intact egg). "This is your brain on drugs" (visual image of an egg being cracked and fried in a sizzling frying pan). "Any questions?"

These brief directives diffused the idea of abstinence throughout the populace, but they suffered from an obvious lack of detail in just how one actually stays away from drugs. In 1983, however, a more complex, multiphased program was founded in Los Angeles that has since been implemented by more than 70 percent of school districts throughout the country. Aimed at teaching children behavioral skills that will help them to enact abstinence, the Drug Abuse Resistance Education, or D.A.R.E., has as "the centerpiece . . . a 17-week drug education and prevention curriculum taught to elementary school children" in the fifth or sixth grades (D.A.R.E. America). The acronym itself conveys meaning—dare to resist, dare to be strong, dare to be different from your peers who give in. The information taught to grade-schoolers by police officers is, according to the precepts of the program, to be reiterated in other contexts by teachers, parents, and other community figures. Refresher lessons are provided to the children in junior and senior high school as well. The program claims to teach kids about the dangers of drugs, to assertively say no, to have self-confidence, to keep their bodies healthy, to control their feelings when angry or under stress, to avoid participation in gangs, and to decide whether to take a risk (D.A.R.E. America).

Communication researcher Everett Rogers (1993), in his analysis of the D.A.R.E. program, attributes the remarkably successful diffusion of this campaign—throughout the United States as well as internationally—to its unique collaboration between school systems and police departments. His summary indicates that many evaluations of the program have shown D.A.R.E. to be moderately effective in terms of participating students having lower rates of subsequent drug use than nonparticipating students. Rogers cautions, however, that these studies do not show "very powerful effects" (p. 150), a conclusion that has been affirmed by other analyses of the cumulative program evaluations (Tobler, 1993). Unfortunately, despite the long-term, widespread availability of D.A.R.E. educational programs in the public schools, overall drug usage by middle- to high-school-aged children in the United States increased during the first half of the 1990s (Substance Abuse and

Mental Health Services Administration, 1996). In sum, U.S. public information campaigns have directed their resources toward prevention of and reduction in the overall prevalence of drug use, emphasizing over and over the position that one must not begin drugs—nearly to the exclusion of alternative messages.

An interesting contrast is a health communication program in Canada that also focuses on illegal drug use. Taking a cue from earlier efforts in Europe, "in 1987, the Canadian government adopted **harm reduction** as the framework for Canada's National Drug Strategy. It defined harm as 'sickness, death, social misery, crime, violence and economic costs to all levels of government'" (Riley, 1994, p. 2). The harm reduction approach takes as a given that the prevalence of drug abuse is widespread; furthermore, the advocates of harm reduction make the point that some drug use is even beneficial and appropriate (Marlatt, 1998). Thus, the top priority is to decrease the negative consequences of already occurring drug use. While not precluding the possibility of abstinence, this perspective adopts a wider range of tolerance and more realistic goals, in which the inevitability of less than a drug-free world becomes the starting point. In line with this philosophy, the program provides information about the effects of controlled and illegal substances in a neutral tone, and it focuses on providing advice for those situations most likely to be dangerous to those who partake in them. So, for instance, in a pamphlet entitled "Drug Use: A Guide for Women," which is presented in a feminine visual style with an embellished typeface and flowery illustrations, readers are advised how to plan breastfeeding a baby to minimize the effects of drug use on the infant and how to stop or cut back on using drugs during pregnancy. This publication and several others in the campaign explain first the dangers of injecting drugs, then how to inject drugs more safely and what to do if someone overdoses. The campaign forthrightly endorses needle-exchange programs, a concept that has been hotly contested and widely rejected in the United States.

Proponents of the harm reduction approach offer evidence that it reduces HIV infection among IV (intravenous) drug users; that it decreases the incidence of other drug-related problems, such as crime, non-HIV disease, and accidental death; that it is cost-effective; and that it does not encourage initiation of or increased drug use (Riley, Teixeira, & Hausser, 1999). Advocates also note, however, that the efficacy of this approach depends on a commitment to long-term efforts; sensitivity to local communities, issues, and populations; and extension of the program to underdeveloped countries and indigent constituencies (Riley & O'Hare, in press). Studies that specifically compare harm reduction to abstinence-based campaigns have not yet been done.

This case study shows the U.S. prioritization on idealism (achieving the ideal of total resistance) versus Canada's acceptance of pragmatism (accepting the practical reality that some people will use drugs and so minimizing the adverse effects).

This comparison of two national public drug information strategies underscores the importance of foundational values in health messages.

To further consider how values function in the communication of public health messages, Theorizing Practice 9.2 probes the processes underlying a health campaign that has touched your life.

## QUESTIONS OF ACCESSIBILITY

A third issue regarding complexities of health information involves the tension between professionals and laypersons over who controls the information based on specialized knowledge and in what forms accessibility occurs.

### ▓ Restricting Information

Dating back to the Greek physician Hippocrates (1923), health professionals traditionally have been regarded as the keepers of—and the experts on—specialized information related to disease. They have been regarded as the ones to make decisions not only about how much information patients would want to know, but also about how well patients could understand what they were being told and if the information would prove harmful in some way. For example, as recently as the mid-1970s, it was common practice for doctors to decide whether to be candid with patients about a potentially fatal diagnosis. The decision *not* to tell the truth to a patient who had an inoperable tumor that had spread extensively and who probably would not live more than two years was thought to be justified if the physician felt this evasion would bolster the patient's will to live or the patient's emotional fortitude could not withstand such bad news. Making decisions on the patient's behalf about revealing information is now known as paternalism, and it has fallen out of favor in lieu of **patient autonomy** or **patient-doctor partnerships** in which information is understood to be an invaluable element (see, for example, Beck, 1997; Deber, 1994; Quill, 1983; Roter, 1987).

Physicians, nurses, pharmacists, and other providers have had communication training as an official part of their curriculum for the last two or three decades, with a heavy emphasis on asking questions (alternately called "data gathering" and "taking a history"). More recently, information-giving skills and negotiating with patients about differences in agenda-setting and treatment decisions during consultations have begun to be included in medical education (Cohen-Cole, 1991; Stewart et al., 1995). This addition to the curriculum represents an increased emphasis on the quality of practitioner-patient interaction and on achieving shared understandings.

## The Values that Persuade Us . . . Or Not

Persuasion theories teach that there are varying levels of difficulty in using communication to gain the cooperation of others. For instance, people may adopt certain responses to persuasive efforts to avoid feelings of dissonance, to resist the difficulties of enacting change, to demonstrate blasé or skeptical feelings about incoming messages, or to react to perceived confusion. The easiest—though still by no means simple—task for designers of persuasive campaigns is to raise awareness about a topic, enabling others to understand its importance. The next level of complexity involves convincing others to change their opinions or beliefs about that topic or issue. The most difficult job is to persuade others to alter their behaviors. This latter task is the goal of many, if not most, public health information campaigns, in which people are asked to make long-term changes in how they live their lives.

Think about specific public health campaigns in which you felt *yourself* to be part of the targeted audience. The campaign may have been carried out through one or a variety of media, such as TV, billboards, radio spots, magazine ads, and so on. Possibilities for such programs abound: antismoking, healthier diets, regular exercise, safe sex, use of seat belts and motorcycle helmets, and many more. Pick one that you recall in detail, and then respond to the following questions:

- What main messages were intended for you to "take home"?

- What values were underlying these messages?

- What strategies were used to communicate these messages?

- How well did this campaign work with you? If you made lifestyle changes in the direction the campaign intended, what factors helped convince you to do so? If you did not make such changes, why do you think you were not convinced to do so?

- In what ways would you suggest improving this information campaign?

Nonetheless, the lopsided power dynamics inherent in the patient–doctor relationship tend to create what physicians Howard Waitzkin and John Stoeckle (1976) have called the micropolitics of **information control.** That is, by deciding what the patient should know of biomedical knowledge, a physician can still maintain relational dominance and expert status. Furthermore, when making explanations, physicians frequently use language that has been characterized as mystifying (Barnlund, 1976) and distancing (Mintz, 1992) rather than as clarifying and helpful. Others (Beckman & Frankel, 1984; West, 1984) have described a "high control" style exhibited by many physicians, typified by a majority of doctor-initiated questions, interruptions of patients' statements, and neglect of patients' psychosocial concerns.

In addition to dramatic situations, such as lying to patients about impending death, the micropolitics of information control frequently occur on a much subtler, routine basis during clinical encounters. Previous research has indicated that physicians tend to underestimate how much information patients desire to know and to overestimate how much time they spend providing information to patients (Waitzkin, 1984). Socioeconomic class also affects how much information is given to patients. Specifically, patients from upper- and upper-middle-class backgrounds receive more time and more detailed explanations from doctors than do individuals from lower-middle- or lower-class backgrounds. Importantly, class does *not* determine the degree of desire that people have for information. Most want as much information as possible, though less educated or poorer patients frequently are less assertive in asking for it. Practitioners often mistakenly assume that if people do not ask, then they do not want to know. Not asking for information may result for many reasons, however, including poor language skills or nonfluency in English, perceiving that the doctor may be too rushed or busy to entertain questions, or feeling that one's questions may be viewed as "dumb."

Similarly, researchers and practitioners involved with public health campaigns report a **knowledge gap** among "the chronically uninformed." That unflattering label tends to apply demographically to people who are nonwhite, less educated, and old (and, correspondingly, of a lower socioeconomic background). Sadly and coincidentally, this same group is at greater risk than the rest of the population for many common diseases and health problems. Furthermore, as health information increasingly proliferates in volume and availability on the Web, the **digital divide**—a concept referring to lack of access to computers, online connections, and training in how to use new technologies—furthers the knowledge gap even more. Public health communication specialist Vicki Freimuth (1990) suggests several ways to address this problematic situation, including educational programs to improve reading and media literacy; better design and targeting of media messages, especially taking into account the cultural contexts of audiences; more reliance on TV and other nonliterary media in lieu of written brochures; and greater use of informal, community-based channels of communication.

Restriction of information creates problems not only between doctors and patients but among health professionals as well. Allusions to "the health care team" create an implicit expectation that a variety of professionals work together and share a commonly understood, coordinated set of goals during patient care. The more frequent reality in our highly complex system of health care, however, is that professionals from different specialties, who have limited—or even no—communication with one another, contribute to the care of a single patient. This lack of communication is not necessarily an intentional omission. Obstacles of geographic location, time constraints, work shifts, specialized idioms and practices, and organizational lines of reporting preclude optimal sharing of information. We described in Chapter 2 the alarming example of how a patient's instruction not to be given anesthesia during a surgical procedure that had been discussed by her and the physician she assumed would be the anesthesiologist in attendance were disregarded just a few hours later during the surgery by a different anesthesiologist and nurse (Geist & Gates, 1996). In essence, the patient's refusal to give informed consent for anesthesia was disregarded because of a change in personnel and a resulting discontinuity in the communication of pertinent information. Presumably, the agreement not to use anesthesia during the surgery should have been recorded in this patient's chart and then read by the replacement anesthesiologist. A patient's written medical record is supposed to serve as a repository of information about that person within a specific health care institution, but a case study of one such chart revealed that the various specialists writing clinical notes about a particular patient each constructed a distinct and different narrative which affected the care of this person (Poirier, Rosenblum, Brauner, Sharf, & Stanford, 1992). Furthermore, it is not at all clear that clinicians read one another's chart notes to get a fuller picture of what is going on with a patient.

Thus far, we have discussed the dynamics of control between providers and patients that restrict the flow of information as well as social structural issues that disadvantage certain segments of society in regard to health information. It is essential to recognize, however, that laypersons increasingly have many sources of health-related information in addition to that received from medical practitioners and public health agencies. This broadening of potential channels for information can be helpful or confounding to an individual, and it can enhance—and even cause—tensions in relationships within the health care system.

## Increasing Information

There has always been an informal system of health advice in which people discuss their problems within a personal network of family, neighbors, friends, and colleagues. In response, they may receive suggestions of what to do (for example, special diets), home remedies, or even unfinished bottles of prescription medicines. Indeed, many minor ailments are resolved in this way. Even in social settings that ostensibly have nothing to do with illness per se, information seeking related to health is often ongoing. For instance, observations of interactions among a group of "stay-at-home moms," whose common interests center on child care, reveal that a good deal of their communication revolves around issues of women's health, especially pregnancy as well as birthing, and on children's health. The more maternal experience that a particular woman had, the more status as an "opinion leader" was attributed to her within this informal network (Tardy & Hale, 1998b).

*News and entertainment media.* Mass media have developed into a ubiquitous source of health information, and the media frequently serve as a common-language interpreter of research that first appears in specialized journals. Newspapers and popular magazines carry health news and special features regularly. Walk into any library or large bookstore, and you will find entire health sections (for example, medicine, women's health, mental and spiritual health, alternative healing, and so on) taking up a sizable portion of the store's space. While there is a demonstrated danger that brief "sound bites" can distort the meaning of scientific studies, there is also a history of popular media alerting audiences to important findings and new possibilities. For instance, *McCall's* published articles during the 1970s through which many American women first learned about lumpectomy (removal of the tumor and surrounding breast tissue) as an alternative to mastectomy (the total removal of the breast ) for treating breast cancer. Three decades later, women's magazines continue to serve similar functions in communicating health news to their readerships.

Health reports are now incorporated in TV and radio news programs as well, and medical controversies are a staple of talk shows, prime-time dramas, movies, soap operas, and even situation comedies. Even though much of this programming is primarily intended for entertainment, a good deal of information is simultaneously—and intentionally—communicated to audiences. Communication researchers Arvind Singhal and Everett Rogers (1999) document the growth of **entertainment-education,** which is the use of a variety of entertainment media, including TV and radio soap operas and popular music, to promote educational messages that "show individuals how they can live safer, healthier, and happier lives" (p. xii). Their research indicates impressive effects on social change in areas such as family planning, prevention of HIV infection, environmental clean-up, organ donation, and expansion of choices in women's lives. Though Singhal and Rogers' work focuses on entertainment-education campaigns in developing countries in Latin America, Africa, and Asia, similar efforts have been documented in Europe and the United States. The narratives that started this chapter are two prime examples. Nancy Weston's struggle with ovarian cancer on prime-time TV taught American viewers about this disease and how to cope with it (Sharf et al., 1996), while the story of Augusto and Michaela Odone, as told in a major motion picture, implanted the idea that ordinary citizens can impact the course of medical research. Theorizing Practice 9.3 lets you try developing such programming strategies yourself.

## Showtime

Choose a conceptually difficult health concept (for example, organ donation or advanced directives) that is both of interest to you and that you feel is of significance to the public at large. Now, it's time to get creative. Using an entertainment-education format, how would you develop this idea to help others both understand *and* undertake specific actions or behaviors? What audiences would you most like to target, and how would you gain their attention and involvement?

*Telecommunication and computer technologies.* In the mid-1970s, the Cancer Information Service, an arm of the National Cancer Institute, initiated a nationally accessible, toll-free telephone number (1-800-FOR-CANCER). With this telephone system, individual citizens and practitioners can access the most recent research findings, referrals to specialists, government publications, and responses to specific queries (Freimuth, Stein, & Kean, 1989). Since that program was established, many other health-related phone systems have also been created to facilitate people's informational searches.

The advent of computer technology and proficiency has, in many ways, gone several steps further than radio, TV, print media, and the telephone in terms of communicating health-related information. With the Internet, citizens can access news headlines and selected magazine and newspaper articles, and they can also contact different agencies in the National Institutes of Health, major medical research centers, or voluntary agencies, such as the Alzheimer's Disease Association or the Multiple Sclerosis Association. Computer users can read reports from medical journals, find the latest clinical trials for experimental treatments, learn about medications, and check on alternative healing approaches to a particular problem. Bibliographic and archival searches are also possible, and on some Web sites, you can even communicate directly with a health care specialist about problems and questions.

Perhaps the most widely used function thus far is the ability to interact with others who are experiencing or otherwise concerned with a specific health issue, both to share information and to provide mutual social support. The Comprehensive Health Enhancement Support System (CHESS), developed at the University of Wisconsin, combines several of these functions in versions tailored specifically for survivors of breast cancer, HIV infection, sexual assault, and parental alcoholism as well as those for people dealing with an academic crisis and other kinds of stress, and all provide encouraging outcomes—including cutting health care costs. Another interesting finding about CHESS is that, given access, disadvantaged people will use health information technology as much as—or even more than—more privileged groups (Hawkins et al., 1997). Almost certainly, the resources now available via the World Wide Web would have enhanced and facilitated the kinds of searches for specialized information that Nancy Weston and Augusto Odone were depicted doing a decade or more ago.

On the other hand, computer-based access to health information also carries both old and new dangers for health citizens, including unreliability of sources and information, because anyone can set up a Web site or post a message; undesired commercial targeting, especially for vulnerable people, whose main concern is relief from suffering and pain; security breaches involving private medical records; and probably some problems still unforeseen that will arise with the evolution of electronic media (Katz & Rice, 2001).

***Health advertising.*** Although most diagnostic technology remains primarily under the control of biomedical specialists, some instruments, such as blood pressure cuffs and home pregnancy or HIV tests, are directly available for consumer use, providing results that previously had been available only from physicians. In terms of treatment options, pharmaceutical companies are also, to some degree, bypassing physicians with DTC (direct-to-consumer) media advertising, especially televised spots that rely on striking audiovisual messages to create a demand for a product.

One notable example is the Claritin campaign. Initially, the drug was introduced to the public on TV and in magazines by what is called a "reminder ad" (Kaplan, 1998, p. 45), featuring several repetitions of its name, along with striking images of attractive people walking through a bright, spring-time landscape. Mysteriously, no explanation was given about what this medication was for. Consumers were simply instructed to ask their physician about it—and, thus, the seeds of demand had been planted. In a later round of commercials, a catchy pop tune ("I'm walking on sunshine, uh huh, and don't it feel good?") was added, along with more explicit information about the drug as an allergy remedy, an obligatory list of possible contraindications and side effects, and directions for obtaining more details. In a short period of time, Claritin became a top-selling product, with widespread name recognition among professionals and laypersons alike. In the first half of 1998, Schering-Plough Pharmaceuticals, the manufacturer, spent more than $57 million on marketing, making Claritin the most advertised DTC product for that time period. As a result, 31 percent of physicians reported an increase in discussions about this medication, and patient requests for the drug were honored by doctors 86 percent of the time (Marcinko, 1998). FYI 9.3 shows what both health consumers and health professionals think about DTC advertising.

***Health citizen evaluation.*** With so much information readily available from so many places, it becomes increasingly incumbent on health citizens to be discriminating about the credibility of sources, the context in which the information

## DOCTORS' COMMENTS ON DTC

A cardiologist: "Initially, DTC advertising seemed a little invasive and annoying. However, it is probably appropriate for the information age that we live in. If it's an effective marketing tool for companies and it isn't illegal, then it seems reasonable."

A podiatrist: "[The ads] bring in patients and make them aware there are treatments for their conditions."

A psychologist: "Anything that decreases the stigma of mental illness and increases the number of people who get help is worth it."

Another cardiologist: "DTC advertising must avoid giving patients false or inflated expectations."

General practice: "I think it gives the patient the idea that all problems can be treated with pills. It implies a simple solution to a complex problem."

Psychiatrist: "Helps those who are suffering recognize that they may have an illness and get help."

## CONSUMER COMMENTS ON DTC

"I feel the fact that I can learn about different drugs without having to ask a doctor who is always too busy for questions about drugs I may not need. It is very convenient to pick up a magazine and learn, so if I ever need them I will have some knowledge about what to ask for."

"I have nail fungus and never knew what it was until I saw an ad in a magazine (with a picture) for a medication."

"It is nice to know you have options; if one prescription isn't working or you can't afford it, you know you have options."

"Everyone needs to know what they are putting into their bodies and what type of reactions could occur when taken with other medications."

"Prescription products should not be advertised to the public; this is what doctors are paid for!"

"They're not even advertised in a convincing way and half the time you don't even know what they're for."

"It enables people to know what is available to consumers without having to speak with a doctor first."

"Helps you understand the product; what it is used for; what to expect from the product."

"It allows us to be more aware of prescription drugs that could be helpful with certain health problems. It can also make us more aware that symptoms we are experiencing may be something [more serious], and that we could contact our physician to discuss the health issue."

(Marcinko, 1998, pp. 53–54)

originally appeared, and the appropriateness of applications about which they read, see, or hear. Data, opinions, and uncorroborated rumors need to be distinguished. Are there sensible explanations and sufficient supporting evidence? Have the recommendations been tried, and if so, were there unintended consequences? The availability of health knowledge outside the medical context may enhance provider–patient interaction or cause tension or confusion if the information from other sources challenges the health professional's perspective. The following example looks at a situation that illustrates such conflict surrounding the availability of information.

### Case Study: Control of the Internet

Some health professionals are only now becoming accustomed to the notion that patients may have extensively researched a health problem through the World Wide Web. While some providers may feel threatened that people they treat have uncontrolled access to all sorts of materials, others are more open to the idea (Kahn, 1997). Even so, some are worried that patients may be misled by erroneous, unproven, or biased information (Bulkeley, 1995; Rogers, 1998), as sometimes has occurred. FYI 9.4 pokes fun at the phenomenon of patients obtaining medical information on the Web.

This concern was the basis of a controversy that caused dissension within the University of Pennsylvania and protest from many computer users. The case centered on Loren Buhle, an assistant professor of physics in the medical school at the university, who had experienced the diagnosis and treatment of leukemia for his young daughter several years earlier. As a parent in this painful situation, he discovered firsthand the difficulties of trying to access up-to-date information that would help him and his wife to understand what was going on and aid them in making decisions they hoped would help their child. As a result of this trauma in his own life, in the early 1990s he established a Web site called OncoLink, using the computer resources of the university. As he conceived it, OncoLink was a repository of cancer-related materials spanning a wide range of interests: studies of basic science, clinical trials, research on psychosocial problems, personal narratives, material on alternative treatments, even drawings by children with cancer. The site was intended to help laypersons dealing with a family member who had cancer, so that they would not have to struggle to obtain pertinent information as he and his wife had. Although he originally was the sole editor and manager of OncoLink, within a short time his department head assigned two other colleagues, both physicians, as coeditors. At first, he welcomed this move. After all, OncoLink was a successful venture that had won awards for computer-based achievement and was greatly utilized by computer users.

"Well, ***www.what'swrongwithme?.com*** says it's just a virus, but I came to you for a second opinion."

*Reprinted by permission of Wm. Hoest Enterprises, Inc.*

Eventually, however, the three editors began to disagree about the requirements for posting material on the site. The two physicians felt that only credible scientific studies, which had been refereed or reviewed and approved by other scientists, should be there. Based on his own personal knowledge and experiences as a person seeking cancer information, Buhle continued posting "unscientific" documents, such as accounts of personal coping, and unrefereed reports of unorthodox treatments and medications that had not been approved by his physician colleagues. In December 1994, officials within the university removed him from his position as coeditor, a controversial move that caused the site to go off-line for a brief period of time and drew a deluge of angry complaints from several users (Goodman, 1994). Since then, OncoLink has remained an informative online site. The two physicians continue as editors-in-chief and, interestingly, have retained many features (for example, survivor stories, artwork by people with cancer) that were first instituted by their ousted colleague.

This story raises many questions about the Internet as a source of health information. Is it good to mix rigorously conducted studies with anecdotal accounts when offering resources to the public? Asked another way, are citizens equipped to differentiate among such varied sources of information? On the other hand, do medical experts have the right to select what information should be readily available to the public? Who should decide how to organize and display information? Are there better ways of combining professional and lay concerns to make information accessible? Ever-increasing use of the computer for both posting and seeking health information continues to fuel debates between professionals and nonprofessionals—as well as among specialists—and raises important questions about the process of communicating scientific knowledge (Pear, 1999).

We have been discussing issues of balance, conflict, and complexity that are inherent in the communication of health information, and we have used a variety of examples and case studies. Specifically, we have considered questions of quality and quantity of information, of values, and of accessibility. Theorizing Practice 9.4 deals with the question of how the kind of media used to convey information may uniquely shape both the content and the understanding of messages about a particular topic.

The overriding themes of this discussion have been how information may empower or confound the people who are touched by it and the struggle between health professionals and nonprofessionals to control the flow and availability of specialized knowledge. We now shift from these points of tension to some important, functional consequences of seeking and sharing health information.

## CONSEQUENCES OF COMMUNICATING INFORMATION

During the time this book was written, each of the three authors faced difficult decisions concerning her own health or that of a close family member. For generations, menopause was a topic that had not been publicly discussed, but today, it is widely aired among both women and health care providers. For me (Barbara), the question of eventually taking HRT (hormone replacement therapy) is an issue I've been actively investigating, trying to integrate a wealth of recent information—much of it contradictory. Taken as a woman ages, HRT has been reported to have the significant long-term benefits of protecting against heart disease (although at the time of this publication, that claim continues to be hotly disputed), osteoporosis, and possibly, Alzheimer's disease and colon cancer. Simultaneously, HRT medicalizes what many women consider to be a natural stage of life, and it can increase the risk of breast cancer (see, for example, Brody, 1998; "Menopause," 1999).

## The Medium and the Message

Cultural critic Marshall McLuhan (McLuhan, 1964; McLuhan & Fiore, 1967) became known for his public declaration that the medium is the message (or more precisely, in a play on words, "the medium is the massage"). In other words, the medium through which we communicate shapes the meanings of the messages that are created. Keeping this idea in mind over the next week, seek out information about a current health issue (for instance, HMOs [health maintenance organizations], genetic research, or nutritional guidelines, just to name a few possibilities); use at least three different media or ways of accessing the information. You might explore the topic interpersonally, such as by talking with a friend or family member who has experience in this area, interviewing an expert scholar on your campus, or asking questions of a local health provider. You might use the computer, such as by checking to see what Web sites exist related to this subject and then exploring one or more of them. You might investigate recent newspaper, radio, and/or TV coverage. Once you have collected the information, respond to the following questions:

- Which aspects of the issue are addressed through each of the different media? In what ways do these complement one another? Do any conflict with each other?

- How have your understanding of and feelings about the topic been affected by the various media approaches you just explored? In other words, for example, how did watching a movie about cloning influence your thinking about that issue, and how did that experience differ from reading an article about cloning in the *New York Times*?

- What gaps in information on this topic still remain for you, and where do you think you need to turn to investigate these?

Many women underestimate their risk of heart and bone disease and overestimate their risk of breast cancer. In my case, however, there is a pronounced family history of breast cancer. Information from a variety of sources (several of which are contradictory or inconclusive), including scientific studies, mass media presentations, personal testimonials, and professional recommendations, are available to me, but in the end, it is my responsibility to integrate these data, balance the risks against the benefits, and make a judgment call that could affect the longevity and quality of the rest of my life.[1]

---

[1] In July 2002 a National Institutes of Health Study on the efficacy of HRT was prematurely halted in light of overwhelming evidence that the health risks far outweigh the benefits for women taking HRT long time.

## ▮ Information and Decision Making

As already mentioned, people generally desire to have information about their own health-related problems, though individuals vary considerably in how assertive, vocal, and articulate they are in seeking that knowledge. How individuals make use of information once they have it also varies greatly.

Increasingly, citizens are challenged to apply their own priorities to health-related information that is often ambiguous and open to revision. Many have developed some degree of skepticism about the constant outpouring of such information to the public. Often the information is contradictory: Is it healthy to eat fish or not? At what point should women start having regular mammograms—at 35, 40, or 50? Is it safe to have silicone breast implants or not? Do diet drugs cause heart disease, or don't they? Conversely, suspicions also arise that important health information is not being made public. In part, this has been spurred by long-delayed disclosures about government-sponsored experiments on uninformed human subjects in Tuskegee, Alabama, concerning the effects of untreated syphilis, or about the effects of radiation on people unknowingly involved in the early testing of atomic weapons. This information became public years after the events had occurred and serious, sometimes even fatal, damage had been done. At another level, the desire to cut costs, which is the hallmark of managed care systems, has aroused many doubts among the public in general—and among individual subscribers to those plans in particular—that the full range of treatments is not being shared if some of those options are deemed too expensive. One of the most significant applications of information pertains to how people choose to participate—or not to participate—in making decisions that affect health care and health maintenance.

A concept often used to explain how involved a person chooses to become in seeking health information, actively taking part in decision making, and enacting preventive behaviors is called the **health locus of control** (Lefcourt, 1982; Wallston, Maides, & Wallston, 1976). This construct posits that an individual has an internal or an external perception of where control related to health resides. Those who perceive that control is internal (residing within themselves) tend to seek out more information, to have a greater desire to participate in decisions affecting their own health, and to feel greater motivation to enact preventive behaviors to lower the risk of disease and disability. Those who perceive that control is external (due to forces outside themselves, such as the environment, heredity, or fate) tend to make less effort to gain information, to maintain healthy behaviors, and to participate in decision making (Brenders, 1989). Note, however, that we must be cautious in generalizing too much from these trends, because the research in this area is somewhat inconsistent.

Furthermore, research indicates that not everyone who wants health information necessarily uses that knowledge to make decisions about their own health care (Strull, Lo, & Charles, 1984). Other studies have shown that rather than not wanting to participate at all, most people are willing to apply information in choosing among or prioritizing possible options already identified by expert professionals (Deber, 1994). In other words, after decades of physicians controlling all the pertinent health information and making all the decisions for their patients, the public now demands more autonomy—but not *complete* autonomy. Many people want to take part in decisions that affect their health, but especially in the case of severe or life-threatening illness, they prefer to have the expert input of trusted health professionals (Kolata, 1997).

Finally, having received and understood health information does not ensure that people will use that knowledge to guide or change their own behaviors. A well-known case in point involves college students who practice unsafe sex despite their exposure to a wealth of materials related to HIV transmission and the availability of condoms (Sheer & Cline, 1995). Health communication scholar Kim Witte (1992, 1995) has developed a theory called the **Extended Parallel Process Model** that predicts whether people's behaviors will change based on how they channel their fear of threats to their health (this model was briefly discussed in Chapter 6). She explains:

> [Health] campaign messages should contain a threat component and an efficacy component. The threat portion . . . tries to make the audience feel susceptible to a severe threat. The efficacy portion . . . tries to convince individuals they are able to perform the recommended response . . . and that the recommended response effectively averts the threat. (Witte, Cameron, Lapinski, & Nzyuko, 1998, p. 347)

In one of several studies illustrating this principle, Witte and her colleagues (1998) examined an HIV/AIDS prevention campaign in Kenya. They found that participants who already considered themselves at high risk for infection responded in different ways to a variety of prevention campaign materials. Posters emphasizing the threat but no specific course of action resulted in denial and defensiveness (similar to the college students participating in unsafe sex). In contrast, pamphlets providing explicit information on self-protection (how to negotiate condom use, correct usage, and where to get them) prompted changes toward the enactment of preventive behavior. Like the Canadian harm reduction approach to drug abuse, this AIDS prevention program openly recognizes existing health risks and emphasizes practical methods that enable people to feel they can do something to help themselves.

In short, for the individual citizen, motivation for health information seeking may be influenced by the strength of source credibility, the degree of overall skepticism, the locus and perception of control. Having access to information and understanding it may—or may not—be directly connected to a person's active participation in making health-related decisions or in taking actions based on that information. As health communication scholar Rajiv Rimal and his colleagues

(Rimal, Ratzan, Arntson, & Freimuth, 1997) point out, "Not only do citizens have to be made aware of their rights and responsibilities, they have to assume and perceive control over their lives, and feel empowered to bring about change" (p. 64).

## Information and Disclosure

Patients are frequently in the position of divulging personal information to health professionals that, because of its embarrassing or sensitive nature, would not be shared in most other situations. This situation of sensitive **disclosure** is the basis for some of the more troubling ethical and communicative dilemmas in medical practice. Asking such questions is typically one of the more challenging tasks for novice health professionals to learn, as the following autobiographical excerpt illustrates. Dr. Perri Klass (1987), a pediatrician and professional writer, describes in a short story called "Invasions" one such moment during her medical school training, when she was commanded by her resident to report on a patient she had examined.[2]

> *"Mr. Z. is a seventy-eight-year-old white male who presents with dysuria and intermittent hematuria of one week's duration." In other words, for the past week Mr. Z. has experienced pain with urination, and has occasionally passed blood. I rocket on, thinking only about getting through the presentation without being told off for taking too long, without being reprimanded for including nonessential items—or for leaving out crucial bits of data. Of course, fair is fair, my judgment about what is critical and what is not is very faulty. Should I include in this very short presentation (known as a "bullet") that Mr. Z. had gonorrhea five years ago? Well, yes, I decide, and include it in my sentence, beginning, "Pertinent past medical history includes . . ." I don't even have a second to remember how Mr. Z. told me about his gonorrhea, how he made me repeat the question three times last night, my supposedly casual question dropped in between "Have you ever been exposed to tuberculosis?" and "Have you traveled out of the country recently?"*

> *"Five years ago?" The resident interrupts me. "When he was seventy-three? Well, good for him!"*

> *Feeling almost guilty, I think of last night, of how Mr. Z.'s voice dropped to a whisper when he told me about the gonorrhea, how he then went on, as if he felt had no choice, to explain that he had gone to a convention and "been with a hooker—excuse me, miss, no offense," and then how he infected his wife, and so on. I am fairly used to this by now, the impulse people sometimes have to confide everything to the person examining them as they enter the hospital. I don't know whether*

---

[2]"Invasions," from *A Not Entirely Benign Procedure* by Perri Klass, © 1987 by Perri Klass. Used by permission of G. P. Putnam's Sons, a division of Penguin Putnam, Inc.

*they are frightened by suggestions of disease and mortality, or just accepting me as a medical professional and using me as a comfortable repository for secrets. I have had people tell me about their childhoods and the deaths of relatives, about their jobs, about things I have needed to ask about and things that have no conceivable bearing on anything that concerns me.*

*In we charge to examine Mr. Z. The resident introduces himself and the other members of the team, and then he and the interns listen to Mr. Z.'s chest, feel his stomach. As they pull up Mr. Z.'s gown to feel his genitals, the resident says heartily, "Well now, I understand you had a little trouble with VD not so long ago." And immediately I feel like a traitor; I am sure Mr. Z. is looking at me reproachfully. I have betrayed the secret he was so hesitant to trust me with.*

*I am aware that my scruples are ridiculous. It is possibly relevant that Mr. Z. had gonorrhea; it is certainly relevant to know how he was treated, whether he might have been reinfected. (pp. 111–113)*

Disclosing information of a very personal nature, such as the fact that one has a sexually-transmitted infection, is necessary to the diagnosis and treatment of illness, but it may be potentially harmful to the patient. Therefore, the ethical and legal principle of doctor–patient confidentiality has been developed. Nevertheless, confidentiality is not always a clear-cut pathway. Klass, the medical student, ponders how much of the patient's sexual history to record in his chart, weighing the value of a complete history against the uncertainty of who will eventually read the medical record. Physicians and nurses are sometimes asked to elicit—and to report—information that could jeopardize an individual's insurance, job opportunities, or ability to receive worker's compensation or continue driving an automobile. Other times, they learn information that might be the cause of potential harm to others.

Peter Northouse and Laurel Northouse (1992), professors of communication and nursing, respectively, point out a variety of circumstances that contribute to difficulties of disclosing sensitive information within clinical settings. These include lack of environmental privacy, self-doubt, fear of negative sanctions (especially impacting the receipt of health services), and lack of trust. Unlike self-disclosure in other relationships and intimate situations, the risky information volunteered by patients to health professionals typically is not mirrored by reciprocal disclosures from providers to patients. Furthermore, patients often experience a lack of receptivity for certain types of disclosures regarding personal feelings, problems, and narrative details that health professionals may judge to be tangential information, not pertinent to diagnosis, treatment, or prevention (even though the disclosing individual may regard this information as essential to their health or to the quality of care they are receiving). For their part, physicians and other providers tend to marginalize such disclosures, either because they lack a

## Disclosing Personal Information

Self-disclosure as a communicative process involves a combination of risk, insofar as this involves personal information that may be harmful or dangerous if brought out into the open, and trust that one's integrity and confidentiality of the content disclosed will be respected. Consider what types of personal information about yourself may need to be disclosed for health or medical purposes. Perhaps you have already made such disclosures, or you may hypothesize doing so in the future. Some examples of risky personal information might include a substance abuse history; sexual practices or sexually transmitted diseases, mental illness, or other kinds of illness history, like cancer; a physical deformity; and so forth. Once you have done so, respond to the following questions:

- Why do you consider these items as possibly being harmful or dangerous? What risks are entailed in disclosing them?

- What factors might prompt you to self-disclose this information despite the risks? (These factors might be institutional, like an insurance or employment requirement, as well as personal.)

- Are there certain situations or people you would feel more trust in than others when disclosing this information? What/who are these, and why?

- What would the repercussions be of withholding the information?

conceptual framework to incorporate such forms of information or because they feel powerless to affect such problems as domestic abuse, financial shortages, or workplace conditions—even if they also recognize that these issues clearly have health consequences (Waitzkin, 1991).

During the past two decades, the public disclosure of personal, potentially stigmatizing health information has become increasingly prevalent. This change has been aided by TV talk and news magazine shows as well as by the popularity of published autobiographical illness narratives. At their best, such public admissions legitimize the health issue under discussion and encourage others with similar problems to seek help. One prominent example is Tipper Gore (wife of former Vice-President Al Gore) coming forward to say that she had been treated for severe depression. Her admission was meant to provide an event to initiate a governmental campaign to remove the shame from mental illness and to publicize the potential success of psychiatric treatment. Theorizing Practice 9.5 raises questions about the disclosure of sensitive information for health purposes at a more interpersonal level.

One of the most serious implications of disclosure is currently being debated at the institutional level of health policy. Since 1990, the Human Genome Project (the U.S. research effort to analyze the DNA of human beings) has made tremendous progress toward identifying the components of the human genetic structure. In the process, the genes responsible for or correlated with many diseases have been identified, and tests have been developed to confirm the existence of a suspected gene within a particular person. For diseases with no known cure, however, of what the value is such a predictive test? Even when treatments are available, the knowledge that a person is at heightened risk for heart disease, cancer, dementia, or other undesirable conditions can be used to stigmatize or behave with prejudice against that person (Murphy & Lappé, 1994). Thus, a number of questions regarding disclosure about genetic susceptibility have surfaced: Who wants to know? Who has a right to know? And what are the implications, both in terms of benefits and harms, of such disclosure?

## SUMMARY

In this chapter, we have sought to describe the ways in which the communication of health information may be empowering, confusing, overwhelming, and even dangerous. We first addressed three major categories of questions that help to define the dynamics inherent in the communication of information: (a) questions of quality and quantity, or tensions over just what and how much information is relevant and useful to include in such contexts as consumer education as well as in determining what or whom is the source of expertise; (b) questions of values, specifically in terms of what and whose values predominate within informational messages and how these values influence meaning and knowledge; and (c) questions of accessibility, or of restricting or expanding the flow of information. We then examined the functional consequences of communicating health information. Specifically, we looked at the relationship between having information and using it to make health-related decisions, and we considered the implications of disclosing personal health data.

In the next chapter, we will look within health care systems and the variety of structures through which medical care is "managed." Our focus will be on the various organizations through which health care is made available and how health communication practices differ within these systems.

## KEY TERMS

| | | |
|---|---|---|
| health literacy | laypersons | informed consent |
| adequacy of health information | explanatory models | foundational values |
| critical incident | subjective-objective dichotomy | quality of life |
| | | abstinence |

harm reduction

patient autonomy

patient–doctor partnership

information control

knowledge gap

digital divide

entertainment-education

health locus of control

Extended Parallel Process Model

disclosure

## DISCUSSION QUESTIONS

1. Name an instance in which health information has been confusing or overwhelming to you. Then identify another situation in which such information has been empowering.

2. What are your main sources of information regarding health issues? How do you prioritize among these in terms of usefulness? Credibility? Skepticism?

3. In what ways do you consider yourself to be a source of expert health information? How have you put this information to use?

4. Think of an important decision you have made concerning your health. Did you rely primarily on an internal or an external locus of control framework in making this decision?

5. What topics related to personal health do you consider to be risky disclosures?

6. What, if any, circumstances have discouraged you from seeking further information about an issue relevant to your own health?

## INFOTRAC COLLEGE EDITION

1. The January 2001 article "Additional Side Effects" in *Promo* provides a detailed review of DTC advertising of pharmaceutical products. Referring to this piece and any others that you deem useful (taking care to properly cite all sources), write a two-page evaluation of how this trend in communicating drug-related information to the public may, in turn, affect communication between patients and health providers. In concluding, take a position as to whether you think DTC advertising is good idea; be sure to state why or why not.

2. Using the key words *health education* and *television* to search the InfoTrac database, identify and describe three different examples of how entertainment TV programming has been used for purposes of health education and/or health promotion.

3. In an article in *Better Home & Gardens* entitled "Quick Clicks to Health," Nick Gallo offers consumers several criteria to use as a way of ensuring that they have accessed trustworthy health information through the World Wide Web. Using the InfoTrac database to identify recent articles (Gallo's as well as others) that list the most frequently used health information sites on the Internet, choose one of those sites to visit and explore its contents. Apply the guidelines suggested by Gallo to write a one-page assessment of that site.

# 10

## Navigating Health Care Organizations

After Belva Johnson, an 88-year-old from Kensington, Calif., had a stroke during a hospital visit last fall, her doctor sent her to a nursing home to receive physical, speech and occupational therapy for 45 days. Within the first two weeks, she got a bladder infection and started vomiting several times a day. On the 16th day, Health Net, her northern California HMO [health maintenance organization], notified her that it would stop paying the bills after her 20th day, according to her son, Dick. Medicare would have paid—and ultimately did pay—for 74 more days at the nursing home. But Johnson's son had to take his mother out of the plan and lobby to get Health Net to pay the nursing home for 20 days, and is now wrangling over a $6000 bill.

(SPRAGINS, 1995, pp. 56, 58)

Sandy Bergevin has a terrific internist, and she adores the ophthalmologist who has treated her glaucoma for the past 15 years. "It takes a long time to build up the trust," she says. "I feel he's taking care of me and is not going to let anything happen to me." But the 55-year-old hospital worker is not so sure about her HMO. Because its vision plan stipulates only three office visits a year, getting the care she needs usually involves a long series of appeals. And she worries constantly that things could get worse. Not long ago she learned that her employer is planning to switch to a different health plan—one that may not even do business with the doctors she knows and trusts.

("HMO Hell," 1999, p. 58)

Plagued by anxiety, Christine felt she was making progress in therapy when her HMO pulled the plug after less than a year. The West Hartford mother had to stifle her nervousness last March as she sat in her psychiatrist's office and pleaded with three health plan reviewers over a speakerphone for continued coverage.

"I basically had to throw myself at their feet to convince them my treatment is necessary," said Christine, calling it a "telephone tribunal . . . All I could think of was the Dark Ages."

Since then, the health plan has approved a handful of sessions at a time for Christine, who doesn't want her real name used.

(LEVICK, 1998, p. A1)

All of us are familiar with stories like Belva's, Sandy's, and Christine's. We read them in popular magazines and newspapers. We hear them on TV or radio. We experience it ourselves or through family or friends. A quick look in any bookstore sets the stage for a potentially negative or traumatic experience in health care organizations. Our best defense is an offense; we approach our health care armed with at the least knowledge and, at best, with a friend or family member who will not leave our bedside. Books with titles like *Don't Let Your HMO Kill You* (Theodosakis & Feinberg, 2000), *How to Get Out of the Hospital Alive* (Blau & Shimberg, 1997), and *Surviving Modern Medicine* (Clarke & Evans, 1998) reinforce this image.

As medical technology, education, specialization, and federal funding have increased, so has the **corporatization of health care.** Health care is viewed as big business, from a corporation mentality, with success being determined by how "efficient" or profitable the business is. We now have many for-profit health care centers, companies buying local hospitals and private practices, with investors interested in maximizing the return on their investment (Miller, 1996). Nonprofit hospitals have had to compete, and the result has been health care being run like a business, with the focus now on the financial bottom line. It is not surprising, then, that providing quality care and making a profit often positions health care providers or organizations and their patients as adversaries.

With cost containment as the goal, hospitals have tried to cut costs by outsourcing services to "alternate-site specialty care." These sites may provide physical therapy, kidney dialysis, rehabilitation, or outpatient surgery. While these satellite sites may be geographically convenient for patients, families may be forced to move a loved one from the hospital prematurely or to provide hands-on care at home. Today, it is not unusual for parents to bring their child home from the hospital while still on IV lines, with the parents having to learn how to hook up the IVs, administer medication, and essentially, act as trained nurses for several weeks. The outcome of the child's treatment rests, in large part, on the parents' shoulders.

Sometimes families are forced to make decisions with less than adequate information. After my (Eileen's) father had brain surgery, about a year before this chapter was written, my family found itself overwhelmed, needing to make critical decisions with little information and little time. After about a week in the hospital, he had stabilized enough that he didn't need constant attention. We were then told to find a short-term nursing home that could take him within two days and could provide the therapy he needed.

Fifteen years ago, my father would have stayed in the hospital until he had recovered and completed a physical therapy regimen while recuperating there. He would have come home only when he was well enough to do so, and if he needed additional therapy, he could have returned to the hospital as an outpatient or hired a therapist to come to his home. Today, however, the choices have changed. He was allowed to stay in the hospital until he was well enough to walk and take care of his daily needs, but he did not do any physical therapy at the hospital. He could have stayed in the hospital's physical therapy ward, but this was now run privately and he would have had to pay for that just like he would for the short-term nursing home. And there were no openings at the time. We quickly toured nursing homes in his neighborhood but weren't sure what we were looking for—or even what questions to ask. We viewed this as a potentially important decision, because we didn't know if he would ever recover enough to return home. Our criteria varied depending on that concern, because we wanted to minimize the need for moving him to different homes. We finally picked one, but we were very confused by the process.

When we seek medical care today, we are dealing with multiple organizations. Decisions about our treatment may differ according to what health care plan you belong to—or if you even have a plan. Of people who are insured, between 80 and 90 percent are enrolled in managed care plans (Brider, 1996). In this chapter, we look at the impact of these plans on communicating health between the care-providing organizations and the patients as well as among health care providers within their organizations. We begin with a discussion of two types of managed care plans and of fee-for-service. The type of plan that we have is important, because they vary in our access to care providers and the treatments they provide, which clearly impacts both the information provided and the provider–patient messages that are exchanged.

# HEALTH CARE PLANS

*In 1995, the suit [against Physicians Health Services] says Physicians Health insisted that 15-year-old Nitai Moscovitch, who had tried to hang himself and then took an overdose of anti-depressants, should be switched from Danbury Hospital to a drug treatment center. About five hours after the transfer, Nitai blocked the door to his room, hanged himself with his belt and died.*

*Stewart Moscovitch—Nitai's father—recalls a Danbury Hospital doctor warned him that Physicians Health would not approve a stay of more than three to five days. The doctor said he "had to play the PHS game because they control where Nitai goes and how long he stays," Moscovitch said. . . .Wracked with regret, Moscovitch says he had to spend more time in his son's final days trying to find a place for him than being by his side. "You have to focus on getting him into the hospital instead of taking care of him and loving him and hugging him," Moscovitch said, weeping. "You have to focus instead on getting him into a safe place."*

*Psychiatrists claim that nearly every member of their profession has had a similar run-in with an insurer.*

(Levick, 1998, p. A1)

**Managed care** refers to "health care systems that integrate financing and delivery of appropriate health care services to covered individuals by arrangements with selected providers, formal programs for ongoing quality assurance and utilization review, and significant financial incentives for members to use providers and procedures associated with the plan" (Harden, 1994, p. vii). As of 2001, 177.9 million Americans were enrolled in a managed care plan (Managed care facts sheets, 2002). Managed care is a **prospective system,** which means that care providers receive a set amount of money (usually an annual allocation) regardless of the actual costs of their services. Whatever the managed care plan, they share the goal of **cost containment,** of trying to keep their financial risk minimal. If they run over their budget, they lose money. If they spend less, they make a profit.

You are probably most familiar with HMOs (**health maintenance organizations**) and PPOs (preferred provider organizations), which provide full care to their subscribed patients on a prepaid basis through a limited panel of providers (Bernstein & Bernstein, 1996). When these organizations work properly, patients get adequate care and resources are used efficiently. When they fail, however, the results can be serious (see Theorizing Practice 10.1).

Let's walk through an example to see how managed care plans differ in their treatments. Suppose that you subscribe to Wonder Care HMO. You have a chronic

## Analyzing a Health Care Plan

Pick and research a specific health care plan. What does it cover? What does it exclude? How does it deal with mental health coverage? With substance abuse? Second opinions? Analyze the plan as it is given to subscribers. What is clear? What is unclear? How might people interpret this plan differently from the written documents (e.g., if they are older or younger, lower or higher in social economic status [ses])? What concrete changes could you make? What are some advantages of this plan? What are some weaknesses?

sore throat, so you go to see Dr. Smith. Her bosses are the higher-up administrators at Wonder Care. They pay her salary and provide her staff and office. In return, she doesn't have to deal with insurance claims, and patient load is dispersed among all the doctors at Wonder Care. She only sees patients who are members of Wonder Care, and her bosses make sure the care that she gives stays within budget. If Dr. Smith wants you to have a certain treatment that is costly, the Wonder Care executives can decide not to approve it. At that point, Dr. Smith can either agree or appeal and argue the need for this treatment—and here is where she may run into problems. A frequently mentioned concern of doctors is that the higher-ups tend to be business people with little or no medical training. Or, they may be retired general practitioners who are making decisions about areas of medicine in which they have little or no training, such as neurology, gynecology, or oncology. Dr. Smith may find that she and her office staff spend much of their time and energy arguing with the HMO executives.

Dr. Smith's HMO may pay her a set salary or a capitated fee. Under **capitation,** she receives a set amount of money each year for each patient. Each time she sends a patient to a specialist or orders a test, it comes out of that money. Her general operating expenses (for example, office rental and staff) also come out of this money. If most of her patients are healthy, she will have excess funds at the end of the year, but if her costs run over her annual allocation, those extra costs come out of her pocket. Obviously, this can put Dr. Smith in an uncomfortable situation. Her salary is determined by how much of the money is left at the end of the year. Therefore, she may hesitate to refer patients to specialists, and by the time she finally makes a referral, the disorder may have become more serious and more difficult to treat.

A subset of HMOs is **Medicare HMOs,** which are designed for people 65 and older who are on Medicare. The idea is for Medicare patients to switch to the HMO, where they will not have to deal with bills or paperwork and will get their services for less. The government has contracts with various plans, and people with Medicare choose one of these plans (Managed care fact sheets, 2002). These

*Reprinted by permission of Mike Smith, Las Vegas Sun, North America Syndicate.*

HMOs make their money by signing up the healthiest senior citizens who live in the areas of the country with the highest average medical costs. For seniors who rarely see doctors, these plans can be excellent deals. For those with chronic illnesses, however, the quality of care tends to be worse (Miller & Luft, 1997). As with other HMOs, problems occur when patients are denied costly medical care. At that point, members can appeal the decision, but this typically requires a significant commitment of time, energy, and patience.

**Preferred provider organizations (PPOs)** are another type of managed care, but are set up differently from HMOs. Here, Dr. Smith runs her own practice and can treat patients who do—and do not—subscribe to the health care plan. She has to treat members at a rate less than her actual fee, however, so she will probably make less money than she would under fee-for-service. The PPO members must first see Dr. Smith (their primary care doctor) for medical care. If she refers them to a specialist within the provider network, the costs are usually covered. If, however, they choose to go outside the caregiver network, they usually are only reimbursed for a percentage of the fee.

**Fee-for-service** used to be the main system of health care in the United States. Unlike managed care, the more services you require in this system, the more money your provider gets. In this system, you purchase health insurance, either through work or privately, and this puts you in the driver's seat. You can seek care from whomever you choose and pay each caregiver as you go. In this case, you can see Dr.

---

Smith or go directly to a specialist, file an insurance claim, and some portion of the charge will be paid to the doctor. Depending on your policy, you may pay a deductible or co-pay, with certain tests, treatments, and prescriptions covered either fully or partially. You are responsible for the costs not covered by your insurance plan.

## (OMMUNICATING IN HEALTH CARE ORGANIZATIONS

**Organizational communication** refers to messages and information exchanged among those who are members within or between organizations. For our purposes, we can include nursing staff, doctors, custodial staff, technicians, pharmacists, HMOs, insurance carriers, and patients as organization members.

We do not want to paint a negative picture of what may happen when we communicate within health care organizations. In most cases, all goes well from our admission to our discharge. Medical and support staff are helpful, considerate, and do their jobs well. In this era of profit as the bottom line, however, they are sometimes thwarted in their best efforts to provide care. One potential outcome is a shift from a conciliatory to an adversarial relationship between providers and patients.

In this section, we first look at the impact of managed care on our communication with providers in a health care organization. We then focus on those who work in the organizations, specifically examining job stress and how it may lead to burnout. Finally, we discuss how supportive communication can mediate this relationship in positive ways, and how sometimes what appears to be support is actually dysfunctional to the recipient and, subsequently, to both permanent and transient members of the organization.

### ▨ Impact on Provider–Patient Communication

Communication researchers John Lammers and Patricia Geist (1997) identified six ways that managed care has changed the relationship between providers and patients. It has: (a) transformed patients from sufferers to quasiconsumers, (b) transformed health care facilities into factories, (c) transformed individuals into population members within health care plans, (d) shifted cost risks from third parties to patients and providers, (e) limited the reach of caring, and (f) transformed providers into bureaucrats. Managed care forces us to make decisions about coverage and providers before we get sick, and it is up to us to gather information, develop criteria, and choose, usually within a narrow set of options. We are more dehumanized, reduced to an illness within a category of treatments, and have little continuity of care providers. Marketing is targeted to our shared aggregate characteristics, not to our individual variations. Costs have shifted from payment by insurance companies after our treatment to prepayment by providers and ourselves. People who don't meet specific criteria (such as below poverty level for Medicaid, not covered by Medicare, or work in small organizations not required to provide health coverage) end up without coverage and must either buy their own insurance or get treatment in emergency rooms. And because of all the new regulations, doctors are more rule-bound, resulting in a more formal provider–patient relationship.

The changes brought about by managed care have a significant impact on communication among care providers. They have always had to cope with high stress, but now they have added stressors caused by the directive of cost containment. In the next sections, we look at the impact of these stressors on communicating in health care organizations and the relationship of job stress to burnout. Later, we examine how supportive communication may mediate this relationship.

## Job Stress

*It has become unbearable and I plan to quit medicine. So many stupid things compromise my patient care that I'm ready to practically give my practice away. . . . When I see a Medicare patient, 110,000 pages of regulations come between us. . . . Keeping up with medicine is tough enough, but I'm also expected to read the Federal Register every day looking for new rules from the bureaucrats.*

Physician after being asked how the medical profession has
changed (Laster, 2001, p. B3)

*It is tougher than ever, therapists say, to get health plans to approve hospitalizing patients—and slashed wrists may not be enough. Fights are routine over the length of hospitalization, outpatient therapy and drug dosages, and patients suffer. . . .*

*Managed care companies acknowledge they push for the least intensive setting possible for care and that multiyear outpatient [mental health] therapy is generally insurance history.*

(Levick, 1998, p. A1)

*It is disheartening to know that the focus of health care service is changing when the personal evidence available to nurses suggests that the patient in the bed still has a set of needs and demands that must be met, regardless of the degree of shift toward outpatient care.*

(Mason & Leavitt, 1998, pp. 261–262)

As these quotes show, managed care has significantly changed the focus of health care in ways that frustrate many providers. Before managed care, doctors requested whatever tests or treatments they felt were necessary, hospitals carried out these orders, and hospitals were reimbursed for these services. Doctors made these decisions autonomously, and being the experts, were not questioned by the insurance companies who paid the customers' claims. Today, however, doctors' decisions under managed care must be approved by the HMO, doctors are forced to limit time with patients, and they have huge amounts of paperwork. FYI 10.1 captures what doctors who take Medicare patients are faced with.

---

**FYI 10.1**  **A LOOK AT HOW MANAGED CARE WORKS**

Leonard Laster (2001, p. B3), Distinguished University Professor of Medicine and Health Policy and Chancellor Emeritus of University of Massachusetts Medical Center, describes how the process of billing Medicare works.

> After seeing a Medicare patient, a doctor has to classify and document his [sic] services in sufficient detail for HCFA [Health Care Financing Administration] (or its contracted regional agents, called "carriers") to determine what to pay him. . . . Having first put the visit into the subcategory "new patient" or "established patient," the doctor must rank a patient's history as problem-focused (PF), expanded problem-focused (EPF), detailed (D) or comprehensive (C). He does the same for the physical examination (PF, EPF, D, C). Then he labels the medical decision-making process as straightforward (S), low complexity (LC), moderate complexity (MC) or high complexity (HC).
>
> These aren't casual choices; HCFA and its carriers have specific requirements for each. For instance, a detailed (D) physical examination must cover two or more body systems and areas and include 12 or more specified procedures, such as listening for heart murmurs and examining the retina for evidence of diabetes. Each procedure, whether it revealed anything or not, must be recorded.
>
> Then the doctor uses these alphabetical classifications to derive a code number, which he submits to his HCFA carrier. A "new patient" visit with a detailed and low complexity (LC) decision making might qualify for a code number such as 99203 for reimbursement. A high complexity (HC) decision would have a different number, say 99205, and a higher payment . . .
>
> If a random audit by a carrier finds that fewer than the required 12 tests are noted, that doctor has officially been overpaid . . .
>
> At any time, a carrier can demand "documentation of the history, examination and decision making which support the level of the evaluation and management service rendered." If the carrier should decide that the doctor "upcoded" his bill, then government agents can enter his office without warning and conduct a full-scale audit.
>
> Suppose random audits of 15 records turn up five instances of upcoding. The carrier can then extrapolate back for a period of time, perhaps a year, and rule that during that entire back period, one-third of Medicare's payments to the doctor were too high. Then HCFA can demand that the doctor make immediate restitution. (p. B3)

---

*Intraorganizational stress.* **Intraorganizational stress** refers to stress that is caused by people or factors within the organization. Some degree of **job stress** is inherent in any health care work. Providers find themselves, for example, taking care of seriously ill patients (children and adults) in an intensive care unit, staffing hospices, and caring for people with Alzheimer's disease, burns, AIDS, and more. (See FYI 10.2 for communication strategies related to intensive care units.) People typically choose health care professions because they want to make a difference in people's lives, and they often say they see their career choice as a calling. They are aware of the stress, at least cognitively, but once they're actually in the field, they are likely to experience stressors such as workload (both underload and overload), role conflict, role ambiguity, scarce resources, understaffing, physical strain (for example, lifting and moving patients), working with seriously or terminally ill patients, and a lack of participation in decision making (Ford & Ellis, 1998).

As the health care environment has changed, so have the expectations for care providers. Nurses, for example, have seen their role shift from expensive, intensive, late-stage health care to less costly, less invasive, preventive care in a managed environment. Now they must coordinate patient services, integrate services among different providers, build effective teams, and facilitate relationships between nurses, staff, and doctors (Mason & Leavitt, 1998). Today, they must straddle the lines of care provider and cost container. Doing so may require them to discharge patients too early to a short-term care facility or home, with the burden of medical care then falling on the family. I (Eileen), for example, personally know of two

---

**FYI 10.2** **COMMUNICATION STRATEGIES IF A LOVED ONE IS IN AN ICU**

1. Make friends with the ICU staff and plead for every extra opportunity for a quick visit.

2. Keep the lines of communication open at all times.

3. Don't add to the staff's stress of doing their job.

4. Be sympathetic to staff. They're dealing with constant life and death situations with extremely ill patients.

5. Bring in bagels, cookies, or snacks to munch on to lower their stress levels.

6. Don't bring flowers or other gifts. There is no place to put them, and chances are the patient wouldn't notice or appreciate them anyway.

7. Make sure a family member or friend is there to look out for the patient's well-being.

(Blau & Shimberg, 1997, p. 31)

seriously ill children who were sent home from the hospital early (because of insurance), with IV lines still in, and whose parents (who had no medical training) had to learn to administer medicine, change and clean the IV line, and essentially, provide care that should have been done by trained professionals.

Because of these changes, many providers are finding that working hands-on with patients has become secondary to completing paperwork or choosing care options based on cost. One example deals with on-floor nursing care. Once, most patient care was done by RNs (registered nurses), who found their relationships with the patients and their families rewarding. Now, however, LPNs (licensed practical nurses) or nursing assistants, rather than RNs, are more likely to do much of the hands-on care in hospitals and nursing homes. RNs find themselves filling out paperwork and spending more and more time away from the patients. These kinds of changes in job responsibilities are causing many to re-evaluate their commitment, and desire to continue, to provide hands-on health care. We should note, however, that one person's stress may be another person's motivator. Research by Kathy Miller, Lori Joseph, and Julie Apker (2000) suggests that some nurses report role ambiguity or job uncertainty as a significant stressor, whereas others see it as enhancing their empowerment and creativity.

Stress within health care organizations also affects allied health and support staff. Physical therapists, for example, may feel caught between incompatible demands from patients and coworkers. Social workers report more stress as they try to balance relationships between patients, patients' families, and other caregivers. Even those not in direct-care jobs may be affected. Communication scholars Kathy Miller, Eric Zook, and Beth Ellis (1989) found that food service, housekeeping, and administrative workers in a retirement center reported role stress similar to that of their direct-care counterparts.

In summary, caregivers in health organizations are often spread thinly, dealing with patients who are acutely ill and not allowed lengthy stays, serving more and more patients, and performing more and varied tasks. Many organizations have downsized and restructured job responsibilities, causing the remaining providers to experience more role conflict and ambiguity. In addition to the actual characteristics of their professions, care providers must also maintain a particular image with the public when enacting their roles. Their portrayal of this image has been referred to as emotional labor.

***Emotional labor.*** **Emotional labor** refers to managing feelings to create a particular public image. Arlie Hochschild (1983) says that workers have to "induce or suppress feeling in order to sustain the outward countenance that produces the proper state of mind in others" (p. 7). This is especially relevant for people in service occupations. Imagine a surly nurse or a verbally aggressive anesthesiologist—or maybe you've actually experienced them. We expect certain behavior, at least when they're performing their roles, from our care providers. Imagine also a nurse or a doctor having to manage their emotions when telling you a devastating diagnosis. Providers who are better able to manage these emotions through **empathic concern** (feeling *for* the other) rather than **emotional contagion** (feeling *with*, or parallel to, the other) are less likely to burn out (Miller, Stiff, & Ellis, 1988). This may be difficult to do, however. In addition to managing their emotions when dealing with patients, they must maintain this front when dealing with families, doctors, coworkers, and support staff. A patient or family doesn't want to hear their doctor talk about how incompetent the hospital lab is or the nursing assistants bad-mouth the RNs. They are expected to suppress these feelings when performing their job, and without effective coping strategies to manage their emotions, this suppression can seriously impact their own emotional health. Stress is not limited to the organization, however; most health care providers must also cope with life outside of work.

*Extraorganizational stress.* **Extraorganizational stress** refers to stress that comes from outside the organization. Home–work stress is very real for many health care providers. Role conflict between work and child or elder care has become a concern as more and more parents find themselves becoming members of the "sandwich generation," caught between caring for their children and their aging parents. Juggling these multiple care-giving roles is likely to result in high stress levels. The number of children or marital status is not necessarily a determining factor either. For example, one study of nursing aides in a nursing home found that the number of children didn't matter; simply having *any* children was stressful (Ray & Miller, 1994). In addition, aides who were cohabitating reported the most stress—even more than those who were married. Juggling work and home responsibilities is a difficult task when all is going smoothly and everyone is healthy. Imagine being understaffed at work, having a sick child or parent at home, and having to decide who gets your time and energy. Research suggests that this role conflict is particularly stressful for health care workers, and can be a predictor of burnout.

Stress from work can spill over to home, straining relationships with spouses and children. However, communication with family and friends about problems at work can act to buffer stress and burnout. **Instrumental support,** such as having hired help or relatives perform household tasks, and strong support from spouses with child care also can reduce stress. **Informational support,** such as friends or family telling us how to find resources or sharing stories of similar experiences and successful coping strategies, can also reduce stress.

Physicians also find themselves caught in home–work role conflict. Women make up about 45 percent of medical students but are still disproportionately in the lower-status, lower-pay specialties, such as family medicine and internal medicine. They are faced with a major decision. Are they willing to put in the long, intense years necessary to reach the top tier (such as surgery, neurology, or orthopedics)? The implications of this decision are clear. The intensity of effort will require a level of commitment not conducive to maintaining personal relationships or to raising children. Even pursuing other specialties, however, does not promise the career they originally had in mind. Instead, they are arranging to work less and to have more flexible hours. One study, for example, found that 25 percent of female doctors surveyed said that they worked less than 40 hours a week, compared to 12 percent of male doctors. Seventeen percent of female doctors said they worked 30 hours a week or less, while only 8 percent of male doctors worked this little (Steinhauer, 1999). Research indicates that the primary source of stress for female doctors is home–work conflict, with women reporting their success with this balancing act as being a greater determinant of their job satisfaction than male doctors did (McMurray et al., 1997).

*Interorganizational stress.* **Interorganizational stress** refers to stress between organizations. In addition to stressors at work and at home, changes in health care have impacted interorganizational communication. Differences in goals and difficulties in coordination often result in provider stress that spills over into patient care. As we've already discussed, cost containment strategies result in outside organizations, not the health care provider, dictating the length of hospital stays, coverage of treatments, and care. This leads to frustration, because "nurses often feel that the dismantling of 'hard won,' high-quality patient care merely in the interest of cost containment and constraining resource availability is completely unacceptable" (Mason & Leavitt, 1998, pp. 261–262).

Managed care also has impacted physicians' relationships with their colleagues and patients as well as control over their work. Doctors report having to negotiate with third-party managed care or government systems about patient care as a major job stressor, resulting in feelings of less professional autonomy and less job satisfaction. Research examining the relationship between managed care, communication problems, and physician satisfaction found that managed care organizations can be a factor in predicting communication problems leading to lower satisfaction among physicians (Lammers & Duggan, in press). Additional managed care stressors include an increased workload that involves charting, paperwork, and keeping up on and complying with ever-changing regulations (Post, 1997).

One example of an interorganizational stressor is reflected in DRGs (diagnosis-related groups), which were designed to contain costs for Medicare patients. Implemented in 1984, DRGs were set up to "control cost increases in Medicare, to achieve some predictability over [Social Security] expenditures, and ultimately to avoid the bankruptcy—perhaps even the destruction—of this program for helping the nation's elderly receive adequate health care" (Morreim, 1985, p. 30). Like managed care, DRGs is a prospective system. Hospitals set a flat rate for the costs of care for specific illnesses before that care is needed for a specific patient. The rate is based on the average cost of providing treatment for anyone with that particular illness. If costs repeatedly exceed the reimbursement rate, hospitals will lose money. If costs are repeatedly less than the rate, hospitals benefit by sharing in the profit. So, hospitals clearly have an incentive to stay at—or below—the reimbursement level. The impact of this system (and of others like it) on the entire organization is pervasive. Medicare patients are assigned a DRG when they enter the hospital, and subsequent care is determined based on this diagnosis. As Geist and Hardesty (1992) note, "under DRGs, the premise that quality patient care will be delivered regardless of cost loses ground to cost containment" (p. 238).

The implications for communication are pervasive. Care is streamlined, and work roles are redefined. Communication between patients and care providers is impacted as well. Explaining how DRGs affect a patient's care is considered **dirty work,** work that no one wants to perform (Hughes, 1971), and usually falls to the nurses (Hardesty & Geist, 1992). This means that the people having the most contact with patients and their families are also the people telling you that Aunt Lil, who is 80 and lives alone, is only allowed five days in the hospital for her pneumonia, after which she must leave or be diagnosed with a different illness (and a new DRG). Obviously, family members are not happy about this. Our dear aunt may be forced to go to a short-term nursing home or to her own home, where she must hire home health care nurses.

Imagine coming up against these kinds of restraints daily. These organizational obstacles, on top of the usual stressors, are enough to put some care providers "over the top." And for some of these providers, the result can be job burnout. Theorizing Practice 10.2 asks you to explore issues of stress and burnout and ways health care providers cope.

## ▓ Burnout

**Burnout** is a reaction to chronic job-related stress and may manifest as emotional exhaustion, depersonalization, and a feeling of a lack of accomplishment (Maslach, 1982). **Emotional exhaustion** refers to a feeling of being emotionally drained, having little or no resources to give to yourself or to others. **Depersonalization** occurs when you stop seeing patients as people and start viewing them as their illness, like "the bladder in room 420." This objectifies the person and creates distance between the care provider and the patient. **Lack of personal accomplishment** is the feeling that you're not making a difference, that you're not doing anyone any good.

Burnout can have a number of negative effects on both care providers and patients. For providers, burnout is associated with physical, psychological, and

## Interviewing Someone in a Health Care Organization

Find someone who works in a health care organization. The organization may be a hospital, HMO, private doctor's office, or ambulatory care center, or it may be a mental health clinic, blood donation center, dialysis center—wherever health care must be coordinated among providers. This should not be a relative, friend, coworker, or boss. Set up a face-to-face interview, lasting between 45 and 60 minutes. Tape record it if possible. Ask questions about the person's job responsibilities, what is stressful about the work, changes in stressors over time, how they manage their stress, if they've experienced burnout and, if so, how they dealt with it, what kinds of support they got and from whom, and how communication increases or reduces their stress. Relate this person's answers to what you've read in this chapter.

behavioral repercussions. Illnesses such as stomach problems, migraines, psychosomatic ailments, depression, and anxiety are common. Burned-out providers report a higher incidence of alcohol and substance abuse, marital conflict, job absenteeism and turnover. Obviously, burnout among health care professionals will affect the health care we receive. (I don't know about you, but I don't want any burned-out provider caring for my family or for me.)

There are several things to consider regarding the job stress–burnout relationship. First, burnout can be a good thing. It can send a strong message to someone that he or she is in the wrong career. Second, chronic job stress does not always result in burnout. Some providers cope successfully using individual-level strategies, such as exercise or prayer. Others cope thanks to their interpersonal relationships at work or at home (or both). In our next section, we discuss how this supportive communication may mediate the relationship between job stress and burnout.

# SUPPORTIVE COMMUNICATION

In Chapter 6, we discussed the types and functions of social support. Just to refresh your memory, recall that supportive communication may be emotional, instrumental, or informational. Here, we look at these different functions and sources of support in the context of health care organizations. See Figure 10.1 for an example of how this supportive communication may mediate the relationship between job stress and burnout. This model suggests that stressors such as role conflict, role ambiguity, participation in decision making, and workload can lead to the emotional exhaustion, depersonalization, and lack of personal accomplish-

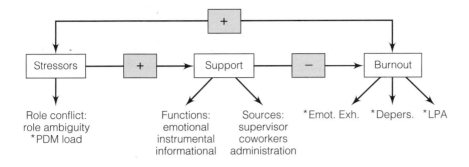

PDM = Participation in Decision Making
Emot. Exh. = Emotional Exhaustion
Depers. = Depersonalization
LPA = Lack of Personal Accomplishment

**FIGURE 10.1** Job stress-communicative support–burnout model.

ment that characterize burnout. However, emotional, instrumental, or informational supportive communication from supervisors, coworkers, or administrators can buffer these stressors so that burnout is less likely to result.

## ■ Sources of Supportive Communication

Sources of support inside the organization include coworkers, support staff, bosses, as well as transient members of the organization. The most obvious transient members are physicians and patients and patients' families. Outside the organization, support may come from friends, spouses, partners, family members, and even acquaintances. Coworkers may have the benefit of shared knowledge (Ray, 1987), while friends or family members may be more objective. Some research indicates that relationships at work offer more tangible, instrumental, informational, and emotional support than relationships outside of work (Metts, Geist, & Gray, 1994).

Intraorganizational communication occurs between and among all levels in health care organizations. It may be asymmetrical, such as between doctors and nurses, or symmetrical, such as between two doctors or two pharmacists. Research suggests that support from coworkers, especially peers and supervisors, is an effective coping mechanism for job stress. For nurses, coworker support may decrease burnout by reducing emotional exhaustion, while support from both coworkers and supervisors may reduce feelings of depersonalization (Miller et al., 1989). For social workers, however, coworker support appears to reduce burnout more than support from supervisors. Nurses who feel a sense of personal control by being assertive and participating in decisions with doctors report less burnout (Ellis & Miller, 1993).

Kathy Miller and I (Eileen) (Ray & Miller,1994) looked at how social support from sources both within and outside organizations reduced stress and burnout among nursing home nurses. We found that those nurses with children and those-who were cohabitating were the most vulnerable to home–work stress. Not surprisingly, other research has found that supervisors who are supportive of their employees' demands outside of work, such as by instituting flexible scheduling, help to reduce job stress.

The importance of social support from interpersonal relationships for health care providers' coping with work-related stress has been well documented (Ellis & Miller, 1993; Ray & Miller, 1994). We generally assume that supportive messages are given with the best of intentions, but sometimes, that's not the case. Sometimes what appears to be support is actually masking a hidden agenda. This is more likely in hierarchical organizations or when resources are scarce, both common in many health care organizations. In the next section, we consider how supportive communication may actually be dysfunctional.

## ▓ Dysfunctions of Supportive Communication

Sometimes what appears to be support may actually be a stressor (see Theorizing Practice 10.3). I (Eileen) have observed that within the organizational context, "relationships [are] embedded in differing levels of power, which may influence the intent and implications of social support" (Ray, 1993b, p. 108). Several dysfunctions of support can be identified: (a) support as commodity, (b) support as information retrieval, (c) support as codependency, and (d) support as hegemony.

**Support as commodity** establishes a situation in which the recipient of the support owes the provider. This type of "support may act as political currency, allowing providers to dictate to recipients when they are ready to 'cash in their chips'" (Ray, 1993b, p. 108).

**Support as information retrieval** involves an assumption of a hidden agenda for providers to uncover information they couldn't get otherwise. This requires providers to get the recipients to disclose while the providers share little, thereby maintaining their power in the organization.

**Support as codependency** may function to perpetuate communicative and organizational norms, so that newcomers quickly learn their roles within the organization. In this case, behavior that appears to be supportive "may actually be individuals enacting their own addictive behaviors, enabling them to repeat familiar patterns. Ostensible social support must maintain the closed system in a way that is acceptable to organizational members . . . maintaining the status quo is a key defining characteristic of support as codependency" (Ray, 1993b, p. 109).

Hegemony refers to "the process by which one group actively supports the goals and aspirations of another dominant group, even though those goals may not be

**THEORIZING PRACTICE 10.3**

## Health Communication and Dysfunctional Support

Choose a health care organization, such as a hospital, nursing home, blood bank, dialysis center, and so on. What are the functions this organization provides? Who are the permanent and transitory members? What are some of the organizations they must coordinate their activities with? What might be some of the advantages and some of the constraints of this coordination?

Within your chosen organization, develop situations to represent each of the possible dysfunctions that may be embedded in supportive communication (commodity, information retrieval, codependency, and hegemony). Discuss how each may function to initiate newcomers, provide socialization, and impact how health care is delivered.

in the subordinate group's interest" (Mumby, 1988, p. 55). **Support as hegemony** occurs when communication is used by those in power to maintain the status quo so that they remain in power.

Support does not always serve these four functions, of course. Health care organizations, however, that are based on asymmetrical relationships, competition for resources, and capitation provide a fertile breeding ground for dysfunctional communication.

## SUMMARY

Clearly, the days are gone when we knew our insurance companies would not question our doctor's medical decisions and we could feel confident that our care provider's goal was to make us better, not to come in under budget. These were not necessarily the "good old days," however, because the system was often abused, health care costs skyrocketed, the uninsured did not receive adequate care, and many needless tests and procedures were done on patients. The new era in health care brings many changes, including our need to be vocal health citizens rather than passive patients. We need to have advocates—or be one to someone else—to ensure that we get proper tests and treatment. This requires some skill at navigating our way through health care organizations—a skill that we usually don't learn until we have to. When a loved one experiences a health crisis, we learn firsthand about hospital care and limits, what insurance will pay, and how understaffing and overload impacts the care of our loved one.

As we cope with our own sets of stressors, care providers deal with theirs. As we've discussed in this chapter, chronic job stress may lead to burnout. Along the way, there is spillover onto patient care. Their stress, multiplied by our own, can become highly combustible. Perhaps most frustrating of all is that most of this additional stress is coming from people outside the health care organization who have little or no medical background.

It appears that emotional, informational, and instrumental support can help to reduce job stress and mediate its relationship with burnout. This varies, however, depending on the type and the source of support. In addition, sometimes what appears to be support is actually dysfunctional manipulation by the so-called supporter.

As mentioned earlier in this chapter, there is no shortage of popular books telling us how to enter a health care organization and come out alive. As users of the health care system, we clearly face many new challenges. We may find ourselves fighting for an experimental treatment for a loved one or having to forgo our medication because it's too expensive and not covered by insurance. So far, little actual research has examined the relationship of these factors to communication and successful outcomes as determined by patient health, not by dollar amount (although ideally both would happen). Clearly, however, in most cases providers are as frustrated with the changes in health care as we are. Their goal of providing quality care is thwarted. Their stresses are more likely to be chronic and to impact our care. At a broader level, changes in health care are impacting who chooses medicine as a career and who remains in it. We are in the midst of a turbulent transformation, and the best we can do is to be enlightened, to listen to those who have been through it, and to watch the evolution of health care in the United States.

## KEY TERMS

corporatization of health care

managed care

prospective system

cost containment

health maintenance organizations (HMOs)

capitation

Medicare HMOs

preferred provider organizations (PPOs)

fee-for-service

organizational communication

intraorganizational stress

job stress

emotional labor

empathic concern

emotional contagion

extraorganizational stress

instrumental support

informational support

interorganizational stress

dirty work

burnout

emotional exhaustion

depersonalization

lack of personal accomplishment

support as commodity

support as information retrieval

support as codependency

support as hegemony

## DISCUSSION QUESTIONS

1. What is managed care? What are some of the different types? Compare it with fee-for-service. What are some of the strengths of each? What are some of the weaknesses?

2. How might different sources and types of support interact to be perceived as the most supportive? To be perceived as the least supportive?

3. What are some issues you need to address if you or a loved one is entering a health care organization, such as a hospital, nursing home, or rehabilitation center?

4. What, if any, are some advantages of job stress? What are some of its disadvantages? What, if any, are some advantages of burnout? What are some of its disadvantages?

5. What are some potential conflicts of interest for health care providers working in managed care systems? Are these inevitable or avoidable? Why?

## INFOTRAC COLLEGE EDITION

1. Read Mary K. Pratt's 2001 article, "'Differentiation' Is Key Word for Health Plans' Marketers." What are some of the recent public health care campaigns you've seen? Who and what were they targeting? Were they persuasive? What are some of the conceptions people have about managed care that a campaign would have to address? What are some of the implications of health care organizations advertising to get patients?

2. Read Tom Majeski's 1995 article, "Chaplains Try to Keep Pace with Patients as Hospital Stays Get Shorter." What is your reaction to this article? What implicit values of those managing health care are reflected in the concerns raised in this article? How do chaplains have to adapt their communication to meet the new demands? Can you think of any additional adaptations that could be used?

# 11

## Empowering Citizens and Advocating Issues

**Scar**
A gray day in February
Some flecks of white
But mostly brown
Purple surprises
riding in on a nerve
Begins to excite you
before it settles down

It's after the knives and
the sutures and needles
I'm left with an arrow that
points at my heart

I call it the seat of my
sentimental sorrow
Gone seems to be one of
the sum of my parts

And the night is cold
as the coldest nights are
There's a wise woman, she
comes from an evening star
She says, "Look for the signs,
you won't have to look far
Lead with your spirit and
follow, follow your scar."

A man I knew once said
he wanted to see me
I said I'd been sick
but was on the mend
I told him a few
of the overall details
He said, "That's too bad."
And he's never called me again

What a gift in disguise,
that poor little puppy
So scared of misfortune
and always on guard
A big man will love you
even more when you're hurtin'
And a really big man
loves a really good scar.

'Cause the dawn breaks
and it's breaking your heart
There's a wise woman she
sits at the end of the bar
She says, "Look for the signs,
you won't have to look far
Lead with your sprit and
follow, follow your scar"

A gray day in February
Some flecks of white
But mostly brown
The world has tilted but
the world has expanded
And the world has turned
my world upside down.

'Cause the night is
warm and all full of stars
There's a wise woman
she's moved right
into my heart

She says "Look for the signs,
you won't have to look far
Lead with your spirit
and follow, follow,
Follow . . . your scar."

CARLY SIMON (2000)

If we are to translate the silence surrounding breast cancer into language and action, then the first step is that women with mastectomies must become visible to each other, for silence and invisibility go hand in hand with powerlessness.

(LORDE, 1980, p. 61)

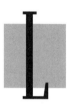aura Evans, an apparently healthy, fit woman in her mid-thirties, found a lump on her breast and went to her doctor. He did a mammogram and told her it was nothing to worry about; she went home reassured and relieved. A few months later, however, Laura found a second lump under her arm. This time, she had a surgical biopsy performed, was diagnosed with cancer, and was told she had only a 15 percent chance of survival. Determined to fight the disease in her own way, she climbed Mt. Kiliminjaro as part of her physical and spiritual recovery. During that experience, she and her mountain-climbing guide conceived the idea of Expedition Inspiration, a climb to the top of Mt. Aconcagua in Argentina to be made by a group of breast cancer survivors. Rising 23,000 feet, snow-covered Aconcagua is one of the highest and most formidable mountains in the world.

As the expedition became reality, it was chronicled through participants' reports to the media as well as by a documentary film later shown on public TV ("Expedition Inspiration," 1995). Laura and six other survivors comprised the Summit Team, those who would attempt to climb to the top of the mountain. Eleven other survivors comprised the Trek Team, those who would climb to a lower-level base camp and provide emotional support to the summit climbers. The survivors ranged in age from 22 to older than 60.

What was the purpose of Expedition Inspiration? PBS commentator Bill Curtis explained that it represented two climbs, one literal and one symbolic. He compared the process of getting to the top of one of the world's tallest, most rugged mountains to the struggle to conquer breast cancer: "It takes the same energy, the same courage. If they [the women] can reach one summit, science can reach the other."[1] The expedition group members discussed many kinds of motivation. At a personal level, the adventure was a celebration of life, an affirmation that, despite surgeries, chemotherapy, and debilitating side effects, they were still alive and able to take part in this incredible experience. Beyond this, the women wanted to convey to the public that breast cancer is not an automatic death sentence, that people do survive and go on to live fully. They wished to call attention to the topic, to stimulate public discussion and support, and to raise awareness, which they hoped would save lives. The oldest team member wanted people to know that 70 percent of women with this disease are over the age of 60. Another woman participated "in honor of kids who've lost a mother to breast cancer." Another wished to represent younger women as well as those who have suffered a recurrence, as she had, emphasizing that it did not connote "the beginning of the end." Tributes to others, both living and dead, were an essential aspect of this journey. At base camp, the Trek Team displayed a long string of colorful Himalayan prayer flags, each one dedicated to a woman who had suffered or died from breast cancer. Each member of the Summit Team carried personal mementos given to her by others, including gifts from young children, in support of their cause—what Curtis called "totems of spiritual connection"—to leave at the top of the mountain.

The goal these survivors set for themselves was extremely difficult and dangerous as well as exhilarating. They invested a great deal of time and effort in preparation before going to Argentina, then struggled against the difficulties in breathing, weakness, headaches, and swelling that are symptomatic of mountain sickness (problems that required two of the Summit Team to turn back before reaching the top) in addition to severe winds and a snowstorm. Yet, as the summit guide observed, these people were sufficiently strong to endure such hardships because of the illness and harsh treatments that they had already experienced. Many, like Laura, had already surpassed their predicted chances of survival. Their belief was that conquering Aconcagua would serve as a bulwark, an inspiration for others to keep going. As one member of the Summit Team said while pushing against the gale-force wind, "[Women who have just been diagnosed] are having their own windy day. . . . If I'm hurting, they're hurting." Thus, reaching the summit was a triumph, both personally and for the whole group, as well as a symbol for everyone touched by this disease. As Curtis concluded the narrative of Expedition Inspiration, "The summit may seem far out of reach, but it's not. . . . You get there one step at a time. And you are never alone."

Throughout this text, we have highlighted several specific kinds of **communication competencies,** combinations of knowledge and skills aimed at enabling

---

[1]All quotes used in this discussion are from "Expedition Inspiration" (1995).

you to better navigate the health care system and to become an effective health citizen. These have included competencies in understanding how health issues help to shape our sense of public and private identity (Chapter 2); interacting cross-culturally (Chapter 3); applying insights about the power dynamics within health care situations (Chapter 4); meeting the communicative challenges of health crises arising through birthing, childhood, and adolescence (Chapters 5 and 6); coping with disability and chronic illness (Chapter 7); communicating about dying and death (Chapter 8); evaluating health information (Chapter 9); and strategizing within the complexities of health care organizations (Chapter 10). In this final chapter, we concentrate on improving your own sense of empowerment and advocating on your own behalf, as a member of a larger community, and for the health issues about which you feel most strongly. We begin by defining key terminology, then take a closer look at health activism in three contexts—patienthood, community well-being, and political advocacy.

## ACTIVISM, ADVOCACY, AND EMPOWERMENT

Climbing mountains may be the extreme in **health activism,** but it is an interesting example of the wide range of behaviors people have chosen for becoming consciously engaged in health-related issues. We use the word *activism* in this book to mean how individuals become actively engaged in:

- Taking responsibility for their own health maintenance and care.

- Working to improve health conditions for a defined group or community.

- Making efforts to change and improve policies and standards that affect large populations.

In recent years, activism has taken a wide variety of creative forms, including public demonstrations; written essays and poetry, art exhibits, and films; political lobbying; foot races and other sports events; fund-raising of all sorts; and special items of attire, such as caps, t-shirts, and jewelry, with both literal and symbolic messages. We would also add to this list other, less visible behaviors, such as maintaining personal files that document key events in one's health history, asking for clearer explanations from health professionals, and helping a friend or family member to cope with a health crisis. Activism, by its very nature, is an effort to exert influence and to make one's voice heard for the purpose of bettering the status quo. Not always, but frequently, such endeavors are grassroots activities, undertakings beginning from the bottom up as opposed to top-down actions taken by those in official or authoritative positions.

A specific type of activism is **advocacy,** in which actions are taken in support of a specific cause, such as a disease or disability like muscular dystrophy or spinal cord injury or a health care issue like universal health insurance. Health advocacy is often political, because it tends to focus on changes in legislation and other forms of policy or funding allocations. Health advocacy has been in existence for at least the past century, especially in the form of voluntary organizations such as the American Heart Association or the March of Dimes, which have worked to provide services for those afflicted as well as to help raise money for medical research. In the past two decades, however, the voices of citizen-activists have become more distinct in terms of influencing matters that had formerly been the sole concerns of biomedical scientists, clinical practitioners, and professional public health experts, such as standards of care, research priorities, and health-related legislation. FYI 11.1 gives a historical background to the evolution of contemporary health activism.

Some of the most recognizable and influential advocates are people with celebrity status, such as the actors Christopher Reeve, whose work on behalf of spinal cord injuries we discussed in Chapter 2, and Michael J. Fox, who decided to forego work in a popular, award-winning TV series to devote time to his family and working toward a cure for Parkinson's disease (Cowley, 2000). Several other well-known people who suffer from Parkinson's, such as former Attorney General Janet Reno, Pope John Paul II, and international sports hero Muhammad Ali, have remained very much in the public eye even while visibly experiencing the tremors and stiffness that are characteristic of this degenerative disease. In consciously deciding to become an advocate for this cause, however, Fox has gone further, appearing before Congress to ask for funding increases that he feels are necessary to find a cure and arguing in favor of stem cell research. Fox has also appeared on TV and magazine covers, and worked with the Parkinson's Action Network (recently renamed the Michael J. Fox Foundation for Parkinson's Research) to produce public service announcements that will raise social awareness, as well as a Web site to provide information. In taking these steps, Fox, like Christopher Reeve, is using his likeable, widely recognized media persona to destigmatize his condition and to work toward an eventual remedy. In doing so, he joins the efforts of hundreds, even thousands, of other noncelebrity citizens actively working toward the same ends. It's important to realize, however, that the prominence celebrities bring to health issues may eventually become a double-edged sword insofar as diseases and health problems must compete among themselves for limited health care dollars (Kalb, 2000; Sharf, 2001). Additional research funds for one disease can come at the expense of funding an equally devastating disease.

*Photo reprinted courtesy of Michael J. Fox.*

As we've stated throughout this text, all of us, whether as citizens or as those who work in the health professions, are touched by health issues. Thus, health professionals also may choose to become advocates. For instance, the group Physicians for Social Responsibility has for many years championed nuclear disarmament and, more recently, gun control legislation as a strategy for reducing global and domestic violence, which that group defines as a menacing threat to

The concept of health activism was heightened and changed forever with the advent of the AIDS epidemic in the 1980s. Initially, this disease was first identified with gay (male homosexual) communities in large cities, but gays were eventually followed by other "at-risk" groups, such as hemophiliacs and intravenous drug users. Until the retrovirus that caused AIDS was identified, allowing medications to be developed to treat the disease, every person who became infected died, usually within a few years. As the number of fatalities increased rapidly, the general population responded with extreme fear, and people who became infected were treated as outcasts. Scientists at the Centers for Disease Control and Prevention worked with local public health officials and clinicians to solve the mysteries of what the virus was and how it was transmitted, but their efforts remained severely underfunded for several years while then-President Reagan and other federal leaders seemingly appeared to be indifferent to the devastation (Shilts, 1987). Clearly, the gay community had to organize to help itself. Some of the earliest activist groups worked to provide services and housing for the sick and to develop public health education about lifestyle changes that were needed to curb the tide of infection.

As the death toll mounted and those afflicted were socially stigmatized (a few states like Colorado even tried to enact mandatory quarantines), some AIDS advocates felt that more "in your face," confrontational tactics were needed. Probably best known among these activist groups is ACT UP (AIDS Coalition to Unleash Power), which was founded in New York in 1987 and has chapters in many locations today. Self-described as "a diverse, non-partisan group of individuals united in anger and committed to direct action to end the AIDS crisis" (ACT UP New York Web site) with the motto "silence = death," ACT UP used attention-grabbing, irreverent—some said outrageous—tactics, such as exaggerated theatrics, ironic language, masked identities, and social disruptions to draw public attention SILENCE = DEATH to key issues and to force responses from pharmaceutical companies, government officials, and scientific researchers. Rhetorical critics Adrienne Christiansen and Jeremy Hanson (1996) argue that the effectiveness of this strategy stemmed from framing the tragedy of this disease in a comic way. While their actions offended some onlookers, they also produced increased funding, a faster drug-approval process, and other important accomplishments.

Nonviolent demonstrations have been interwoven throughout American history, from the Boston Tea Party to Dr. King's civil rights bus boycott and March on Washington to the student strikes against the War in Vietnam. ACT UP, however, with its predominantly—and openly—gay membership, introduced protest and political action into health care, and as health advocacy groups proliferate, things haven't been the same since.

public health. The American Academy of Pediatrics focuses on advocacy for children, with programs promoting such topics as breastfeeding, child safety seats, infant immunizations, literacy promotion, and firearms injury prevention.

A byproduct of health activism is the self-perception of **empowerment,** that is, feeling more powerful and in control of our own lives because we have chosen to devote time, energy, and resources to bettering the health-related problems that have an impact on ourselves and those we care about. Conversely, **disempowerment** is the feeling of having little or no control, that one's life is being determined by other people or circumstances beyond one's influence. Empowerment is a popular term nowadays that has been discussed in various ways. One feminist researcher (Shields, 1995) identifies three central themes in women's individual experiences of empowerment: (a) connectedness to other women, (b) an internal sense of self, and (c) a resulting ability to take action. Brazilian educator Paulo Freire (1970), who dedicated himself to the psychological liberation of poor and oppressed people, focused on the importance of consciousness (*conscientizacáo* in Portuguese), the bringing into our awareness factors that we have not previously realized. Sharry Erzinger (1994), a public health consultant in Latin America, points out that the Spanish language has no equivalent term for empowerment, because *power* in that language connotes authorities—especially the military—dominating others. More appropriate translations include such terms as self-determination (*auto-determinación*) and self-esteem (*auto-estima*). She also points out that, in Latin America, individuals do not stand alone; rather, people think of themselves within the context of family and community. Thus, another word used by community groups in relation to the notion of empowerment is appropriation (*apropiación*), meaning to make this issue ours.

In a study that I (Barbara) conducted about Internet communication on the Breast Cancer Listserv, empowerment was operationalized as the ways in which feedback from other people enabled individuals to make more informed decisions and to take actions that they might not have otherwise (Sharf, 1997). Subscribers to this listserv supplied me with specific examples of how they felt empowered through their participation, including being better informed, having their feelings validated by other survivors, reassurance that life continues after the diagnosis, and the abilities to mobilize action and to influence others. Reflected in the song lyrics that began this chapter, popular singer and songwriter Carly Simon speaks of the hard-earned empowerment that resulted from her own breast cancer experience. She tells us that she has learned to trust in her own spirit despite negative reactions from others and, perhaps, because of the pain and the scar that is a constant reminder of the ordeal she has survived. Theorizing Practice 11.1 asks you to think about how empowerment has played out in your own health-related experiences.

In the next section, we examine how the ideas of advocacy and empowerment have activated patients to communicate in new and assertive ways. We give special emphasis to patienthood competencies, concerned with how to most effectively interact with your health care providers, and health consumer competen-

## Power Play

Describe a health-related situation in which you have felt empowered. What factors helped you to feel this way? What actions did you take? What impact did the feeling of empowerment have on your health? Do you continue to feel empowered? If not, why?

Now consider a situation in which you have felt disempowered. What differences existed between these circumstances versus those of the first situation that you described? As you think about being disempowered in retrospect, is there anything you would have chosen to say or do differently that might have changed the situation for the better?

cies, concerned with maximizing coordination among the varied segments of health care and maintenance.

# BEING A PROACTIVE PATIENT: THE ROLE OF HEALTH PARTNER

A few years ago, the popular newsmagazine *Newsweek* began carrying a feature called "Patient Power," which headlines articles about what patients can do to manage—and to improve—the quality of their health care. This is one very public sign of a change that has been ongoing in the relationship between patients, physicians, and other health care providers. Traditionally, the state of **patienthood** has not been associated with having much power. Patients, perceived both by themselves and by health professionals as being in a vulnerable and dependent condition, are expected to report their complaints, which a health professional then evaluates and classifies with a diagnosis. Having determined what is wrong, the provider issues an order or a prescription, with which a "good" patient is expected to comply. Patients who are perceived as being uncooperative or irresponsible are still widely labeled as **noncompliant** in the medical context, a term that carries a very negative connotation among health professionals (Heymann, 1995).

Research indicates, however, that noncompliant individuals are not at all uncommon: "Estimates of noncompliance [in taking medications] range from 20% among patients who are required to follow a short-term treatment for an acute, symptomatic problem, to 50% for a longer-term, symptomatic condition (e.g., arthritis), and up to 70% or more for a long-term, asymptomatic condition requiring lifestyle change [e.g., high cholesterol]" (Schooler & Henderson, 2000, sec. 1,

p. 2, citing Sherbourne, Hays, Ordway, DiMatteo, & Kravitz, 1992). **Mindful non-adherence** (Brashers, Haas, & Neidig, 1999a) is a concept that implies patients may have their own well-considered reasons for not following through on practitioners' recommendations. Such reasons may include difficult side effects from prescribed medications, differing perceptions about the nature of the problem, lack of trust between the practitioner and patient, and problems incorporating medical recommendations within the patient's everyday life. Health communication researchers Sharon Hammond and Bruce Lambert (1994) point out that a good deal of noncompliance stems from lack of information and poor explanations.

As a result of a complex combination of social, political, and economic factors that include the increasing shift of care for chronic illnesses to the home, bureaucratization of health care systems, availability of health-related information through a variety of mass media, and questioning attitudes toward biomedical authority, patients have concurrently assumed a greater responsibility—and a greater voice—concerning the health care decisions affecting them. We call this competency of being more aware and better prepared to play a role in the medical encounter and one's own health care being a **proactive patient.** Communication researcher Dale Brashers and his associates (Brashers et al., 1999a; Brashers & Klingle, 1992) have identified three dimensions of this competency: (a) increased education or knowledge about one's health problems; (b) increased assertiveness, especially with one's health practitioners; and (c) the potential for mindful nonadherence, that is, the choice to reject treatments or to be noncompliant when treatments fail to meet the patient's expectations. Most of us have been noncompliant with health authorities' recommendations from time to time. Theorizing Practice 11.2 asks you to consider the circumstances and reasons of your own choice to resist compliance.

It can be difficult to gauge the technical expertise of the doctors we go to with our health problems, but most people have definite opinions about the interpersonal skills of their health providers—their capacities to listen, to empathize, and to explain (Cegala, Socha McGee, & McNeilis, 1996). In Chapter 4, we examined a wide variety of factors that may influence the nature and the quality of patient-provider relationships; these understandings come from more than 30 years of research on this subject. As a result, some form of communication training is now included in the education of nearly every kind of health professional who has direct contact with patients. More recently, attention is being given to the notion that the communication abilities of patients may also be honed to make a difference (Cegala, 1997; Sharf, 1987). We now take a closer look at the potential of proactive patients to be health care partners during interactions with practitioners. In particular, we look at the communicative behaviors associated with this role.

Contemporary medical ethics and health law stress the importance of physicians, nurses, and other health professionals respecting patient autonomy, that is,

## To Comply or Not to Comply—That Is the Question!

The word *noncompliance* is widely used by health professionals to refer to the behavior of patients who refuse a recommended treatment or do not follow through on what the provider believed was an agreed-on plan to manage a health problem or to promote or maintain a healthy condition. Because the term connotes obeying a command or an order, it implicitly assumes the compliant patient to be a relatively passive participant in the health care transaction, a person who does what she is told. Conversely, the noncompliant patient who does not do as she is instructed (for her own good) is viewed as problematic, as a negative element in the health care environment. Recently, however, the word has come under scrutiny and criticism, with many scholars and practitioners searching for a phrase that will denote the patient as a more equal and active partner. Suggested replacements have included *adherence* and *cooperation,* the idea being that people are more likely to adhere to or cooperate with a management plan that they helped to develop.

Think back to a specific incident in which you decided *not* to comply with the recommendation of a physician, other practitioner, or public health message, and then consider the questions that follow. Examples of such incidents might include stopping antibiotics when you started to feel better rather than continuing throughout the prescribed ten-day period, not returning for a requested follow-up appointment, driving your car after having had a beer or a mixed drink, or having unprotected sex.

- Why did you decide to go against the advice of a health authority?
- Would you make the same decision again? If so, why? If not, why not?
- Did you/would you feel okay discussing this incident (after the fact) with your primary care practitioner? With your family? With close friends? In each case, why, or why not?
- Under what circumstances do you think medical noncompliance is justified? Under what circumstances is it a bad idea?
- If you disagree with a health provider during a clinical visit, are you willing to state your disagreement? How do you typically handle this situation?

patients' rights and abilities to make decisions that determine the most appropriate of the health care options provided to them. The principle of autonomy is especially salient when the provider and the patient hold different views of how treatment should proceed. This principle, however, doesn't speak to the processes of relationship and interchange—in other words, communication. Therefore, we prefer to highlight the concept of **partnership** between patients and health care professionals. From a partnership perspective, both parties see themselves as competent and responsible to collaboratively produce mutually acceptable solutions to the health problems afflicting the patient. Timothy Quill, an internist who has written extensively on the patient-physician relationship, was one of the earliest to use the term *partnership,* which he envisioned as a kind of contract that is developed though interaction. According to Quill (1983), to qualify as a partnership, both participants must have unique responsibilities, be willing to negotiate, and gain something through the interchange. Jody Heymann (1995), a pediatrician, is especially interested in the notion of promoting patient-doctor partnerships because of her own experience with suffering through a dangerous brain tumor surgery and a lengthy recuperation just weeks after her graduation from Harvard Medical School. She recommends a partnership model that gives prominence to patient voices not only in clinical interactions but in treatment decisions and medical education as well (Heymann & Kerr, 2000). Health providers bring to this relationship specialized knowledge of disease, diagnostic technologies, treatment options, and prevention strategies. Patients bring specialized knowledge of their own bodily sensations, lifestyles and stressors, resources and limitations, and family and community contexts. A combination of both kinds of knowledge is needed for medical problem solving that patients can incorporate and sustain in their daily lives (Sharf, 1984).

A number of communication skills have been identified that enable individuals to enact the role of partner in their interactions with health professionals (Street, 2001). As you read through the following descriptions of these skills, think of your own experiences in interacting with health care providers. To what degree are you consciously aware of practicing these behaviors? Which behaviors have you intentionally attempted to use with some success? Which behaviors have you attempted that have been less successful? Are there some that you've never considered at all? What resources do you think would be helpful in increasing your abilities to be an effective health partner?

### ■ Agenda-setting

Too often, patients leave a health care encounter feeling that they haven't had a chance to talk about all their concerns. This can happen for many reasons. There is a tendency to focus on the first problem that is mentioned or on the one that the health professional feels is most important. Sometimes patients have difficulty due to fear or embarrassment of mentioning what is most troubling to them (for example, "Does this genital pain mean that I have a sexually transmitted disease?"). In addition, administrative pressure is increasing in many health care environments to keep these encounters brief, so that if patients have, for example, three concerns that they wish to discuss, there may be an opportunity to address only one of these in sufficient detail. Therefore, it is crucial for patients to think out in advance of the interview which items they wish to bring to their provider's attention and to be able to lay these out at the beginning of the interview. A program called Consultation Planning and Recording at the University of California at San Francisco is being developed for just this purpose. In addition, patients with breast cancer who received help in setting an agenda before seeing their doctors, as well as a summary of the clinical visit afterward, were more satisfied and felt they had made better-quality decisions about complicated treatments than did patients who did not participate in this experimental program (Sepucha, Belkora, Tripathy, Esserman, & Aviv, 2000).

Stating your concerns up front does not ensure that they will all be addressed, but this initial communication does invite health professionals to respond with their own priorities. For example, you may wish to discuss an annoying cough that has continued despite medications prescribed at your last visit as well as several recent incidents of digestive upset. The physician acknowledges your concerns and also brings up the desirability of getting a flu shot. With each participant's items "on the table," an agenda can be jointly formulated in terms of what can be dealt with during the current encounter (for example, re-evaluating the nature and severity of the cough and getting the flu shot) and what less-urgent items can be dealt with during a successive appointment (for example, advice to keep a written record of foods that seem to be associated with the stomach upsets until the digestive problem can be more fully addressed at a future visit).

## Sharing Information

As we've already noted, each partner in a health care interaction brings specific kinds of information that are necessary for effective medical problem solving. It is the job of proactive patients to "tell the story" of their health status or complaints. After all, no one but you can describe the pain or discomfort that you may be feeling; the travel or life stress or change in routine that occurred in conjunction with your symptoms; or the contextual factors of home, job, community, and culture that may influence your efforts in health maintenance. Though you seek the services of health professionals to evaluate or to help prevent specific problems, your own "explanatory model" of your health status may be very helpful in achieving these objectives.

This is not to say that telling your story is necessarily an easy task. Most contemporary texts on clinical interviewing instruct students of the health professions to elicit patients' narratives, but in practice, many still use a series of closed-ended, checklist-type questions to obtain a patient's medical history, statement of the current problem(s), and review of body systems. If a patient fails to provide information in ways that fit with a clinician's expectations (for example, key events arranged in chronological order), she may be labeled as a "poor historian." On the other hand, some patients are not very forthcoming with the information they possess; not crediting themselves with having special knowledge, they expect the health provider to figure out what is going on. As always, time constraints also present another limitation. You won't always be able to predict—or to influence—the communication style of your clinicians, but you can be well prepared for your own contribution to the interaction. In short, it is important to be able to tell your story succinctly yet assertively, highlighting those factors that describe your concerns, symptoms, and ideas about what is going on. Effective practitioners will ask you questions that help to complete the story in ways that may help them to understand well enough to help you (Stewart et al., 1995).

## ■ Questioning

The traditional format of a medical interview is for the physician, nurse, or other health professional to ask questions that are designed to elicit pertinent information from the patient. A significant aspect missing from this picture is the patient's questions that facilitate the provider's explanations and clarifications, enabling the patient to understand the biomedical problems and issues as well as the treatment options to be considered or an agreed-on plan of management. Until recently, clinical training has been remiss in emphasizing the importance of making explanations (Whaley, 2000), and patients have not been well prepared to ask questions. In addition to the critical element of power differential between patient and provider—it is often difficult to question an individual who is perceived as having special expertise regarding your health—not feeling well or being fearful about one's state of health can also deter patients from asking questions. The inability of providers to give clear explanations, as well as the lack of demand for sufficient information by patients, has had serious results for patients, including lack of understanding about side effects from medication, impact of treatment, and confusion about whom to approach for help (Heymann & Kerr, 2000).

Within the past two decades, research has indicated that patients who receive preparatory training in understanding their medical record, in the logic of medical decision making, and in asking questions about their concerns not only ask more questions during their visits with physicians (Roter, 1977) but also experience improved health outcomes, including briefer recovery from illness, decreased discomfort, improvement in chronic symptoms, and decreased need for medication (Kaplan et al., 1989). In other words, with increased awareness and practice in questioning skills, proactive patients achieve a more equitable partnership with health providers and have better long-term results in health status (Street, 2001).

When is it appropriate for you to ask questions of a health practitioner? Whenever you find the technical terminology to be mystifying or need a better explanation of a diagnosis, test result, or recommended treatment. Whenever you have ideas of your own that may affect your health condition, such as hypotheses about problems, the usefulness of over-the-counter remedies and complementary modes of healing, or new approaches you have been alerted to via the mass media, the Internet, or interpersonal contacts. Your goal should be to voice such questions and concerns before ending your conversation with the provider. It is natural, however, for more questions to occur after a clinical encounter, so you may need to continue with subsequent queries during the next appointment or with a follow-up phone call or note. When the health issue at stake is complex or of an especially serious nature, many people find it helpful to talk through their questions with a trusted friend or family member first and then bring a written list of questions to the clinical visit. Again, there is no guarantee that a particular practitioner will give satisfactory responses to your questions, but clearly, not raising those questions has negative consequences.

## Negotiating Decisions

Decisions about how to attempt to solve medical problems are made in many ways. In the traditional model of physician-patient relationships, the doctor makes a decision and instructs the patient what to do next. Many people still prefer to defer entirely to the health professional's authority and expertise. Others will do so under certain conditions, such as when they trust that practitioner completely, when the approach to treatment seems exceedingly simple or exceedingly confusing, or when they feel too ill to do much thinking on their own.

The traditional stance, however, has gradually been challenged and changed over many years. There also are more treatment options to choose among, nearly all of which have inherent benefits and risks involving the primary illness, problematic side effects, and changes in quality of life. Physicians remain respected authorities (we all want our own doctors to be excellent!), but we also now realize that they are not the only source of health information nor are they omnipotent.

This change in patients' attitudes has been reflected in the research literature. One often-cited survey of patients indicated that most people wanted to know as much information as possible about their health conditions, but that many stopped short of wanting to make key decisions (Strull, Lo, & Charles, 1984). A more contemporary study, however, indicates that a majority of North American patients now think medical decision making should be a shared, participatory process (Deber, Kraetschmer, & Irvine,1996). Cross-cultural studies indicate that the same trend toward patient participation can be found in China, Hong Kong, and Australia (Bennett, Smith, & Irwin, 1999). Increasingly, physicians are aware that trust with their patients may be better served by working together to devise a reasonable course of medical management that is effective, feasible, and desirable within the scale of the patient's life values.

At times, patient priorities may differ considerably from the treatment course that providers perceive as being most efficacious from a biomedical perspective. These differences between health professionals and patients of how best to proceed may be due to a variety of underlying factors, such as cultural beliefs (see Chapter 3 ), credibility of information (see Chapter 9), and how we wish to identify ourselves in terms of core values and public personas (see Chapter 2). For example, consider a star professional basketball player who had planned on a 15-year career in the NBA but sustains a number of joint injuries during his first seven years. His physician advises that, in the best interests of his long-term health, he should quit the game as soon as possible. In discussing this advice, the player considers such factors as the likelihood of future injuries, the medical therapies available, his concern for his family's well-being, and his own psychological happiness. In the end, the player decides to limit his professional career to one more season, during which he agrees to participate in a special physical therapy program aimed at strengthening the joints judged to be most at-risk for future injury. His choice limits—but does not eliminate—the health dangers, acknowledges his respect for the doctor's advice, yet honors his own values and needs.

There are many such differences of opinion in which life concerns may conflict with medical judgments. Instead of a stand-off directed at right and wrong, the health of patients is better served by, when possible, **negotiated decision making,** which provides a degree of mutual (if imperfect) satisfaction for each person who participates. In some circumstances, other participants, such as various health care specialists, the patient's family, or even a medical ethicist or spiritual advisor, may be invited into the decision-making discussion. Negotiation in this context requires that both patient and provider make clear statements about their preferences and their underlying reasoning. They must be willing to listen to the other's point of view with openness, respect, and an effort to understand implicit values and priorities. Of course, not all decision making will be resolved in a manner equally satisfying to all participants. For instance, in the example of the basketball player, the physician may remain convinced that even one more season of play could prove substantially detrimental to the player's health, but negotiation offers the opportunity for *mutual* influence between patient and providers (Smith & Pettegrew, 1986) and a full hearing of various perspectives as part of the decision-making process.

Theorizing Practice 11.3 asks you to apply your understanding of the elements of proactive patient competency to a real-life clinical interchange.

## Doctor–Patient Talk: You Be the Judge!

The following conversation is an excerpt from an actual clinical interchange between a patient and a physician. The patient (P) is a middle-aged woman who has been diagnosed with rheumatoid arthritis, a serious, chronic disease that typically accelerates over time. She is suffering with chronic pain as well as experiencing multiple side effects from the prescribed drugs. The doctor (D) is a young male resident (a doctor-in-training) who is seeing the patient in the outpatient clinic in the absence of her regularly assigned doctor. Once you've read through the interchange, consider the questions that follow.

D: When you say no relief of pain, it [prescribed medication] hasn't helped at all?

P: No.

D: Did it ever help when you were on three of them [medications] at one time?

P: No. . . . I'm constantly in pain. The only time I'm not in pain is when he [the other doctor] gives me shots and then I'm pain-free for a week to a week and a half, and then I'm back in pain.

D: Has your pain been worse than it is now?

P: On a scale of one to ten, I'm at a ten all the time. . . . It's one continuous flare-up.

D: Are you saying it's worse?

P: It hasn't gotten any better.

D: So it's stabilized then?

P: If you want to call pain constantly, I guess you can call it stabilized. I don't call it stabilized. I call it being in constant pain. If you're taking three drugs, I can't understand why the pain's not gone.

D: The reason is—

P: (*voice rising*) What is this medication doing besides nothing for me because it's not relieving the pain. And it certainly isn't—and you can look at my hands—taking the swelling down.

D: First of all, the medications that we have is not a cure-all.

P: I know that.

D: Just because we're giving you medication doesn't mean it will cure your rheumatoid arthritis.

P: There is no cure for it.

D: Of course. All the medications do is help control the disease and try to help to prevent it from getting any worse. Now, the thing is we don't have control of the weather. There are other reasons like stress . . . that can cause re-exacerbations. So those are hard to control. All the medications are really gonna do at this point is to try and control it and minimize it as much as possible. The ideal situation is to have you be pain-free, but we may never have you pain-free.

*(continued)*

---

*(continued from previous page)*

P: That's terrible!

D: Well, that's terrible, but that's what the disease is all about. . . . We may increase the medication . . . to help stabilize it, but you will always have the disease.

P: Well, I know that I will always have the disease, but what I'm thinking is why do I have to be in so much pain with the disease? There's other diseases out there that people have that are ten times worse than rheumatoid arthritis, the doctors can give 'em pills and they're not in as much pain as what I'm in all the time.

D: One of the things you have to understand that makes our job kind of hard is that not only is every disease different, but every patient is different, too. And every patient has a different pain tolerance. . . .

P: I think the whole medication should be changed and I should be on something different. It's not arresting this and it's not slowing this down because for—I've had rheumatoid arthritis for over three years now and first it was in my right side, my hand and my foot. Now, this summer, it has come into both elbows and into my left hand and my left foot. So the medication that I'm taking, doesn't seem to me like it's slowing it down. So I do think that I need to be put on a different medication.

D: . . . So your main concern is getting this pain under control.

P: Right.

D: Bringing it down from a ten to at least a five.

- Clearly, the doctor and the patient are expressing different points of view about the patient's problem. How would you summarize each person's understanding of the situation?

- How competent is this patient in terms of being proactive? In what ways, if any, do you see the communicative skills of agenda-setting, question asking, information sharing, and negotiating decisions being used in this interchange?

- Do you judge this conversation to fit the concept of a partnership? Why, or why not?

(Adapted from Sharf, Stanford, Montgomery, & Kahler, 1998)

# BEING A PROACTIVE HEALTH CONSUMER: INFORMATION COORDINATION AND SELF-ADVOCACY

To be a patient implies that one is being cared for by a health professional, but much that we do for ourselves regarding health does not specifically depend on our relationships with health care providers. From this perspective, we are

**consumers of health information and health services,** including both mainstream and complementary practices. We engage in activities that we expect will promote well-being or facilitate health care. As with patienthood, specific communication skills enable us to be proactive consumers on our own behalf.

## Coordinating Health Information

One form of health information that may be critical to the care we receive over time is our written health records. In today's world, however, people move to take new jobs; switch doctors, clinics, or hospitals due to personal preference or changes in insurance coverage; and receive health care from a variety of specialists. Therefore, it is unwise to assume that our personal health information will be accessible whenever or wherever it is needed. We should request and keep copies of diagnostic test results, inoculations, radiological imaging reports, and prescribed medication records. Some health analysts even suggest requesting a copy of the chart notes after each clinical visit (Spragins, 1997). In other words, it is important to understand our own health histories and to maintain a repository of our own health records. After all, at some key point in time, consumers may be the only people who can produce an accurate history and holistic picture of their own health status. While different health facilities have a variety of procedures for requesting copies of medical records, all of us should keep in mind that these records contain information specific to us that we (or our insurance company) have paid for—and we have a right to be able to access them.

A second way in which consumers often act as coordinators of health information is by integrating data and advice received through a wide variety of sources, such as physicians, nurses, pharmacists, chiropractors, neighbors, media news reports, books, and the Internet. The way in which such information is brought to our attention and understood often becomes a primary basis for significant health decisions. Given the complexity and ever-changing nature of the information now available to us, individuals commonly process such material through interpersonal discussions, not only with providers but also with family, friends, and networks of others who share similar health concerns (Rimal, Ratzan, Arntson, & Freimuth, 1997).

## Advocating in Our Own Self-interest

As we discussed in Chapter 10, we are living in a time of great transition for the organizational structures of health care services. For the vast majority of us, medical care and pharmaceuticals are now "managed" in some way. Both providers and consumers are subject to rules and structures that are geared to the health

## Self-Advocacy and Managed Care

Imagine yourself as the patient/consumer in one of the following situations:

- While taking a shower in the morning, you notice a hard lump on the right side of your throat. You assume it's a swollen lymph node—perhaps just a minor infection—but as the day goes on, you find yourself becoming increasingly anxious, checking the lump every few minutes. You call your health plan, requesting an emergency appointment with Dr. Kohler, your primary care physician, whom you've seen for the past five years (for mostly minor complaints) and with whom you feel quite comfortable. You're told, however, that Dr. Kohler is booked solid for the next week. You can either wait to see him in another eight days or, alternatively, meet today with a nurse specialist whom you've never met before. Now, in addition to being anxious, you feel frustrated and angry.

- You are a committed runner who exercises nearly every day. You feel out of sorts on days when you don't run. Over the past month, however, you've experienced a sharp pain in your left knee that has made running increasingly difficult. In the last three days, the knee has become red and swollen. When you see one of the orthopedic surgeons from your HMO, you ask to have an MRI (magnetic resonance image) done on your knee. The doctor doesn't feel the MRI is necessary; instead, she suggests that you refrain from running and generally keep weight off that knee for at least two weeks. You suspect she is trying to save the health plan money—at your expense.

In either case, what factors will determine if you advocate for the option you think is best for your care? If you decide to complain, what will you say, and to whom? If you decide to accept the other option, why?

---

(Adapted from Levinson et al., 1999)

needs of large populations and to cost constraints. In the best of all worlds, your primary care provider (the health professional you turn to as the first contact for health concerns and problems) would coordinate all your health care, help you to integrate information and make important decisions, and above all, look out for your best interests. Unfortunately, providers who receive reimbursement though corporate structures are increasingly caught in a dilemma of divided loyalties—to their employers' profits, to the needs of their patients, to the needs of the organizational membership at large, and to their own salaries (Degnin, 1999; Emanuel & Dubler, 1995). Thus, consumers must be alert to organizational interests that might conflict with their own, and they must bring their concerns and complaints to the attention of their physicians and health plan administrators.

Representing one's own interests within a health care decision-making process is the essence of **self-advocacy** (Brashers et al., 1999a; Brashers & Klingle, 1992). In other situations, however, we might act as advocates on behalf of family or close friends who are too anxious or ill to negotiate difficult health care dilemmas on their own. Advocating for others often involves helping to formulate key questions about the nature of the diagnosis, the risks and benefits of treatment options, and the quality of case management; accompanying them on clinical visits to provide support and to function as a witness in terms of understanding what transpires; helping to search for information relevant to the situation at hand; and helping to ensure that a hospitalized or institutionalized patient receives timely and adequate care. Theorizing Practice 11.4 invites you to think through the complexities of being one's own advocate through the organizational barriers that are often encountered in managed care situations.

So far, we've discussed empowerment and activism at the individual and interpersonal levels—that is, what you can do for yourself. We now move to issues of public health motivated by the force of people coming together.

## CONCEPTUALIZING COMMUNITY HEALTH

In December 1996, two of us (Patricia and Barbara) traveled to Cuba with a group of ten other U.S. scholars and health practitioners who had been granted a special license to study the health care system of that country. Our interest was based on Cuba's reputation for having an outstanding system of primary and preventive care that has resulted in national health statistics equivalent to those of the United States and other First World countries despite its dire Third World economy brought about by political isolation, aided by the American-enforced embargo. It is not our purpose here to debate the political disparities and historical problems that have separated the two nations for more than 30 years but, instead, to report some firsthand observations regarding community-based health care as practiced in Cuba.

We saw many things that were quite inadequate by American standards: outdated medical equipment; greatly restricted diets, with certain items rationed only to children and pregnant women; an appalling lack of basic supplies and medications; and public health campaigns severely hampered by a scarcity of such necessities as paper on which to print flyers and brochures and condoms with which to enact the safe sex behaviors widely advertised in AIDS prevention posters.

Left: "The Couple's Best Friend," one of several popular AIDS prevention posters used throughout Cuba. Right: Author Patricia Geist Martin (upper left) at a CDR reception.

At the same time, we were favorably impressed by other observations, particularly by how seamlessly health care was integrated within the routine social interactions of communities (Waitzkin, 1991). There is free universal health care. A family doctor and nurse work—and often live—within nearly every city block, apartment complex, or rural community center. At a symbolic level, the family doctor is held up to the populace as one of the main accomplishments of the Cuban Revolution. In terms of ordinary, daily life, family doctors are quite familiar with the 700 individuals (125 families) assigned to each for primary care. Not only do patients come to the physician's office for care, the doctor makes home visits to understand family dynamics and living conditions and work visits to assess occupational health issues. Because medications are so scarce, disease prevention and health promotion are greatly emphasized. In addition, family doctors maintain a health census of their neighborhood and are required to report cases of infectious disease to the government.

The family doctor also works closely with the local community council, called the Committee for the Defense of the Revolution (CDR). This collaboration results in group solutions to individual problems. For example, when a physician in one area had a difficult time convincing an elderly family member about the necessity of a hospitalization, the family, friends, and neighbors joined in the effort to persuade that person to accept proper treatment. In another case, the CDR enlisted community help to provide child care and household help when a high-risk, pregnant mother needed to be hospitalized earlier than her expected delivery date. We were also told that the CDRs take an active role in social health problems, such as negatively sanctioning abusive husbands or teenage girls seeking to make money through prostitution. Concerted efforts are made to train and to rehabilitate people hospitalized for mental illnesses so that they can re-establish residence in home communities. Even the treatment of patients with AIDS is changing from permanent quarantine to encouraging the afflicted to maintain outpatient treatment while living in normal communities.

The Cuban health care system that we observed was a mixed bag. Health care is more available (no long waits for appointments!) but with far fewer resources than most Americans expect. There is also more government intrusiveness than most of us are accustomed to, but we remain impressed with the involvement of local communities and the implicit understanding that home, work, and social networks are all important parts of the health constellation of any individual.

## A Model of Empowered Communities

*Community* is one of those words that is bandied about without much clear understanding of its meaning. We talk about the African-American community, the disability community, the university community, the Shaker Heights (substitute the name of your local neighborhood) community, or the substance abuse community. In recent years, we have increasingly spoken about virtual communities, referring to people who are connected though computer-aided communication. So, what is a community? In this section, we define a community as being geographically bounded, such that members of a particular community share a physical, historical, and social environment and have the potential for face-to-face contact.

Communication researchers Mara Adelman and Larry Frey (1997), who worked with people with AIDS in a communal residence, note that community also implies a common way of viewing the self and others, emotional connection, interdependence, and mutual influence. Thus, **community health** concerns may include infectious diseases that can easily spread within a geographical area, but such concerns also encompass issues of public and personal safety, environmental hazards and resources, adequate shelter and nutrition, accessibility of health services, and a variety of other factors related to both quality of life and longevity. The economic status of a particular community is often equated with the nature of its public health, which frequently justifies our assumptions that conditions in low-income communities are indicators of greater public health problems, such as higher infant mortality, decreased longevity, epidemic substance abuse, more injuries due to gun violence, environmental hazards, and more. Higher socioeconomic status, however, does not necessarily ensure better community health. Consider, for instance, the shocking school gun violence in Columbine, Colorado, or the extremely high rate of breast cancer in Long Island, New York—both of which are solid, middle-class communities.

At the Northwestern University Center for Urban Affairs and Policy Research, social policy analysts John Kretzmann and John McKnight (Kretzmann & McKnight, 1993; McKnight, 1987) observe that many have approached the social health problems of communities through a negative conceptual framework focused on deficits, problems, and needs. Solutions, then, are in the form of institutional services that put community members in the role of dependent clients. Kretzmann and McKnight offer an alternative model that—while acknowledging the existence of problems—emphasizes the capacities, gifts, and assets of community residents. These residents include not only the individual inhabitants, with acceptance of all their resources and fallibilities, but also local institutions, such as schools and libraries, as well as voluntary citizens associations, such as churches and clubs. They explain that this view of community is characterized by a recognition of what individual members can bring to the table, collective effort, informality and spontaneity, rituals of celebration and tragedy, and communication through storytelling.

Similarly, Putnam (2000) refers to the connections among individuals, as they occur in political, civic, social, religious, and workplace participation, as **social capital** (in contrast to the typical use of the word *capital* to denote money or other property, though social capital can still result in financial gain). Such social networks have the potential to promote communicative norms of reciprocity and trustworthiness.

Putnam as well as Kretzmann and McKnight have proposed a perspective of community health that is premised on genuine, internal empowerment of residents, trusting that they can mobilize the resources necessary to deal with the problems they regularly face. This model also incorporates partnership, largely within but also with entities outside the community, such as universities, government agencies, and public health professionals. The processes of change that can arise from such empowering partnerships include the development of self-help mechanisms, specific problem-solving implementation, and basic institutional changes that permanently shift both power and resources to community members (Bracht, Kingsbury, & Rissel, 1999).

Empowerment partnerships that strive to improve the health of communities and assume that communities *are* healthy in terms of their composite assets and capacities are, unfortunately, not as prevalent as deficit models. Nonetheless, such efforts have been implemented and documented in a wide variety of places, including Brazil (Freire, 1970), Canada, New Zealand, Australia (Labonte, 1994), and in urban as well as rural areas throughout the United States.

Westside Health Authority Safe Summer Kickoff at a local play lot. *Courtesy of the Westside Health Authority in Chicago.*

## ■ The Model in Action

One example that we have some personal familiarity with is the WHA (Westside Health Authority) in Chicago. The Westside of Chicago contains neighborhoods with dilapidated buildings and overgrown vacant lots; drug dealers, gang warfare, and a high crime rate; and broken sidewalks as well as rutted streets. Its discouraging health statistics include high infant mortality, increased rates of low-birth-weight babies and teen mothers, and higher incidences of sexually transmitted diseases, AIDS, and tuberculosis than the rest of the city. This is a deficit, problem-focused description of this community.

Community resident and organizer Jacqueline Reed had a different view: "to reach out to those demoralized by urban decay and inspire confidence in their own community, trust in their neighbors, and a commitment to a new vision" (Westside Health Authority Web site). Her plan, strongly defined by social capital, mobilized the community by organizing block leadership; creating networks for employment opportunities, child care, and transportation; and reaffirming community values and standards. The accomplishments of the WHA over the past decade have included raising the funds necessary to purchase a neighborhood hospital that had closed, placing nearly 300 young people in health career opportunities, helping local businesses gain access to potential hospital contracts, and reducing neighborhood violence by an impressive 20 percent.

In one of its newest initiatives, called Every Block a Village Online, the WHA has focused on Austin, one of its poorest and most troubled neighborhoods. FYI 11.2 identifies the goals of this program. Supplying each block leader with a Web TV and a series of Web pages, "community members can provide information to others on their block, teach each other new skills, and become connected with other communities around the world" (Every Block a Village Online Web site). Despite a litany of serious challenges facing this community, the program also recognizes a variety of assets, including established, supportive block clubs and an array of educated, respected professionals in the area. In other words, while Austin has many social problems and a lack of material assets, it is rich in "human capital."

Using a capacities model of community development and communication strategies that include local leadership development and recognition, personal networking, and computer interaction, the WHA is a successful role model for a self-empowerment approach: "This is not a question of holding hands out; i is the reality of holding hands together" (Westside Health Authority Web site).

---

**FYI 11.2** **EVERY BLOCK A VILLAGE ONLINE: HEALTH AND SAFETY GOALS**

1. Reduce maternal medical risk factors which complicate pregnancy.

2. Reduce the proportion of low birth weight infants born in the target area.

3. Increase first trimester initiation of prenatal care.

4. Reduce area emergency department visits through increased access to primary care.

5. Reduce annual index crimes in the target area.

(Every Block a Village Online Web site)

---

**THEORIZING PRACTICE 11.5**

## Assessing Your Community

- Identify the primary community of which you consider yourself to be a member. This may be the neighborhood in which you grew up, your current neighborhood, university campus, dormitory, and so on.

- List the social health problems, needs, and deficits of your community.

- Now think about your community in terms of its capacities, assets, and gifts. Who are the constituent members, local institutions, and voluntary associations that can be mobilized to help with social health concerns?

- How do you fit into this picture?

Theorizing Practice 11.5 encourages you to think about empowerment in a community of which you are a member.

# PUBLIC ADVOCACY AND HEALTH ACTIVISM

Having explored the potential for proactivity in patienthood, in health consumerism, and in community organization, we wish to address one more venue for empowerment through health care activism. This is the public realm, or **political advocacy,** the realization of partnerships from local grassroots through national policy formation. In this final section, we look at how groups affiliated via common health concerns have made efforts to have their voices heard and their needs met. Public advocacy encompasses strategies including prioritization of vital issues, collaboration among key "players," various forms of interpersonal and mass media, and participation in national decision-making processes.

The fact that health care issues have emerged as some of the most prominent political themes over the past decade should come as no surprise. Health care reform, particularly that involving some version of a patient's bill of rights, has been championed by a variety of citizens organizations and both major U.S. political parties. Topics that continue to be debated include preserving a patient's choice of providers, access to primary and specialty care, economic availability of needed prescription medicines, continuity of care, provision of quality-assurance standards, nondiscrimination in delivery of services, fair appeals mechanisms for health care denials, protection of patient confidentiality, and accountability of managed care organizations for patient outcomes (U.S. Senate Web site). Clearly, these are important health policy issues that affect all of us, but we'd like to turn our attention to the communicative and rhetorical processes used by grassroots health communities in bringing their ideas to prominence and, perhaps, to fruition.

In 1990, a collaboration among several disease- and disability-related groups, in conjunction with receptive members of government, resulted in passage of the ADA (Americans with Disabilities Act). Since its approval into law, the implementation of this legislation has been imperfect, but the ADA has made some real differences in the patterns of American life. Perhaps as significant as the end result was the process that helped the constituencies publicly articulate their positions. So, for our last example, we go back to the context with which we began this chapter: breast cancer advocacy. While the women of Expedition Inspiration worked as a team, for the most part their achievements were individually defined. Now let's examine how another kind of partnership has made breast cancer a very visible and influential point on the national radar screen.

## ■ Political Advocacy in Action

In 1990, despite an escalating occurrence rate and no decrease in mortality, breast cancer received only about $90 million in federal funding and limited attention in the media and other places, except for an occasional "bump" in visibility when a well-known person fell prey. Many voluntary organizations had formed support groups, special programming, fund-raising strategies, and information clearinghouses, but national momentum to make significant changes in the status quo was lacking.

Much akin to how Jacqueline Reed envisioned capability and assets in her local Westside community, breast cancer survivor Fran Visco foresaw the possibilities inherent in forming an umbrella organization that would integrate and unite the energies and resources of concerned individuals and member groups. The result was the 1991 formation of the National Breast Cancer Coalition (NBCC), which is now composed of more than 500 organizations and 60,000 individuals. With the motto "grassroots advocacy in action," the NBCC's goals include promoting research into causes, treatments, and cure; improving access to high-quality screening and treatment, especially for the underserved and uninsured; and increasing the influence of breast cancer survivors in legislation, regulation, and clinical trials. These goals were forged during an unprecedented gathering of governmental officials, clinicians, scientists, and survivors in 1993, resulting in a National Action Plan on Breast Cancer (Proceedings, 1993). Initially, the scientific community resented the inclusion of survivors—laypersons who they did not perceive as being qualified to participate in such meetings. In a brief period of time, however, the activists proved that they brought a unique expertise and perspective to the discussions based on their own difficult experiences. Additionally and importantly, the NBCC has undertaken a variety of educational programs to ensure that its representatives are well prepared to participate in significant decision-making situations.

Since 1992, the NBCC has sponsored an annual advocacy training conference, attended by hundreds of people. Participants are provided a great deal of information, including updates on current issues such as new medications, research initiatives, and the legislative process, to enable them to speak with credibility about the legislative priorities identified by the Coalition. People attending the meeting are well briefed on the top five or six priorities that the organization has chosen to highlight for the next year. The culmination of this four-day program is Lobby Day, in which participants make a noisy demonstration outside the Congressional Office Building, followed by state delegations talking with their elected representatives about the prioritized issues. To ward off intimidation, the activists are repeatedly advised by NBCC staff to stand up tall during their Congressional visits and to remember that the legislators have been elected to work for them—that it is their right to talk about their concerns with the legislators.

National Breast Cancer Coalition Lobby Day activists. *Photo reprinted with permission of the National Breast Cancer Coalition.*

A second, more intensive training program called Project Lead is held three to four times a year, in various locations around the country, with smaller groups of participants who are chosen on a competitive basis. Having made a commitment to activism, attendees receive in-depth instruction in research methodology and evaluation as well as about recent developments in the basic science and clinical investigations of breast cancer. Many graduates of Project Lead go on to participate in the selection process of awarding grant funds, and some even make presentations, alongside researchers and clinicians, at scientific meetings.

The gatherings and publications sponsored by the NBCC make frequent use of personal narratives, memorializing the contributions of activists who have died from breast cancer while motivating survivors to make a greater investment and fight even harder to achieve their goals. The poignant stories effectively serve a variety of purposes—honoring the fallen advocates, emphasizing that the organization's agenda has a life-or-death dimension, and reminding members that behind the statistics are real people.

The accomplishments of the NBCC have been considerable so far. The NBCC has increased the amount of money directed toward breast cancer research nearly eight-fold, aided in the recruitment of sufficient numbers of participants to conduct crucial clinical trials, influenced the nature and implementation of relevant legislation, and created much more visibility of breast cancer issues in the mass media. Perhaps just as important, this group has achieved an unprecedented role for including survivors as key decision makers in health policy and planning, a huge step forward in empowering people to take an active role in changing a health problem that previously had merely victimized them. Just as the breast cancer advocates learned from the AIDS activists before them, other health-related advocacy groups are sure to follow—and to surpass—the NBCC's example.

## SUMMARY

In this final chapter, we have focused on the health citizen competencies of self-empowerment and advocacy in three health-related contexts: (a) patienthood, (b) community development, and (c) political advocacy. We have explored a variety of forums for health activism, one of which is advocacy, as well as how these may lead to perceptions of empowerment and why noncompliance often occurs. As patients, we can choose to interact as partners with our health practitioners in setting agendas, sharing information, asking questions, and negotiating decisions. As activist health consumers, we can coordinate our own health information and can advocate on behalf of ourselves within complex health institutions. As members of communities, we can benefit ourselves and others by framing health issues within a capacities—rather than within a deficits—perspective. At the macrolevel of health advocacy, individual citizens work together to formulate strategies of influence, to develop interpersonal and organizational networks, to build leadership, and to affect policy decisions.

## KEY TERMS

communication competencies
health activism
advocacy
empowerment
disempowerment
patienthood

noncompliant
mindful nonadherence
proactive patient
partnership
negotiated decision making
health consumer

self-advocacy
community health
social capital
political advocacy

## DISCUSSION QUESTIONS

1. Assess your position—and your accompanying behavior—regarding participation in health care decision making. How active are you in partnering with

your providers for key decisions affecting your health? What decisions do you choose to make without talking to a clinician?

2. How do the communities of which you are a member affect your health and well-being? Think about this question in terms of specific examples.

3. What forms of public health activism are you aware of? Have you been influenced by activist communication in any way, such as giving money, signing a petition, searching for more information, or altering your own health behaviors?

4. Have you been—or could you anticipate being—an advocate for a particular health issue? If so, which one, and why is it important to you? What communication strategies do you think would be most effective in enlisting attention and effecting change?

## INFOTRAC COLLEGE EDITION

1. Choose at least three periodical citations under the subject heading "Patient Advocacy" that discuss how patients can advocate in their own best interests for themselves or for a loved one with health care providers. Based on what you read, create a list of patient advocacy communication skills.

2. Read the 2000 article by Henderson et al. entitled "'It Takes a Village' to Promote Physical Activity." Now describe an example of your own in which community interaction impacts on an individual's health practices.

# REFERENCES

Abbey, A., Andrews, F. M., Halman, J. J. (1992). Infertility and subjective well-being: The mediating roles of self-esteem, internal control, and interpersonal conflict. *Journal of Marriage and the Family, 54,* 408–418.

Abrams, D. B., & Biener, L. (1992). Motivation characteristics of smokers at the workplace: A public health campaign. *Preventative Medicine, 21,* 679–687.

ACT UP New York Web site. Downloaded on May 13, 2002, from http://www.actupny.org

Addington, T., & Wegescheide-Harris, J. (1995). Ethics and communication with the terminally ill. *Health Communication, 7,* 267–281.

Adelman, M. B. (1992). Healthy passion: Safer sex as play. In T. Edgar, M. A. Fitzpatrick, & V. S. Freimuth (Eds.), *AIDS: A communicative perspective* (pp. 69–89). Hillsdale, NJ: Erlbaum.

Adelman, M. B., & Frey, L. R. (1997). *The fragile community: Living together with AIDS.* Mahwah, NJ: Erlbaum.

Adelman, M. B. (Producer), Moytl, H. D. (Technical Director), & Downs, D. (Acting Director). (1988). *Safe-sex talk* [video]. Department of Communication Studies, Northwestern University, Evanston, IL.

Adler, J. (1998, November 2). Tomorrow's child. *Newsweek,* pp. 54–64

Albrecht, T. L., & Adelman, M. (1987). Communicating social support: A theoretical perspective. In T. L. Albrecht & M. Adelman (Eds.), *Communicating social support* (pp.18–39). Newbury Park, CA: Sage.

Allen, M., & Marks, S. (1993). *Miscarriage: Women sharing from the heart.* New York: Wiley.

Altman, I. (1993). Dialectics, physical environments, and personal relationships. *Communication Monographs, 60,* 26–34.

Altman, I., Vinsel, A., & Brown, B. B. (1981). Dialectical conceptions in social psychology: An application to social penetration and privacy regulation. In L. Berkowitz (Ed.), *Advances in experimental social psychology* (Vol. 14, pp. 257–274). New York: Wiley.

Altman, L. K. (1995, June 2). Actor thrown from horse is dependent on respirator. *New York Times,* p. A12.

American Academy of Pediatrics, Committee on Communications. (1995, October). Children, adolescents, and television. *Pediatrics, 96,* 95–96.

American Cancer Society. (2001). *Cancer facts & figures 2001.* Document 01-300M-No. 5008-01. New York: American Cancer Society.

American Psychiatric Association. (1987). *Diagnostic and statistical manual of mental disorders* (3rd ed.). Washington, DC: American Psychiatric Press.

American Psychiatric Association. (1994). *Diagnostic and statistical manual of mental disorders* (4th ed.). Washington, DC: American Psychiatric Association.

Andersen, P. A., & Guerrero, L. K. (Eds.). (1998a). *Handbook of communication and emotion: Research, theory, applications, and contexts.* San Diego: Academic Press.

Andersen, P. A., & Guerrero, L. K. (1998b). Principles of communication and emotion in social interaction. In P. A. Andersen & L. K. Guerrero (Eds.), *Handbook of communication and emotion: Research, theory, applications, and contexts* (pp. 49–96). San Diego: Academic Press.

Anderson, J., & Geist-Martin, P. (in press). Narratives and healing: Exploring one family's stories of cancer survivorship. *Health Communication.*

Anderson, J. M., Waxler-Morrison, N., Richardson, E., Herbert, C., & Murphy, M. (1991). Conclusion: Delivering culturally sensitive health care. In N. Waxler-Morrison, J. M. Anderson, & E. Richardson (Eds.), *Cross-cultural caring: A handbook for health professionals in Western Canada.* Vancouver: University of British Columbia.

Andriote, J. M. (1998, March 10). Getting personal. *Washington Post,* p. 10 (Health Section).

Aptheker, B. (1989). *Tapestries of life: Women's work, women's consciousness and the meaning of daily experience.* Amherst: University of Massachusetts Press.

Arnston, P. (1989). Improving citizens' health competencies. *Health Communication, 1,* 29–34.

Arntson, P., & Droge, D. (1987). Social support in self-help groups: The role of communication in enabling perceptions of control. In T. L. Albrecht & M. D. Adelman (Eds.), *Communicating social support* (pp. 148–171). Newbury Park, CA: Sage.

Arrington, M. I. (2000a). Thinking inside the box: On identity, sexuality, prostate cancer, and social support. *Journal of Aging and Identity, 5,* 151–158.

Arrington, M. I. (2000b). Sexuality, society, and senior citizens: An analysis of sex talk among prostate cancer support group members. *Sexuality and Culture, 4,* 46, 57.

Arrington, M. I. (2002). *Recreating ourselves: Stigma, identity changes, and narrative re-construction among prostate cancer survivors.* Unpublished doctoral dissertation, University of South Florida, Tampa, FL.

Askham, J. (1976). Identity and stability within the marriage relationship. *Journal of Marriage and the Family, 38,* 535–547.

Atkinson, P. (1995). *Medical talk and medical work.* London: Sage.

Atkinson, P. (1997). Narrative turn or blind alley? *Qualitative Health Research, 7,* 325–344.

Avalos-C'de Baca, F., Geist, P., Gray, J. L., & Hill, G. (1996). The baby shower: Rituals of public and private joy and sorrow. In E. B. Ray (Ed.), *Case studies in communication and disenfranchisement: Applications to social health issues* (pp. 59–73). Mahwah, NJ: Erlbaum.

Babrow, A., Hines, S., & Kasch, C. R. (2000). Illness and uncertainty: Problematic integration and strategies for communicating about medical uncertainty and ambiguity. In B. B. Whaley (Ed.), *Explaining illness: Messages, strategies and contexts* (pp. 41–67). Hillsdale, NJ: Erlbaum.

Baeck, L. (1978). Meditation 12. In *Gates of Repentance: The new union prayer book for the days of awe* (pp. 5–6). New York: Central Conference of American Rabbis and Union of Liberal and Progressive Synagogues.

Bakhtin, M. M. (1986). *Speech genres and other late essays* (C. Emerson & M. Holquist, Eds.; V. McGee, Trans.). Austin: University of Texas Press.

Baltes, M. M., & Wahl, H. W. (1996). Patterns of communication in old age: The dependency-support and independence-ignore script. *Health Communication, 8,* 217–231.

Bansen, S. S., & Stevens, H. A. (1992). Women's experiences of miscarriage in early pregnancy. *Journal of Nurse-Midwifery, 35,* 84–90.

Barbash, I., & Taylor, L. (1997). *Cross-cultural filmmaking.* Berkeley: University of California Press.

Barna, L. M. (1993). Stumbling blocks in intercultural communication. In L. A. Samovar and R. E. Porter (Eds.), *Intercultural communication: A reader* (6th ed., pp. 345–353). Belmont, CA: Wadsworth.

Barnes, D. B., Taylor-Brown, S., & Wiener, L. (1997). "I didn't leave y'all on purpose": HIV-infected mothers' videotaped legacies for their children. *Qualitative Sociology, 20,* 7–32.

Barnland, D. C. (1976). The mystification of meaning: Doctor-patient encounters. *Journal of Medical Education* (now *Academic Medicine*), *51,* 716–725.

Barroso, J. (1997). Reconstructing my life: Becoming a long-term survivor of AIDS. *Qualitative Health Research, 7,* 57–74.

Bauer, C., Deering, M. J., & Hsu, L. (2001). E-health: Federal issues and approaches. In R. E. Rice & J. E. Katz (Eds.), *The Internet and health communication* (pp. 355–383). Thousand Oaks, CA: Sage.

Baxter, L. A. (1988). A dialectic perspective on communication strategies in relationship development. In S. Duck (Ed.), *Handbook of personal relationships: Theory, research, and interventions* (pp. 257–273). New York: Wiley.

Baxter, L. A. (1990). Dialectical contradictions in relationship development. *Journal of Social and Personal Relationships, 7,* 69–88.

Baxter, L. A. (1991, November). *Bakhtin's ghost: Dialectical communication in relationships.* Paper presented at the Speech Communication Association, Atlanta, GA.

Baxter, L. A., & Montgomery, B. M. (1996). *Relating: Dialogues and dialectics.* New York: Guilford.

Baxter, L. A., & Montgomery, B. M. (1997). Rethinking communication in personal relationships from a dialectical perspective. In S. Duck (Ed.), *Handbook of personal relationships* (pp. 325–349). Sussex, England: John Wiley.

Baxter, L. A., & Simon, E. P. (1993). Relationship maintenance strategies and dialectical contradictions in personal relationships. *Journal of Social and Personal Relationships, 10,* 225–292.

Bayne-Smith, M. (Ed.). (1996). *Race, gender, and health.* Thousand Oaks, CA: Sage.

Beach, W. A. (1996). *Conversations about illness: Family preoccupations with bulimia.* Mahwah, NJ: Erlbaum.

Beach, W. A., & LeBaron, C. (in press). Body disclosures: Attending to personal problems and reported sexual abuse during a medical encounter. *Journal of Communication, 52* (3).

Beaudry, M., Dufour, R., & Marcoux, S. (1995). Relation between infant feeding and infections during the first six months of life. *Journal of Pediatrics, 126,* 191–197.

Beck, C. S. (1997). *Partnerships for health: Building relationships between women and health caregivers.* Mahwah, NJ: Erlbaum.

Becker, G., & Nachtigall, R. D. (1991). Ambiguous responsibility in the doctor-patient relationship: The case of infertility. *Social Science and Medicine, 32,* 875–885.

Beckman, H. B., & Frankel, R. M. (1984). The effect of physician behavior on the collection of data. *Annals of Internal Medicine, 101,* 692–696.

Bellah, R., Madsen, R., Sullivan, W., Swidler, A., & Tipton, S. (1985). *Habits of the heart.* Berkeley: University of California Press.

Benjamin, J. (1986). A desire of one's own: psychoanalytic feminism and intersubjective space. In T. de Lauretis (Ed.), *Feminist studies/critical studies* (pp. 78–101). Bloomington: Indiana University Press.

Bennett, K., Smith, D. H., & Irwin, H. (1999). Preferences for participation in medical decisions in China. *Health Communication, 11,* 261–284.

Bergstrom, M., & Nussbaum, J. (1996). Cohort differences in interpersonal conflict:

Implications for the older patient-younger care provider interaction. *Health Communication, 8,* 233–248.

Bernstein, A. B., & Bernstein, J. (1996). HMOs and health services research: The penalty of taking the lead. *Medical Care Research and Review, 53,* S18–S43.

Bird, J. A., Otero-Sabogal, R., Ha, N. T., & McPhee, S. J. (1996). Tailoring lay health worker interventions for diverse cultures: Lessons learned from Vietnamese and Latina communities. *Health Education Quarterly, 23,* 105–133.

Bitzer, L. F. (1968). The rhetorical situation. *Philosophy and Rhetoric, 1,* 1–14.

Black, D. (2000, July 28). All drugs are not created equal: Women's health may be at risk due to gender bias in drug testing. *The Toronto Star,* p. LI-1.

Bland, J. H. (1997). Live long, die fast: Playing the aging game to win. Minneapolis: Fairview Press.

Blau, S. P., & Shimberg, E. F. (1997). *How to get out of the hospital alive: A guide to patient power.* New York: Macmillan.

Blazer, D. G. (2002). *Depression in late life.* New York: Springer.

Blum, S., Sing, T. P., Gibbons, J., Fordyce, J., Lessner, L., Chiasson, M. A., Weisfuse, I. B., & Thomas, P. A. (1994). Trends in survival among persons with acquired immunodeficiency syndrome in New York City. *American Journal of Epidemiology, 139,* 351–361.

Bochner, A. (1997). It's about time: Narrative and the divided self. *Qualitative Inquiry, 3,* 418–438.

Bochner, A. P., Ellis, C., & Tillmann-Healy, L. M. (1996). Relationships as stories. In S. Duck (Ed.), *Handbook of personal relationships* (pp. 307–324). Sussex, England: John Wiley.

Book, P. L. (1996). How does the family narrative influence the individual's ability to communicate about death? *Omega-Journal of Death and Dying, 33,* 323–341.

Booth-Butterfield, M., & Sidelinger, R. (1998). The influence of family communication on the college-aged child: Openness, attitudes and actions about sex and alcohol. *Communication Quarterly, 46,* 295–310.

Bordo, S. (1990). Reading the slender body. In M. Jacobus, E. Fox Keller, and S. Shuttleworth (Eds.), *Body politics* (pp. 83–112). New York: Routledge.

Bordo, S. (1993). *Unbearable weight: Feminism, Western culture, and the body.* Berkeley: University of California Press.

Bordo, S. R. (1989). The body and the reproduction of femininity: A feminist appropriation of Foucault. In A. M. Jaggar & S. R. Bordo (Eds.), *Gender/body/knowledge* (pp. 13–33). New Brunswick, NJ: Rutgers University Press.

Botta, R. A., & Pingree, S. (1997). Interpersonal communication and rape: Women acknowledge their assaults. *Journal of Health Communication, 2,* 197–212.

Bowman, D. (1995). Nurses build cultural bridges with patients. *The University of Iowa Spectator, 28* (2), 2.

Boyle, J. S. (1991). Transcultural nursing care of Central American refugees. *Imprint, 38,* 73–79.

Bracht, N., Kingsbury, L., & Rissel, C. (1999). A five-stage community organization model for health promotion: Empowerment and partnership strategies. In N. Bracht (Ed.), *Health promotion at the community level: New advances* (2nd ed., pp. 83–104). Thousand Oaks, CA: Sage.

Bradley, R. A. (1975). *Husband-coached childbirth.* New York: Harper & Row.

Braithwaite, D. O. (1986, February). *Redefinition of disability and identification as a subculture by persons with physical disabilities.* Paper presented at the annual meeting of the Western Speech Communication Association, Tucson, AZ.

Braithwaite, D. O. (1990). From majority to minority: An analysis of cultural change from able-bodied to disabled. *International Journal of Intercultural Relations, 14,* 465–483.

Braithwaite, D. O. (1991). Just how much did that wheelchair cost? Management of privacy boundaries by persons with disabilities. *Western Journal of Speech Communication, 55,* 254–274.

Braithwaite, D. O. (1996). Persons first: Exploring different perspectives on communication with persons with disabilities. In E. B. Ray (Ed.), *Communication and disenfranchisement: Social health issues and implications* (pp. 449–464). Hillsdale, NJ: Erlbaum.

Braithwaite, D. O., & Braithwaite, C. A. (1997). Understanding communication of persons with disabilities as cultural communication. In L. A. Samovar & R. E. Porter (Eds.), *Intercultural communication* (8th ed., pp. 154–164). Belmont: Wadsworth.

Braithwaite, D. O., & Labrecque, D. (1994). Responding to the Americans with Disabilities Act: Contributions of interpersonal communication research and training. *Journal of Applied Communication Research, 22,* 287–294.

Braithwaite, D. O., & Thompson, T. L. (Eds.). (2000). *Handbook of communication and people with disabilities: Research and application.* Mahwah, NJ: Erlbaum.

Brashers, D. E., Haas, S. M., & Neidig, J. L. (1999a). The patient self-advocacy scale: Measuring patient involvement in health care decision-making interactions. *Health Communication, 11,* 97–122.

Brashers, D. E., & Klingle, R. S. (1992, October). *The influence of activism on physician-patient communication.* Paper presented at the annual meeting of the Speech Communication Association, Chicago.

Brashers, D. E., Neidig, J. L., Cardillo, L. W., Dobbs, L. K., Russell, J. A., & Haas, S. M. (1999b). "In an important way, I did die": Uncertainty and revival in persons living with HIV or AIDS. *AIDS Care, 11,* 201–219.

Breast implants: An information update 2000. (2000). Chronology of FDA breast implant activities. U.S. Food and Drug Administration—Center for Devices and Radiological Health. Downloaded July 11, 2002, from http://www.fda.gov/fdac/departs/2001/601_upd.html

Brenders, D. A. (1989). Perceived control and the interpersonal dimension of health care. *Health Communication, 1,* 117–135.

Brennan, P. F., & Fink, S. V. (1997). Health promotion, social support, and computer networks. In R. L. Street, W. R. Gold, & T. Manning (Eds.), *Health promotion and interactive technology* (pp. 157–170). Mahwah, NJ: Erlbaum.

Brider, P. (1996). Huge job loss projections shock health professionals. *American Journal of Nursing, 96,* 61–64.

Brislin, R. W. (1991). Prejudice in intercultural communication. In L. A. Samovar and R. E. Porter (Eds.), *Intercultural communication: A reader* (6th ed., pp. 366–370). Belmont, CA: Wadsworth.

Brody, H. (1987). *Stories of sickness.* New Haven, CT: Yale University Press.

Brody, H. (1992). *The healer's power.* New Haven, CT: Yale University Press.

Brody, J. (1998, September 8). Weighing the pros and cons of hormone therapy. *New York Times,* p. F7.

Brooks, P. (1993). *Body work: Objects of desire in modern narrative.* Boston: Harvard University Press.

Broom, B. C. (2000). Medicine and story: A novel clinical panorama rising from a unity mind/body approach to physical illness. *Advances in Mind-Body Medicine, 16,* 161–177.

Broyard, A. (1992). *Intoxicated by my illness and other writings on life and death.* New York: Clarkson Potter.

Brumberg, J. J. (2000). *Fasting girls: The history of anorexia nervosa.* New York: Vintage Books.

Bruner, J. (1986). *Actual minds, possible worlds.* Cambridge, MA: Harvard University Press.

Bruner, J. (1987). Life as narrative. *Social Research, 54,* 11–32.

Buckman, R. (1992). *How to break bad news: A guide for health care professionals.* Baltimore, MD: Johns Hopkins University Press.

Bulger, R. J. (Ed.). (1987). *In search of the modern Hippocrates.* Iowa City: University of Iowa Press.

Bulkeley, W. M. (1995, February 27). Untested treatments, cures find stronghold on on-line services. *The Wall Street Journal,* pp. A1, A7.

Burleson, B. R., & Goldsmith, D. J. (1998). How the comforting process works: Alleviating emotional distress through conversationally induced reappraisals. In P. A. Andersen & L. K. Guerrero (Eds.), *Handbook of communication and emotion: Research, theory, application, and contexts* (pp. 245–280). San Diego: Academic Press.

Burrell, G. (1988). Modernism, postmodernism, and organizational analysis. 2: The contribution of Michel Foucault. *Organization Studies, 9,* 221–235.

Butler, R. R., & Koraleski, S. (1990). Infertility: A crisis with no resolution. *Journal of Mental Health Counseling, 12,* 151–163.

Byock, I. (1977). *Dying well: The prospect for growth at the end of life.* New York: Riverhead Books.

California Wellness Foundation. (1997, April 21). Teen pregnancy. It's a problem so complex most people just see part of it. *San Diego Union-Tribune,* p. A-9.

Callahan, D. (1987). *Setting limits: Medical goals in an aging society.* New York: Simon & Schuster.

Callahan, M., & Kelley, P. (1992). *Final gifts: Understanding the special awareness, needs, and communications of the dying.* New York: Bantam Books.

Campo, R. (1996). *What the body told.* Durham, NC: Duke University Press.

Cantor, C. (1999, October). Teen suicides, up: Cause? Elusive. CBSHealthWatch-Library. Downloaded on January 25, 2000, from http://cbshealthwatch.health.aol.com/aol.../article.asp?RecID=200648&ContentType=Library

Carovano, K. (1991). More than mothers and whores: Redefining the AIDS prevention needs of women. *International Journal of Health Services, 21,* 131–142.

Carver, M. H. (1993). Women and HIV/AIDS education. In F. C. Corey (Ed.), *HIV education: Performing personal narratives* (pp. 34–40). Tempe: Arizona State University.

Cegala, D. J. (1997). A study of doctors' and patients' patterns of information exchange and relational communication during a primary care consultation: Implications for communication skills training. *The Journal of Health Communication, 2,* 169–194.

Cegala, D. J., Socha McGee, D., & McNeilis, K. S. (1996). Components of patients' and doctors' perceptions of communication competence during a primary care medical interview. *Health Communication, 8,* 1–28.

Center, S. A. (1998, May 8). *Alternative medicine: From fringe to mainstream.* Lecture presented to faculty/staff/students, San Diego State University, San Diego, CA.

Centers for Disease Control and Prevention. (2001, September 24). HIV Surveillance Report, Year-end 2000 edition, Vol. 12, No 2, Divisions of HIV/AIDS Prevention. Downloaded on April 10, 2002, from http://www.cdc.gov/hiv/stats/hasr1202.htm

Centers for Disease Control and Prevention. (2002, May 6). Suicide in the United States. Downloaded on May 9, 2002, from http://www.cdc.gov/ncipc/factsheets/suifacts.htm

Charmaz, K. (1983). Loss of self: A fundamental form of suffering in the chronically ill. *Sociology of Health and Illness, 5,* 168–195.

Charmaz, K. (1987). Struggling for a self: Identity levels of the chronically ill. In J. Roth & P. Conrad (Eds.), *Research in the sociology of health care: A research manual* (Vol. 6, pp. 249–281). Greenwich, CT: JAI Press.

Charmaz, K. (1991). *Good days, bad days: The self in chronic illness and time.* New Brunswick, NJ: Rutgers University Press.

Charmaz, K. (1994). Identity dilemmas of chronically ill men. *Sociological Quarterly, 35,* 269–288.

Charmaz, K. (1995). The body, identity, and self: Adapting to impairment. *Sociological Quarterly, 36,* 657–680.

Chenail, R. J. (1991). Heartfelt stories. In R. J. Chenail (Ed.), *Medical discourse and systemic frames of comprehension* (pp. 1–18). Norwood, NJ: Ablex.

Cheney, G. (1999). *Values at work: Employee participation meets market pressure at Mondragón.* Ithaca, NY: Cornell University Press.

Children's Defense Fund. (1994). *The state of America's children: Yearbook 1994.* Washington, DC: Children's Defense Fund.

Children's Miracle Network. (1992). Keloland TV, Channel 11, Sioux Falls, SD.

Christiansen, A. E., & Hanson, J. J. (1996). Comedy as cure for tragedy: ACT UP and the rhetoric of AIDS. *Quarterly Journal of Speech, 82,* 157–170.

Christopher Reeve Homepage (http://www.geocites.com/Hollywood/Studio/4071/sp-wc1999.htm).

Chu, S., Buehler, J., & Berkelman, L. (1990). Impact of the human immunodeficiency virus epidemic on mortality of women of reproductive age, United States. *Journal of the American Medical Association, 264,* 225–229.

Ciabattari, J. (1999, December 12). A great reward is coming. *Parade Magazine,* p. 10.

"Cigars linked to higher disease risks." (1999, June 10). *The Dallas Morning News,* p. 9A.

Cissna, K., Cox, D. E., & Bochner, A. P. (1990). The dialectic of marital and parental relationships within the stepfamily. *Communication Monographs, 57,* 46–61.

Clarke, P., & Evans, S. H. (1998). *Surviving modern medicine: How to get the best from doctors, family & friends.* Piscataway, NJ: Rutgers University Press.

Clifford, J. (1988). *The predicament of culture: Twentieth century ethnography, literature, and art.* Cambridge: Harvard University Press.

Cline, R. J., Freeman, K. E., & Johnson, S. J. (1990). Talking among sexual partners about AIDS: Factors differentiating those who talk from those who do not. *Communication Research, 17,* 792–808.

Cline, R. J. W., & McKenzie, N. J. (1996a). HIV/AIDS, women, and threads of discrimination: A tapestry of disenfranchisement. In E. B. Ray (Ed.), *Communication and disenfranchisement: Social health issues and implications* (pp. 365–386). Mahwah, NJ: Erlbaum.

Cline, R. J. W., & McKenzie, N. J. (1996b). Women and AIDS: The lost population. In R. L. Parrott & C. M. Condit (Eds.), *Evaluating women's health messages: A resource book* (pp. 382–401). Thousand Oaks, CA: Sage.

"Clinton taps Foster to fight teen pregnancy." (1996, January 30). *San Diego Union-Tribune,* p. A-7.

Cohen-Cole, S. A. (1991). *The medical interview: The three-function approach.* St. Louis: Mosby–Year Book.

Coles, R. (1989). *The call of stories: Teaching and the moral imagination.* Boston: Houghton Mifflin.

Collins, K. S., Hughes, D. L., Doty, M. M., Ives, B. L., Edwards, J. N., & Tenney, K. (2002, March 6). Diverse communities, common concerns: Assessing health care quality for minority Americans. The Commonwealth Fund 2002 Health Care Quality Survey Release. Downloaded on May 3, 2002, from http://www.cmwf.org

Colt, G. H. (1996, September). The healing revolution. *Life*, pp. 35–50.

Conant, M. (1997, February 3). This is smart medicine. *Newsweek*, p. 26.

Condor, B. (1998, February 23). Salud! Latinas and medical establishment: They're learning more about each other. *San Diego Union-Tribune*, pp. E-1, E-3.

Connick, H. (1994). Booker. On *She* [CD]. New York: Columbia Records.

Conquergood, D. (1988). Health theatre in a Hmong refugee camp: Performance, communication, and culture. *TDR: Journal of Performance Studies, 32*, 174–208.

Conquergood, D. (1991). Rethinking ethnography: Towards a critical cultural politics. *Communication Monographs, 58*, 179–194.

Conquergood, D. (1994). Homeboys and hoods: Gang communication and cultural space. In L. R. Frey (Ed.). *Group communication in context: Studies of natural groups* (pp. 23–55). Hillsdale, NJ: Erlbaum.

Corea, G. (1985a). *The hidden malpractice: How American medicine mistreats women* (2nd ed.). New York: Harper & Row.

Corea, G. (1985b). *The mother machine: Reproductive technologies from artificial insemination to artificial wombs.* New York: Harper & Row.

Corey, F. C. (1996). Gay men and their physicians: Discourse and disenfranchisement. In E. B. Ray (Ed.), *Communication and disenfranchisement: Social health issues and implications* (pp. 331–346). Mahwah, NJ: Erlbaum.

Coupland, N., Coupland, J., & Giles, H. (1991). *Language, society and the elderly: Discourse, identity and aging.* Oxford, UK: Blackwell.

Cousins, N. (1981). *Anatomy of an illness as perceived by the patient: Reflections on healing and regeneration.* New York: Bantam.

Coward, R. (1989). *The whole truth: The myth of alternative health.* Boston: Faber and Faber.

Cowley, G. (2000, May 22). The new war on Parkinson's. *Newsweek*, pp. 52–58.

Czarniawska, B. (1997). A four times told tale: Combining narrative and scientific knowledge in organization studies. *Organization, 4*, 7–30.

Dalton, H. L. (1989, Summer). AIDS in blackface. *Daedalus*, 205–227.

Dan, A. J. (Ed.). (1994). *Reframing women's health: Multidisciplinary research and practice.* Thousand Oaks, CA: Sage.

Daniels, A., & Hoover, M. (1974). *When children ask about sex.* New York: Child Study Press.

Daniels, M. J., & Parrott, R. L. (1996). Prenatal care from the woman's perspective: A thematic analysis of the newspaper media. In R. L. Parrott & C. M. Condit (Eds.), *Evaluating women's health messages: A resource book* (pp. 222–233). Thousand Oaks, CA: Sage.

Daniluk, J., Leader, A., & Taylor, P. J. (1985). The psychological sequelae of infertility. In J. H. Gold (Ed.), *The psychiatric implications of menstruation* (pp. 77–85). Washington, DC: American Psychiatric Press.

Daniluk, J. C. (1988). Infertility: Intrapersonal and interpersonal impact. *Fertility and Sterility, 49*, 982–990.

D.A.R.E. America. The Official Website. Downloaded on January 18, 2002, from http://www.dare.com/D_OFFI/dare_results_shell.htm

Davis-Floyd, R. E. (1992). *Birth as an American rite of passage.* Berkeley: University of California Press.

Deber, R., Kraetschmer, N., & Irvine, J. (1996). What role do patients wish to play in treatment decision-making? *Archives of Internal Medicine 156*, 1414–1420.

Deber, R. B. (1994). Physicians in health care management: 8. The patient-physician partnership: Decision making, problem solving and the desire to participate. *Canadian Medical Association Journal, 151*, 423–427.

Deetz, S. A. (1992). *Democracy in an age of corporate colonization: Developments in communication and the politics of everyday life.* Albany: New York: State University of New York Press.

Degnin, F. D. (1999). Between a rock and a hard place: Ethics in managed care and the physician-patient relationship. *Managed Care Quarterly, 7,* 15–22.

Delgado, J. (1997). *Salud!: A Latina's guide to total health—Body, mind, and spirit.* New York: Harper/Perennial.

DeLoach, C., & Greer, B. G. (1981). *Adjustment to severe physical disability: A metamorphosis.* New York: McGraw-Hill.

Denzin, N. K. (1992). Whose cornerville is it, anyway. *Journal of Contemporary Ethnography, 21,* 120–132.

Denzin, N. K. (1997). *Interpretive ethnography: Ethnographic practices for the 21st century.* Thousand Oaks, CA: Sage.

DeWitt, P. M. (1993). The pursuit of pregnancy. *American Demographics, 15,* 48–51.

DiClemente, R. J., Hansen, W. B., & Ponton, L. E. (Eds.). (1996). *Handbook of adolescent health risk behavior.* New York: Plenum Press.

Dietz, W. H. (1990). You are what you eat: What you eat is what you are. *Journal of Adolescent Health Care, 11,* 76–81.

Do, T. P. (1997). In my shoes for life: A disabled woman's journey. In L. A. M. Perry & P. Geist (Eds.), *Courage of conviction: Women's words, women's wisdom* (pp. 129–143). Mountain View, CA: Mayfield.

Do, T. P., & Geist, P. (2000). Othering the embodiment of persons with physical disabilities. In D. Braithwaite & T. Thompson (Eds.), *Handbook of communication and people with disabilities: Research and application* (pp. 49–65). Mahwah, NJ: Erlbaum.

Dockrell, C. (2000, February 16). Teen tactic. *Boston Globe,* p. C2.

Doka, K. J. (1989) (Ed.). *Disenfranchised grief: Recognizing hidden sorrow.* Lexington, MA: Lexington Books.

Donnelly, W. J., & Brauner, D. J. (1992). Why SOAP is bad for the medical record. *Archives of Internal Medicine, 152,* 481–484.

Dorsey, A. M., Scherer, C. W., & Real, K. (1999). The college tradition of "Drink 'Til you Drop": The relation between students' social networks and engaging in risky behaviors. *Health Communication, 11,* 313–334.

Dossey, L. (1982). *Space, time, and medicine.* Boston: New Science.

du Pré, A. (2000). *Communicating about health: Current issues and perspectives.* Mountain View, CA: Mayfield.

Duerksen, S. (1997, March 31). 2nd opinion: Tibetan lets doctors here view traditional medicine. *San Diego Union-Tribune,* pp. B-1, B-4.

Duh, S. V. (1991). *AIDS and blacks.* Newbury Park, CA: Sage.

Dunphy, J. E. (1976). Annual discourse: On caring for the patient with cancer. *New England Journal of Medicine, 295,* 313–319.

Edgar, T. (1992). A compliance-based approach to the study of condom use. In T. Edgar, M. A. Fitzpatrick, & V. S. Freimuth (Eds.), *AIDS: A communicative perspective* (pp. 47–67). Hillsdale, NJ: Erlbaum.

Eisenberg, D. M., Davis, R. B., Ettner, S. L., Appel, S., Wilkey, S., Van Rompay, M., & Kessler, R. C. (1998). Trends in alternative medicine use in the United States, 1990–1997: Results of a follow-up national survey. *Annals of Internal Medicine, 127,* 61–69.

Eisenberg, D. M., Kessler, R. C., Foster, C., Norlock, F. E., Calkins, D. R., & Delbanco, T. L. (1993). Unconventional medicine in the United States: Prevalence, costs, and patterns of use. *New England Journal of Medicine, 328,* 246–252.

Eisenberg, E. M., & Goodall, H. L. (2001). *Organizational communication: Balancing creativity and constraint* (3rd ed.) New York: St. Martin's Press.

Eisler, R. M., & Hersen, M. (Eds.). (2000). *Handbook of gender, culture, and health.* Mahwah, NJ: Erlbaum.

Elkin, E. F. (1990). When a patient miscarries: Implications for treatment. *Psychotherapy, 27,* 600–606.

Elkind, D. (1967). Egocentrism in adolescence. *Child Development, 38,* 1025–1034.

Elkind, D. (1978). Understanding the young adolescent. *Adolescence, 13,* 127–134.

Ellis, B. H., & Miller, K. I. (1993). The role of assertiveness, personal control, and participation in the prediction of nurse burnout. *Journal of Applied Communication Research, 21,* 327–342.

Ellis, C. (1991). Sociological introspection and emotional experience. *Symbolic Interaction, 14,* 23–50.

Ellis, C. (1993). "There are survivors": Telling a story of sudden death. *The Sociological Quarterly, 34,* 711–730.

Ellis, C. (1995a). *Final negotiations: A story of love, loss, and chronic illness.* Philadelphia: Temple University Press.

Ellis, C. S. (1995b). Speaking of dying: An ethnographic short story. *Symbolic Interaction, 18,* 73–81.

Ellis, C. (1996). On the demands of truthfulness in writing personal loss narratives. *Journal of Personal and Interpersonal Loss, 1,* 157–177.

Ellis, C. (1997). Evocative autoethnography: Writing emotionally about our lives. In Y. Lincoln & Tierney (Eds.), *Voice in text: Reframing the narrative* (pp. 115–139). Thousand Oaks, CA: Sage.

Ellis, C. (2000). Negotiating terminal illness: Communication, collusion, and coalition in caregiving. In J. H. Harvey & E. D. Miller (Eds.), *Loss and Trauma: General and close relationship perspectives* (pp. 284–304). Philadelphia: Brunner-Routledge.

Ellis, C., & Bochner, A. (2000). Autoethnography, personal narrative, and reflexivity: Researcher as subject. In N. K. Denzin & Y. S. Lincoln (Eds.), *Handbook of qualitative research* (2nd ed., pp. 733–768). Thousand Oaks, CA: Sage.

Elwood, W. N. (1999a). *Power in the blood: A handbook on AIDS, politics, and communication.* Mahwah, NJ: Erlbaum.

Elwood, W. N. (1999b). Victories to win: Communicating HIV/AIDS prevention and tolerance. In W. N. Elwood (Ed.). *Power in the blood: A handbook on AIDS, politics, and communication* (pp. 415–421). Mahwah, NJ: Erlbaum.

Emanuel, E. J., & Dubler, N. N. (1995). Preserving the physician-patient relationship in the era of managed care. *Journal of the American Medical Association, 273,* 323–329.

Emry, R., & Wiseman, R. L. (1987). An intercultural understanding of able-bodied and disabled persons' communication. *International Journal of Intercultural Relations, 11,* 7–27.

Engelberg, M., Flora, J. A., & Nass, C. I. (1995). AIDS knowledge: Effects of channel involvement and interpersonal communication. *Health Communication, 7,* 73–91.

Enkin, M., Keirse, M. J. N. C., & Chalmers, I. (1989). *A guide to effective care in pregnancy and childbirth.* Oxford, UK: Oxford University Press.

Erzinger, S. (1994). Empowerment in Spanish: Words can get in the way. *Health Education Quarterly 21,* 417–419.

Every Block a Village Online Web site. Downloaded on January 7, 2002, from http://www.ebvonline.org

"Expedition Inspiration." (First aired July 12, 1995). *The New Explorers* (Producer, Bill Curtis). PBS.

Fadiman, A. (1997). *The spirit catches you and you fall down: A Hmong child, her American doctors, and the collision of two cultures.* New York: Farrar, Straus, and Giroux.

Faludi, S. (1991). *Backlash: The undeclared war against American women.* New York: Crown Publishers.

Faux, M. (1984). *Childless by choice: Choosing childlessness in the eighties.* Garden City, NY: Anchor Press/Doubleday.

Federal Register. (1997, September 24). U.S. Department of Health and Human Services, Food and Drug Administration, Vol. 62, No. 185. Proposed Rules. Downloaded on April 24, 2002, from http://www.fda.gov/oashi/aids/womcl.html

Fernandes, M. (1999, August 4). La Leche League walks to promote breast-feeding. *The St. Louis Post-Dispatch,* p. E5.

Fibromyalgia and ruptured silicone gel breast implants. (2001). U.S. Food and Drug Administration—FDA Consumer Magazine, Nov–Dec. Downloaded July 11, 2002, from http://www.fda.gov/fdac/departs/2001/601_upd.html

Field, D. (1989). Nurses' accounts of nursing the terminally ill in a coronary care unit. *Intensive Care Nursing, 5,* 114–122.

Fiese, B. H., & Grotevant, H. D. (2001). Introduction to special issue on "Narratives in and about relationships". *Journal of Social and Personal Relationships, 18,* 579–581.

Fine, M. (1988). Sexuality, schooling, and adolescent females: The missing discourse of desire. *Harvard Educational Review, 58,* 29–53.

Fine, M. (1994). Working the hyphens: Reinventing self and other in qualitative research. In N. K. Denzin & Y. S. Lincoln (Eds.), *Handbook of qualitative research* (pp. 70–82). Thousand Oaks, CA: Sage.

Fisher, M. (1995). *I'll not go quietly: Mary Fisher speaks out.* New York: Scribner.

Fisher, S. (1986). *In the patient's best interest: Women and the politics of medical decisions.* New Brunswick, NJ: Rutgers University Press.

Fisher, W. (1984). Narration as human communication paradigm: The case for public moral argument. *Communication Monographs, 51,* 1–22.

Fisher, W. (1985). The narrative paradigm: An elaboration. *Journal of Communication, 35,* 74–89.

Fisher, W. (1987). *Human communication as narration: Toward a philosophy of reason, value, and action.* Columbia: University of South Carolina Press.

Fitzsimmons, B. (1997, August 2). A labor union. *San Diego Union-Tribune,* pp. E-1, E-3.

Fitzsimmons, B. (1998, September 19). Birth rights. *San Diego Union-Tribune,* pp. E-1, E-4.

Food and Drug Administration. (1995). Gender Studies in Product Development. Downloaded on April 24, 2002, from http://www.fda.gov/womens/executive.html

Food and Drug Administration. (1997, March). A status report on breast implant safety. Downloaded on April 24, 2002, from http://www.fda.gov/fdac/features/99r_implants.htm

Ford, L. A., & Ellis, B. H. (1998). A preliminary analysis of memorable support and nonsupport messages received by nurses in acute care settings. *Health Communication, 10,* 37–63.

Ford, L. A., Ray, E. B., & Ellis, B. H. (1999). Translating scholarship on intrafamilial sexual abuse: The utility of a dialectical perspective for adult survivors. *Journal of Applied Communication Research, 27,* 139–157.

Ford, L. A., & Yep, G. A. (in press). Working along the margins: Developing community-based strategies for communication about health with marginalized groups. In T. Thompson, A. Dorsey, K. Miller, & R. Parrott (Eds.), *Handbook of health communication.* Mahwah, NJ: Erlbaum.

"Formula ads shorten breastfeeding." (2000, April). *The nation's health.* Washington, DC: American Public Health Association, p. 1.

Foss, S. K. (1989). Generic criticism. In S. K. Foss (Ed.), *Rhetorical criticism: Exploration and practice* (pp. 111–150). Prospect Heights, IL: Waveland.

Foss, S. K., & Griffin, C. L. (1995). Beyond persuasion: A proposal for an invitational rhetoric. *Communication Monographs, 62,* 2–18.

Foucault, M. (1977). *Discipline and punish: The birth of the prison* (A. Sheridan, Trans.). New York: Vintage Books.

Foucault, M. (1978). *The history of sexuality: An introduction* (Vol. 1). New York: Vintage Books.

Frank, A. W. (1991). *At the will of the body: Reflections on illness.* Boston: Houghton Mifflin.

Frank, A. W. (1993). The rhetoric of self change: Illness experience as narrative. *The Sociological Quarterly, 34,* 39–52.

Frank, A. W. (1995). *The wounded storyteller: Body, illness, and ethics.* Chicago: University of Chicago Press.

Fraser-Vaselakros, D. (2002). What is the clothesline project? Downloaded on April 1, 2002, from http://www.clothesline.org

Freimuth, V. S. (1990). The chronically uninformed: Closing the knowledge gap in health. In E. B. Ray & L. Donohew (Eds.), *Communication and health: Systems and applications* (pp. 171–186). Hillsdale, NJ: Erlbaum.

Freimuth, V. S., Stein, J. A., & Kean, T. (1989). *Searching for health information: The Cancer Information Service model.* Philadelphia: University of Pennsylvania Press.

Freire, P. (1970). *Pedagogy of the oppressed* (Trans. M. B. Ramos). New York: Continuum.

Freudenheim, J. L., Marshall, J. R., Graham, S., Laughlin, R., Vena, J. E., Bandera, E., Muti, P., Swanson, M., & Nemoto, T. (1994). Exposure to breast milk in infancy and the risk of breast cancer. *Epidemiology, 5,* 324–331.

Frey, L. R., Query, J. L., Flint, L. J., Adelman, M. B. (1998). Living together with AIDS: Social support processes in a residential facility. In V. J. Derlega & A. P. Barbee

(Eds.), *HIV and social interaction* (pp. 129–146). Thousand Oaks, CA: Sage.

Furnham, A. (1994). Explaining health and illness: Lay perceptions on current and further health, the causes of illness, and the nature of recovery. *Social Science and Medicine, 39,* 715–725.

Galanti, G. (1997). *Caring for patients from different cultures: Case studies from American hospitals* (2nd ed.). Philadelphia: University of Pennsylvania Press.

Galewitz, P. (2000, March 6). Prozac's reign as top antidepressant ending. Downloaded on April 28, 2002, from http://www.canoe.ca/Health0003/06_prozac.html

Gallup Organization, Inc. (February, 1993). *The American public's attitudes toward organ donation and transplantation.* Conducted for The Partnership for Organ Donation, Boston, MA.

Gates, L. R. (1995). *Reproducing selves: Contradiction, control and identity in natural childbirth.* Unpublished doctoral dissertation, University of Southern California, Los Angeles.

Gates, L. R. (1997). The mystery and mystique of natural childbirth. In L. A. M. Perry & P. Geist (Eds.), *Courage and conviction: Women's words, women's wisdom* (pp. 185-200). Mountain View, CA: Mayfield.

Geertz, C. (1973). *The interpretation of culture.* New York: Basic Books.

Geist, P. (1999). Communicating health and understanding in the borderlands of co-cultures. In L. Samovar & R. E. Porter (Eds.), *Intercultural communication: A reader* (9th ed., pp. 341–354). Belmont, CA: Wadsworth.

Geist, P., & Dreyer, J. (1993a). The demise of dialogue: A critique of the medical encounter. *Western Journal of Communication, 57,* 233–246.

Geist, P., & Dreyer, J. (1993b). Juxtapositioning accounts: Different versions of different stories in the health care context. In S. Herndon & G. Kreps (Eds.),

*Qualitative research: Applications in organizational communication* (pp. 79–105). Cresskill, NJ: SCA Applied Communication Series/Hampton Press.

Geist, P., & Gates, L. (1996). The poetics and politics of re-covering identities in health communication. *Communication Studies, 47,* 218–228.

Geist, P., Gray, J. L., Avalos-C'de Baca, F., & Hill, G. (1996). Silent tragedy/social stigma: Coping with the pain of infertility. In E. B. Ray (Ed.), *Communication and disenfranchisement: Social health issues and implications* (pp. 159–183). Mahwah, NJ: Erlbaum.

Geist, P., & Hardesty, M. (1990). Ideological positioning in professionals' narratives of quality medical care. In N. Denzin (Ed.), *Studies in symbolic interaction: A research annual* (Vol. 11, pp. 255–281). Greenwich, CT: JAI Press.

Geist, P., & Hardesty, M. (1992). *Negotiating the crisis: DRGs and the transformation of hospitals.* Hillsdale, NJ: Erlbaum.

Geist-Martin, P., & Dreyer, J. (2001). Accounting for care: Different versions of different stories in the health care context. In S. Herndon & G. Kreps (Eds.), *Qualitative research: Applications in organizational communication* (2nd ed., pp. 121–149). Cresskill, NJ: SCA Applied Communication Series/Hampton Press.

Giddens, A. (1991). *Modernity and self identity: Self and society in the late modern age.* Stanford, CA: Stanford University Press.

Giger, J. N., & Davidhizar, R. E. (1991). *Transcultural nursing: Assessment and intervention.* St. Louis: Mosby-Year Book.

Giles, K. L. (1998). "Real women can": The breastfeeding backlash. In A. B. Brown & K. R. McPherson (Eds.), *The reality of breastfeeding* (pp. 188–192). Westport, CT: Bergin & Garvey.

Gillotti, C. M., & Applegate, J. L. (2000). Explaining illness as bad news: Individual differences in explaining illness-related

information. In B. Whaley (Ed.), *Explaining illness: Research, theory, and strategies* (pp. 101–120), Mahwah, NJ: Erlbaum.

Gladwell, M. (1997, June 6). The estrogen question. *The New Yorker,* pp. 54, 55, 58–61.

Glaser, B., & Strauss, A. (1966). *Awareness of dying.* Chicago: Aldine.

Glover, T. D., & Barratt, C. L. R. (Eds.). (1999). *Male fertility and infertility.* Cambridge, UK: Cambridge University Press.

Goffman, E. (1963). *Stigma: Notes on the management of spoiled identity.* Englewood Cliffs, NJ: Prentice Hall.

Goldsmith, D. (1990). A dialectical perspective on the expression of autonomy and connection in romantic relationships. *Western Journal of Speech Communication, 54,* 537–556.

Goldsmith, D. J., & Dun, S. A. (1997). Sex differences and similarities in the communication of social support. *Journal of Social and Personal Relationships, 14,* 317–337.

Goldsmith, J. (1990). *Childbirth wisdom: From the world's oldest societies.* New York: East West Health Books.

González, M. C. (1994). An invitation to leap from a trinitarian ontology in health communication research to a spiritually inclusive quatrain. In S. A. Deetz (Ed.), *Communication yearbook 17* (pp. 378–387). Thousand Oaks, CA: Sage.

González, M. C. (1997). There must have been a place. In L. A. M. Perry & P. Geist (Eds.), *Courage of conviction: Women's words, women's wisdom* (p. 168). Mountain View, CA: Mayfield.

Goodman, H. (1994, December 14). Power struggle cuts Penn's on-line cancer link. *Philadelphia Inquirer,* p. A1.

Gorrie, M. (1989). Reaching clients through cross cultural education. *Journal of Gerontological Nursing, 15* (10), 29–31.

Granovetter, M. S. (1973). The strength of weak ties. *American Journal of Sociology, 78,* 1360–1380.

Greenberg, B. S., Brown, J. D., & Buerkel-Rothfuss, N. (1993). *Media, sex and the adolescent.* Cresskill, NJ: Hampton.

Greene, K., Rubin, D. L., Hale, J. L., & Walters, L. H. (1996). The utility of understanding adolescent egocentrism in designing health promotion messages. *Health Communication, 8,* 131–152.

Greil, A. L. (1991). *Not yet pregnant: Infertile couples in contemporary America.* New Brunswick, NJ: Rutgers University Press.

Grinspoon, L., & Bakalar, J. B. (1997). *Marijuana, the forbidden medicine.* New Haven, CT: Yale University Press.

Grogan, S. (1999). *Body image: Understanding body dissatisfaction in men, women, and children.* New York: Routledge.

Gudykunst, W. B., Ting-Toomey, S., & Chua, E. (1988). *Culture and interpersonal communication.* Newbury Park, CA: Sage.

Guerrero, L. K., Andersen, P. A., & Trost, M. R. (1998). Communication and emotion: Basic concepts and approaches. In P. A. Andersen & L. K. Guerrero (Eds.), *Handbook of communication and emotion: Research, theory, applications, and contexts* (pp. 5–27). San Diego: Academic Press.

Guinan, M., & Leviton, L. (1995). Prevention of HIV infection in women: Overcoming barriers. *Journal of the American Medical Women's Association, 50,* 74–77.

Guttman, N. (2000). *Public health communication interventions: Values and ethical dilemmas.* Thousand Oaks, CA: Sage.

Haffner, D. W., Kelly, M., & Bozell, L. B. (1987). The media affect teen sexuality. In B. Leone, T. O'Neill, & K. Swisher (Eds.), *Teenage sexuality: Opposing viewpoints* (pp. 33–40). San Diego: Greenhaven Press.

Hammond, S. L., & Lambert, B. L. (1994). Communicating with patients about medication. *Health Communication, 6,* 247–252.

Hanne, M. (1994). *The power of the story: Fiction and political change.* Providence, RI: Berghahn Books.

Harden, S. L. (1994). *What legislators need to know about managed care* [brief]. Denver: National Conference of State Legislatures.

Hardesty, M., & Geist, P. (1990). Physicians' self-referent communication as management of uncertainty along the illness trajectory. In G. L. Albrecht (Ed.), *Advances in medical sociology* (Vol. 1, pp. 27–55). Greenwich, CT: JAI Press.

Hardesty, M., & Geist, P. (1992). Communication as hospital dirty work: The neglected task of informing patients about DRGs. In E. B. Ray (Ed.), *Case Studies in health communication* (pp. 237–248). Hillsdale, NJ: Erlbaum.

Hathaway, M., Hathaway, J., & Bek, S. H. (1989). *The Bradley method: Student workbook.* Sherman Oaks, CA: American Academy of Husband-Coached Childbirth.

Haug, F., et al. (1987). *Female sexualization.* London: Verso.

Hawkins, R. P., Pingree, S., Gustafson, D. H., Boberg, E. W., Bricker, E., McTavish, F., Wise, M., & Owens, B. (1997). Aiding those facing health crises: The experience of the CHESS Project. In R. L. Street, W. R. Gold, & T. Manning (Eds.), *Health promotion and interactive technology* (pp. 79–102). Mahwah, NJ: Erlbaum.

Healthy People 2010. (2001). *Health Communication.* Downloaded on December 20, 2001, from http://www.healthgov/healthypeople/document/pdf/Volume1/11HealthCom.pdf

Helm, A., & Mazur, D. J. (1989). Death notification: Legal and ethical issues. *Dimensions of Critical Care Nursing, 8,* 382–385.

Helman, C. G. (1990). *Culture, health, and illness: An introduction for health professionals.* Boston: Wright.

Henriksen, L., & Jackson, C. (1998). Antismoking socialization: Relationship to parent and child smoking status. *Health Communication, 10,* 87–101.

Herek, G. M. (1999). AIDS and stigma. *American Behavioral Scientist, 42,* 1106–1116.

Heymann, J. (1995). *Equal partners*. Boston: Little Brown & Co.

Heymann, S. J., & Kerr, C. (2000). We need partners: Forging strong relationships with patients. In W. B. Bateman, E. J. Kramer, & K. S. Glassman (Eds.), *Patient and family education in managed care and beyond: Seizing the teachable moment* (pp. 203–227). New York: Springer.

Hines, S., Babrow, A., Badzek, L., & Moss, A. H. (1997). Communication and problematic integration in end-of-life decisions: Dialysis decisions among the elderly. *Health Communication, 9,* 199–217.

Hippocrates. (1923). *On decorum and the physician* (Vol. 2). London: Heinemann Medical Books.

"HIV-positive girl, 8, is finally welcomed into a Scout troop" (1998, December 4). *Star Tribune* (Minneapolis, MN), p. 21A.

"HMO hell." (1999, November 8). *Newsweek*, p. 58.

Hochhauser, M. (1988, August). *AIDS: It's not what you know, it's what you do.* Paper presented at the annual meeting of the American Psychological Association, Atlanta.

Hochschild, A., with Machung, A. (1989). *The second shift: Working parents and the revolution at home.* New York: Viking-Penguin Press.

Hochschild, A. R. (1983). *The managed heart: Commercialization of human feelings.* Berkeley: University of California Press.

hooks, b. (1991). Theory as liberatory practice. *Yale Journal of Law and Feminism, 4,* 1–12.

Horwood, L. J., & Ferguson, D. M. (1998). Breastfeeding and later cognitive and academic outcomes. Downloaded on April 25, 2002, from http://www.pediatrics.org/cgi/content/full/101/1/e9

House, J. S., Landis, K. R., & Umberson, D. (1988). Social relationships and health. *Science, 241,* 540–545.

Howe-Murphy, R., Ross, H., Tseng, R., & Hartwig, R. (1989). Effecting change in multicultural health promotion: A systems approach. *Journal of Allied Health, 18,* 291–305.

Hsu, F. L. K. (1985). The self in cross-cultural perspective. In A. J. Marsella, G. DeVos, & F. L. K. Hsu (Eds.), *Culture and self: Asian and western perspectives* (pp. 24–55). New York: Tavistock Publications.

Hughes, E. (1971). *The sociological eye.* Chicago: Aldine.

Humbert, M. (2000, February 7). Hillary Clinton formally begins race to become senator from New York. *San Diego Union-Tribune*, p. A-2.

Humphry, D. (1991). *Final exit: The practicalities of self-deliverance and assisted suicide for the dying.* Eugene, OR: Hemlock Society.

Hunt, D. J. (1996). Break the silence. Downloaded on April 1, 2002, from http://www.webistry.net/jan/abuse.html

Hunter, K. M. (1991). *Doctors' stories: The narrative structure of medical knowledge.* Princeton, NJ: Princeton University Press.

Hyde, M. J. (1990). Experts, rhetoric, and the dilemmas of medical technology: Investigating a problem of progressive ideology. In M. J. Medhurst, A. Gonzalez, & T. R. Peterson (Eds.), *Communication and the culture of technology* (pp. 115–136). Pullman: Washington State University.

Hynes, G. J., Callan, V. J., Terry, D. J., & Gallois, C. (1992). The psychological well-being of infertile women after a failed IVF attempt: The effects of coping. *British Journal of Medical Psychology, 65,* 269–278.

Iley, C. (2000, January 28). Britney is 18 and she's already had breast implants. *The Scotsman*, p. 22.

Illich, I. ( 1976). *Medical nemesis: The expropriation of health.* New York: Pantheon Books.

Ingram, D., & Hutchinson, S. A. (1999). Defensive mothering in HIV-positive mothers. *Qualitative Health Research, 8,* 243–258.

Ingrassia, M. (2000, December 21). Plastic surgery Santa. *New York Daily News,* p. 60.

Inlander, C. B., Levin, L. S., & Weiner, E. (1988). *Medicine on trial: The appalling story of medical ineptitude and the arrogance that overlooks it.* New York: Pantheon.

Institute of Medicine. (1994). *AIDS and behavior.* Washington, DC: National Academy Press.

Irwin, B. R. (Executive Producer), & Rodriguez, D. R. (Director). (1995). *Prostate cancer treatment: Understanding your options* [Videocassette]. (Available from MEDCOM, Inc., P. O. Box 6003, Cypress, CA 90630)

Jackson, M. (1989). *Paths toward a clearing: Radical empiricism and ethnographic inquiry.* Bloomington: Indiana University Press.

Jacobsen, P., Perry, S., & Hirsch, D. (1990). Behavioral and psychological responses to HIV antibody testing. *Journal of Counseling & Clinical Psychology, 58,* 31–37.

Jacobson, N. (2000). *Cleavage: Technology, controversy, and the ironies of the manmade breast.* New Brunswick, NJ: Rutgers University Press.

Jagger, A. (1994). Sexual differences and sexual equality. In D. L. Rhode (Ed.), *Theoretical perspectives on sexual difference* (pp. 239–254). New Haven, CT: Yale University Press.

Jefferson, T. (1782). Notes on the state of Virginia: Query XVII. In P. L. Ford (Ed.). (1894), *The writings of Thomas Jefferson, Volume III: 1781–1784.* New York: G. P. Putnam's Sons.

Jhally, S. (Writer, Editor, Narrator). (1987). *Dream worlds: Desire/sex/power in rock video* [video]. Media Education Foundation, Northampton, MA 01060.

Jhally, S. (Writer, Editor, Narrator). (1995). *Dream worlds 2: Desire/sex/power in music video* [video]. Media Education Foundation, Northampton, MA 01060.

Johnston, L. D., O'Malley, P. M., & Bachman, J. G. (1994). *National survey results on drug use from the Monitoring the Future Study, 1975–1993.* Rockville, MD: National Institute on Drug Abuse.

Jones, C. M., & Beach, W. A. (in press). "I just wanna know why": Patients' attempts and physicians' responses to premature solicitation of diagnostic information. In M. Maxwell (Ed.), *Diagnosis as cultural practice.* New York: Mouton de Gruyter.

Jones, J. H. (1981). *Bad blood: The Tuskegee syphilis experiment.* New York: Free Press.

Joy, J. E., Watson, S. J., & Benson, J. A. (Eds.). (1999). *Marijuana and medicine: Assessing the science base.* Washington, DC: National Academy Press.

Kahn, G. (1997). Digital interactive media and the health care balance of power. In R. L. Street, W. R. Gold, & T. Manning (Eds.), *Health promotion and interactive technology* (pp. 187–208). Mahwah, NJ: Erlbaum.

Kalb, C. (2000, May 22). Stars, money and medical crusades. *Newsweek,* pp. 58–60.

Kanter, R. M. (1972). *Commitment and community: Communes and utopias in sociological perspective.* Cambridge, MA: Harvard University Press.

Kaplan, H. I., & Sadock, B. J. (Eds.). (1985). *Comprehensive textbook of psychiatry* (4th ed.). Baltimore: William & Wilkins.

Kaplan, R. T. (1998). It's time to remove the brief summary from DTC print ads. *Medical Marketing & Media, 33* (5), 44–48.

Kaplan, S. H., Greenfield, S., & Ware, J. E. (1989). Assessing the effects of physician-patient interaction on the outcomes of chronic disease. *Medical Care 27 (suppl),* S110–S127.

Kar, S. B, Alcalay, R., & Alex, S. (2001a). Communicating with multicultural populations: A theoretical framework. In

S. B. Kar, R. Alcalay, & S. Alex (Eds.), *Health communication: A multicultural perspective* (pp. 109–137). Thousand Oaks, CA: Sage.

Kar, S. B, Alcalay, R., & Alex, S. (2001b). Preface. In S. B. Kar, R. Alcalay, & S. Alex (Eds.), *Health communication: A multicultural perspective* (pp. ix–xxi). Thousand Oaks, CA: Sage.

Karp, D. A. (1994). The dialectics of depression. *Symbolic Interaction, 17,* 341–366.

Karp, D. A. (1999). Illness and identity. In K. Charmaz & D. A. Paterniti (Eds.), *Health, illness, and healing* (pp. 83–94). Los Angeles: Roxbury.

Kastenbaum, R. J. (1995). *Death, society, and human experience* (5th ed.). Boston: Allyn and Bacon.

Katz, J. (1984). *The silent world of doctor and patient* (pp. 48–84). New York: Free Press.

Katz, J. E., & Rice, R. E. (2001). Concluding thoughts. In R. E. Rice & J. E. Katz (Eds.), *The Internet and health communication: Experiences and expectations* (pp. 417–429). Thousand Oaks, CA: Sage.

Kaysen, S. (1993). *Girl, interrupted.* New York: Vintage Books.

Kellehear, A., & Lewin, T. (1988–1989). Farewells by the dying: A sociological study. *Omega, 19,* 275–292.

Kelleher, K. (1998a, December 5). Is there a right time to get pregnant? *San Diego Union-Tribune,* p. E-3.

Kelleher, K. (1998b, December 5). Pros and cons to conceiving at any age. *San Diego Union-Tribune,* p. E-3.

Kettl, P. A. (1999). Major depression: The forgotten illness. *Hospital Medicine, 35,* 31–38.

Kim, Y. M., Odallo, D., Thuo, M., & Kols, A. (1999). Client participation and provider communication in family planning counseling: Transcript analysis in Kenya. *Health Communication, 11,* 1–19.

Kim, Y. Y. (1991). Communication and cross-cultural adaptation. In L. A. Samovar and R. E. Porter (Eds.), *Intercultural communication: A reader* (6th ed., pp. 401–411). Belmont, CA: Wadsworth.

Kinder, M. (1999). *Kids' media culture.* Durham, NC: Duke University Press.

Kistenberg, C. J., & Shaw, C. M. (1993). What she does know won't hurt her: Women's words on HIV. In F. C. Corey (Ed.), *HIV education: Performing personal narratives* (pp. 79–86). Tempe: Arizona State University.

Klass, P. (1987). *A not entirely benign procedure: Four years as a medical student* (pp. 111–116). New York: Plume/Penguin.

Klaus, M. H., Kennell, J. H., & Klaus, P. H. (1993). *Mothering the mother.* Reading, MA: Addison-Wesley.

Kleinfield, S. (1977). *The hidden minority: A profile of handicapped Americans.* Boston: Little, Brown and Company.

Kleinman, A. (1980). *Patients and healers in the context of culture: An exploration of the borderland between anthropology, medicine, and psychiatry.* Berkeley: University of California Press.

Kleinman, A. (1988). *The illness narratives: Suffering, healing, and the human condition.* New York: Basic Books.

Kleinman, A., Eisenberg, L., & Good, B. (1998). Culture, illness, and care: Clinical lessons from anthropologic and cross-cultural research. *Annals of Internal Medicine, 88,* 251–258.

Kolata, G. (1997, June 22). Women want control, just not all of the time. *New York Times Women's Health Special Edition,* p. WH3.

Kolb, R. H., & Albanese, P. J. (1997). The functional integration of sole-media images into magazine advertisement. *Sex Roles, 36,* 813–836.

Kopfman, J. E., Smith, S. W., Ah Yun, J. K., & Hodges, A. (1998). Affective and cognitive reactions to narrative versus statistical evidence organ donation messages. *Journal of Applied Communication Research, 26,* 279–300.

Korda, M. (1997). *Man to man: Surviving prostate cancer.* New York: Vintage Books.

Korsch, B. M., & Negrete, V. F. (1972). Doctor-patient communication, *Scientific American, 227 (2),* 66–74.

Kotarba, J. A., & Hurt, D. (1995). An ethnography of an AIDS hospice: Toward a theory of organizational pastiche. *Symbolic Interaction, 18,* 413–438.

Krajewski-Jaime, E. R. (1991). Folk-healing among Mexican-American families as a consideration in the delivery of child welfare and child health care services. *Child Welfare, 70,* 157–167.

Kramer, P. D. (1993). *Listening to Prozac: A psychiatrist explores antidepressant drugs and the remaking of the self.* New York: Penguin Books.

Kreps, G. L., & Kunimoto, E. N. (1994). *Effective communication in multicultural health care settings.* Thousand Oaks, CA: Sage.

Kreps, G. L., & Thornton, B. C. (1992). *Health communication: Theory and practice* (2nd ed.). New York: Longman.

Kretzmann, J. P., & McKnight, J. L. (1993). *Building communities from the inside out: A path toward finding and mobilizing a community's assets.* Chicago: ACTA Publications.

Kubler-Ross, E. (1969). *On death and dying.* New York: Macmillan.

Kuipers, J. C. (1989). "Medical discourse" in anthropological context: Views of language and power. *Medical Anthropology Quarterly, 3,* 88–123.

Labonte, R. (1994, Summer). Health promotion and empowerment: Reflections on professional practice. *Health Education Quarterly, 21,* 253–268.

Labov, W. (1972). *Sociolinguistic patterns.* Philadelphia: University of Pennsylvania Press.

Lamaze, F. (1956). *Painless childbirth.* Chicago: Contemporary Books, Inc.

Lambert, B. L., Street, R. L., Cegala, D. J., Smith, D. H., Durtz, S., & Schofield, T. (1997). Provider-patient communication, patient-centered care, and the mangle of practice. *Health Communication, 9,* 27–43.

Lammers, J. C., & Duggan, A. (in press). Bringing physicians back in: Communication predictors of physicians' satisfaction with managed care. *Health Communication, 14.*

Lammers, J. C., & Geist, P. (1997). The transformation of caring in the light and shadow of "managed care." *Health Communication, 9,* 45–60.

Landa, A. (1990). No accident: The voice of voluntarily childless women: An essay on the social construction of fertility choices. In J. P. Knowles & E. Cole (Eds.), *Woman-defined motherhood* (pp. 139–158). New York: Harrington Park Press.

Lannin, D. R., Mathews, H. F., Mitchell, J., Swanson, M. S., Swanson, F. H., & Edwards, M. S. (1998). Influence of socioeconomic and cultural factors on racial differences in late-stage presentation of breast cancer. *Journal of the American Medical Association, 279,* 1801–1807.

Larry King Live. (1998, May 6). *Still Me.* Christopher Reeve: "I have never been disabled in my dreams" (http://www.cnn.com/books/dialogue/9805/reeve/index.htm).

Laster, L. (2001, January 21). A look at quitting medicine: It's not the job, it's the OIG and the 99203s. *Washington Post,* p. B3.

Laumann, E. O., Gagnon, J. H., Michael, R. T., & Michaels, S. (1994). *The social organization of sexuality: Sexual practices in the United States.* Chicago: University of Chicago Press.

Leash, R. M. (1994). *Death notification: A practical guide to the process.* New York: Upper Access, Inc.

Leboyer, F. (1975). *Birth without violence.* New York: Knopf.

Leder, D. (1990). *The absent body.* Chicago: University of Chicago Press.

Lee, J. (1997). Never innocent: Breasted experiences in women's bodily narratives of puberty. *Feminism and Psychology, 7,* 453–474.

Lee, J., & Sasser-Coen, J. (1996). *Blood stories: Menarche and the politics of the female body in contemporary society.* New York: Routledge.

Lefcourt, H. M. (1982). *Locus of control: Current trends in theory and research* (2nd ed.). Hillsdale, NJ: Erlbaum.

Leininger, M. (1991). Transcultural nursing: The study and practice field. *Imprint, 38* (2), 55–66.

Lemp, G. F., Hirozawa, A. M., Cohen, J. B., Derish, P. A., McKinney, K. C., & Hernandez, S. R. (1992). Survival for women and men with AIDS. *Journal of Infectious Disease, 166,* 74–79.

Levick, D. (1998, November 8). When slashed wrists are not enough: Insurers tighten access to mental health care, *Hartford Courant,* p. A1.

Levinson, W., Gorawara-Bhat, R., Dueck, R., Egener, B., Kao, A., Kerr, C., et al. (1999). Resolving disagreements in the patient-physician relationship: Tools for improving communication in managed care. *Journal of the American Medical Association, 282,* 1477–1483.

Levy-Warren, M. H. (1996). *The adolescent journey: Development, identity formation, and psychotherapy.* Northvale, NJ: Jason Aronson.

Lindquist, G. J. (1990). Integration of international and transcultural content in nursing curricula: A process for change. *Journal of Professional Nursing, 6,* 272–279.

Link, P. W., & Darling, C. A. (1986). Couples undergoing treatment for infertility: Dimensions of life satisfaction. *Journal of Sex and Marital Therapy, 12,* 46–59.

Lisle, L. (1996). *Without child: Challenging the stigma of childlessness.* New York: Ballantine Books.

Littlejohn, S. W. (1996). *Theories of human communication* (5th ed.). Belmont, CA: Wadsworth.

Littlewood, R. (1991). From disease to illness and back again. *The Lancet, 337,* 1013–1015.

Liu, A. (1979). *Solitaire.* New York: Harper and Row.

Liu, J., Grove, K., & Kelly, D. P. (1997). "I'm alive, thank you": Women's accounts of HIV/AIDS. In L. A. M. Perry & P. Geist (Eds.), *Courage of conviction: Women's words, women's wisdom* (pp. 283–299). Mountain View, CA: Mayfield.

Loeser, J. D. (1991). What is chronic pain? *Theoretical Medicine, 12,* 214–215.

Long, S. O. (1997). *Reflections on becoming a cucumber: Images of the good death in Japan and the United States.* Paper presented at the Center for Japanese Studies, University of Michigan, Ann Arbor, MI, September 11.

Long, S. O. (1999). Family surrogacy and cancer disclosure in Japan. *Journal of Palliative* Care, *15* (3), 31–42.

Lorde, A. (1980). *The cancer journals.* San Francisco: Aunt Lute Books.

"Losing a son: One family's spiritual ordeal." (2000, July 30). *The Plain Dealer,* National Section, pp. A1–A10.

"Losing Lisa." (1998, November 1-26), *The Plain Dealer,* 26-part series, Section A. Downloaded on November 19, 1998, from http://www.cleveland.com/losinglisa/

Love, S., & Lindsey, K. (1997). *Dr. Susan Love's hormone book: Making informed choices about menopause.* New York: Random House.

Lowenberg, J. S. (1989). *Caring and responsibility: The crossroads between holistic practice and traditional medicine.* Philadelphia: University of Pennsylvania Press.

Lupton, D. (1994). Toward the development of critical health communication praxis. *Health Communication, 6,* 55–67.

Lyons, R., Sullivan, M., & Ritvo, P. (1994). *Close relationships and chronic health problems.* Thousand Oaks, CA: Sage.

Lyons, R. E., & Meade, D. (1995). Painting a new face on relationships: Relationship remodeling in response to chronic illness. In S. Duck & J. T. Wood (Eds.), *Confronting relationship challenges* (pp. 181–210). Thousand Oaks, CA: Sage.

MacPherson, P. (1996). A pitch for organ donation. *Hospitals & Health Networks, 70* (4), 76.

Managed care facts sheets. (2002). Downloaded on May 14, 2002, from http://www.mcareol.com/factshts/factover.htm

Marcinko, T. (1998). What we've learned from 11 years of strategic studies. *Medical Marketing & Media, 33* (11), 53–54, 56.

Marlatt, G. A. (1998). Highlights of harm reduction: A personal report from the First National Harm Reduction Conference in the United States. In G. A. Marlatt (Ed.), *Harm reduction* (pp. 3–29). New York: Guilford Press.

Marshall, A. A. (1993). Whose agenda is it anyway? Training medical residents in patient-centered interviewing techniques. In E. B. Ray (Ed.), *Case studies in health communication* (pp. 15–29). Hillsdale, NJ: Erlbaum.

Marshall, A. A., & McKeon, J. K. (1996). Reaching the "unreachables": Educating and motivating woman living in poverty. In E. B. Ray (Ed.), *Communication and disenfranchisement: Social health issues and implications* (pp. 137–156). Mahwah, NJ: Erlbaum.

Martin, E. (1987). *The woman in the body: A cultural analysis of reproduction.* Boston: Beacon Press.

Martin, J. N., & Nakayama, T. K. (1999). Thinking dialectically about culture and communication. *Communication Theory, 9,* 1–25.

Martin, K. A. (1996). *Puberty, sexuality, and the self: Boys and girls at adolescence.* New York: Routledge.

Maslach, C. (1982). *Burnout: The cost of caring.* Englewood Cliffs, NJ: Prentice Hall.

Mason, D. J., & Leavitt, J. K. (1998). *Policy and politics in nursing and health care* (3rd ed.). Philadelphia: W. B. Saunders.

Mason, M. (1993). *Male infertility—Men talking.* New York: Routledge.

Masheter, C., & Harris, L. (1986). From divorce to friendship: A study of dialectical relationship development. *Journal of Social and Personal Relationships, 3,* 177–179.

Mathieson, C. M., & Barrie, C. M. (1998). Probing the prime narrative: Illness, interviewing, and identity. *Qualitative Health Research, 8,* 581–601.

Mathieson, C. M., & Stam, H. J. (1995). Renegotiating identity: Cancer narratives. *Sociology of Health and Illness, 17,* 283–306.

Mathre, M. L. (1997). Introduction. In M. L. Mathre (Ed.), *Cannabis in medical practice: A legal, historical and pharmacological overview of the therapeutic use of marijuana* (pp. 1–10). Jefferson, NC: McFarland & Company.

Maybury, K. K. (1995–1996). Invisible lives: Women, men and obituaries. *Omega, 32* (1), 27–37.

Mazor, M. D., & Simons, H. F. (Eds.). (1984). *Infertility: Medical, emotional and social considerations.* New York: Human Sciences Press, Inc.

McAllister, M. P. (1992). AIDS, medicalization, and the news media. In T. Edgar, M. A. Fitzpatrick, & V. S. Freimuth (Eds.), *AIDS: A communication perspective* (pp. 195–221). Hillsdale, NJ: Erlbaum.

McCaffrey, B. R. (1997, February 3). We're on a perilous path. *Newsweek,* p. 27.

McDaniel, S. H., Hepworth, J., & Doherty, W. (1992). Medical family therapy with couples facing infertility. *The American Journal, 20,* 101–122.

McEwan, K. L., Costelli, C. G., & Taylor, P. G. (1987). Adjustment to infertility. *Journal of Abnormal Psychology, 96,* 108–116.

McGowin, D. F. (1993). *Living in the labyrinth: A personal journey through the maze of Alzheimer's.* San Francisco: Elder Books.

McKnight, J. L. (1987, Winter). Regenerating community. *Social Policy,* 54–58.

McLuhan, M. (1964). *Understanding media: The extensions of man.* New York: McGraw-Hill.

McLuhan, M., & Fiore, Q. (1967). *The medium is the massage.* New York: Random House.

McMurray, J. E., Williams, E., Schwartz, M. D., et al. (1997). Physician job satisfaction: Developing a model using qualitative data. *Journal of General Internal Medicine, 12,* 711–714.

Meckler, L. (1999, September 15). Increase in multiple births unprecedented. *San Diego Union-Tribune,* p. A-8.

"Menopause: A guide to smart choices." (1999, January). *Consumer Reports, 64,* 50–54.

Metts, S., & Fitzpatrick, M. A. (1992). Thinking about safer sex: The risky business of "Know Your Partner" advice. In T. Edgar, M. A. Fitzpatrick, & V. S. Freimuth (Eds.), *AIDS: A communicative perspective* (pp. 1–19). Hillsdale, NJ: Erlbaum.

Metts, S., Geist, P., & Gray, J. L. (1994). The role of relationship characteristics in the provision and effectiveness of supportive messages among nursing professionals. In B. R. Burleson, T. L. Albrecht, & I. H. Sarason (Eds.), *Communication of social support: Messages, interactions, relationships, and community* (pp. 229–246). Thousand Oaks, CA: Sage.

Metts, S., & Manns, H. (1996a). Coping with HIV and AIDS: The social and personal challenges. In E. B. Ray (Ed.), *Communication and disenfranchisement: Social health issues and implications* (pp. 347–364). Mahwah, NJ: Erlbaum.

Metts, S., & Manns, H. (1996b). Living with HIV and AIDS: Personal accounts of coping. In E. B. Ray (Ed.), *Case studies in communication and disenfranchisement: Applications to social health issues* (pp. 179–194). Mahwah, NJ: Erlbaum.

Metzger, D. (1992). Tree. In *Tree and the woman who slept with men* (p. 91). Berkeley, CA: Wingbow Press.

Michal-Johnson, P., & Bowen, S. P. (1992). The place of culture in HIV education. In T. Edgar, M. A. Fitzpatrick, & V. Freimuth (Eds.), *AIDS: A communication perspective* (pp. 147–172). Hillsdale, NJ: Erlbaum

Miller, B. C., Norton, M. C., Fan, X., Christopherson, C. R. (1998). Pubertal development, parental communication, and sexual values in relation to adolescent sexual behaviors. *Journal of Early Adolescence, 18,* 27–52.

Miller, K. I., Ellis, B., Zook, E., & Lyles, J. (1990). An integrated model of communication, stress, and burnout in the workplace. *Communication Research, 17,* 300–326.

Miller, K. I., Joseph, L., & Apker, J. (2000). Strategic ambiguity in the role development process. *Journal of Applied Communication Research, 28,* 193–214.

Miller, K. I., & Ray, E. B. (1994). Beyond the ties that bind: Exploring the "meaning" of supportive messages and relationships. In B. Burleson, T. Albrecht, & I. Sarason (Eds.), *Communication of social support: Messages, interactions, relationships, and community* (pp. 215–228). Thousand Oaks, CA: Sage.

Miller, K. I., Stiff, J. B., & Ellis, B. H. (1988). Communication and empathy as precursors to burnout among human service workers. *Communication Monographs, 55,* 250–265.

Miller, K. I., Zook, E. G., & Ellis, B. H. (1989). Occupational differences in the influence of communication on stress and burnout in the workplace. *Management Communication Quarterly, 3,* 166–190.

Miller, R. H. (1996). Health system integration: A means to an end. *Health Affairs, 15* (2), 92–106.

Miller, R. H., & Luft, H. S. (1997). Does managed care lead to better or worse quality of care? *Health Affairs, 16* (5), 7–25.

Miller, T. (2000). Losing the plot: Narrative construction and longitudinal childbirth research. *Qualitative Health Research, 10,* 309–323.

Miller, V. D., & Knapp, M. L. (1986). The post-nuntio dilemma: Approaches to communicating with the dying. In M. McLaughlin (Ed.), *Communication yearbook 9* (pp. 1124–1136). Beverly Hills, CA: Sage.

Mintz, D. (1992). What's in a word: The distancing function of language in medicine. *Journal of Medical Humanities, 13,* 223–233.

Mishler, E. G. (1984). *The discourse of medicine: Dialectics of medical interviews.* Norwood, NJ: Ablex.

Mitford, J. (1998). *The American way of death revisited.* New York: Alfred A. Knopf.

Montgomery, B. M., & Baxter, L. A. (Ed.). (1998). *Dialectical approaches to studying personal relationships.* Mahwah, NJ: Erlbaum.

Morell, C. M. (1994). *Unwomanly conduct: The challenges of intentional childlessness.* New York: Routledge.

Morreim, E. H. (1985). The MD and the DRG. *Hastings Center Report, 15,* 30–38.

Morris, D. B. (1998). *Illness and culture in the postmodern age.* Berkeley: University of California Press.

Morris, J. (1991). *Pride against prejudice: Transforming attitudes to disability.* Philadelphia: New Society Publishers.

Morrison, K. H. (1996, October). *"The sacred circle of life": A value analysis of the Native American Women's Health Education Resource Center's poster "Prevent Fetal Alcohol Syndrome."* Paper presented at the annual meeting of the Organization for the Study of Communication, Language, and Gender, Monterey, CA.

Mullally, B. (1997). Law to change on organ donor requests. *The Times Herald Record* [Online]. Downloaded on November 16, 1998, from http://www.th-record.com/9-26/97/organver.htm

Mullan, F. (1975). *Vital signs.* New York: Laurel.

Mumby, D. (1988). *Communication and power in organizations: Discourse, ideology, and domination.* Norwood, NJ: Ablex.

Murphy, T., & Lappé, M. (1994). *Justice and the Human Genome Project.* Berkeley: University of California Press.

Myerson, A. R. (1996, April 22). Trickle-down health care: Many executives go first class as workers get cut-rate benefits. *San Diego Union-Tribune,* pp. C-1–C-2.

Nadesan, M. H., & Sotirin, P. (1998). The romance and science of "Breast Is Best": Discursive contradictions and contexts of breastfeeding choices. *Text and Performance Quarterly, 18,* 217–232.

Nagro, M. J. (1998). The first lesson. In A. B. Brown & K. R. McPherson (Eds.), *The reality of breastfeeding* (pp. 144–148). Westport, CT: Bergin & Garvey.

National Advisory Mental Health Council. (1996). Basic behavioral science research for mental health: Vulnerability and resilience. *American Psychologist, 51,* 22–28.

National Clearinghouse for Alcohol and Drug Information. (2001). Alcohol and other drugs & suicide. Downloaded on January 10, 2002, from http://www.health.org/govpubs/m1009/index.htm

"National data on HIV prevalence among disadvantaged youth in the 1990s." (1998, September). Center for Disease Control. Downloaded on December 31, 2001, from http://www.cednpin.org/cgi-bin

National Institutes of Health. (1993). Revitalization Act of 1993 (Public Law 103-43). Downloaded on April 24, 2002, from www4.od.nih.gov/orwh/inclusion.html

National Spinal Cord Association. (1999). Downloaded on August 3, 1999 from http://www.spinalcord.org

Needleman, J. (1985), *The way of the physician.* San Francisco: Harper & Row.

Nelson, E. J. (1996). The American experience of childbirth: Toward a range of safe choices. In R. L. Parrott & C. M. Condit

(Eds.), *Evaluating women's health messages: A resource book* (pp. 109–123). Thousand Oaks, CA: Sage.

Newcomb, P. A., Storer, B. E., Longnecker, M. P., Mittendorf, R., Greenberg, E. R., Clapp, R. W., et al. (1994). Lactation and reduced risk of premenopausal breast cancer. *The New England Journal of Medicine, 330,* 81–87.

Newman, J. (November 1997). At your disposal. *Harper's Magazine,* 61–71.

Norbeck, J. (1995). Who is our consumer? Shaping nursing programs to meet emerging needs. *Journal of Professional Nursing, 11.*

Northouse, P. G., & Northouse, L. L. (1992). *Health communication: Strategies for health professionals* (2nd ed.). Norwalk, CT: Appleton & Lange.

Nuland, S. B. (1995). *How we die: Reflections on life's final chapter.* New York: Alfred A. Knopf.

Nussbaum, J. F., Pecchioni, L. L., Robinson, J. D., Thompson, T. L. (2000). *Communication and aging* (2nd ed.). Mahwah, NJ: Erlbaum.

Oakley, A. (1984). *The captured womb: A history of the medical care of pregnant women.* New York: Basil Blackwell.

O'Brien, K. (1999, October 10). *Minneapolis Star Tribune,* p. 1E.

Office of National Drug Control Policy. (2000). Summary of current situation: National household survey. Downloaded on May 28, 2002, from http://www. whitehousedrugpolicy.gov/drugfact/index. html

O'Moore, M. A., & Harrison, R. F. (1991). Anxiety and reproductive failure: Experiences from a Dublin fertility clinic. *The Irish Journal of Psychology, 12,* 276–285.

Oppenheimer, G. M. (1988). In the eye of the storm: The epidemiological construction of AIDS. In E. Fee & D. M. Fox (Eds.), *AIDS: The burden of history* (pp. 267–300). Berkeley: University of California Press.

"Organ donation: Donate life." Downloaded on April 28, 2002, from http://www. organdonor.gov/

Orque, M., Block, B., & Monroy, L. (1983). *Ethnic nursing care: A multicultural approach.* St. Louis: C. V. Mosby.

Orr, J. (1993). Panic diary: (Re)constructing a partial politics and poetics of disease. In J. Holstein & G. Miller (Eds.), *Reconsidering social constructionism: Debates in social problems theory* (pp. 441–482). New York: Aldine.

Ott, J. K. (1999). *Emotional experiences embraced: Communicating identity and illness survivorship.* Unpublished master's thesis. San Diego State University.

Pappert, A. (2000). What price pregnancy? *Ms. Magazine, 10,* 43–49.

Paradis, L. F. (1985). The development of hospice in America: A social movement organizes. In L. F. Paradis (Ed.), *Hospice handbook: A guide for managers and planners* (pp. 3-24). Rockville, MD: Aspen.

Park, K. Y., & Peterson, L. M. (1991). Beliefs, practices, and experiences of Korean women in relation to childbirth. *Health Care for Women International, 12,* 261–267.

Parrott, R. (1994). Exploring family practitioners' and patients' information exchange about prescribed medications: Implications for practitioners' interviewing and patients' understanding. *Health Communication, 6,* 267–280.

Parrott, R. L., & Condit, C. M. (Eds.). (1996). *Evaluating women's health messages: A resource book.* Thousand Oaks, CA: Sage.

Parrott, R. L., & Daniels, M J. (1996). Promoting prenatal and pregnancy care to women: Promises, pitfalls, and pratfalls. In R. L. Parrott & C. M. Condit (Eds.), *Evaluating women's health messages: A resource book* (pp. 205–221). Thousand Oaks, CA: Sage.

Parry, J. K. (1987). The significance of open communication in working with terminally ill clients. *The Hospice Journal, 3* (4), 33–49.

"Patient cleared in marijuana case." (2001, January 30). *San Diego Union-Tribune,* p. A-3.

Payer, L. (1988). *Medicine and culture: Varieties of treatment in the United States, England, West Germany, and France.* New York: Penguin Books.

Pear, R. (1999, June 8). N.I.H. plan for journal on the Web draws fire. *New York Times,* p. D1.

Pennebaker, J. W. (1993). Putting stress into words: Health, linguistic, and therapeutic implications. *Behaviour Research & Therapy, 31,* 539–548.

Pennebaker, J. W. (1995). Emotion, disclosure and health: An overview. In J. W. Pennebaker (Ed.), *Emotion, disclosure, and health* (pp. 3–10). Washington, DC: American Psychological Association.

Pennebaker, J. W., & Beall, S. K. (1986). Confronting a traumatic event: Toward an understanding of inhibition and disease. *Journal of Abnormal Psychology, 95,* 274–281.

Pennebaker, J. W., Kiecolt-Glaser, J. K., & Glaser, R. (1988). Disclosure of traumas and immune function: Health implications for psychotherapy. *Journal of Counseling and Clinical Psychology, 56,* 239–245.

Pepler, C. J., & Lynch, A. (1991). Relational messages of control in nurse-patient interactions with terminally ill patients with AIDS and cancer. *Journal of Palliative Care, 7,* 18–29.

Perloff, R. M. (2001). *Persuading people to have safer sex: Applications of social science to the AIDS crisis.* Mahwah, NJ: Erlbaum.

Phoenix, A., Woollett, A., & Lloyd, E. (Eds.). (1991). *Motherhood: Meanings, practices and ideologies.* Newbury Park, CA: Sage.

Pines, D. (1990). Emotional aspects of infertility and its remedies. *International Journal of Psychoanalysis, 71,* 561–568.

Poirier, S. (1995). *Chicago's war on syphilis, 1937–1940: The times, the Trib, and the clap doctor.* Urbana: University of Illinois Press.

Poirier, S., Rosenblum, L., Brauner, D., Sharf, B. F., & Stanford, A. F. (1992). Charting the chart—An exercise in interpretation(s). *Literature and Medicine, 11,* 1–22.

Polce-Lynch, M., & Meyers, B. J., Kilmartin, C. T., Forssmann-Falck, R., & Kliewer, W. (1998). Gender and age patterns in emotional expression, body image, and self-esteem: A qualitative analysis. *Sex Roles, 38,* 1025–1048.

Polkinghorne, D. E. (1988). *Narrative knowing and the human sciences.* Albany: State University of New York Press.

Pollock, D. (1999). *Telling bodies, performing birth: Everyday narratives of childbirth.* New York: Columbia University Press.

Ponton, L. E. (1996). Disordered eating. In R. J. DiClemente, W. B. Hansen, & L. E. Ponton (Eds.), *Handbook of adolescent health risk behavior* (pp. 83–113). New York: Plenum.

Porter, C. P., Oakley, D. J., Guthrie, B. J., & Killion, C. (1999). Early adolescent sexual behaviors. *Issues in Comprehensive Pediatric Nursing, 22,* 129–142.

Porter, R. E., & Samovar, L. A. (1998). Cultural influences on emotional expression: Implications for intercultural communication. In P. A. Andersen & L. K. Guerrero (Eds.). *Handbook of communication and emotion: Research, theory, applications, and contexts* (pp. 452–472). San Diego: Academic Press.

Post, D. M. (1997). Values, stress and coping among practicing family physicians. *Archives of Internal Medicine, 6,* 252–255.

"Postpartum blues and breastfeeding." (1998, August 31). *San Diego Union-Tribune,* p. E-3.

Poussaint, A. F. (1997, April). Prostate cancer: Male killer hits famous and not so famous. *Ebony, 52* (6), 116–120, 134.

Powell-Cope, G. M. (1995). The experiences of gay couples affected by HIV infection. *Qualitative Health Research, 5,* 36–62.

"Pregnant facts." (2000, July 9). *Boston Globe,* p. F6.

Price, R. (1994). *A whole new life: An illness and a healing.* New York: Atheneum.

*Proceedings of the Secretary's Conference to establish a national action plan on breast cancer.* (1993, December 14–15). Bethesda, MD: National Institutes of Health.

Purnell, L. D., & Paulanka, B. J. (Eds.). (1998a). *Transcultural health care: A culturally competent approach.* Philadelphia: F. A. Davis Company.

Purnell, L. D., & Paulanka, B. J. (1998b). Transcultural diversity and health care. In L. D. Purnell & B. J. Paulanka (Eds.), *Transcultural health care: A culturally competent approach* (pp. 1–6). Philadelphia: F. A. Davis Company.

Purnell, L. D., & Paulanka, B. J. (1998c). Purnell's model for cultural competence. In L. D. Purnell & B. J. Paulanka (Eds.), *Transcultural health care: A culturally competent approach* (pp. 7–51). Philadelphia: F. A. Davis Company.

Purtilo, R. (1999). *Ethical dimensions in the health professions* (3rd ed.). Philadelphia: W. B. Saunders.

Putnam, R. D. (2000). *Bowling alone: The collapse and revival of American community.* New York: Simon & Schuster.

Quill, T. (1983). Partnerships in patient care: A contractual approach. *Annals of Internal Medicine, 98,* 228–234.

Rabinow, P., & Sullivan, W. M. (Eds.). (1987). *Interpretive social science: A second look.* Berkeley: University of California Press.

Radner, G. (1989). *It's always something.* New York: Simon and Schuster.

Rawlins, W. K. (1983). Negotiating close friendship: The dialectic of conjunctive freedoms. *Human Communication Research, 9,* 255–266.

Rawlins, W. K. (1989). A dialectical analysis of the tensions, functions, and strategic challenges of communication in young adult friendships. In J. A. Anderson (Ed.), *Communication yearbook 12* (pp. 157–189). Newbury Park, CA: Sage.

Rawlins, W. K. (1992). *Friendship matters: Communication, dialectics, and the life course.* New York: Aldine.

Ray, E. B. (1987). Supportive relationships and occupational stress in the workplace. In T. L. Albrecht & M. B. Adelman (Eds.), *Communicating social support* (pp. 172–191). Newbury Park, CA: Sage.

Ray, E. B. (Ed.). (1993a). *Case studies in health communication.* Hillsdale, NJ: Erlbaum.

Ray, E. B. (1993b). When the links become chains: Considering dysfunctions of supportive communication in the workplace. *Communication Monographs, 60,* 106–111.

Ray, E. B. (Ed.). (1996a). *Case studies in communication and disenfranchisement: Applications to social health issues.* Mahwah, NJ: Erlbaum.

Ray, E. B. (Ed.). (1996b). *Communication and disenfranchisement: Social health issues and implications.* Mahwah, NJ: Erlbaum.

Ray, E. B., Ellis, B. H., & Ford, L. A. (2000). Sharing the secret: Social support among adult incest survivors. In D. O. Braithwaite & J. T. Wood (Eds.), *Case studies in interpersonal communication: Processes and problems* (pp. 218–226). Belmont, CA: Wadsworth.

Ray, E. B., & Miller, K. I. (1994). Social support, home/work stress, and burnout: Who can help? *Journal of Applied Behavioral Science, 30,* 357–373.

Ray, M. C. (1997). *I'm with you now: A guide through incurable illness for patients, families, and friends.* New York: Bantam Books.

Read, G. D. (1944). *Childbirth without fear: The principles and practice of natural childbirth.* New York: Harper.

Redfield, J. (1997). Tigger. In R. Shah, K. Brown, & R. Martinoff (Eds.), *Body Electric, XIII* (p. 2). Chicago: Department of

Medical Education, University of Illinois College of Medicine-Chicago.

Reeve, C. (1998). *Still me.* New York: Ballantine Books.

Reindl, S. M. (2001). *Sensing the self: Women's recovery from bulimia.* Cambridge, MA: Harvard University Press.

Remen, R. N. (1988, Autumn). Spirit: Resource for healing. *Noetic Sciences Review,* pp. 5–9.

Remen, R. N. (1994). The recovery of the sacred: Some thoughts on medical reform. *ReVision, 16,* 123–129.

Reuters Health Information (2001, January 5). UK doctor says 15-year-old too young for breast op. Downloaded on April 26, 2002, from http://www.reutershealth.com/frame2/arch.html

Rice, R. E., & Katz, J. E. (Eds.). (2001). *The Internet and health communication: Experiences and expectations.* Thousand Oaks, CA: Sage.

Richardson, L. (1997). *Fields of play: Constructing an academic life.* New Brunswick, NJ: Rutgers University Press.

Riessman, C. K. (1987). Women and medicalization: A new perspective. In H. D. Schwartz (Ed.), *Dominant issues in medical sociology* (2nd ed., pp. 101–121). New York: Random House.

Riessman, C. K. (1993). *Narrative analysis.* Newbury Park, CA: Sage.

Riley, D. (1994). *The harm reduction model.* Toronto: Harm Reduction Network.

Riley, D., & O'Hare, P. (in press). Harm reduction: History, definition and practice. In J. Inciardi & L. Harrison (Eds.), *Harm reduction and drug control.* Thousand Oaks, CA: Sage.

Riley, D., Teixeira, P., & Hausser, D. (1999). HIV/AIDS policy issues related to large-scale targeted interventions for injection drug users. Paper presented at the UNAIDS/Health Canada dialogue on policy dilemmas facing governments of high-income countries regarding HIV/AIDS, Montebello, Quebec.

Rimal, R. N., Ratzan, S. C., Arntson, P., & Freimuth, V. S. (1997). Reconceptualizing the "patient": Health care promotion as increasing citizens' decision-making competencies. *Health Communication, 9,* 61–74.

Roback, G., Randolph, L., & Seidman, B. (1992). *Physician characteristics and distribution in the U.S.* Chicago: American Medical Association.

Robbins, P. R. (1998). *Adolescent suicide.* Jefferson, NC: McFarland & Company.

Roberts, E. J. (Ed.). (1980). *Childhood sexual learning: The unwritten curriculum.* Cambridge, MA: Ballinger.

Rogers, A. (1998, August 24). Good medicine on the web. *Newsweek,* p. 60.

Rogers, E. M. (1993). Diffusion and reinvention of Project D.A.R.E. In T. E. Backer & E. M. Rogers (Eds.), *Organizational aspects of health communication campaigns: What works?* (pp. 139–162). Newbury Park, CA: Sage.

Romney, S. L. (1999). Can we talk? Downloaded on May 5, 2002, from http://www.prch.org/News%20sep%2099.html

Ronan, R. (1982). *Narratives from America.* Port Townsend, WA: Dragon Gate.

Rosenthal, D. A., & Feldman, S. S. (1999). The importance of importance: Adolescents' perceptions of parental communication about sexuality. *Journal of Adolescence, 22,* 835–851.

Rosenthal, E. (2001, December 30). With ignorance as fuel: AIDS speeds across China. *New York Times,* pp. A1, A8.

Ross, J. L., & Geist, P. (1997). Elation and devastation: Women's journeys through pregnancy and miscarriage. In L. A. M. Perry & P. Geist (Eds.), *Courage of conviction: Women's words, women's wisdom* (pp. 167–184). Mountain View, CA: Mayfield.

Roter, D. (1977). Patient participation in the patient-provider interaction: The effects of patient question asking on the quality of the interaction, satisfaction, and compliance. *Health Education Monographs, 5,* 281–315.

Roter, D. (1987). An exploration of health education's responsibility for a partnership model of client-provider relations. *Patient Education and Counseling, 10,* 25–31.

Rothman, B. K. (1989). *Recreating motherhood: Ideology and technology in a patriarchal society.* New York: Norton.

Rothman, B. K. (1991). *In labor: Women and power in the birthplace.* New York: Norton.

Ruben, B. D. (1990). The health caregiver-patient relationship: Pathology, etiology, treatment. In E. B. Ray & L. Donohew (Eds.), *Communication and health: Systems and applications* (pp. 51–68). Hillsdale, NJ: Erlbaum.

Rubin, D. L., Healy, P., Gardiner, T. C., Zath, R. C., & Moore, C. P. (1997). Nonnative physicians as message sources: Effects of accent and ethnicity on patients' responses to AIDS prevention counseling. *Health Communication, 9,* 351–368.

Rummans, T. A., Frost, M., Suman, V. J., Taylor, M., Novotny, P., Gendron, T., et al. (1998). Quality of life and pain in patients with recurrent breast and gynecologic cancer. *Psychosomatics, 39,* 437–445.

Ryan, A. (1997). The resurgence of breastfeeding in the United States. *Pediatrics, 99,* 596.

Ryan, E. B., & Butler, R. N. (1996). Communication, aging, and health: Toward understanding health provider relationships with older clients. *Health Communication, 8,* 191–197.

Rychlak, J. F. (Ed.). (1976). *Dialectic: Humanistic rationale for behavior and development.* Basel, Switzerland: D. Karger.

Saarinen, U. M., & Kajosaari, M. (1995). Breastfeeding as prophylaxis against atopic disease: Prospective follow-up study until 17 years old. *The Lancet, 346,* 1065–1069.

Saenger, E. (1999). Depression, age, and ethnicity. CBS HealthWatch-Library. Downloaded on December 18, 2001, from http://cbshealthwatch.health.aol.com/aolmeds.../article.asp?RecID=15&ContentType=Library

Scaer, R. M. (1993). Three social interventions to dramatically improve the quality and outcomes of maternity care. *International Journal of Childbirth Education, 8,* 7–9.

Scheerhorn, D. (1997). Creating illness-related communities. In R. L. Street, W. R. Gold, & T. Manning (Eds.), *Health promotion and interactive technology* (pp. 171–186). Mahwah, NJ: Erlbaum.

Scheman, N. (1993). *Engenderings: Constructions of knowledge, authority, and privilege.* New York: Routledge.

Schiff, H. S. (1996). *How did I become my parent's parent?* New York: Viking Books.

Schooler, C., & Henderson, V. (2000). *Summary report: Patient compliance with cholesterol-lowering drug regimens.* Miami Beach, FL: Patient Compliance Experts Panel.

Schwartz, J. L. (1999). Foreword. In J. Medina (Ed.), *What you need to know about Alzheimer's* (p. xi). Oakland, CA: CME & New Harbinger Publications.

Scripps Howard News Service. (1997, April 7). Nearly 60% of new moms say they are breastfeeding. *San Diego Union-Tribune,* p. A-6.

Seals, B. F., Sowell, R. L., Demi, A. S., Moneyham, L., Cohen, L., & Guillory, J. (1995). Falling through the cracks: Social service concerns of women infected with HIV. *Qualitative Health Research, 5,* 496–515.

Segrin, C., & Fitzpatrick, M. (1992). Depression and verbal aggressiveness in different marital types. *Communication Studies, 43,* 79–91.

Sells, C. W., & Blum, R. W. (1996). Current trends in adolescent health. In R. J. DiClemente, W. B. Hansen, & L. E. Ponton (Eds.), *Handbook of adolescent health risk behavior* (pp. 5–34). New York: Plenum Press.

Sengupta, S. (1996). Understanding less educated smokers' intention to quit smoking: Strategies for antismoking communication aimed at less educated smokers. *Health Communication, 8,* 55–72.

Sennett, R. (1976). *The fall of public man: On the social psychology of capitalism.* New York: Vintage.

Sepucha, K., Belkora, J., Tripathy, D., Esserman, L., & Aviv, C. (2000). *Proceedings of the Era of Hope Department of Defense Breast Cancer Research Program Meeting* (Vol. II, p. 771). Atlanta: U.S. Army Medical Research and Materiel Command.

Sexton, J. (Fall, 1997). The semantics of death and dying: Metaphor and mortality. *Et cetera,* 333–345.

Shapiro, J. P. (1993). *No pity: People with disabilities forging a new civil rights movement.* New York: Random House.

Sharf, B. F. (1984). *The physician's guide to better communication.* Glenview, IL: Scott, Foresman.

Sharf, B. F. (1987). Teaching patients to speak up: Past and future trends. *Patient Education & Counseling, 11,* 95–108.

Sharf, B. F. (1990). Patient-physician communication as interpersonal rhetoric: A narrative approach. *Health Communication, 2,* 217–231.

Sharf, B. F. (1995). Poster art as women's rhetoric: Raising awareness about breast cancer. *Literature and Medicine, 14,* 72–86.

Sharf, B. F. (1997). Communicating breast cancer online: Support and empowerment on the Internet. *Women & Health, 26,* 65–84.

Sharf, B. F. (2001). Out of the closet and into the legislature: The impact of communicating breast cancer narratives on health policy. *Health Affairs, 20,* 1–6.

Sharf, B. F., & Freimuth, V. S. (1993). The construction of illness in entertainment television: Coping with cancer on *thirtysomething. Health Communication, 5,* 141–160.

Sharf, B. F., Freimuth, V. S., Greenspon, P., & Plotnick, C. (1996). Confronting cancer on *thirtysomething*: Audience response to health content on entertainment television. *Journal of Health Communication, 1,* 157–172.

Sharf, B. F., & Kahler, J. (1996). Victims of the franchise: A culturally sensitive model of teaching patient-doctor communication in the inner city. In E. B. Ray (Ed.), *Communication and disenfranchisement: Social health issues and implications* (pp. 95–115). Hillsdale, NJ: Erlbaum.

Sharf, B. F., Stanford, A. F., Montgomery, K., & Kahler, J. (1998). *"So your main concern is getting this pain under control": A clinical case as text and performance.* Paper presented at the annual meeting of the International Communication Association, Jerusalem, Israel.

Sharf, B. F., & Street, R. L. (1997a). The patient as a central construct: Shifting the emphasis. *Health Communication, 9,* 1–11.

Sharf, B. F., & Street, R. L. (Eds.). (1997b). Special issue: The patient as a central construct in health communication research. *Health Communication, 9,* 1–93.

Shaw, J., & Waller, G. (1995). The media's impact on body image: Implications for prevention and treatment [Special issue: Body experience]. *Eating Disorders: The Journal of Treatment and Prevention, 3,* 115–123.

Sheer, V. C., & Cline, R. J. (1994). The development and validation of a model explaining sexual behavior among college students: Implication for AIDS communication campaigns. *Human Communication Research, 21,* 280–304.

Sheer, V. C., & Cline, R. J. W. (1995). Individual differences in sensation seeking and sexual behavior: Implications for communication intervention for HIV/AIDS prevention among college students. *Health Communication, 7,* 205–223.

Shelton, D. L. (1996). Physicians hold key to boosting organ donation, awareness. *American Medical News, 39* (17), 11.

Sherbourne, C. D., Hays, R. D., Ordway, L., DiMatteo, M. R., & Kravitz, R. L. (1992). Antecedents of adherence to medical recommendations: Results from the medical outcomes study. *Journal of Behavioral Medicine, 15,* 447–468.

Shields, L. E. (1995). Women's experiences of the meaning of empowerment. *Qualitative Health Research, 5,* 15–35.

Shilling, C. (1993). *The body and social theory.* Newbury Park, CA: Sage.

Shilts, R. (1987). *And the band played on: Politics, people, and the AIDS epidemic.* New York: St. Martin's Press.

Shorter, E. (1985). *Bedside manners: The troubled history of doctors and patients.* New York: Simon and Schuster.

Siegel, K., & Raveis, V. (1997). Perceptions of access to HIV-related information, care, and services. *Qualitative Health Research, 7,* 9–31.

Signorielli, N., & Staples, J. (1997). Television and children's conceptions of nutrition. *Health Communication, 9,* 289–301.

Simon, C. (2000). Scars. *The bedroom tapes* [CD]. New York: Arista Records.

Singhal, A., & Rogers, E. M. (1999). *Entertainment-education: A communication strategy for social change.* Mahwah, NJ: Erlbaum.

Smith, D., & Pettegrew, L. (1986). Mutual persuasion as a model for doctor-patient communication. *Theoretical Medicine, 7,* 127–146.

Smith, J. W., & Kandath, K. P. (2000). Communication and the blind or visually impaired. In D. O. Braithwaite & T. L. Thompson (Eds.), *Handbook of communication and people with disabilities: Research and application* (pp. 389–403). Mahwah, NJ: Erlbaum.

Smith, K. K., & Berg, D. N. (1987). *Paradoxes of group life: Understanding conflict, paralysis, and movement in group dynamics.* San Francisco: Jossey-Bass.

Smith, M. L. (2000, October). *Entitlement, injunction, or sacred act: Women's decisions to have or not have breast implants.* Paper presented at the annual meeting of the Organization for the Study of Communication, Language, and Gender, Milwaukee, WI.

Smith, S. W., Morrison, K., Kopfman, J. E., & Ford, L. A. (1994). The influence of prior thought and intent on the memorability and persuasiveness of organ donation message strategies. *Health Communication, 6,* 1–20.

Sofaer, S. (1996). *Five scenarios for the public's health.* Unpublished manuscript, George Washington University.

Somers, M. R. (1994). The narrative constitution of identity: A relational and network approach. *Theory and Society, 23,* 605–649.

Sontag, S. (1978). *Illness as metaphor.* New York: Farrar, Strauss, and Giroux.

Sontag, S. (1989). *Illness as metaphor and AIDS and its metaphors.* New York: Doubleday.

Sparkes, A. C. (1996). The fatal flaw: A narrative of the fragile body-self. *Qualitative Inquiry, 2,* 463–494.

Sparkes, A. C. (1997). Reflections on the socially constructed physical self. In K. Fox (Ed.), *The physical self: From motivation to well-being* (pp. 83–110). Champaign, IL: Human Kinetics.

Sparkes, A. C. (1998). Athletic identity: An Achilles' heel to the survival of self. *Qualitative Health Research, 8,* 644–664.

Spector, R. (1996). *Cultural diversity in health and illness* (4th ed.). Stanford, CT: Appleton & Lang.

Spitzberg, B. H. (1999a). An analysis of empirical estimates of sexual aggression: Victimization and perpetration. *Violence and Victims, 14,* 241–260.

Spitzberg, B. H. (1999b). Intercultural communication competence. In L. A. Samovar & R. E. Porter (Eds.), *Intercultural communication: A reader* (9th ed., pp. 353–365). Belmont, CA: Wadsworth.

Spitzberg, B. H., & Cupach, W. R. (in press). Interpersonal skills. In M. L. Knapp & J.

Daly (Eds.), *Handbook of interpersonal communication* (3rd ed.). Thousand Oaks, CA: Sage.

Spragins, E. (1997, July 28). When your HMO says no. *Newsweek, 73.*

Spragins, E. E. (1995, June 19). Simon says, join us! *Newsweek,* p. 55.

Stamper, J. (1998, March 4). Shrinking world making Americans sick, surgeon general says. *The San Diego Union-Tribune,* p. A-11.

Stanton, A. L., & Dunkel-Schetter, C. (Eds.). (1991). *Infertility: Perspectives from stress and coping research.* New York: Plenum Press.

Starr, P. (1982). *The social transformation of American medicine: The rise of a sovereign profession and the making of a vast industry.* New York: Basic Books.

"Statement of purpose." (1998). *PSP Advocate, 9* (3), 2.

Steinhauer, J. (1999, April 2). Life vs. work: For female doctors, a difficult choice. *San Diego Union-Tribune,* p. E-3.

Sterk, H. M. (1996). Contemporary birthing practices: Technology over humanity? In R. L. Parrott & C. M. Condit (Eds.), *Evaluating women's health messages: A resource book* (pp. 124–134). Thousand Oaks, CA: Sage.

Stewart, M., Brown, J. B., Weston, W. W., McWhinney, I. R., McWilliam, C. L., & Freeman, T. R. (1995). *Patient-centered medicine: Transforming the clinical method.* Thousand Oaks, CA: Sage.

Stoddard, S. (1992). *The hospice movement: A better way of caring for the dying.* New York: Vintage Books.

Strasburger, V. C. (1995). *Adolescence and the media: Medial and psychological impact.* New York: Ballantine Books.

Street, R. L. (2001). Active patients as powerful communicators: The linguistic foundation of participation in health care. In W. P. Robinson & H. Giles (Eds.), *The new handbook of language and social psychology* (2nd ed., pp. 541–560). Chichester, U.K.: John Wiley.

Street, R. L., Gold, W. R., & Manning, T. (Eds.). (1997). *Health promotion and interactive technology: Theoretical applications and future directions.* Mahwah, NJ: Erlbaum.

Street, R. L., & Rimal, R. N. (1997). Health promotion and interactive technology: A conceptual foundation. In R. L. Street, W. R. Gold, & T. Manning (Eds.), *Health promotion and interactive technology: Theoretical applications and future directions* (pp. 1–18). Mahwah, NJ: Erlbaum.

Strull, W. N., Lo, B., & Charles, G. (1984). Do patients want to participate in medical decision making? *Journal of the American Medical Association, 252,* 2990–2994. [AU: Or 2442–2446?]

"Study links culture, some cancer rates" (June 10, 1998). *The San Diego Union-Tribune,* p. A-7.

Stumpf, S. H., & Bass, K. (1992). Cross cultural communication to help physician assistants provide unbiased health care. *Public Health Records, 107,* 113–115.

Styron, W. (1990). *Darkness visible: A memoir of madness.* New York: Vintage Books.

Substance Abuse and Mental Health Services Administration. (1996). *Preliminary estimates from the 1995 National Household Survey on Drug Abuse.* Rockville, MD: U.S. Department of Health and Human Services.

Suchman, A. L. (2000). Story, medicine, and health care. *Advances in Mind-Body Medicine, 16,* 193–198.

"Talk to your patients about organ donation." (1998). *American Medical News, 41,* 17.

Tardy, R. W., & Hale, C. L. (1998a). Bonding and cracking: The role of informal, interpersonal networks in health care decision making. *Health Communication, 10,* 151–173.

Tardy, R. W., & Hale, C. L. (1998b). Getting "plugged in": A network analysis of health information seeking among "stay-at-home moms." *Communication Monographs, 65,* 336–357.

Theodosakis, J., & Feinberg, D. T. (2000). *Don't let your HMO kill you: How to wake up your doctor, take control of your health, and make managed care work for you.* New York: Routledge.

Thompson, T. L. (1982). "You can't play marbles—you have a wooden hand": Communication with the handicapped. *Communication Quarterly, 30,* 108–115.

Thompson, T. L. (1989). Communication and dying: The end of the life-span. In J. F. Nussbaum (Ed.), *Life-span communication* (pp. 339–359). Hillsdale, NJ: Erlbaum.

Thompson, T. L. (1996). Allowing dignity: Communication with the dying. In E. B. Ray (Ed.), *Communication and disenfranchisement: Social health issues and implications* (pp. 387–404). Mahwah, NJ: Erlbaum.

Thompson, T. L., & Gillotti, C. (1993). From labor to the NICU: The journey of a premature baby and her parents. In E. B. Ray (Ed.), *Case studies in health communication* (pp. 87–100). Hillsdale, NJ: Erlbaum.

Thorne, B. (1993). *Gender play: Girls and boys in school.* New Brunswick, NJ: Rutgers University Press.

Tiggemann, M., & Pennington, B. (1990). The development of gender differences in body-size dissatisfaction. *Australian Psychologist, 25,* 306–313.

Tillich, P. (1952). *The courage to be.* New Haven, CT: Yale University Press.

Tillmann-Healy, L. M. (1996). A secret life in a culture of thinness: Reflections on body, food, and bulimia. In C. Ellis & A. P. Bochner (Eds.), *Composing ethnography: Alternative forms of qualitative writing* (pp. 76–108). Walnut Creek, CA: Altamira.

Tinder, G. (1995). *Tolerance and community.* Columbia: University of Missouri Press.

Tobler, N. S. (1993). Meta-analysis of adolescent drug prevention programs: Results of the 1993 meta-analysis. *National Institute on Drug Abuse Monograph,* no. 170.

Tourigny, S. C. (1998). Some new dying trick: American youths "choosing" HIV/AIDS. *Qualitative Health Research, 8,* 149–167.

Treichler, P. A. (1988). AIDS, gender, and biomedical discourse: Current contests for meaning. In E. Fee & D. M. Fox (Eds.), *AIDS: The burden of history* (pp. 190–266). Berkeley: University of California Press.

Treichler, P. A. (1989). What definitions do: Childbirth, cultural crisis, and the challenge to medical discourse. In B. Dervin, L. Grossberg, B. J. O'Keefe, & E. Wartella (Eds.), *Rethinking communication* (pp. 424–453). Newbury Park, CA: Sage.

Turow, J. (1989). *Playing doctor: Television, storytelling, and medical power.* New York: Oxford University Press.

United Network for Organ Sharing. (2002). Critical data: U.S. facts about transplantation. Downloaded on April 28, 2002, from http://www.unos.org/Newsroom/critdata_main.htm

U.S. Census Bureau. (2001). *Statistical abstracts of the United States.* Downloaded on April 10, 2002, from http://www.census.gov/prod/2001pubs/statab/sec01.pdf

U.S. Department of Commerce. (1994). *Statistical abstract of the United States 1994.* Washington, DC: U.S. Government Printing Office.

U.S. Department of Health and Human Services. (2001). Life expectancy hits new high in 2000; mortality declines for several leading causes of death. Downloaded on April 28, 2002, from http://www.hhs.gov/news

U.S. Immigration & Naturalization Service (2001). Immigrants admitted by selected country of birth: Fiscal Year 1998. Downloaded on April 10, 2002, from http://

www.ins.usdoj.gov/graphics/aboutins/
statistics/imm98list.htm

U.S. Senate Web site. Bipartisan Patients' Bill
of Rights Act of 2001. Downloaded on
January 27, 2002, from http://thomas.
loc.gov/cgibin/query/D?c107:1:./temp/
~c107KZLP3M

Uslander, A., & Weiss, C. (1975). *Dealing
with questions about sex.* Palo Alto, CA:
Learning Handbooks.

Vanderford, M. L., & Smith, D. H. (1996).
*The silicone breast implant story: Com-
munication and uncertainty.* Mahwah,
NJ: Erlbaum.

Varallo, S. M., Ray, E. B., & Ellis, B. H.
(1998). Speaking of incest: The research
interview as social justice. *Journal of
Applied Communication Research, 26,*
254–271.

Verge, C. F., Howard, N. J., Irving, L., Simp-
son, J. M., Mackerras, D., & Silink,
M. (1994). Environmental factors in
childhood IDDM: A population-based,
case-control study. *Diabetes Care, 17,*
1381–1389.

Wagner, M. K. (2001). Behavioral characteristics related to substance abuse and
risk-taking, sensation-seeking, anxiety
sensitivity, and self-reinforcement. *Addictive Behaviors, 26,* 115–120.

Waitzkin, H. (1979). Medicine, superstruc-
ture and micropolitics. *Social Science and
Medicine, 13A,* 601–609.

Waitzkin, H. (1983). *The second sickness:
Contradictions of capitalist health care.*
New York: The Free Press.

Waitzkin, H. (1984). Doctor-patient communication: Clinical implications of social scientific research. *Journal of the
American Medical Association, 252,*
2441–2446.

Waitzkin, H. (1985). Information giving in
medical care. *Journal of Health and Social Behavior, 26,* 81–101.

Waitzkin, H. (1991). *The politics of medical
encounters: How patients and doctors deal
with social problems.* New Haven, CT:
Yale University Press.

Waitzkin, H. (2000). *Second sickness: Contradictions of capitalist health care* (Revised and updated edition). New York:
Rowman & Littlefield.

Waitzkin, H., & Britt, T. (1989). A critical
theory of medical discourse: How patients and health professionals deal with
social problems. *International Journal of
Health Services, 19,* 577–597.

Waitzkin, H., & Stoeckle, J. (1976). Information control and the micropolitics of
health care. *Social Science and Medicine,
10,* 263–276.

Waitzkin, H. B., & Waterman, B. (1974). *The
exploitation of illness in capitalist society.*
New York: Bobbs-Merrill.

Wallerstein, E. (1982). *Circumcision: An American health fallacy.* New York: Springer.

Wallerstein, E. (1990). *The circumcision decision.* Seattle: Pennypress, Inc.

Wallis, C. (1991, November 4). Why new age
medicine is catching on. *Time,* 68–76.

Wallston, K. A., Maides, S., & Wallston, B. S.
(1976). Health related information seeking as a function of health related locus
of control and health value. *Journal of
Research in Personality, 10,* 215–222.

Warren, P. M. (1999, May 21). A cap and
gown—and new breasts. *Los Angeles
Times,* p. E1.

Waxler-Morrison, N., Anderson, J., &
Richardson, E. (1991). *Cross-cultural caring: A handbook for health professionals
in Western Canada.* Vancouver: University of British Columbia.

Webb, R. E., & Daniluk, J. C. (1999). The end
of the line: Infertile men's experiences of
being unable to produce a child. *Men
and Masculinities, 2,* 6–25.

Weber, P. (1994). Organ donation. *Kidney
Health* [Online]. Downloaded on March
18, 2002, from http://www.health-line.
com/articles/kp940107.htm

Wekesser, C. (Ed.). (1996). *Reproductive technologies.* San Diego: Greenhaven Press.

Werner, C. M., & Baxter, L. A. (1994). Tempo-
ral qualities of relationships: Organismic,

transactional, and dialectical views. In M. L. Knapp & G. R. Miller (Eds.), *Handbook of interpersonal communication* (2nd ed., pp. 323–377). Thousand Oaks, CA: Sage.

West, C. (1984). *Routine complications: Troubles with talk between doctors and patients.* Bloomington: Indiana University Press.

Westside Health Authority Web site. Downloaded on January 7, 2002, from http://www.healthauthority.org

Whaley, B. (1994). "Food is to me as gas is to cars??": Using figurative language to explain illness to children. *Health Communication, 6,* 193–204.

Whaley, B. (1999). Explaining illness to children: Advancing theory and research by determining message content. *Health Communication, 11,* 185–193.

Whaley, B. (Ed.). (2000). *Explaining illness: Research, theory, and strategies.* Mahwah, NJ: Erlbaum.

Whitcomb, J. (1994). *Teaching natural birth: Deciding to teach and establishing your own successful business.* San Diego: Thornwood Gardens Publishing.

White, H. (1981). The value of narrativity in the representation of reality. In W. J. T. Mitchell (Ed.), *On narrative* (pp. 1–23). Chicago: University of Chicago Press.

Wiener, L. S. (1991). Women and human immunodeficiency virus: A historical and personal psychosocial perspective. *Social Work, 36,* 375–378.

Wilkie, D. (2002, July 12). Teenage birthrate declines to lowest level ever recorded. *San Diego Union Tribune,* A1, A12.

Wilmot, W. W. (1987). *Dyadic communication* (3rd ed.). New York: Random House.

Wilson, H. S., Hutchinson, S. A., & Holzemer, W. L. (1997). Salvaging quality of life in ethnically diverse patients with advanced HIV/AIDS. *Qualitative Health Research, 7,* 75–97.

Windle, M., Shope, J. T., & Bukstein, O. (1996). Alcohol use. In R. J. DiClemente,

W. B. Hansen, & L. E. Ponton (Eds.), *Handbook of adolescent health risk behavior* (pp. 115–159). New York: Plenum.

Winter, B. (1991, April 18). Happy birthday! Heart problems plague toddler's first three years. *Rock County Star Herald,* Luverne, MN, p. B1.

Witte, K. (1992). Putting the fear back in fear appeals: The Extended Parallel Process Model. *Communication Monographs, 59,* 330–349.

Witte, K. (1995). Fishing for success: Using the persuasive health message framework to generate effective campaign messages. In E. Maibach & R. Parrott (Eds.), *Designing health messages: Approaches from communication theory and public health practice* (pp. 145–166). Newbury Park, CA: Sage.

Witte, K. (1997). Preventing teen pregnancy through persuasive communication: Realities, myths, and the hard-fact truths. *Journal of Community Health, 22,* 137–154.

Witte, K. (1998). Fear as motivator, fear as inhibitor: Using the extended parallel process model to explain fear appeal successes and failures. In P. A. Andersen & L. K. Guerrero (Eds.). *Handbook of communication and emotion: Research, theory, applications, and contexts* (pp. 424–450). San Diego: Academic Press.

Witte, K., Cameron, K. A., Lapinski, M. K., & Nzyuko, S. (1998). A theoretically based evaluation of HIV/AIDS prevention campaigns along the Trans-Africa Highway in Kenya. *Journal of Health Communication, 3,* 345–363.

Witte, K., Sampson, J., Liu, W. Y., & Morrison, K. (1995). *Addressing cultural orientations in fear appeals: Promoting AIDS-protective behaviors among Hispanic immigrant and African-American adolescents.* Unpublished manuscript.

Wong-Wylie, G., & Jevne, R. F. (1997). Patient hope: Exploring the interactions between physicians and HIV seropositive individuals. *Qualitative Health Research, 7,* 32–56.

Wood, J. T. (1994). *Who cares? Women, care, and culture.* Carbondale: Southern Illinois University Press.

Wood, J. T., & Dindia, K. (1998). What's the difference? A dialogue about differences and similarities between women and men. In D. J. Canary & K. Dindia (Eds.), *Sex differences and similarities in communication: Critical essays and empirical investigations of sex and gender in interaction* (pp. 19–39). Mahwah, NJ: Erlbaum.

Workman, T. A. (2001). Find the meanings of college drinking: An analysis of fraternity drinking stories. *Health Communication, 13,* 427–447.

World Health Organization (2001). Downloaded on December 20, 2001, http://www.who.int/home-page/ and http://www.who.int/m/topicgroups/who_organization/en/index.html

World Health Organization Executive Board. (1979). *Formulating strategies for health for all by the year 2000: Guiding principles and essential issues.* Geneva: World Health Organization.

Wright, A. L., Bauer, M., Naylor, A., Sutcliffe, E., & Clark, L. (1998). Increasing breastfeeding rates to reduce infant illness at the community level. *Pediatrics, 101,* 837–844.

Yoshikawa, R. L. (Ed.). (1995). The double-swing model of intercultural communication between the East and the West. In D. L. Kincaid (Ed.), *Communication theory: Eastern and Western perspectives* (pp. 319–329). San Diego: Academic Press.

Young, M., & Klingle, R. S. (1996). Silent partners in medical care: A cross-cultural study of patient participation. *Health Communication, 8,* 29–53.

Zola, I. K. (1982). *Missing pieces: A chronicle of living with a disability.* Philadelphia: Temple University Press.

Zook, E. G. (1994). Embodied health and constitutive communication: Toward an authentic conceptualization of health communication. In S. A. Deetz (Ed.), *Communication yearbook 17* (pp. 344–377). Thousand Oaks, CA: Sage.

Zuckerman, M. (1979). *Sensation seeking: Beyond the optimal levels of arousal.* Hillsdale, NJ: Erlbaum.

Zukerman, D., & Nassar, S. (2000, August 31). FDA warns of dangers of breast implants. Washington, DC: National Center for Policy Research for Women and Families.

Zuniga, M. E. (1992). Using metaphors in therapy: Dichos and Latino clients. *Social Work, 37,* 55–60.

# PICTURE CREDITS

This page constitutes an extension of the copyright page. We have made every effort to trace the ownership of all copyrighted material and to secure permission from copyright holders. In the event of any question arising as to the use of any material, we will be pleased to make the necessary corrections in future printings. Thanks are due to the following authors, publishers, and agents for permission to use the material indicated.

**Front matter. xxv:** Reprinted with permission from Ruth Zittrain

**Chapter 1.1:** Reprinted with permission from Deena Metzger

**Chapter 2. 26:** Photo by Don Flood/reprinted with permission from the Christopher Reeve Paralysis Foundation

**Chapter 3. 67:** Native American Women's Health Education Resource Center

**Chapter 4. 105:** John O'Brien, *The New Yorker*

**Chapter 5. 165, 166, 169:** Reprinted with permission from Staci, Monte, and Zachary Zwaan

**Chapter 6. 186:** Reprinted from the 1997 Public Education Campaign

**Chapter 7. 209:** Photo reprinted with permission from Heather Reich  **212:** Photo reprinted with permission from Ruth Zittrain  **215:** Photo reprinted with permission from June Ray and Jim Feehan

**Chapter 8. 232:** Photo reprinted with permission from Erica Goldfarb  **233:** Photo reprinted with permission from Barbara Verlezza

**Chapter 9. 264:** Courtesy of MGM Clip and Still  **289:** Reprinted by permission of Wm. Hoest Enterprises, Inc.

**Chapter 10. 305:** MIKE SMITH reprinted by permission of United Feature Syndicate, Inc.

**Chapter 11. 326:** Courtesy of Michael J. Fox  **342:** HIV prevention in Cuba/photo by Barbara Sharf  **342:** Courtesy of Barbara Sharf  **345:** Courtesy of the Westside Health Authority in Chicago  **349:** National Breast Cancer Coalition

# NAME INDEX

Valleya, Karen, 119–120
Vanderford, Marsha L., 118, 120–123
Varallo, S. M., 4, 223
Veciana-Suarez, Ana, 227
Velezza, Barbara, 232–253
Vena, J. E., 150
Verge, C. H., 150
Vinsel, A., 82n
Visco, Fran, 348

Wagner, M. K., 189
Wahl, H. W., 216
Waitzkin, Howard, 83, 108–109, 281–282, 296, 342
Wallace, Mike, 4
Waller, G., 176
Wallerstein, E., 145, 150
Wallis, C., 12, 86
Wallston, B. S., 292
Wallston, K. A., 292
Ware, J. E., 334
Warren, P. M., 115
Waterman, B., 108

Watson, S. J., 96–97, 99
Waxler-Morrison, N., 66, 69, 83
Webb, R. E., 158, 160
Weber, P., 247–248
Wegescheide-Harris, J., 234
Weiner, E., 69
Weir, Kerri, 173–174
Weisfuse, I. B., 75
Weiss, C., 183
Wekesser, C., 160
Welby, Marcus, 13
Werner, C. M., 82n
West, C., 281
Weston, Nancy, 263–265
Weston, W. W., 280, 334
Whaley, Bryan B., 170–171, 334
Whitcomb, J., 148
White, H., 27
Wiener, L., 80
Wilke, D., 187
Williams, E., 312
Wilmot, W. W., 82n
Wilson, H. S., 79
Windle, M., 193–194
Winter, B., 163–164

Wise, M., 286
Wiseman, R. L., 65
Witte, Kim, 89–90, 293
Wittman, Juliet, 262
Wong-Wylie, G., 79
Wood, J. T., 222, 241
Woollett, A., 161
Workman, Thomas A., 194–195
Wright, A. L., 150

Yep, Gust, 110
Yoshikawa, R. L., 82
Young, M., 91

Zath, R. C., 63
Zeman, David, 261
Zola, Irving, 44–45
Zook, Eric G., 6, 10, 16, 83, 267, 310, 315
Zuckerman, M., 189
Zukerman, D., 117
Zuniga, M. E., 84
Zwann, Staci, Monte, and Zachary, 163–171

Embodiment, 40–41
  narratives of, 39–48
Emotional contagion, 311
Emotional exhaustion, 313
  coping mechanisms for, 315
Emotional expression
  during adolescence, 176
  of men, 176
Emotional labor, 310–311
Emotional support, 221. *See also*
  Social support; Supportive
  communication
  for parents who miscarry,
  157–158
Emotions, cognitive, behavioral,
  and physiological
  components of, 89
Empathic concern, 311
Emphysema, 38–39
Empowerment
  of communities, 343–346
  of health citizens, 328
  through health activism,
  346–350
Empty Cradle, 62, 157–158, 163
End-of-life care, 253–260
End-of-life (EOL) decisions,
  255–256
Ending life passages, 228–229.
  *See also* Death and dying
Enema, 145
Entertainment-education, 284
Epilepsy, 54–57
Episiotomy, 145, 149–150
*ER*, 13
Erectile dysfunction (ED), 276
Ethical dilemmas, 110
Ethnicity. *See also* Culture
  access to information and
  care, influence on, 75
  women, cancer, and, 66
Ethnocentrism, acknowledging,
  69–70
Ethnocultural/Familial Layer of
  Meaning, 70–72
  of AIDS, 78–79
*Evaluating Women's Health
  Messages* (Parrott and
  Condit), 155
Every Block a Village Online,
  346
Exclusion of terminally ill, 237
Expedition Inspiration,
  322–323, 347
Expertise
  challenges to, 268–270

subjective-objective
  dichotomy, 269–270
Experts, 7
  dialogue with public, 16
  technological knowledge,
  reliance on, 85
Explanatory models, 268–270
  eliciting, 59
Extended Parallel Process
  Model, 89, 293
Extraorganizational stress,
  311–312

Familial Layer of Meaning,
  70–72
  of AIDS, 78–79
Family
  narratives of, 38–39
  organ donation decisions,
  246–249
  as primary caregivers,
  240–241
  rejection/support of persons
  with AIDS, 80–81
  role in health care, 15–16
  smoking, communication
  about, 195
  spiritual and cultural values
  focus of, 71–72
  support groups and, 224–225
Fateful moments, 49
Fear
  communicating to others, 31
  of illness and disease, 89–90
  reducing, with
  communication, 143
  of terminal illness, 236
Federal Drug Administration
  (FDA) drug approval
  process, 101–102
Fee-for-service, 305–306
Fertility drugs, 162
Fetal alcohol syndrome
  prevention programs,
  66–67
*Final Exit* (Humphry), 254
Folk medicine, 86
Food and Drug Administration
  (FDA), 101, 115
Formative life passages, 115
  adolescence, 175–181
  death of a parent, 173
  risk-taking behaviors,
  188–195
  sense of self, communicating,
  175–181

sex education during,
  181–188
  suicide attempts, 173–174
Foundational values, 274

Gamete intrafallopian transfer
  (GIFT), 161
Gay community, stigmatization
  related to AIDS, 74, 76
Gender
  education about, 182–183
  gender bias in clinical drug
  trials, 101–102
  social support and, 222
  stereotypes of, media
  perpetuation of, 177
Genetic susceptibility, disclosure
  of, 296–297
Geriatric medicine, 217
*Girl, Interrupted* (Kaysen),
  175–176
Government-sponsored
  experiments, 292
Grief
  communicating symbolically,
  157
  disenfranchised grief, 250–254
  emotional support for,
  157–158
  following miscarriage,
  156–157
Guided visual imaging, 86

*Handbook of Gender, Culture,
  and Health* (Eisler and
  Hersen), 126–127
Harm reduction programs for
  drug use, 279
Healing
  cultural influences on, 83
  politics of, 107–111
  theory as location for, 5
Health
  beyond medicine, 15–17
  and identity, interdependence
  between, 213–214
  interpretations of, 63
  representing in everyday life,
  8–10
  social support effect on, 219
  symbolic representation of, 8
Health activism, 324–325,
  346–350
Health advertising, 286
Health behavior
  cultural influences on, 12

Homosexuality, pathologization of, 11
Hormone replacement therapy (HRT), 11, 290–291
Hospice, 241–242
Hospice of Connecticut, 241
Hospital procedures, communicating, 148–150
Hospitals
cost containment focus, 301
outsourcing of services from, 301–302
*How Did I Become My Parent's Parent?* (Schiff), 214–215
*How to Get Out of the Hospital Alive* (Blau and Shimberg), 301, 309
Human Genome Project, 296–297
Humanistic knowledge
subordination of, 86
technological knowledge, balancing with, 85
technological knowledge, dialectics of, 85–90
understanding of communication and emotion component, 89
Humor, as coping strategy, 210
Husband-coached childbirth, 144
Hysterectomies, 88

Identity, 30. *See also* Self-identity
and health, interdependence between, 213–214
narrating, 39–42
Identity work, 42–43
Ideological Layer of Meaning, 70–72
about AIDS, 73–74
Illness
ambivalence about, 45
as biocultural construction, 92
chronic, 199
denial of, 220
explaining to children, 170–171
interpretations of, 63
knowledge and experience of, 11–12
narratives, changing identities, and, 43–46
normalcy explanation of, 171
self-identity, renegotiation of, 42–43

uncertainty caused by, 220–221
and wellness, boundary between, 9–12
writing the body, 103
Illness identity, multiple cultural community membership and, 68
Immigrants to United States, 60–61
In vitro fertilization, 160, 162
Incest, 4
survivor stories of, 222–223
Independence-ignore interaction, 216
Independence-support interaction, 216
Infants
circumcision of, 150
monitoring heartbeat of, 148–149
Infertility, 134–135
communicating through, 155–163
men's stories of, 158–160
negative treatment effects, 161–162
reproductive technologies for, 160–163
stigmatizing messages about, 158
technological treatment of, 110
Information
control of, 281–282
sharing in patient-doctor partnership, 333–334
Informational support, 221, 311
Informed consent process, 270–274
Institute of Medicine, 75
Institutional policies, provider focus on, 71–72
Institutional/Professional Layer of Meaning, 70–72
of AIDS, 77–78
Instrumental support, 221, 311
Insurance policies, limitations of, 31
Integrated health theory, 212–213
Interaction, sensitivity to, 237
Interactive technology
health promotion with, 128
uses of, 225
Intercultural interactions, dialectics of, 82

Intergenerational communication, 214–219
International medical graduates, 63
Internet
control of, 288–290
digital divide, 282
health information on, 285–286, 288–290
impact on health care, 128
impact on health communication, 225
support groups and information on, 225
Interorganizational stress, 312–313
Interpersonal Layer of Meaning, 70–72
of AIDS, 79–81
Intraorganizational stress, 309–310
Isolation of terminally ill, 237

Job burnout, 313–314
Job stress of providers, 307–313
coping mechanisms for, 315

Kaiser Family Foundation, 188
Kenyan HIV/AIDS prevention campaign, 293
Knowledge, discourse, and power, interaction of, 108
Knowledge gap, 282

La Leche League, 144
Labeling of depression, 203–206
Labor, inducing, 149
Lack of personal accomplishment, 313
Language
in epidemics of stigmatization, 112–122
in medical settings, 108
Latina women, health belief system of, 84
Layers of meaning, 70–72
Laypersons, expertise of, 268
Lee family, 55–58
Leukemia, online resources for, 288–290
Licensed practical nurses (LPNs), 310
Life-adjusting passages, 134
parenting a disabled child, 163–171
Life-affirming passages, 134
breastfeeding, 150–151

Terminally ill persons
  (continued)
  isolation and exclusion of, 237
  nearing death awareness of,
    242–245
  reflexivity in communication
    with, 231, 242
Theorizing health practices, 4–5
Therapeutic power, 106
*thirtysomething,* 263
Three-phase model of
  adjustment to disability,
  208–210
Traditional medicine, 86
Transformation
  communication as vehicle for,
  41–42
  communication of, 42–48
Traumatic events, talking about,
  222
Treatment
  consent for, 270–274
  cultural bias in, 88–89
  cultural miscommunication
  of, 56–57
  patient priorities for, 336
  risks of, warning patients of,
  271
*Tree* (Metzger), 2
Tuskegee experiment, 292
TV viewing, links to unhealthy
  eating habits, 189

Uncertainty, stress of, 220
Unconditional listening, 222
Unhealthy eating habits,
  189–190
United Nations breastfeeding
  recommendations, 150
United Network for Organ
  Sharing, 246
United States
  ageism in, 217–218
  assisted reproductive
  technologies controversy,
  162
  birthing in, 141–147
  death rate in, 228

graying of, 212
history of medicine in,
  104–107
immigrants admitted to,
  60–61
international medical
  graduates in, 63
physician authority in, 104
teenage pregnancy rate in,
  185
Unplanned pregnancy, 134–135
U.S. Census Bureau, 60
U.S. Department of Commerce,
  63
U.S. Department of Health and
  Human Services, 65, 199,
  212
U.S. Immigration and
  Naturalization Service, 61

Vagina, 145
Value orientation of health
  messages, 274–280
Ventura County Clothesline
  Project, 47–48
Verbal communication of
  health, 2
Verbicide, 10
Viagra, 276
Victims
  blaming of, 200–201
  humanizing, 46
Victims of Abuse Hotline, 48
Vietnam War, 47
Vietnamese women, cervical
  cancer rates in, 66
Voice of medicine, 36
Vulva, 145

Webster Work, 10
Well-being, 2
  sexual and overall, 178
Wellness
  and illness, boundary
  between, 9–12
  interpretations of, 63
  knowledge and experience of,
  11–12

Wellness identity, multiple
  cultural community
  membership and, 68
Westside Health Authority
  Every Block a Village Online,
  346
  Safe Summer Kickoff,
  345–346
Women
  abuse of, 47–48
  with AIDS, 75–76
  breast development in,
  179–180
  depression in, 202
  disordered eating in, 192
  empowerment experiences,
  328
  ethnicity, cancer, and, 66
  health care needs of, 128
  home-work role conflict of,
  311–312
  infertility research and
  treatment for, 162
  medicalization of natural
  experiences of, 146
  menarche, 180
  music videos depiction of,
  177
  preparation for childbirth,
  148
  as primary caregivers,
  240–241
  second shift for, 241
Workplace health site, 16
World Health Organization
  (WHO), 8
  breastfeeding
  recommendations, 150
  disease outbreak surveillance
  and investigation program,
  77
Writing the body, 103
Written health records, 339

Zona cracking or drilling, 161
Zygote intrafallopian transfer
  (ZIFT), 160